Texas Legacy Narrators*

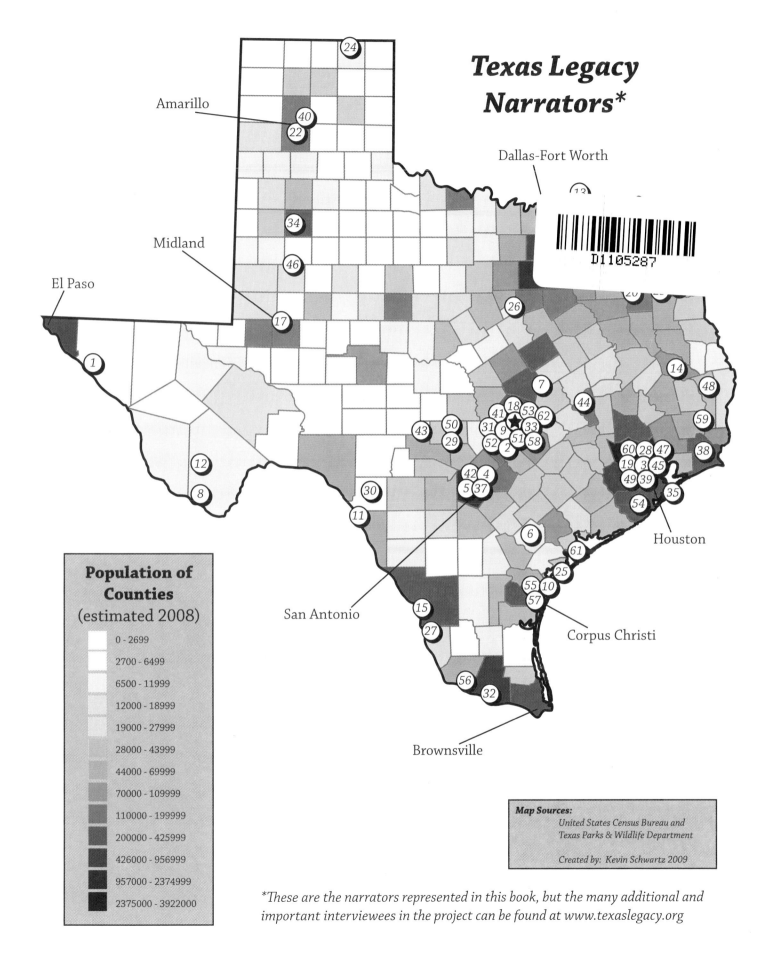

Amarillo

Midland

El Paso

Dallas-Fort Worth

D1105287

San Antonio

Corpus Christi

Houston

Brownsville

Population of Counties
(estimated 2008)

	0 - 2699
	2700 - 6499
	6500 - 11999
	12000 - 18999
	19000 - 27999
	28000 - 43999
	44000 - 69999
	70000 - 109999
	110000 - 199999
	200000 - 425999
	426000 - 956999
	957000 - 2374999
	2375000 - 3922000

Map Sources:
United States Census Bureau and
Texas Parks & Wildlife Department

Created by: Kevin Schwartz 2009

*These are the narrators represented in this book, but the many additional and important interviewees in the project can be found at www.texaslegacy.org

The Texas Legacy Project

The
TEXAS
LEGACY
Project

Stories of Courage & Conservation

EDITED BY DAVID TODD AND DAVID WEISMAN

Foreword by Carter Smith

TEXAS A&M UNIVERSITY PRESS   •   *College Station*

LIBRARY OF CONGRESS CATALOGING-IN-PUBLICATION DATA

The Texas Legacy Project : stories of courage and conservation /
edited by David Todd and David Weisman ; foreword by Carter
Smith.—1st ed.
       p. cm
Includes index.
ISBN-13: 978–1-60344–200–8 (pb-flexibound : alk. paper)
ISBN-10: 1-60344–200–6 (pb-flexibound : alk. paper)
1. Environmentalists—Texas—Interviews.   2. Conservation of
natural resources—Texas—History—20th century.   3. Texas Legacy
Project.   I. Todd, David, 1959-   II. Weisman, David, 1961-
III. Conservation History Association of Texas.
GE55.T48   2010
333.72092'2764—dc22
2010003498

In memory of Ned Fritz,
organizer, advocate, and author
for Texas conservation;
and in honor of George Stoney,
teacher, filmmaker,
and storyteller.

Contents

List of Illustrations

Foreword

To borrow a line from a Texas singer/songwriter of some repute, my heroes have always been conservationists. They always have been and still are today.

Thanks to the seminal efforts of the Conservation History Association of Texas, there is now a book that tells their stories—sixty-two, to be precise. Inside these pages, you will find the stories emanating from the actions of an impressive coterie of fellow Texans. There are attorneys, scientists, game wardens, landowners, politicians, environmental advocates, and seemingly ordinary citizens, who did extraordinary things on behalf of our state's lands, waters, fish, and wildlife. Some risked their lives, others their livelihoods, and still others their families, reputations, community standings, and savings. And, regardless of whether their call to action was borne out of their vocation or avocation, they all share a common denominator. They all made a difference in keeping the Texas we know and love a little wilder for a little longer.

God bless 'em.

For those not well initiated in the conservation battles and politics of yore, one should know that their journey was, as Robert Penn Warren once famously wrote, "not exactly like Easter week in a nunnery." Just ask those involved with efforts to prohibit commercial gill netting of redfish on the coast, or the game wardens charged with shutting down deer hunting with dogs in the deep East Texas woods, or the battles fought over nuclear waste dumps out around Sierra Blanca, or the contention surrounding the plight of several obscure endangered invertebrates dependent upon the deep limestone crevices and waters of the Edwards Aquifer. This book tells those stories.

Suffice to say, for all of us who were born here, reside here, work here, play here, and plan to die here, we owe these citizen conservationists a great debt of gratitude. I know I do. As a seventh generation Texan, I hail from a family with a deep stake in our state's past, and just as importantly, its future. My forefathers have been farmers, ranchers, shopkeepers, mill operators, teachers, attorneys, professors, and probably a few other things in between. All have had a connection to the land. A strong sense of place and stewardship was passed along to me at birth. A love for the out-of-doors came with it. I will always be indebted to my parents for enabling that.

I also have the extraordinary good fortune of making my passion for conservation my profession. Many in this book have aided me along the way, some knowingly and others perhaps unwittingly so. For instance, as a kid, I read and re-read John Graves's *Goodbye to a River* and *Hard Scrabble.* I could think of nothing more adventuresome than a canoe trip down a still-wild river with a dog and shotgun as my companions. I relished his observations on the land, stock, game, and ranch people gleaned from his beloved perch on the patch of Hill Country "hard scrabble" that he called home. It was abundantly clear that he knew of what he wrote. And, through his written words, his love for a sense of place helped shape my own love for my own sense of place.

Andy Sansom, who was executive director of the agency I now have the privilege of serving, gave me my first job when I graduated from college. He didn't have to, and candidly didn't need to, but he did anyway. He found a job for me working in the realm of private lands conservation, an exciting place to be in the early 1990s as interest in wildlife management on private lands was rapidly growing and conflicts over how to manage endangered species were about to reach their crescendo. At some point, he then counseled me to return to graduate school to pursue my education and to go out and explore the universe of opportunities across the country and even the world. I will always be grateful for how generously he has given of his experience, wisdom, and counsel.

Carl Frentress, a wise man of the woods if ever there was one, took me under his wing while I was at the Texas Parks and Wildlife Department as a rookie intern. He taught me about the magic of bottomland hardwoods, the mysteries of wetlands, and the rich natural and cultural history behind the pine curtain. He also made sure I was able to meet and interact with Dan Lay, one of the great pioneers in wildlife management and a custodian of the rich and bountiful heritage that encompassed the eastern part of our state. Carl is the consummate and ever patient teacher, and as a biologist, there is hardly one finer.

And how could I forget the contributions of that fiery redhead with the indomitable spirit, Ann Hamilton, from over Houston way. As a grants officer for the Houston Endowment, she arguably had more influence over more conservation projects in the state than any single person. Her passion for all things conservation was legendary and her intensity even greater. Time and time again, she stood beside me and supported me as we tackled conservation projects big and small from the Katy Prairie to the Rio Grande. She has been an extraordinary partner and most importantly, a dear friend.

There are plenty of others here I could and should mention, but the constraints of space will keep me from doing so. Never mind though. I doubt they will notice the omission, because such things aren't really of much interest to all those featured in this book. What this collection of conservationists really cares about is the present and future state of our woods and waters, prairies and pastures, springs and streams, and bays and bottomlands. Texas is blessed with an extraordinary amount of natural treasures. These individuals have been their guardians.

On behalf of all of us at Texas Parks and Wildlife, I offer my heartfelt thanks to those featured within these pages. Our wild things and wild places have been well served by their courage and their convictions.

CARTER SMITH
Texas Parks and Wildlife Department

Acknowledgments

We wish to thank the friends and supporters of the Conservation History Association of Texas, and their effort to recognize and document the many contributions of conservationists in the state.

First, of course, we owe a great debt of gratitude to the hundreds of narrators who have participated in the project, lending their time, experience, expertise, and patience. This work is for them, and by them. Please see Appendix 2 for a full listing of their names.

We feel very obliged to our fellow interview crew members, Gary Spalding, Jody Horton, and Eric Acevedo, who took such care and interest in making the recordings that form the basis of the entire project. We have been especially fortunate to be able to rely on Mr. Spalding for his skill, resourcefulness, and good humor during *nine* of our tours. We would also like to extend thanks to those who gave us completed interviews for the archive, including Christopher Cook, Craig Damuth, Tonya Kleuskens, Randy Mallory, Jessica Schoenbaechler, Sandra Skrei, J. B. Smallwood, and the University of North Texas.

We appreciate the help from the Texas Parks and Wildlife Department, especially Richard Roberts, Lydia Saldana, Chase Fountain, and Cecilia Nasti, who have been so generous in providing the video footage, still images, and sound editing support that were crucial to improving and illustrating our interview recordings. And now, later in the process, we are grateful to the Department's director, Carter Smith, for his insightful and generous foreword to this book.

We would like to note the efforts of the many people involved in making our tapings into something that can be understood, distributed, and preserved for years to come. This long list would certainly include our very patient transcribers, Robin Johnson and Judy Holloway, our friends at the School of Information at the University of Texas who have supported our digital archive and outreach (among others, Bill Aspray, Phil Doty, Pat Galloway, Gary Geisler, Thomas Kiehne, Luis Francisco-Revilla, Quinn Stewart, and Yan Zhang), and our colleagues at the Briscoe Center for American History at the University of Texas (particularly Kate Adams, Allison Beck, Brenda Gunn, and Zach Vowell) who have been excellent stewards of our transcripts, videotapes, and other artifacts collected during our tours.

Since conservation is, at its core, a story about a sense of place, we would be remiss if we did not thank our cartographer, Kevin Schwartz, and the many photographers who contributed to the book. Mr. Schwartz prepared the maps that you see in the endpapers of this book, showing the Texas communities, lands, and waters that the narrators have cared for so much. As you look through the rest of the book, you will also see the fine eye and camerawork of Cody Austin, Ronald Billings, Tammy Cromer-Campbell, David Bezanson, Richard Donovan, Howard Eskin, Karen Gallagher, Daniel Iggers, Neil Kelley, James Kennedy, Sam Kittner, Stuart Klipper, Martin Labar, Dan LaMee, Amber MacPherson, George Marsh, Doc McGregor, Ville Miettinen, Alan Pogue, Ed Schipu, Peter Shanks, Larry Shelton, Sharon Stewart, Jaap van der Veer, Carol Von Canon, and John Young.

This broad circle of friends has been critical to whatever success our little non-profit can claim. Of course, within our group, we owe thanks to the Trustees of the Conservation History Association of Texas, Janice Bezanson, Susan Petersen, and Ted Siff, as well as our Board of Advisors, Laura Dunn, Stephen Klineberg, Louis Marchiafava, Martin Melosi, Char Miller, and

Paul Stekler. We cannot forget the help from our emeritus board members, including Sue Bumpous, John Hamilton, Beth Hudson, and Helen Thorpe.

While we have relied heavily on volunteers, donated equipment, and in-kind help, we've also been fortunate to have steadfast financial supporters, including the Brown Foundation, Clayton Fund, Environmental Defense, Friends of the Texas Historical Commission, Houston Endowment, Hershey Foundation, Humanities Texas, Magnolia Charitable Trust, Meadows Foundation, Price Foundation, Stillwater Foundation, Summerlee Foundation, Susan Vaughan Foundation, Wray Charitable Trust, and numerous individuals.

Finally, we would like to thank Shannon Davies, Patricia Clabaugh, Kim Withers, Holli Estridge, Mary Ann Jacob, and their many fine colleagues at Texas A&M Press for their enthusiasm and wisdom as they guided us through the long and fascinating process of bringing this book to print.

The Texas Legacy Project

Introduction

The stories in this book are excerpts from informal and unscripted interviews with Texas conservationists, collected from 1997 through 2008 by the Conservation History Association of Texas. We see value in them as personal reminiscences, as citizen journeys, and as first-hand histories of conservation in Texas during the past sixty years. In a sense, we see them as a useful conversation between the narrators and you, the reader, about the recent history of environmental issues in this state, and what the future might hold.

Private Individuals and Public Citizens

We hope you enjoy these chapters simply as tales of interesting people's youth and maturity, lives and careers, family and friends, accomplishments and disappointments, passions and frustrations, lessons learned and lessons passed on. They represent the voice of experience, the seed stock of ideas, the intellectual property of skills, and the legacy for a new generation.

Beyond reading these conversations as stories of individual lives, we hope you might also see them as pictures of what it means to be a citizen, and how important that role is. As Supreme Court Justice Felix Frankfurter once wrote, "In a democracy, the highest office is the office of citizen."[1] We think you will find that the narrators have used every tool possible to press our democracy to address national and, indeed, global environmental problems through scientific research, business acumen, legal pleadings, community organizing, and political pressure.

History

We believe that the passages presented here have value for what they tell about the history of a particular place, time, and cause. The place, of course, is Texas, a diverse, dynamic, and endlessly fascinating region with a long history of notable events that influenced our conservation legacy (see Appendix 1). The time is principally the post–World War II era, a span of two generations that brought exciting changes and great challenges to the state. The cause is the conservation movement, the broad grassroots effort to protect habitat and wildlife, promote public health, and ensure environmental justice.

History of a Place

Texas, and particularly Texas in the twentieth century, serves as a wide-ranging case study on how the country's conservation themes have played out. This place offers a sample of the nation's full scope of diversity, whether in its people, its government, its laws, or in its natural resources. For example, Texans possess great ethnic diversity.[2] Our largest city, Houston, is now roughly one-third Anglo, one-third Hispanic, one-third African American and one-tenth Asian; and, as of 2004, the entire state had crossed the threshold of having a majority "minority" population.[3] From a political perspective, in the last two hundred years the land of Texas has been under the flags of France, Spain, Mexico, the Texas Republic, the Confederate States and the United States, and has inherited the tenets of both Spanish civil law and English common law.[4] From a biological standpoint, Texas is a collection of twelve main ecological regions that hold more than 180 mammalian species, 600 birds and 6,000 plants, making the state's biodiversity second only to California, with climatic zones that extend from high, virtually rainless deserts to lush, semi-tropical bottomland forests. As a consequence, this state has been the site for a wide variety of environmental challenges and human responses. It has provided a slew of "backyards," big and small, that individuals and communities have worked to understand and protect, as their shared treasure and legacy.

History of an Era

The lives of the 225 participants in our archive encompass the latter two-thirds of the twentieth century and the dawn of the new millennium. From an environmental standpoint, their lives and stories begin shortly after the creation of the first major parks and refuges in Texas,[5] proceed through the Dustbowl and Depression, the post–World War II industrialization and suburbanization boom, the nascent environmental movement (energized by the 1961 publication of Rachel Carson's *Silent Spring*, the 1969 Santa Barbara oil spill and the first Earth Day), the private property rights backlash,[6] and then continue through the challenging, dual phenomena of globalization and global climate change. Throughout this time, the narrators have understood the earth's finite and fragile nature, seen the serious risks to our environment, helped alert and broaden our collective consciousness, and contributed to the success of many conservation efforts.[7]

History of a Cause

The excerpts in this book cover many streams of the conservation movement, including the topics of habitat and wildlife protection; issues of pollution control, public health protection, and environmental justice;

questions of a sustainable economy, and the intertwining themes of philosophy, media, and government. For example, here you can find stories of habitat protection that touch on conservation of the Neches river bottom, East Texas Piney Woods, Central Texas tall grass prairies, South Texas brush country, and coastal beaches and oyster reefs. And, you can read varied tales of work with wildlife, as conservationists manage white-tailed deer, catch game bird poachers, protect endangered piping plovers, and promote ecotourism. In these pages you also can see stories of pollution, public health, and environmental justice as communities oppose high-level nuclear waste disposal in the Panhandle, low-level radioactive waste sites in West Texas, waste blending and deep well injection in deep East Texas, fuel storage in Austin, and toxic air emissions in Houston and Channelview. You can also look at the discussions about resources and sustainability involving wind energy, green building, organic farming, and compact cities. And, at a more abstract level, you can consider the musings of environmental thinkers and religious leaders regarding the meaning of materialism, spirituality, civility, decency, and justice.

History of a Community

The environmental cause is complex, the affected sites are diverse, and the issues are constantly evolving and unfolding through time. For a fuller understanding, we believe it is important to get a broad sample of conservationists, representing the true breadth of Texas' environmental issues and communities. So, while the storytellers in this book share a common conservation ethic, they bring a great diversity of experience, insight, and voice. The narrators include men and women, old and young, African American, Anglo, and Hispanic. They reside in small towns such as Sierra Blanca, Farnsworth, and Rio Grande City, and in the large cities of Houston, Dallas/Fort Worth, Austin, and San Antonio. They include a microbiologist, botanist and ornithologist, a farmer, rancher and fisherman, a politician, attorney and lobbyist, and many others.[8] Each brings a unique perspective, training and skill set to the environmental work that they do.

All together, the Texas Legacy archive currently includes 225 narrators (please see www.texaslegacy.org). This book comprises barely a quarter of that number. In a state of over twenty-three million souls, it is clear that the archive, and certainly the book, can provide only a partial view of the state's environmental movement. Still, we hope that we can give a fair likeness of the full picture, and that the individual narrators are seen, in a sense, as archetypes, as representatives of their many friends, colleagues, mentors, supporters, and of course, the many other participants in the project who could not be included in the book due to space limitations. We do understand that trying to document a movement as broad and varied as environmental conservation, in a place as big and diverse as Texas, is something of a fool's errand. However, we trust that this collection of stories sends a common message, one that is strengthened in being told by many witnesses and participants, all in their own words and with their own experiences and ideas.

History within a Book

Over ten years ago, the Texas Legacy Project was born as an electronic archive. As an online, digital resource (www.texaslegacy.org), the archive allowed each reader/viewer to search, sort, and randomly access any part of hundreds of hours of video interviews or written transcripts. The online reader could easily troll through many excerpts, tying together these various stories of the cause, using different topics and themes that seemed apropos to him or her. There was little hierarchy or sequence imposed on the user.

However, the challenge of placing these same interviews into the linear format of a book required organizing these participants in a more rigid and uniform way.

It needed a way to narrow and tag the category for each story, without losing sight of its context in the broader, shifting, interconnected nature of ecological systems and environmental efforts.

There were many options for organizing the interview excerpts, including placing the pieces within chronological periods, geographic areas, professional careers, or thematic topics. Each of these models presented challenges and limitations. For example, selecting fixed intervals along a timeline was tricky because a given year in a particular community might have less significance than whether the date were before or after the start of a local population boom, industrial project, or waste facility. In that sense, time might mean different things in different areas, and have little shared meaning across all the excerpts of the narrators' stories.

In our view, geographic categories had shortcomings too: for instance, a narrator might have lived and been interviewed in their "home" region, yet typically worked at distant and diverse locations. We found that sorting by professional career had limits as well. A narrator might have had a career as a banker or realtor, yet found their true legacy of service in protecting rivers or monitoring hazardous waste. Categorizing by theme created problems too: some of the narrators had worked on many topics: conserving land, water and habitat; controlling pollution; protecting public health; and developing overarching perspectives and philosophies about environmental matters. To confine them to a single arena seemed too limiting.

In the end, we arrived at a method that we hope will orient and encourage the reader, provide a roomy framework for this diverse collection, and yet not pigeonhole the narrators. The excerpts that follow are organized according to the *tools* of the narrators; that is, the physical or mental gear they use for tackling environmental problems. This system is a nod to the idea of humans as toolmakers, who are, if not unique, at least unusual in the animal kingdom.[9] This approach also recognizes the leveraged power that tools have given us over the natural world, both for good and ill. Some of these tools are mechanical (chain saws and bulldozers), while others may be abstract (corporations and governments), but all have amplified our impact far beyond our home and era. Further, this idea of organizing stories by tools gives some leeway to the narrators who might have picked up one tool for one problem, and then turned to another problem with a different, more suitable implement. Their means may be varied, but they all share the goal of conservation. And finally, we hope that this idea of tool use will show that the conservation "tackle box" is available to all of us: that you do not need to be a commercial fisherman to throw a lure or set a hook on a nearby fish, and that you need not be a professional environmentalist to care for your corner of the natural world.

Thus, these profiles are placed in categories that include the tools, gear, and instruments of law enforcement ("Gavels, Rifles, and Writs"), exploration ("Boots and Compass"), government ("Ballots and Bills"), wildlife management ("Rod, Gun, and Lens"), religion and philosophy ("Pulpit and Lectern"), education ("Slide Rules and Specimens"), public policy ("Alphabet Soup"), agriculture ("Farmstands and Feedlots"), communication ("Pen and Press"), community advocacy ("Watchdogs and Watersheds"), and sustainability ("Satellites and Blueprints").

This is clearly only one way to approach the subject of conservation in Texas. There are certainly many other categories and schemes to use. But, no matter what the era, locale, topic, theme, or tool, all the narrators here speak to their shared effort to understand and protect the many special backyards found in Texas, and to see them as our shared and invaluable legacy.

Audience

We would like to indulge ourselves with a brief speculation about our readers. You are, of course, the point of it all. These memories and predictions and insights are only as useful and valuable as you find them to be. So,

below, please find a few words about how we see our connection with you, and what our hopes are for your reaction.

As one of our interviewees, Char Miller, a former professor of history and urban studies at San Antonio's Trinity University, noted about his students:

My goal is to get students to see why history matters in the work that they're about to do . . . We actually live within history; we just don't always see it. If we want to have more sustainable communities, if we want to have a natural environment in which we build for ourselves and are able to not destroy that place and ourselves; if we want to have economies that function appropriately, then you show them how, in the past, people have struggled with those same issues and have done it better and worse than we will do it . . . We don't just live in the past that other people created: we are conscientious—or we should be. We are politically engaged—or we should be. We should be men and women of integrity and of that, we need to recognize that part of what makes us citizens is not just that we have a right to vote, but that we have an obligation to act.

Here, we hope that you find engaging stories about conservation, life and our shared world that you will enjoy, learn from, and value. Please read on!

1. David Bollier, "Citizen Action and Other Big Ideas, Ch. 3," *Nader.org* (blog comment posted January 6, 2004), http://www.nader.org/index.php?/archives/15-CHAPTER-3-The-Office-of-Citizen.html (accessed November 18, 2009).

2. There are at least 27 ethnic and cultural groups that have settled in the state. University of Texas—San Antonio, "UTSA Hemisfair Park Campus," http://www.utsa.edu/About/Overview/ITC.html (accessed January 28, 2009).

3. As of July 1, 2004, the U.S. Census estimated that Texas had a minority population of 11.3 million, 50.2 percent of its total population, including a 35 percent proportion for Hispanics, a 12 percent share for African-Americans, and a 4 percent part made up of Asians. Robert Bernstein,

"Texas Becomes Nation's Newest "Majority-Minority" State," Washington, D.C.: U.S. Census Bureau (August 11, 2005), http://www.census.gov/Press-Release/www/2005/cb05–118_table1.xls, http://www.census.gov/Press-Release/www/releases/archives/population/005514.html (accessed November 18, 2009). Studies have shown that environmental hazards, such as landfills and industrial facilities, tend to be found more often in minority communities raising questions of unequal treatment and injustice (please see endnote 2 in the Phyllis Glazer excerpts for more discussion).

4. For example, Texas water law reflects a unique combination of English and Spanish traditions. Under English riparian law, developed in the wet climate of the British Isles, riverside landowners were assured access to (presumably plentiful) water in the river. However, under Spain's law of "prior appropriation," originating in a dry climate, limited water rights were assigned by a central authority, with seniority given to the first applicant. In Texas, there is a gesture to the English precedents in the state's grant of a two hundred acre-foot exemption for riparian landowners' domestic and livestock uses, while all other water rights must generally follow the Spanish process of prior appropriation and specific state permit. Andrew Sansom, *Water in Texas: An Introduction* (Austin: University of Texas Press, 2008), 174.

5. Actually, the State acquired and managed its earliest parks through the Board of Control, and did so a generation before the conservationists in this collection first appeared. However, these first parks were more typically small in size, and were saved for their historic value. These earliest protected sites included the Alamo Mission (1883), the San Jacinto (1907) and Fannin (1914) battlegrounds, and Washington-on-the-Brazos (1916), the location of the signing of the Texas Declaration of Independence. Large-scale efforts to protect state lands truly began in 1923, when Governor Neff and the Legislature created the Texas State Parks Board to solicit money for park acquisitions to spur travel, economic development, and outdoor recreation. Under this authority, the State made its first purchases in 1932, securing Longhorn Cavern and Palo Duro Canyon state parks. James W. Steely, *Parks for Texas: Enduring Landscapes of the New Deal* (Austin: University of Texas Press, 1999), 1–9; Texas State Library and Archives Commission, "To Love the Beautiful: The Story of Texas State Parks," *Texas State Library and Archives Commission,* http://www.tsl.state.tx.us/exhibits/parks/index.html (accessed November 18, 2009). Muleshoe National Wildlife Refuge, a key wintering area for migratory waterfowl and sandhill cranes, was the first federal refuge set up in Texas, dating to 1930. Jeanne S. Lively, "Muleshoe National Wildlife Refuge," *Handbook of Texas Online,* http://www.tshaonline.org/handbook/online/articles/MM/gkm1.html (accessed November 18, 2009). Big Bend National Park was the first national park in the state, authorized by Congress in 1935, and established in 1944. National Park Service, "Big Bend National Park 2008 Fact Sheet," http://www.nps.gov/bibe/parknews/upload/BIBE-facts-2008.pdf (accessed January 28, 2009).

6. The property rights movement stemmed from concern over environmental regulations, which were seen as enabling government takings of private property for public use without compensation, in violation of the Fifth Amendment to the U.S. Constitution. The national movement can likely be traced to James Watt's formation of the Mountain States Legal Foundation in 1976, and his 1981 appointment as U.S. Secretary of the Interior. In Texas, this trend was seen in the rise of the Take Back Texas group, started in 1994, led by Marshall Kuykendall, Sr., and inflamed by Hill Country development restrictions. These restrictions were tied to proposed designation of Austin's Barton Creek as an Outstanding Natural Resource Water under the federal Clean Water Act, and Endangered Species Act provisions intended to protect the golden-cheeked warbler. Audrey Duff, "Cowboys & Critters," *Austin Chronicle,* January 26, 1996, http://www.austinchronicle.com/gyrobase/Issue/story?oid=oid%3A530503 (accessed July 1, 2009).

7. The narrators have been part of an unusual time that has seen an abrupt and global change in the long-standing place of humans in nature. Since the start of human history, for over two million years, our fundamental challenge has been to protect ourselves from famine, drought, cold, predators, and other risks of nature; but we are now having to switch rapidly to protecting nature from *us*, from climate change, ozone depletion, biodiversity collapse, and so on. The tables have turned.

8. Choosing the participants who comprise this oral history archive was a humbling task. We hope that the narrators are representative of this large grassroots movement, but we certainly cannot pretend that the list of interviewees in the archive is complete. Perhaps it would help to explain how the archive was built: it was assembled piecemeal, in geographic groups, growing year-by-year as regional interview tours were organized and completed. A typical preparation for a round of interviews would start several months before actually meeting and talking with the area's narrators. The process would start with research on broad topics of local environmental concerns, including agriculture, industry, water and air pollution, land use, development, and resource management. Within that geographical area and list of high-profile topics, the next step involved the identification of the possible narrators. Some candidates were the leading spokespeople on the major topics that we had singled out, or they were the people that had been long active in or broadly recognized by conservation groups, or they were those who had been featured in public media, print, TV, radio, or web publications. Other candidates had simply been personally recommended by leading conservationists, in an informal daisy-chain manner. This initial list was then narrowed down, in a way somewhat like a search engine might do it: by ranking those candidates higher that had been referred more often by others. And then our final culling was often the result of simple logistics: who might be nearby, willing, and available for an interview! More discussion of our approach can be found below in the Methods section.

9. See Kenneth Page Oakley, *Man the Tool-Maker*, 6th edition, (Chicago: University of Chicago Press, 1976).

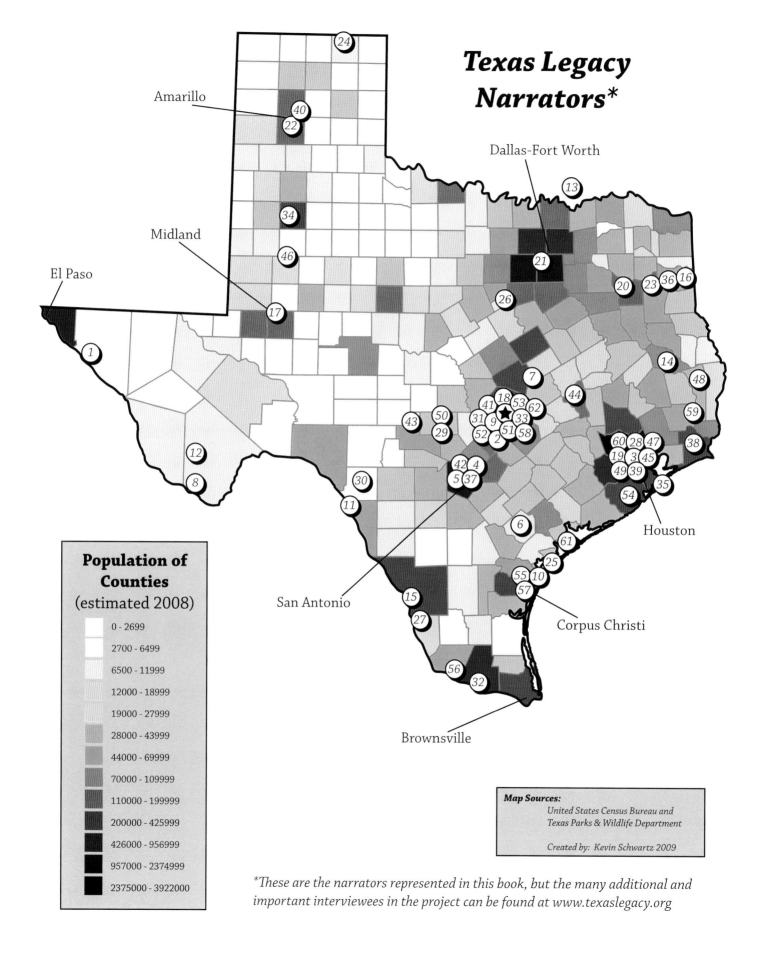

Texas Legacy Narrators*

Amarillo

Midland

El Paso

Dallas-Fort Worth

Houston

San Antonio

Corpus Christi

Brownsville

Population of Counties
(estimated 2008)

	0 - 2699
	2700 - 6499
	6500 - 11999
	12000 - 18999
	19000 - 27999
	28000 - 43999
	44000 - 69999
	70000 - 109999
	110000 - 199999
	200000 - 425999
	426000 - 956999
	957000 - 2374999
	2375000 - 3922000

Map Sources:
United States Census Bureau and
Texas Parks & Wildlife Department

Created by: Kevin Schwartz 2009

*These are the narrators represented in this book, but the many additional and
important interviewees in the project can be found at www.texaslegacy.org

Interview Excerpts

The short passages on the following pages are drawn from the full interviews, and are intended to give some idea of the early and formative experiences of the narrators, as well as a picture of their adult work and insights. They are organized by the conservation tools and strategies that these conservationists came to use most commonly, including law enforcement ("Gavels, Rifles, and Writs"), exploration ("Boots and Compass"), government ("Ballots and Bills"), wildlife ("Rod, Gun, and Lens"), religion and philosophy ("Pulpit and Lectern"), education ("Slide Rules and Specimens"), policy ("Alphabet Soup"), agriculture ("Farmstands and Feedlots"), communication ("Pen and Press"), community politics ("Watchdogs and Watersheds"), and sustainability (Satellites and Blueprints).

LOCATION OF NARRATORS

1. Bill Addington
   Grocer—Sierra Blanca
2. Susana Almanza
   Organizer—Austin
3. LaNell Anderson
   Realtor—Channelview
4. Malcolm Beck
   Agricultural supplier—San Antonio
5. Maria Berriozabál
   Politician—San Antonio
6. Al Brothers
   Wildlife manager—Berclair
7. Bob Burleson
   Attorney—Temple
8. Scooter Cheatham
   Botanist—Lajitas
9. Ernie Cortes
   Organizer—Austin
10. Felix Cox
    Fisherman—Aransas Pass
11. Carol Cullar
    Poet—Eagle Pass
12. Susan Curry
    Activist—Alpine
13. Walt Davis
    Rancher—Bennington, OK
14. Richard Donovan
    Realtor—Lufkin
15. Jim Earhart
    Biologist—Laredo
16. John Echols
    Military Officer—Uncertain

17. Midge Erskine
    Wildlife Rehabilitator—Midland
18. Ted Eubanks
    Ecotourism Consultant—Austin
19. Sissy Farenthold
    Attorney—Houston
20. Carl Frentress
    Biologist—Athens
21. Ned Fritz
    Attorney—Dallas
22. Beverly Gattis
    Retailer—Amarillo
23. Phyllis Glazer
    Rancher—Winona
24. Jeanne Gramstorff
    Banker—Farnsworth
25. Jesse Grantham
    Biologist—Rockport
26. John Graves
    Author—Glen Rose
27. Meg Guerra
    Publisher—San Ygnacio
28. Ann Hamilton
    Philanthropist—Houston
29. Terry Hershey
    Philanthropist—Stonewall
30. Tootsie Herndon
    Activist—Spofford
31. Jim Hightower
    Commentator—Austin
32. Dennis Holbrook
    Citrus farmer—Mission

33. Reggie James
    Attorney—Austin
34. Rob Lee
    Game warden—Lubbock
35. Marvin Legator
    Toxicologist—Galveston
36. Richard LeTourneau
    Machinist—Longview
37. Ruth Lofgren
    Microbiologist—San Antonio
38. Roy Malveaux
    Minister—Beaumont
39. Brandt Mannchen
    Inspector—Bellaire
40. Leroy Matthiesen
    Bishop—Amarillo
41. Craig McDonald
    Political Analyst—Austin
42. Susan Mika
    Nun—San Antonio
43. Bill Neiman
    Farmer—Junction
44. Gerald North
    Physicist—Bryan
45. Terry O'Rourke
    Attorney—Houston
46. Larhea Pepper
    Entrepreneur—O'Donnell
47. Mary Ann Piacentini
    Land trust manager—Houston
48. Billy Platt
    Game warden—Jasper

49. Daniel Quinn
    Author—Houston
50. Andy Sansom
    Administrator—Stonewall
51. Ben Sargent
    Editorial cartoonist—Austin
52. Babe Schwartz
    Politician—Austin
53. Smitty Smith
    Lobbyist—Austin
54. Sharron Stewart
    Coastal Activist—Lake Jackson
55. Pat Suter
    Chemist—Corpus Christi
56. Benito Trevino
    Horticulturalist—Rio Grande City
57. Carlos Truan
    Politician—Corpus Christi
58. Genevieve Vaughan
    Philanthropist—Austin
59. Geraldine Watson
    Botanist—Warren
60. Laverne Williams
    Architect—Houston
61. Diane Wilson
    Shrimper—Sea Drift
62. Billie Woods
    Musician—Rosanky

Gavels, Rifles, & Writs

"The wrongs done to trees, wrongs of every sort, are done in the darkness of ignorance and unbelief, for when the light comes, the heart of the people is always right."[1]

JOHN MUIR[2]

PROTECTING WILDLIFE and the native habitat of Texas is not an occupation for the faint of heart or those lacking nerves of steel. Given the wild and wooly history of the state, with its colorful array of varmints and outlaws, it's no surprise that many a dispute over the territory ended at the barrel of a gun. But in modern times, the outlaws are as likely to be polluters as poachers, and the dispute is more likely to find itself resolved in the chambers of a courtroom. Those who would disrespect the law, from the taking of endangered species to the dumping of hazardous waste, will find dedicated sleuths pursuing their tracks with patience, cunning, and persistence.

1. Linnie Margh Wolfe, ed., *John of the Mountains: The Unpublished Journals of John Muir*, (Madison: University of Wisconsin Press, 1938), 429.

2. The reader will find introductory quotations from John Muir, who is widely held to be the architect of the modern environmental movement, at the start of each of the excerpt sections. Muir's writings on behalf of the California wilderness of the nineteenth century have an uncanny prescience regarding the issues that would face the burgeoning state of Texas during the twentieth and into the twenty-first century. As such, they serve as a reminder that past is often prologue.

Polluters in Court and Heaven in Earth

TERRY O'ROURKE is an attorney and a hydrologist based in Houston, who has worked on numerous civil and criminal environmental prosecutions for the Texas Attorney General's Office and the Harris County Attorney's Office since the early 1970s. In 1973 he went to work for John Hill as an Assistant Attorney General for the State of Texas. He has also had a long interest in alternative energy and energy conservation, serving as an energy spokesman in the Carter White House, and as an educator in the field of environmental and international law. Recently, he has returned to legal prosecution work in Houston.

Interviewed on October 2, 1999, in Houston, Texas

Reel 2031; Time Code 00:01:19

"Hey, Bubba, we're going to trial."

Sometimes in politics, you're just lucky. In 1972, what happened was that there was a new Attorney General, John Hill, from Houston. Hill got elected by saying, "I'm going to clean up pollution." One of the first things that he did was he appointed me, Terry O'Rourke, Assistant Attorney General of the State of Texas. They had a backlog of cases, and he personally went in the office of the Attorney General and carried the cases down and loaded them in the back of my little Toyota car in Austin. He said, "Terry, you just take those cases to Houston, set them for trial, and win them. Need some help, call me." And so I opened up this office here in Harris County and started trying cases. I was twenty-five years old at the time, I'd been a law clerk to a federal judge in Washington, D.C., and I had the opportunity to take on some of the biggest polluters in the United States of America. It's hard for people to think back then what it was like, but these industries were essentially built in World War II to beat the Japanese and the Germans, and so they had no pollution control devices to speak of. Giant smokestacks out in east Harris County like Armco Steel, Tentex Alloy Corporation, Champion Paper just belching out pollution. And back then there was this kind of mentality of a Faustian bargain, you know, "If you're going to get rich, you got to be filthy." It's that kind of "goose that laid the golden egg" mythology and even organized labor was into it. They'd say things like, "Well, where there's smoke, there's jobs." And so I went into that world and of course, as an environmentalist, it didn't matter to me because if you didn't have clean air, you didn't have a right to live from my perspective.

I came down to Houston with the kind of mentality of prosecution that I'd learned in Washington, D.C. I'd spent a year in the United States District Court watching some of the best U.S. prosecuting attorneys who prosecuted under Nixon's Safe Streets Act. They took the power of the government and put it against essentially poor black people who were violent in the streets. Well I took the power of the State of Texas and put it against the powerful, rich corporations that were polluting. I did the same thing that I'd learned except that I was David fighting Goliath; but it didn't

matter to me because maybe I didn't know any better. The first case I had was against Champion Paper Company, and I opened up the file from the State of Texas and there's no evidence, no evidence! The case was four years old and there was no evidence in the file. And I had the joy of meeting Dr. Walter Quebedeaux, truly a saint. If there is a saint in the history of Texas in this entire movement, it was the Director of the Harris County Pollution Control Department, Dr. Walter Quebedeaux. There's a park right over here by the courthouse named in his honor. And he was this eclectic scientist who ran this department. He took no compromises at any time. He would be up in front of Commissioner's Court of the City Council. He'd be on television. He would be demanding that people be prosecuted for polluting, and he kept a most wanted list. Well, I thought that was a great idea, but he never publicized the list. So I took it out and put a ten most wanted list in my office and said, you know, here are the companies and you're the most wanted and I'm going to take you one at a time. Well, they were not used to being dealt with in that way. They had the largest law firms in town, and all of the lawyers had kind of divided

Champion Paper and Fiber Company, Pasadena, Texas (Courtesy Houston Metropolitan Research Center, Houston Public Library, Houston, Texas)

up the pollution defense business. And now here was this twenty-five year old kid coming down here to say things like, "Hey Bubba, we're going to trial." And they tried to keep me from even getting to trial. I had to sue the judge in the case of *State v. James,* if you ever look it up, I had to sue the judge to get the case to go to trial.[1] And I had great help from my boss, John Hill. Hill is a great trial lawyer and he approved of my unorthodox behavior.

For example, in the Champion Paper case, what I did is: I went to the League of Women Voters and I said, "Look, I need to win this case. That plant stinks. It's terrible. It's not Pasadena, Texas, it's *Stinkadena.* I need your help. I need you to man the phones." I didn't have the money in the state budget so I swore in these women on television as special assistants to the Attorney General of Texas. You call this number if you've got evidence about Champion Paper polluting. And I took out ads in the *Houston Chronicle* and the *Houston Post.* The ads said, "The State of Texas is going to trial against the Champion Paper Company, if you have evidence call this number. Special deputies will answer the phone."

Well golly, I mean, you talk about turning the tables. One of the lawyers here in Houston, Larry Feldcamp, wrote a letter to the State Bar complaining of my behavior. Well what did I think? I was, in a way, honored by it, but I was offended at the same time. So instead of going to the State Bar, I went to Marvin Zindler of Channel 13 News and said, "Marvin, can you believe this stuff? A big, giant law firm like Baker and Botts tried to take my law license away for doing the work of the people?" So Marvin had this thing on television. He said, "Larry Feldcamp must go to the board and write twenty-five times, 'I will not try to take the law license away from Terry O'Rourke.'" Of course, it changed and the case only settled on the day of trial for a one hundred thousand dollar penalty and a significant injunction. It seems small by today's standards, but at the time, it was larger than all of the penalties under the Clean Air Act and the Clean Water Act in the whole history of the state in one case.

Reel 2030; Time Code 00:13:48

"This is earth in heaven."

I'm into the theology that this is earth in heaven, and if you're going to say a prayer, that instead of saying, "Our Father who art in heaven," I say, "Our mother who is on earth," or, "Our children who are on earth" instead. I think that we have plenty of hell around us, but we've got plenty of heaven. And, for me, one of the greatest things was the discovery of the heaven right here in Houston. I grew up here with this kind of mentality that Houston is a terrible place. You ask people about Houston, and they say, "Oh man, it's hot. The season's terrible. You make your money, get the hell out and go get your place in Aspen, Colorado or get out and go get a place in Galveston." I discovered that Houston and the area around here is one of the richest ecological areas in the whole world. I've come to live in that and love it and I really sincerely believe that is a possibility for all of us, in some way.

In the ecology movement, they often say, "not in my backyard." Are you familiar with that phrase, NIMBY, Not In My Backyard? Well, what is the one that says *In My Backyard,* you know, IMBY? What do I have in my backyard? And I think that that's, in some measure, a test. Whether we're in offices or homes—it can be what's on the balcony of my apartment, or what's in my office—that we look around. What do I have there that speaks of life when I go in there? I've often thought, why don't we take coffee grounds or something like that and make compost out of them? You know, we have all kinds of material. Why don't we take the paper in our offices and make compost out of it and start growing plants around people? But, you know, maybe that's for tomorrow's generation.

1. *The State of Texas, Relator v. Honorable W. Ervin James, Judge, 127th District Court, Harris County, Texas, Respondent,* 494 S.W.2d 956 (Tex. Civ. App.–Houston [1ˢᵗ Dist.] 1973, no writ).

Wardens, Outlaws, and Wildlife

BILLY PLATT SR. served as a game warden for Texas Parks and Wildlife in East Texas. Especially during his early years, game law enforcement was an unpopular and dangerous effort, as stock laws,[1] bag limits, hunting seasons, and restrictions on hunting with dogs were still new to the area. Mr. Platt worked on numerous cases, ranging from fishing violations to night-hunting, poaching rings, meat-hunting, trespass, and other illegal practices. In the early days before fencing, outlaw hunters roamed the Piney Woods, operating with impunity, and in collusion with some local law enforcement officials—creating some tense situations for the wardens.

Interviewed on March 1, 2008, in Jasper, Texas

Reel 2428; Time Code 00:42:34

I had a seven-year old son, my little Grant, and there was a bunch of gangs over in my country, and maybe four or five of us would kill a hundred deer a year. You know, we killed lots of deer. And I shot my last one and I looked at it and I said, "You know, I've got to quit this."

My son is seven years old and if we keep killing deer like we're killing right now, my son's not going to have a deer to hunt because there's a lot of outlaws and everybody was doing what we were doing and you could see the deer population just going down. I said, "I'm going to quit it," so I quit it. And that was about 1960.

> *"'Yes sir, I know how outlaw hunters work.' He said, 'You're just what we need.'"*

In 1962, there was an advertisement in the paper looking for game wardens.[2] I said, well, you know, I did not like game wardens—I didn't want to see one coming—but I did not dislike them. And all my friends were outlaw hunters and I said well, I'm going to apply, and see what I can do to help this situation. The man who became my boss after I was hired, he came to Livingston first and interviewed me. He said, "Billy, I know of you real well. You're a well-known outlaw hunter." I said, "Yes sir, I know that I got a bad reputation, but I quit two years ago and I want to do something to help." He said, "Well, you know all about it don't you?" I said, "Yes sir, I know how outlaw hunters work." He said, "You're just what we need." I had a high school education and they hired me. And my wife came with me to Tyler, they had a regional office there, and I went in and met my boss. He gave me a law book, a badge, a commission card, and one of the first patrol cars issued: an old six-cylinder Ford, '62 model, two-door sedan with no air-conditioner. He said, "Do you know where Newton County is?" I said, "Yes sir," and he said, "Well, go over there and go to work." I did not have one day of law enforcement experience. I really did not know what a warrant was. So they sent me to Newton County. I bought my own pistol, moved in over there, and it was quite a learning experience.

So I caught my first illegal deer hunter using a shotgun out of season, with his old dogs, and he was running deer. When I caught him, I said, "What are you doing out here?" He said, "Just running my dogs." I said, "Well then, what are you doing with your shotgun?" He said, "I just like to carry it, East Texas tradition." I said, "Well, you're hunting deer out of season." I said what I was going to do with him. I said, "You going to have to load up with me and I'm going to carry you to the sheriff's office and we going to see what you were hunting." So I loaded him up, my first arrest, and carried him into the sheriff, locked him up. And I got my first lesson of politics! The local sheriff and the district attorney or county attorney wouldn't prosecute it, people just hunted like this; in East Texas it was their way of living. And then a few days later, I caught two men with a skinned deer. They had the butchered meat in an Igloo cooler. I carried them in, started the file on them, and told the county attorney, "I've got to file this case in county court." He said, "No, we file that in J.P. [Justice of the Peace] Court." And I said, "No, the law reads I have to file it in county court." He said, "I'm the law in Newton County (this was the county attorney), I'm the law in Newton County." I said, "Well, whatever." He said, "How do you know that was a deer?" I said, "I know a deer carcass when I see it, seen them all my life." He said that it might've been a goat. You know, this has been—how many years ago, 1962? I still remember it to this day real plain. He said, "It might've been a goat!" I said it was a deer. He said, "You can't

prove that, I'm dismissing the case." So that gets a person kind of riled up, when you try to enforce the law and your own people in law enforcement and the prosecution treat you this way because you are a game warden enforcing the game laws. Every other law, DWI, they'd handle it, but not a case from a game warden.

Anyhow, I spent my training period by myself in Newton County; went to game warden school at Texas A&M and they assigned me back to Jasper County. So I went down to meet my judges, stopped at Buna to talk to a judge and I said, "Judge, I'm going to be working down here a lot, a lot of outlaw hunting going on here." I said, "I'm going to be working a lot of days and a lot of nights and I'm going to be bringing you a bunch of cases." He said, "Don't bring me a game case." I said, "Sir?" He said, "Don't bring me a game case." So I walked outside and sat down a minute and says, you know, this is bad. When you get down here and you work your butt off and bring them in here and they dismiss them. No, I'm not going to do that. So I had a judge in Jasper, he was a humdinger. He would say, whatever you want, you'll get, as far as setting fines. So when I caught someone down at the lower end of Jasper County, I had one, two, three Justices of the Peace between there and Jasper. I bypassed them all and went to my judge up here in Jasper. This might not have been right, you know, but I had to get something done. And people back then, really didn't know that I couldn't legally file a case up here. But if they said, "No, I want this case filed where I live," I had to file there, if they requested it. But they didn't know that they could do this. And I would bring them up to my hanging judge and he'd hang them. So, you know, the other judges started looking at the situation and then landowners, like the Withers down at Buna, they used to call that judge right quick and say, "Judge, you need to do something about these outlaw hunters. I live here and these outlaw hunters are eating me up, and then Bill comes by here and he catches these outlaw hunters, they take them in there and ya'll dismiss it." They said, "That's not going to work anymore. We want to see something done with them," and it started changing. When your landowners and your local people started wanting laws enforced, things started changing, and they've been changing for the better ever since. It's a good situation now.

Reel 2428; Time Code 00:51:27

You can't really train a person to be a game warden. You can go to Game Warden Academy for seven months and you learn many, many different laws for many different things, but you can't teach the instincts of an outlaw hunter. And you've got a lot of real good young men that now have a college degree. When I went to work, you had to have a high school degree. You've got a lot of game wardens now, they went from high school straight to college. They haven't had a lot of experience in the woods. Back in my outlaw days on maybe a cold drizzly night, we'd say, "Hey, boy, this is a good night to shoot a deer, let's go tonight." We'd go out and we'd kill a deer. So when I got to be a game warden, I knew all this. I mean, I had been an outlaw hunter and I knew how they operated. If I went to bed at ten o'clock at night and at eleven o'clock at night, I heard a drizzle dripping off my house, I'd think, they're stirring tonight. I'd get up and put my uniform on and I'd go out and I'd usually catch a night hunter because I knew how they operate. But it's changed a lot. The regulations now are stiffer. The penalties are severe for getting out here and shooting an old deer at night off a public road or anywhere. You can be arrested and put in jail for a year! It can be a felony, depending on what kind of case you file. Everything has changed so much, but your experience in the woods, well, I have a lot of young wardens come by here and ask me a lot of questions about the old days, which, you know, you enjoy telling war stories. You've got a lot of good young men but it takes them a long time to really learn the woods and how to really catch an outlaw hunter or fisherman.

1. Local stock laws requiring that cattle, sheep, goats and other livestock be fenced were authorized in Texas as early as 1876, but the open range persisted in parts of East Texas well into the post-WWII era, as late as 1960. The tradition of the free range allowed neighbors to graze their cattle and hogs on neighbors' lands, as well as hunt, fish, and trap, without close regard to the landowners' preferences, or the requirements of state game laws. *General Laws of Texas,* ch. 98 (August 15, 1876); Texas Constitution, art. 16, secs. 22, 23; Thad Sitton, *Backwoodsmen: Stockmen and Hunters along a Big Thicket River Valley* (Norman: University of Oklahoma Press, 1995) 194–232; Thad Sitton and C. E Hunt, *Big Thicket People* (Austin: University of Texas Press, 2008) 3, 9, 40, 46, 52, 70.

2. Mr. Platt came to be a warden when game law enforcement in East Texas was still relatively new and rare, though regulation elsewhere in the state was quite well established. The first game laws in Texas were enacted in 1861, a two-year closed season on bobwhite quail on Galveston Island. Severe decreases in wildlife populations in the latter 1800s and early 1900s led to the creation of the Texas Game, Fish, and Oyster Commission in 1907. The first bag limits were placed on white-tailed deer and turkeys that same year, and the first hunting licenses were issued in 1909. Shawn Bengston, Randy Blankinship, and Craig Bonds, *Texas Parks and Wildlife Department History, 1963–2003* (Austin: Texas Parks and Wildlife, 2003), 72. www.tpwd.state.tx.us/publications/pwdpubs/media/pwd_rp_e0100_1144.pdf (accessed November 11, 2009). However, through the 1950s, each county continued to set its own hunting seasons and the means of taking game, with the commissioner's court and county judge taking on enforcement responsibilities. By the 1960s, the state wildlife agency adopted general laws governing wildlife, standardizing the regulations, and making them less subject to local politics.

Butterflies and Moths, Shotguns and Disguises

ROB LEE trained as a biologist, worked as a Special Agent with the U.S. Fish and Wildlife Service, and volunteered in care and education at the South Plains Wildlife Rehabilitation Center in Lubbock. A winner of the 1998 Guy Bradley award, which recognizes outstanding law enforcement contributions to conservation, Mr. Lee is best known for his ten-year effort to eliminate waste oil hazards to migratory birds in West Texas. Mr. Lee also participated in the prosecution of defendants involved in pronghorn antelope killings, rare insect smuggling, burrowing owl poisoning, and game bird poaching. Some of these investigations involved undercover role-playing and a great deal of intrigue.

Interviewed on October 12, 2002, in Lubbock, Texas

I grew up in the country near Toledo, Ohio, outside the city limits, near a hardwood forest and a small creek. I lived quite a ways from most of the people I went to school with. Few other kids lived near us, so a lot of my time was spent alone walking in the woods and searching in the creek; looking at critters, watching butterflies, and having an insect collection. We were primarily looking for butterflies as I remember, that was the big attraction—and moths. We were fortunate that a lot of the North American silk moths are found in Ohio—those cecropia and polyphemus moths. We would find their cocoons in the winter, collect them, and then they would usually hatch before springtime. Quite often we made those part of our collection, though we tried to let them go, but in the winter they didn't survive very well and so we were more careful. We would also collect praying mantis egg cases sometimes, and that was usually a disaster when they ended up hatching quickly in the early spring when they were in our home. I can remember making our own butterfly nets and chasing around trying to catch the elusive tiger swallowtail butterfly. That was the one that we always wanted to try to catch and we were seldom successful. As a young boy I remember a few old books in our home that had pictures of exotic animals, African animals and such, and I think that's when my interest in wildlife probably started.

I do remember a few instances where, as a typical boy, I would get my hands on a BB gun or something. I thought at that time it might be important for me to go out and try to shoot something. My father was a very quiet man and his lessons to us were usually very subtle. But he didn't really tolerate me going out and shooting anything needlessly. And that was a lesson that I learned early, and it was very meaningful to me and it helped really develop an appreciation for wildlife in its natural state. It was not important for me after that to necessarily have to kill something to be fulfilled.

Thinking about childhood, I haven't really encountered very many young children who weren't excited about learning about wildlife. It's just one of those things that once you are exposed to it, it's sort of easy to comprehend. It's not like having to interpret some complex mathematical formula or trying to visualize some chemical reaction in a test tube, because wildlife is *right there* and it can be part of our lives. If you stop and look around you'd be surprised at how much *is* really around you. This discussion makes me think back to one early encounter in grammar school when we had a man come and present a reptile show. I'd forgotten about that. But he had all these different kinds of snakes up there on the stage in our school, our little inner city school in Toledo, and I was pretty fascinated by that. I remember him and how exciting that was for me, and I think that's sort of what I tried to do when I was involved with educational programs.

I think that being able to be there and be surrounded by natural resources was a big part of what led me into

Polyphemus moth (Earl Nottingham, courtesy Texas Parks and Wildlife Department)

this career: that I was just fortunate to be able to walk outside my door and go right into the forest. I think it meshes very well in my current career enforcing natural resource law. I believe that every encounter I have is an educational experience, both for me and for the person I might be interviewing. And I don't simply have a desire just to catch bad guys. It's important to educate people as well and to help them develop an appreciation for natural resources, because it's going take a lot more people than just one Fish and Wildlife agent to really make a difference. So I look at every encounter as an opportunity to do that.

Reel 2241; Time Code 00:11:45

"They would just kill them and let them lay."

One of the more elaborate Fish and Wildlife undercover investigations I participated in involved some outfitters who were advertising some very exclusive dove hunts in the Permian Basin area of Texas over in Winkler County. They had a large ranch with a lot of historic buildings, a very rustic rural setting, and very good dove hunting. The woman who owned the ranch was quite an accomplished hunter and marksman. She started a business where she would bring in exclusive clients for a three-day dove hunt on her ranch. And then she'd put you up in a little fleabag motel in a little community there and you'd have these dove hunts. But she offered gourmet meals and safari tents with an open bar and everything out on the ranch at night. And she advertised it in such a way that indicated they were probably doing a little more hunting than they're supposed to do there. We were curious and so I decided to open an undercover case against her. I called her up just to see what kind of situation they had there and in talking found out it was one thousand dollars. This was the most expensive dove hunt that any of us had ever heard of. You had to pay one thousand dollars to be a part of this! So I called her and indicated that I had the means to pay her for this kind of a hunt. And in talking with her, she sort of loosened up and was indicating to me that well, "we'll go hunting in the morning and we'll get a limit of birds and then we'll feed you lunch and then you can sack out and then we'll pick you up and we'll go out in the afternoon and we'll kill another limit of birds, and we'll do that a couple of times." And we knew that what she was doing was what we suspected. So we booked some hunts and I got to go out there posing as a rich hunter. I had to get some special clothes and borrow some fancy guns that we had seized in some other cases and mingle with the other customers she had there.

I was able to kill my limit of birds in the morning, and then we still had them in our truck in the afternoon. And it was really interesting, because when we were going out to hunt again in the afternoon, she sent one of her employees over, and he said, "I've got to get your birds out of your truck. We can't let the game warden catch you with the morning's limit." So we had

some pretty good evidence that they were taking over the limit. And then I documented what all of her other clients killed, and they killed two limits on those days. I did that one year and another agent, Nick Chavez, had done it the previous year and made similar cases.

Then, before we were going to take this case down, some of the clients that he hunted with invited him to come to Louisiana for a big duck-poaching weekend. We couldn't turn that down, so we sent him over there! They picked him up at the airport, and wined him and dined him, and then they went out and slaughtered ducks. They would just kill them and let them lay. They were shooting other kinds of birds as well. Nick used a GPS unit and he sent in the coordinates over a cell phone to the pagers of the other agents in Louisiana. So they were able to then use their GPS units to find out where they were and to make those cases. And once we had that established, then it was a few months after that that we let these poachers know that we also hunted with you guys on the illegal dove hunts in Texas. Then we served a warrant on the outfitter and the ranch owner's home. And we uncovered records of other hunters going back five years. So through a variety of telephone interviews and in-person interviews we were able to make cases on over 30 of her clients over a period of five years. It was a fairly significant case affecting lots of people and I ended up citing people from California, Pennsylvania, Boston, Maine, New York, and Kentucky. It was a very interesting case.

What I've encountered with a lot of people that are doing hunting, and this is just one aspect of the people that we deal with, is that they're successful busy people and they have a lot of money, but they don't have a lot of time. It's pretty common among them to say, "I don't have much time, I want the biggest bang for my buck, so let's go out and basically let's see how many things we can kill." They don't really perceive it as being anything like money laundering or bank fraud. It's just a little "game violation," and they don't have any qualms about doing it.

Smokestacks and Asthma, Rights and Rules

BRANDT MANNCHEN served as an environmental investigator for the City of Houston Bureau of Air Quality Control for many years, where he inspected and monitored large industrial facilities for compliance with local, state, and federal air pollution law. He also was a co-founder of the non-profit group GHASP, the Galveston-Houston Association for Smog Prevention', and has filed numerous private citizen comments on the State Implementation Plan, Grand Parkway, and other issues affecting Houston air quality, which struggles with hazardous air emissions and high ozone levels.

Interviewed on October 22, 2003, in Bellaire, Texas

Reel 2281; Time Code 00:01:38

"Without air, you're out of business right away."

The boosters here always talk about Houston being unique, and I totally agree with them. Where else are you going to get this massive amount of petrochemi-cal refinery capacity anywhere else in the world?[2] Now, you know that people breathe approximately twenty thousand quarts of air a day. It's involuntary, so we don't think about it. We just breathe. But when you have a problem like asthma, where you can't catch your breath, then you start realizing just how important it is to breathe because without oxygen, in two or three minutes you're dead. You can go three, four days, maybe even a week without water. Maybe you can go thirty days without food. But without air, you're out of business right away. Now we seem to have a lot more children and a lot of other people developing asthma that just have never had these problems before. I've spoken to a lot of parents and they say, "Yeah, my child has asthma. My child has to take something every day to help them catch their breath or if they have an attack." I just don't believe that what's being emitted by a lot of these large facilities are particularly beneficial things to inhale. I think that complicates the whole situation and the scientific research seems to indicate that also. I feel like I'm on pretty firm ground to say that air pollution hurts you and the more we can reduce it, from my standpoint, the better off we are.

That's why I like "command-and-control" versus these economic arguments like "we'll put a price on pollution" and trading pollution credits.[2] For me, I just want to say, "Here's your limit and if you've got a stack emission, you've got to reduce it to that limit." It seems like that's much easier to do than talk about something that's worth fifty dollars a ton and that this guy can reduce it or this guy can pay some other guy for the amount that he's reduced so he doesn't have to reduce it. I mean, think about the economic and the environmental unfairness of it all. If I lived next to a facility and this facility doesn't want to reduce its sulfur dioxide, for instance, and then buys a credit from somebody else who's reduced that sulfur dioxide, that person living there is still stuck breathing that stuff. Why should they be forced to breathe that? It seems to me a basic tenet, a basic right everyone has, is to breathe, just to live.

So those economic mechanisms of reducing air pollution, I don't like them. I'm an old throw back. I like command-and-control. Put a limit on that sucker and then I can test it, then I can see if it's there. If you have a lot of mumbo-jumbo written on paper, and then you bought pollution credits, for an investigator it's very confusing trying to figure out whether you have met your cap or not met your cap. So, for me, I prefer simplicity. You know, I always tell companies, "The worst thing you can have is a confused investigator in your facility." So whatever you do, make sure it's simple so that we can understand what it is you're doing, because you don't want an investigator who's confused about what it is you're doing. And I think these economic ways of reducing air pollution are very confusing, at least for me. Besides, I think we should maximize pollution reduction.

So far, we haven't found any limit that is good for you, and so I think it's better to err by reducing it than to err and say, "Well, let's allow them to put a little bit more out." That seems to be going in the wrong direction for me. With emissions, I would say you want to get as close as you can to zero as possible. In my opinion that's the way we ought to go because I don't have a choice: I have to breathe the air, *whatever* it is. If you're putting that stuff out there and you're doing

that because you don't want to pay the cost of the air pollution equipment to control that, it doesn't leave me a choice: I've got to breathe your trash and I don't think that's fair. To me that's an insult. It's a nuisance, a trespass on the air, which is a "common good" type of resource. Everybody deserves clean air from the poorest person to the richest person in River Oaks, and it shouldn't be based on where you live and what facility is next to you. While technically that's difficult to do, and in some cases that may be very hard to do, I think we should strive to go in that direction because I'd like to have zero emissions. I'm visionary enough and romantic enough to believe we can do that eventually, but we won't if we always make excuses and say that you can "buy your way out of this." Why do we put a price on air, anyway? I mean, it's priceless. I mean, you can't live without it so why would you want to filth it up? So that's just my perspective.

Reel 2281; Time Code 00:21:52

I guess the reason that I have worked for the City of Houston for almost twenty-nine years, is just because I always wanted to be a public servant. I always wanted to help people and it seemed to me that working as an air quality investigator was one way that I could physically put my hands around helping people. I could actually say, "They fixed that because I called them on it, and that means that stuff is not in the air anymore." For me, I guess, one of the things that's kept me going is that, who else is going to protect the public if not government-sponsored agencies specifically set up to do that? Industry is not going to do it: their highest calling is to their stockholders and to the highest amount of money they can generate in a quarter or a year or whatever. We already know laissez-faire doesn't work, we had that in the late 1800s, early 1900s. That's why we've got a lot of the child labor laws and food safety laws. We know if left strictly on their own, industry will not do the right thing because that's not why they're set up.

Razed house, industrial buffer zone, Port Arthur, Texas—1994 (© Sam Kittner/kittner.com)

At my job, I've been punished for my activities outside of my work, whether as a volunteer worker for the Sierra Club or just on my own. I once had a Bureau Chief who wanted to fire me because of my Sierra Club activities and I outlasted him; just got lucky. I had a "protector" within the City who was bigger than he was and some people were afraid of that person. I managed to slip, kind of, in between the blockers. So I lucked out, but I have been punished for my efforts. I've been told that I don't have good judgment. I've been looked upon suspiciously because I speak on behalf of the Sierra Club sometimes in public and at public hearings before the state on air pollution matters. But when you're in the job itself of dealing with compliance you've got to deal with what rules and laws and regulations you have. You can't create new ones. So I don't personally see a conflict there. When I go out to a company, I don't create a new rule and say, "Gotcha!" I can't do that. My supervisors wouldn't allow me to do that anyway and I don't want to do that. I have to use what's on the books. But there isn't a lot of passion in many of the agencies. People don't think of these jobs as, "Gee, I want to help the public." They think of it as, "Oh, I got a job, thank goodness," and I can understand that.

I, however, think it is a good job for missionary zeal, but unfortunately the people in charge don't necessarily feel that way. I mean, you always have to be fair. You don't want to issue a violation to an industry that they don't deserve. I don't want that any more than the industry does. On the other hand, you've got to call it the way you see it, too. And with our agency, you know, I'm not the only one calling them on it. My supervisor looks at what I do, and we go to the state regulatory agency and ask them to look at what we do, because I sure don't want to be wrong. If I go to a company with something I perceive as a problem, I want them to understand that I know what I'm talking about, and to have at least enough confidence in my abilities to the point where they'll say, "Okay, let's look at this."

1. GHASP merged with the non-profit group Mothers for Clean Air in April 2010 to form Air Alliance Houston.

2. Houston hosts nearly 40 percent of the nation's base of petrochemical manufacturing capacity, with four hundred chemical production facilities. City-Data.com, "Houston: Economy," http://www.city-data.com/us-cities/The-South/Houston-Economy.html (accessed February 5, 2009); Ken Sexton and others, "Comparative Assessment of Air Pollution—Related Health Risks in Houston," *Environmental Health Perspectives* 115, no.10 (2007), http:www.ncbi.nlm.nih.gov/pmc/articles/PM2022677/ (accessed November 16, 2009).

3. Pricing and trading pollution had its first major test under the Acid Rain Program of the 1990 Clean Air Act, where an aggregate level of acceptable sulfur dioxide emissions was calculated, and proportionate shares of that emission total were distributed to major polluters. The polluters, typically coal-fired utilities, then traded these emission rights, with plants that had higher costs of control tending to sell their rights to those with lower costs. As a result, sulfur dioxide (SO_2) emissions were lowered at a price some 80 percent less than a standard command-and-control approach, and are on track for a 50 percent reduction in emissions by 2010 over 1990 levels. U.S. Environmental Protection Agency, "Clean Air Markets: SO_2 Reduction and Allowance Trading under the Acid Rain Program," http://www.epa.gov/airmarkets/progsregs/arp/s02.html (accessed January 28, 2009). The cap-and-trade model has since been applied to controlling nitrogen oxides (NO_x), volatile organic compounds (VOC), and carbon dioxide (CO_2) emissions. Accepting its value, critics of cap-and-trade do show that there are still drawbacks to it—its creation of private rights to use a public resource (to pollute clean air), its uneven effects from one plant and community to another (air quality in communities might hinge on the cost of cleanup at their local plant, not on health risks), and the possibility of fraud and loopholes in its accounting systems.

Boots & Compass

"I only went out for a walk and finally concluded to stay out till sundown, for going out, I found, was really going in."[1]

JOHN MUIR

FOR THE INTREPID, for those whom muck-laden boots, mosquitoes, and poison oak are mere inconveniences, the backwoods, remote streams, and lonely deserts of Texas provide an untold bounty. Overlooked by the impatient, casual tourist, here lay the enigmatic details, rendered in petals, ripples, and strata. To the curiously observant, these reveal not simply frozen moments in evolution, but clues to the past and future of the plant and animal kingdoms. As such, their preservation is invaluable.

It takes perseverance to buck a scorching sun, strong headwinds, and impenetrable brush. These plucky Texans, armed with oars and walking sticks, have brought to the public's attention–often at great personal cost—the richness of their state's biological heritage.

1. Linnie Margh Wolfe, ed., *John of the Mountains: The Unpublished Journals of John Muir* (Madison: University of Wisconsin Press, 1938), 439.

Big Timber and the Big Thicket

GERALDINE WATSON is a self-trained botanist who lives near Silsbee, in southeast Texas. She has made many contributions to protecting the Big Thicket, from her efforts in identifying and collecting plants for the University of Texas and the National Park Service, which went far to document the great biodiversity of the Big Thicket, to her political efforts with the Big Thicket Association to advocate for a federal preserve, to her work restoring a portion of the Thicket on her own land, near Warren. In 2003, the University of North Texas Press released her book, *Reflections on the Neches: A Naturalist's Odyssey Along the Big Thicket's Snow River*. Her advocacy for the creation of the Big Thicket National Preserve—with the aid of colleagues Ned Fritz and Maxine Johnston—occupied most of her time during the 1970s. Although the effort was successful, it came at a great price to her own family and personal well-being.

Interviewed on October 12, 1999, in Warren, Texas

Reel 2056; Time Code 00:01:55

I guess to tell you about my involvement with Big Thicket I need to go a long way back. I was born and raised in this area, spent my childhood in the woods along the streams. In the days before the lumber companies said, "Cut it out," the woods were still virgin. I grew up in these beautiful woodlands, and on Sunday afternoons my mother would take us walking in the woods, picking flowers. We would pick birdfoot violets and winecups and all those things. And Mother would point out plants to us that her mother had made into medicines and dyes. I learned the trees from my father, who worked for a lumber company. He was a machinist at the lumber mill. He loved the outdoors, was a big fisherman. And I followed behind Daddy up and down the streams and through the woods. I learned to appreciate and understand what was there when I was very young.

Wild azalea (Courtesy Dan LaMee)

". . . It all started when we were going to have children. We wanted a little bit of woods for them."

It's been my memory of these forests and this land that has inspired me to try to save a little bit of what's left. And in my own preserve here, I try to restore a little bit of it as it once was. Quite a few years went by before I became really involved in the environmental movement. And, I guess it all started when we were going to have children. We wanted a little bit of woods for them. So we bought this little bit of woods. And I put trails through it and planted azaleas and ferns and all that sort of thing. Then they decided to make a big bypass of Highway 96, and guess where they took the bypass? Right across my woods! So, I was pretty upset over that. Shortly after that I saw a notice in the paper that Lance Rosier was going to reorganize the Big Thicket Association.[1] It said anybody that was interested to come to the church building there in Saratoga the next Sunday. So, I was pretty fired up at the time, so I was there. And, that was the beginning of my involvement with the Big Thicket cause.

Reel 2056; Time Code 00:11:16

The Big Thicket Association began like every other organization: everybody involved had their own ideas about what needed to be done. There was a faction that wanted ten thousand acres in what we call the "Traditional Thicket," which is, dense, thickety wetland. And then there was another faction that was interested in the "ecological" Big Thicket, which included maximum diversity of habitat. There was sort of a war that went on between the proponents of the preserve, at the time. Ned Fritz and I were supporting the ecological Thicket, and there were certain other people who were supporting the other way. But, we did manage to get together and come to a compromise with something to present to the Park Service and Congress to where we could all stand together on it. And our Senator, Ralph Yarborough, was very active in promoting the Thicket. He wanted one hundred thousand acres. Eventually it came down to a plan for a number of different, scattered units, amounting to about seventy thousand acres. But, we managed to work together on it because I suppose we all really wanted to see the bill passed. And we realized it would never get passed as long as we were fighting one another.

"You never go against the powers-that-be in an area that has a one-product economy . . ."

The lumber companies were our bitter enemies. They were saying, "How can you expect us to save the Big Thicket when those people can't even agree on what and where it should be saved?" The lumber companies had full page ads in the local papers telling the local people that if the Big Thicket bill passed, it would take their homes and that they would lose their oil royalties on their property. They also claimed it would stop all hunting and fishing in East Texas and all sorts of things like that. And of course, it would bring a horde of all these Yankees down here, and southeast Texas and especially the Big Thicket area

Village Creek, Big Thicket National Preserve (Photo by David Bezanson)

is a pure, unreconstructed Rebel area. The Civil War isn't over to most of them. These people were really stirred up. All those who lived in the areas of the proposed Big Thicket units thought that they were going to lose their homes: that everything was going to be taken away from them. So everybody hated my guts, and would spit at me when they'd pass me on the street, that sort of thing.

During the ten years that we were trying to get the bill passed to create the Big Thicket, my children, who were growing up in that area, faced a lot of persecution. It would take a book to tell how they were treated. It was pretty bad. If I had known then what it would mean

to my family, I would have never got involved in the Big Thicket. You never go against the powers-that-be in an area that has a one-product economy, because they control the schools, they control the law enforcement people, they control the courts, they control everything, the economy, everything. And nobody is going to go against them. The teachers at school are the wives or daughters of the executives of the lumber companies. And they can really make it hard on kids. My youngest daughter, her life-long friend said to her, "Regina, I'm sorry that I can't invite you to my party, but I'm sure you understand it's because of who your mother is." And, that was one of the milder things.

Just before I was to go to Washington, D.C. to testify at hearings, I got a phone call from a forester, who said that Rosier Park (that was a little park near Saratoga that belonged to the Big Thicket Association) had pine bark beetles infesting it, and that we were going to have to cut down the trees out there. And I said, "Well, I am not an officer in the Big Thicket Association. You'll have to talk to Maxine Johnston about that." Well, he kept on and on about it. And, I said, "Look, they had that area checked out by an entomologist who said there were no pine bark beetles there." And he said, "Well, I am a forester and I say there are and you better do something about it or we'll sue you." And I laughed and I said, "Hey look, you can't sue me. I'm as poor as Job's turkey and the Big Thicket Association doesn't have any money." I said, "Just call Maxine Johnston." And I hung up. Well, I was in Maxine's office the next day and the boy at the [Beaumont] *Enterprise* newspaper called. He had gone up there to cover the story and the forester had given them this terrible story about how this terrible infestation of pine bark beetle[2] was spreading to all the private landowners, and they were going to lose millions of dollars, and all that sort of thing. And when Geraldine Watson, head of the Big Thicket Association, was told of this plight, she merely laughed. "Well," Maxine told him, "Hey, Geraldine is here now, why don't you talk to her yourself?" So, I talked to him. And he said, "Well, this is clearly a case of harassment. We'll forget about it."

A few days after that, my daughter Eden, who was fourteen, and my son, David, who was about fifteen and a half, never in trouble in their lives, real good kids, were in my VW van, and they were stopped by the police. In the van I'd left a box that had some plant specimens I'd taken to the University of Texas Herbarium to study. The police claimed that they were the remnants of marijuana. They also claimed that they found the medium for growing psilocybin mushrooms in my carpet. I had been carrying some manure from my flowerbed, which is all it was. And they threw my two kids in jail. They beat the snot out of David. They put Eden in a cell

between the cells of convicted men criminals. For two days, there was nothing we could do. We did everything we could to get them out and when we finally did, every time the case would come up for resolution, the police would say, "Well, we've misplaced the evidence." It was always one thing or another. This issue hung over their heads for two years. Eden was the first to break down. She had to spent time in a psychiatric hospital. In the meantime they were being really badly treated by the other kids and all. David lasted until he graduated, then he broke down. David couldn't walk down the street without the police grabbing him up and harassing him. After the Big Thicket legislation got signed, that was the end of it. But, this is just one incident of what the family went through. And my husband, who was a really conservative, conservative Republican, somebody began to tell him that all these people I was associating with were Communist. These liberal Democrats who were promoting the Big Thicket were Communists. I didn't intend to get off into that. But that's what happened.

1. Efforts to secure a protected area for the Big Thicket reach far back, and have continued to the present day. In 1936, H. B. Parks and V. L. Cory completed the *Biological Survey of the East Texas Big Thicket Area* (College Station: Texas Agricultural Experiment Station), which was one of the first attempts to document and outline the Thicket, describing it as roughly one million acres in size. In 1966, Senator Ralph Yarborough introduced the first Big Thicket National Park bill, which succeeded in passing the Senate. In 1970, Representative Bob Eckhardt sponsored a bill to establish a park of 191,000 acres, and, in 1973, Congressman Charlie Wilson introduced a bill to protect 75,000 acres. Finally, in 1974, the Big Thicket National Preserve Bill was signed into law, authorizing a sanctuary of 84,550 acres. The Big Thicket Addition Act of 1993 authorized 10,766 acres to be added to the Preserve. Big Thicket Association, "Track Record," http://www.btatx.org/About (accessed January 28, 2009).

2. Southern pine bark beetle infestations can damage standing timber but they tend to peak and trough in normal cycles of perhaps as long as one hundred years, seldom kill infected trees, and often are confined to one acre. Critics have charged that the Forest Service has tended to overreact in their efforts to isolate pine bark beetle outbreaks from affecting merchantable timber, with buffer cuts as large as sixty-eight to one hundred acres at five Texas wilderness areas, and most controversially, fifty-six hundred acres in an area proposed for wilderness designation in East Texas. Robert W. McFarlane, *A Stillness in the Pines: The Ecology of the Red-Cockaded Woodpecker*, (New York: W.W. Norton & Company, 1994), 184, 187.

Plants, Tools, and Civilization

SCOOTER CHEATHAM is an architect and botanist who has managed multi-disciplinary land use studies of the Texas coast for the General Land Office, taught architecture at the University of Texas Austin, rebuilt Native American Caddo and Pamunkey sites, and provided drawings and photographs for various botanical field guides. His major effort over the past thirty years has been to direct, illustrate, write, edit and lay out the *Encyclopedia of the Useful Wild Plants of Texas,* a twelve volume, six thousand page work produced by the Useful Wild Plants Project and designed to find and publicize textile, food, construction, and pharmaceutical uses for native plants, ensuring the survival of the plants and the continued viability of farming and ranching families and communities.

Interviewed on April 1, 2001, in Lajitas, Texas

Reel 2147; Time Code 00:21:58

At the time I was working on a General Land Office study and practicing architecture, I also developed an interest in anthropology. I guess it really began with a research project that another colleague, Glen Goude, and I did in 1971. We studied a primitive culture and were looking at some of its enigmas and mysteries. I think archeologists and anthropologists have more

questions than they have answers. And they've got interesting tools and they've got theories, but often they just kind of leave it at that, they don't test it out. Now, another new term at that time was "experimental archeology." That implies that you take what you know and you try something, you do something with it. If you have a fireboard and a drill and you wonder about it, then you try to make a fire with a similar fireboard and drill and see whether it's possible, how long it takes, and what you can learn from that. So we did that, and we did it with a culture on my grandmother's place at Concrete [a small town in Guadalupe County, Texas]. We felt we were going to solve some of these riddles and what we ended up with was a great many more questions. Glen and I went down there, with this wonderful tool set—these really nice stone tools and bone tools—and we were supposed to be down there for a week. We even wore deerskin clothes! When we got there, we had nice tools but we didn't have anything to eat. I think, over a week's time, we harvested a possum and an armadillo. I didn't eat all the opossum, it was pretty greasy. We were pretty hungry, and we were asking lots of questions that we didn't have answers for.

*"Civilizations are entirely driven
by the plant kingdom."*

One of the questions was, given these wonderful tools from primitive cultures that archeologists had been focusing on for a long time, where does *everything else* come from? If we were starting a civilization anew—and there we were in this wilderness with just these tools—how would you start over? We kept asking that question throughout that week. What became clear, that might not have ever happened otherwise, is that we merely give lip service to the fact that plants are important. However, it became very clear to us that civilizations are entirely driven by the plant kingdom. Almost everything they do has a carbon product involved with it. You may have stone, but you had to cut it with something. If you go back and look at what you cut it with, it may have been steel or a chisel. If it was steel, it had to be pig iron mixed with carbon. If you just start looking more carefully at everything, you find that there's carbon behind it all, which means plants are behind it all.

We'd spent this time doing this experimental project on the Guadalupe River and I became aware for the first time how important the plant kingdom is. And I wanted a reference to explain to me the uses of all these plants that we have down there. And I found out there was no such thing. Along with my colleague, Marshall Johnston, we agreed to take on putting a book together. And we looked at why we would do Texas as an economic botany region. See, if you took away political boundaries and you looked only at biological boundaries, there are eleven zones that come together here. And so if you used something like Texas as a template, then you're really addressing a large part of northern Mexico. I mean, if we didn't have the Rio Grande right over here, this might be considered part of Mexico; the zones are about the same, and we saw the same species in the Mexican side as we were seeing on the Texas side. And in South Texas, we have the Rio Grande Plains that extend all the way down to Monterrey, and we've got the Rocky Mountains coming through as well. So, we're representing a great part of North America by doing Texas.

Carrying an interdisciplinary interest over to this subject, I thought it was very important to bring together all of the sciences that might relate to a plant species: chemistry, phytochemistry, medicine, pharma-ceutical interests, domestic applications, food uses—economic botany on a broader scale. We also decided, thinking ahead that this work might be the first piece in a larger work to cover the entire world, that if we studied a plant, we would treat all of the uses wherever they occurred all around the world. So if we had a species that occurs in Texas, and it occurs in Cuba, maybe even China, we'd cover all those uses everywhere. Eventually, when this is done, anybody, anywhere in the world can find anything they want to know about this plant as it occurs.

Reel 2147; Time Code: 00:34:18

I see the *Encyclopedia* [*of Useful Wild Plants*] as the kind of information that I think would appeal to land-owners and some small business people who are looking for some ways to get some sustainable economic value from their land and maybe not bulldoze their property and damage the land. At the same time, we hope we're educating people about the intrinsic value of each species to just exist for its own right, its great contribution and value to human beings. Each of these species is, in itself, a self-sustaining factory that pro-

Monarch butterfly on milkweed (Courtesy Karen Gallagher)

duces chemicals and alkaloids and, in many cases we've found out how to use those. We really have just begun to understand these "factories" that produce carbon products for us. We're hoping that there will be a strong conservation bent to recognize the importance of these plants and make sure their safety and future is secured.

There may also be commercial applications for the use of native plants—we've estimated a hundred thousand new uses in the *Encyclopedia*—like making perfume. The problem is, you may know what the use is, you may know how to make this new perfume, but how do you get anybody wanting to buy it? In our culture, marketing is such a big factor—distribution and marketing. It requires a whole economic structure to create the market to bring a product into existence. So, for now, the safest thing would be to go with something that already is well-marketed. An example would be something like milkweed fiber. There's already a company called Ogalalla now that makes hypoallergenic pillows and life jackets that are lighter than kapok and comforters and such things using milkweed fiber. In Nebraska, the local farmers there, I'm told by the company president, make more money growing milkweed than they do from growing traditional crops. And they're not able to grow traditional crops in a lot of cases because there is a surplus and they don't have anything to grow. So economically they're coming out much better off. If you grow milkweed that's local to your area it requires very little fertilizer, very little extra water, so there's no question that it's much more energy efficient to grow these things.

A Dam, A Refuge, and a Canoe

RICHARD DONOVAN worked in the timber and real estate industry, and has volunteered more and more of his time to preserve the habitat and way of life that he knew growing up in Zavalla and other parts of East Texas. In recent years, his chief focus has been on securing protection for the free-flowing reaches of the Neches River, which are threatened by impoundment at the Fastrill and Rockland dams. Towards that goal, he has twice boated extended lengths of the Neches, writing about the effort in *Paddling the Wild Neches*.

Interviewed on March 3, 2008, in Lufkin, Texas

Reel 2433; Time Code 00:31:10

I saw that layout of those dams, and it just stunned me. It was just like I'd lost a family friend, because the plan said they would probably start construction of Rockland Dam[1] within ten years. And I didn't know what to do. It didn't really dawn on me at the time that I could do anything. I'm just one person, and East Texas is not really environmentally aware. And I was a part of that culture for a long, long time. We in East Texas like to pummel the earth, it seems to me, and I don't know how we're going to change that mindset. But, we need to be proud of where we live, because we live in a beautiful area. But, we're so close to the forest sometimes we can't see the trees, or so close to the trees we can't see the forest maybe.

Anyway, I saw that plan and I muddled that over in my mind for quite some time. And just perchance I was reading the U.S. Forest Service Forest Management Plan. It's a big thick tome of a book, and all of a sudden, I read that there exists the possibility that the Neches River would qualify for a "wild and scenic river" designation under the Wild and Scenic Rivers Act.[2] And I just couldn't believe that, and then this idea just flashed in my mind: I thought, "If I were to get out and canoe the river and try to get some publicity focused on the river, the people would recognize what a beautiful treasure that we had there. They would just come out of the woodworks and start beating on dish pans and Congress would be forced to act and protect the Neches!" I was pretty naïve about it, to tell you the truth. But anyway, I proceeded with that idea.

I went and talked to the local press and media companies, and of those I talked to, *The Lufkin Daily News, Jacksonville Daily Progress,* and KTRE-TV expressed an interest in it. We devised places that I would meet them along the canoe trip and places I would hand off copy to them. I would keep a journal—a logbook— and I would hand off notes to them at different places along the river. And they would do stories. I was pretty excited about that, we were going to get something done. So I pushed off from Highway 175, northwest of Jacksonville, and came all the way down to Dam B[3] over a period of twenty-four days. It was in the fall of the year, and the river was extremely low with a lot of logs in

the river, treetops, shallow water—it was a very strenuous trip for a sixty-five-year-old man to be making. I
camped out, of course. And had a little one-man tent
that I went and bought purposely for the project.

"Wildlife would never even know I was there."

I wish every person, man and woman, at some point
in their early life could do that. It would change their
whole perspective on the world. You would have a different appreciation for the place in which we live: to see
how it works, to see all the inner workings of nature. For
instance, a log that's rotting on the ground: you'd see
the bugs and the worms just crawling into that log and
gnawing on it, and the fungi that's growing on it. And it's
slowly decaying and decomposing, and going back into
the ground. And maybe at some stage it was a hollow
log and maybe some kind of wild animal had his den in
there, and the termites that are eating that up. All of that
nature at work. You'd see how critical all of this is to our
well-being. When that's destroyed and when those functions are gone, what is going to happen to the world?

I saw so much wildlife: white-tailed deer were in
abundance. I saw numerous otter, and beavers are back
in such numbers that they're causing a problem. We
don't have very many huge hardwood trees left in the
river bottoms, they were cut and hauled away years
ago. So what few we have, the beaver are girdling those
giants. They're just stripping the bark off all the way
around them, as high up as they can reach. That's what
they're eating. And many of the trees are dying. So I'm
afraid that that blessing is going to be a curse as well.
But I saw a lot of beaver, coyotes, raccoons, white-tailed
deer, as I said. Even in the late fall, there were a lot of
birds, particularly shorebirds, and wading birds, bril-
liantly colored wood ducks and mallards, and I even
saw one merganser hen. And the nature that I saw,
squirrels just chattering and whistling, and hawks
circling overhead, and one white-headed eagle! Just a
magnificent display of wildlife that I experienced on
that trip!

The nights were almost unimaginable. I would slip
in with my canoe, pull up on a sandbar or something
for a campsite, and pitch my tent. And I didn't make a
fire, most often. I just had a little propane burner and
I poured hot water over noodles because I wanted to
keep the weight as low as I possibly could in that canoe,
because of dragging it over those treetops and things.
So wildlife would never even know I was there. And
coyotes would come up within a few hundred feet of
me and just bark and howl and yelp. And I'd even hear
the small whelps, the small pups, barking and yapping
at times. And the owls . . . I love owls! And the barred
owls, and the great horned owls, would talk back
and forth, and call back and forth. The nights were
spectacular!

Sometimes it would be totally devoid of sound. And
I don't know how to explain that, but there would be
absolutely no sound whatsoever, and you could just
feel the silence. Then other nights the little miniature
frogs would be chirping real loud. There were still
some crickets at that time of the year, and they would be
chirping—just the whole array of sounds at night that
you could hear. One night I remember particularly, I
camped under a big white oak tree and there was a nest
of flying squirrels in the tree above my head. And flying
squirrels are one of those animals that can see at night.
And they feed at night, unlike an ordinary squirrel, who
cannot see at night and feeds in the daytime. These feed
at night. And they just rained that acorn litter debris
down on my tent all night long, and were chirping up
above, and that was quite interesting to hear as well.

I can't tell you that this first trip was a rousing success, because although the paper did cover it well,
and the TV stations did cover it well, there was no
groundswell. I sat back and waited for it to happen,
and it didn't happen. I was disappointed that it didn't
happen, but I learned a lesson from it. And so, two
years later, after I had talked to the people at Texas
Conservation Alliance who thought that this was a
good event, I decided to do it a second time. And we
decided to extend the trip on down below Lake B. A.

Coyote (Courtesy Texas Parks and Wildlife Department)

Steinhagen, down to the Beaumont Port at the Golden Triangle area. A million people or so live in that area, and also the Big Thicket National Park[4] is part of their heritage, and the Neches nourishes the Big Thicket. So we thought, if we can get them interested in it as well, maybe we'd get a little bit more public participation. So we decided to extend it on down to the Beaumont/ Golden Triangle area. This time, my daughter Gina was going to go with me. So she put in with me and we traveled together and we made the same contacts with the same media, only we went to Beaumont and contacted the *Beaumont Enterprise,* and Channel 6 and Channel 4 television stations in that area. We got them interested in it, and they expressed a lot of interest. So Gina and I put off and traveled together for a few days. And Texas Parks and Wildlife—complete surprise— they showed up and met us. . . . The 1999 trip, as I said, was moderately successful. But the 2001 trip that we took, when we got them all involved, was spectacu-

lar, beyond our wildest dreams. Never did I dream that there would be so much coverage and so much interest in it.

Reel 2434; Time Code 00:08:56

After the publication of the book[5] I wrote about my trip, there's certainly a lot more awareness about the Neches River, and about environmental issues in the broad spectrum. In fact it has been translated into some initiatives that I never dreamed of. At the present time, we're working on a project called the East Texas Experience, of which our hope is to make the people of East Texas aware of what we have here. We will catalog all the interesting and historical places, generate an infrastructure that will accommodate guests to come here and make East Texas a tourist destination and increase the income of people in this area of the state. At the same time, we'd protect these natural resources that we hold so dear. . . . I've been invited to speak to any number of groups around the area; I am well received by all of them.

We had a tremendous impact on the establishment of the Upper Neches River National Wildlife Refuge.[6] That's a spectacular thing. It's about a twenty-five thousand acre wildlife refuge on the upper Neches, and is some of that pristine, rare, almost exotic, hardwood bottomland.[7] It's almost gone. It's almost non-existent in this state, and even in the United States. And that is some beautiful hardwood bottomland forest up there. And the U.S. Fish and Wildlife Service had been working to establish that thing since sometime back in the eighties. But like all bureaucracies, time grinds slowly with them. There are lawsuits and legal issues still to be decided before it is finalized, but that was a great victory. When we heard that the U.S. Fish and Wildlife Service was interested in doing this, our group, the Texas Conservation Alliance, and its affiliate, the Neches River Protection Initiative, generated somewhere between twelve thousand and twenty thousand pieces of mail. The U.S. Fish and Wildlife Service said that it was by far the most correspondence ever generated by the establishment of any wildlife refuge that they had done in the nation. So that shows you the awareness that has been created among the local people for what the environment holds and the value that we have here. There has been some real good environmental awareness generated by the activity that we've done on that river.

1. Rockland Dam was deauthorized as a federal Army Corps of Engineers project in 1990. However, the state sponsor, the Lower Neches Valley Authority, with promotion from the East Texas Water Planning Group, has attempted to reorganize the project as a state-funded effort. In its current configuration, it would cost about seven hundred million dollars and require condemnation of 150 thousand acres. James Cozine, *Saving the Big Thicket: From Exploration to Preservation, 1685–2003* (Denton: University of North Texas Press, 2004), 233–34.

2. The federal Wild and Scenic Rivers Act was passed in 1968, and currently seeks to protect the free flow and natural character of over 150 river segments. A 196-mile reach of the Rio Grande in the Big Bend is the only segment so protected in Texas. *Wild and Scenic Rivers Act of 1968*, Public Law 90-542, *U.S. Statutes at Large* 82 (1968): 906–918; Tom Cassidy and Jack Hannon. "Section 2(a)(ii) of the Wild and Scenic Rivers Act of 1968: An Underutilized Tool to Designate National Wild and Scenic Rivers," *UCLA Journal of Environmental Law & Policy* 17, no. 1 (January 1999): 145; Wikipedia contributors, "Wild and Scenic Rivers Act," *Wikipedia,* http://en.wikipedia.org/wiki/Wild_and_Scenic_Rivers_Act (accessed January 29, 2009).

3. Congress authorized Dam B, later named Town Bluff Dam, and B. A. Steinhagen Reservoir in 1945. Construction of the fifteen thousand acre lake in the forks of the Angelina and Neches rivers was completed in 1953. A small nearby community named "Dam B" recalls the original dam name. U.S. Army Corps of Engineers, "History of Town Bluff and B.A. Steinhagen Lake," http://www.swf-wc.usace.army.mil/townbluff/Information/History.asp (accessed January 27, 2009).

4. The Big Thicket National Preserve was set aside in southeast Texas in 1974 for protection of its great biodiversity, which includes swamp, deciduous forest, prairie, pine savanna, and dry sandhill ecosystems, and comprises more than one hundred species of trees, twenty orchids and carnivorous plants, and three hundred species of migratory and nesting birds. Originally authorized for 84,550 acres, it now covers roughly one hundred thousand acres in a string-of-pearls layout along Little Pine Island Bayou, Big Sandy Creek, Menard Creek, Turkey Creek, and the Neches River. See Pete Gunter, *The Big Thicket: A Challenge of Conservation* (Austin: Jenkins, 1971); Howard Peacock, *The Big Thicket of Texas: America's Ecological Wonder* (Boston: Little, Brown, 1984).

5. Richard N. Donovan, *Paddling the Wild Neches* (College Station: Texas A&M Press, 2006).

6. In 1988, the U.S. Fish and Wildlife Service first proposed creation of a Neches River Wildlife Refuge to protect its rare bottomland hardwood ecosystem. U.S. Fish and Wildlife Service, "North Neches River National Wildlife Refuge Establishment Proposal, Environmental Assessment, Conceptual Management Plan, & Land Protection Plan," (Albuquerque: U.S. Fish and Wildlife Service, National Wildlife Refuge System, Southwest Region, 2005). http://library.fws.gov/CMP/neches_cmp05.pdf (accessed November 11, 2009). In June 2006, the U.S. Fish and Wildlife Service approved creation of a twenty-five thousand acre Neches River National Wildlife Refuge in Anderson and Tyler counties. In September 2008, Federal District Judge George Solis ruled against a lawsuit the City of Dallas and Texas Water Development Board had filed to protect plans to build the thirty thousand acre Fastrill Reservoir in the same reach of the river as outlined for the refuge. The Fifth Circuit affirmed the district ruling and the Supreme Court declined to rehear the case, so it appears that the reservoir will be blocked, and the refuge will proceed. *City of Dallas v. Hall and Texas Water Development Board v. U.S. Dept. of the Interior, et al*, No. 08–10890, (5th Cir 2009); City of Dallas, Texas v. Rowan W. Gould, U.S. Fish and Wildlife Service, et al., 176 L.Ed. 2d 108 (Sup. Ct. 2010).

7. Bottomland hardwoods make up about 3 percent of Texas land area, and have declined 63 percent from the level seen before the West was settled. They continue to decline at a rate of 12 percent per decade, due to reservoir construction, lumbering, cultivation and development. Texas Parks and Wildlife Department, "The Texas Wetlands Plan: Addendum to the 1985 Texas Outdoor Recreation Plan," (Austin: Texas Parks and Wildlife, 1988), 7; Texas Parks and Wildlife Department, "Texas Wetlands Conservation Plan," (Austin: Texas Parks and Wildlife, December 6, 1996) 29. www.tpwd.state.tx.us/publications/pwdpubs/media/pwd_pl_r2000_0005_textonly.pdf (accessed November 11, 2009).

Ballots & Bills

"Everything is governed by laws. I used to imagine that our Sabbath days were recognized by Nature, and that, apart from the moods and feelings in which we learn to love, there was a more or less clearly defined correspondence between the laws of Nature and our own."[1]

JOHN MUIR

FEW PLACES COULD SEEM more antithetical to nature than the floor of the Texas legislature, where the ornate wooden desks and chairs may symbolize for some the highest use for trees. Likewise, the woodpecker and the sea turtle might be similarly ill at ease in the noisy backrooms and bars where crucial decisions affecting their very survival are drafted and debated. Add to that list perhaps another rare species: elected officials of conscience and good heart. Not that these noteworthy exemplars haven't endured the specter of threats, bribes, and compromises, for the rigors of realpolitik are as daunting as a Gulf Coast hurricane. But with courage and conviction, this gallery of legislators and appointees has left a written body of codes that will hopefully give all the residents of Texas—both critters and folk—equal protection under the law.

1. Herbert Franklin Smith, *John Muir*, (New York: Twayne Publishers, 1965), 58.

Populists, Mavericks, and Farmers

JIM HIGHTOWER has been a long-time advocate of agricultural reform, co-founding and running the Agribusiness Accountability Project from 1970 to 1975, writing books titled *Eat Your Heart Out* and *Hard Tomatoes, Hard Times* explaining his concerns, and holding the elected post of commissioner of the Texas Department of Agriculture (TDA) for two terms (1983–91). While at the TDA, he was noted for introducing programs for high-efficiency irrigation, organic and alternative crops, pesticide regulation, farmworker protection, and Texas produce marketing.

Interviewed on April 9, 2002, in Austin, Texas

Reel 2171; Time Code 00:02:47

"The vast majority of people in this country are no longer in shouting distance of the powers at the top."

I grew up in Denison, Texas, a little town due north of Dallas right on the Oklahoma border. We considered ourselves the first line of defense against the "Okies." And I was raised in a small business family. My mother and father both had come off of tenant farms, which is what that area was in the 1950s. It's largely tenant farmers around there, main street merchants. Denison was a railroad town for the Katy Railroad, so a lot of workers were truck drivers, merchants, farmers. Those are kind of the folks that I grew up with. I later learned that they were "Populists" ; that rather than being particularly liberal or conservative, they actually had this classic Texas anti-establishment maverick streak in them. And so that's where my politics came from: experiencing the reality of ordinary folks battling the powers-that-be. My own father and mother having to contend with the bankers to get a loan; going hat-in-hand down there to do that; contend then as the chain stores grew larger. They couldn't deal locally anymore, they had to send forms in triplicate to Dallas, and then the banks began to move out of the city and out of the state. These are people who would call themselves conservative, yet if you talked about the power of the banks to squeeze them, the power of the oil companies in the Texas Legislature, the power of the lobbyists in Washington D.C., you scratched very progressive people, sort of William Jennings Bryant people. And I realized early on, without putting words to it, that the real political spectrum is not right to left. That's theory; that actually divides us. Rather, the real spectrum is top to bottom. That's where folks actually live. That's the experience that they're having. I have learned in my political years and my writings and radio work and travels that the vast majority of people in this country are no longer in shouting distance of the powers at the top, no matter what those powers call themselves, liberal or conservative. And that these are the work-a-day people of the country and these are the folks that have very progressive instincts within them. They are not the hide-bound, xenophobic conservatives that we are taught that they are. And if we develop a politics that appeals directly to their ideals, their idealism as well as their interests, then we've got a very progressive possibility in this country, a progressive possibility economically, socially, and environmentally.

Now, in my upbringing, we didn't call it "the environment." We didn't know that word. But it was right on Lake Texoma, the Red River, where I spent most of my boyhood just running up and down the creeks around that area and finding out about wildlife; seeing my first owl and first rattlesnake; and playing with the terrapins and horn toads and just having a rather idyllic boyhood. And then I also spent time up around Ector, Texas, Bonham, where my Uncle Ernest and Aunt Eula had a little farm. They were tenant farmers also but had a very successful farm: small operation, fifty acres, raising cotton and a little bit of corn; had a dairy cow, you know, a pig and some chickens. Then I had a great-

uncle down at Weatherford who was my father's uncle and he was what we called a truck farmer; basically raised a little bit of watermelon and chickens and veggies and stuff and would go into the farmer's market in Weatherford, Texas with my uncle Ben Fletcher and sell there. And it was a delight for me as a child. This farmer's market was just a phenomenon. It was so bright and so colorful and the smells were so good and the people were so happy.

Reel 2171; Time Code 00:36:37

"'Status quo' is Latin for 'the mess we're in.' And so it's not easy making the break."

Texas is a state that is awash in chemicals.[1] We're the number one pesticide user, surpassing California. And we are the number one chemical producer and pesticide manufacturer, and there is a lot of money riding on all of that; a lot of banks invested in it; a lot of corporate investors into the "status quo" (which, as one farmer told me, "'Status quo' is Latin for the mess we're in."). And so it's not easy making the break. But you have to trust in the common sense of ordinary folks that if you show them something real, they will look at it, they will absorb it, and that is happening. As consumers become more concerned about what's in their food and air and water, people in the cities and farmers themselves become more concerned and ask, "What am I doing to my land and my water and my family and my neighbors and my workers?" I had more than one farmer come to me and say, "I had a farmer get sick. I'm just not going to do that to people," and was looking for help. How can he get off of this?

That created something that you can't create artificially; that created a political climate that allowed changes to be put forth in a serious way and to be received seriously. And so, as Ag Commissioner, I was the chief pesticide regulator of the state. And we did put forth some new pesticide standards that would protect farm workers more than they had been, which was almost nil. I mean, we were doing basic stuff like: here's a list of chemicals that come with a timetable: once they're applied you can't let anybody go into the field until a certain amount of time has passed. And the farm workers have a right to know what you're putting there and what the medical response to a poisoning would be. We were working with the medical profession, county health officers, farm workers, and environmentalists. And then another set of regulations was geared to people who live up against the fields, because the way pesticides are applied in a state as windy as ours, either by air or by a tractor spraying, there's a lot of drift. And you may be saying, "Well, I'm just going to get my cotton sprayed *here,*" but right over *there,* the veggie garden is getting the pesticide and the cat's getting it and the dog's getting it and maybe the kids out in the yard; the grass is getting it; the rose bush is getting it. That was a real problem almost leading to a territorial war, like it used to be in the old cowboy movies of the cattlemen versus the sheep guys. So we proposed regulations of notification of neighbors; the rights of neighbors to know what's being sprayed, and what they should do, and that the very least they could do was shut their windows or leave the house for a while. Ultimately, that's not the answer, but that's how basic the situation was, because none of that was in place. So we proposed these regulations. And because we had natural resource responsibilities for soil and rural water, we began to do some monitoring of what was going on, and then I also had oversight over pesticide spills and contamination by pesticide companies and that sort of thing, so we began to look seriously into this. We became an environmental advocate with farmers and with farm workers and rural people as well as city people, making that coalition central to our effort. You can't just come from a city and say to a farmer, "No chemicals. Thank you very much. Goodbye." You've got to bring them into it.

In addition, Susan DeMarco, who was our Assistant Commissioner for Marketing and Development,

assembled a phenomenal staff from all over who could open up these markets and develop cooperatives for these farmers to move their new commodities: blueberries and wine grapes that were just starting at the time; the specialty vegetables for high-dollar restaurants, the organic production. We had to move that product, because it's no good to say to a farmer, "All right, we know you're losing money raising cotton, so why don't you raise apples?" Well, unless you've got a market for the apples, because there's a whole investment and knowledge and everything that's got to go into making that switch, it's of no use. So we started with markets, for example, Kroger stores. In Houston, they were the dominant supermarket. And we had a bunch of African American farmers raising watermelons over in East Texas right outside of Houston: wonderful melon, just delicious, but they couldn't get in those markets, and so they were selling on the side of the road getting what they could for their melons. Susan DeMarco and her marketing team met the executives at Kroger and said, "We've got better watermelons just two counties away from where your stores are than you're now bringing in from Georgia and California;[2] melons that would be cheaper for you. And these melons would sell." This was our pitch, because Texans have a chauvinistic feeling about our state. And sure enough, to pretty much get us out of the office, they bought a load of watermelons from this co-op. And sure enough that whole bin of watermelons sold out. And then we had a promotion program for them. DeMarco developed a thing called "Taste of Texas" so they could label, "This is a Texas-made product." So we had the Taste of Texas flag and they could use that logo in their newspaper and television ad. And sure enough, that bin of watermelons sold before any other watermelon was touched. And they bought another load and another load, and what we had done was to help organize the market. Initially, Kroger said, "Well, we can't go up and down the road buying watermelons, you know. We're a big company." We said, "No, there's a co-op. We'll deliver the volume;

they'll produce the quality, the standard you want, the size, everything. We'll work with you on it." And suddenly those farmers were in the market. Kroger was making money; the farmers were making money; and so we were out of it. That's government as a catalyst. We didn't run anything. We didn't create anything. We were the catalyst that opened the market up to the enterprise of these good farmers. And we did that in every aspect of our work.

1. Common pesticides in use in Texas include herbicides such as 2,4-D, atrazine, trifluralin, metalachlor, and glyphosate, and insecticides such as malathion, sodium chlorate, ethephon, terbufos, and methyl parathion. Texas Environmental Profiles, "Pesticide Use in Texas," http://www.texasep.org/html/pes/pes_2tex.html (accessed January 28, 2009).

2. The Taste of Texas program was an early example of encouraging local agricultural suppliers and markets to minimize food-miles, the distance between the farmfield and the consumer's plate. Andrea Paxton, email message to Sustag Public Mailing list, alt.sustainable.ag newsgroup, "Hazards of Long-distance Food Transport," October 1,1996, http://www.ibiblio.org/london/agriculture/forums/sustainable-agriculture2/msg02653.html (accessed November 19, 2009). Current estimates are that food travels roughly fifteen hundred to twenty-five hundred miles every time it is delivered to the consumer. Long-food transport distances raise concerns over fossil fuel use, greenhouse gas emissions, foreign food supplier dependence, erosion of local agricultural economies, and, of course, food freshness and safety. Erika Engelhaupt. "Do Food Miles Matter?" *Environmental Science & Technology* 42, no. 10 (2008): 3482. U.S. House of Representatives, Committee on Homeland Security, Subcommittee on Management, Investigation, and Oversight, *Farm to Fork: Partnerships to Protect the Food You Eat: Field Hearing,* Serial No. 110–55, 110th Congress, 1st sess., 2007, 2, http://frwebgate.access.gpo.gov/cgi-bin/getdoc.cgi?dbname=110_house_hearings&docid=f:48929.pdf (accessed November 11, 2009).

Meddlesome Women, Outsiders, and Lobbyists

SISSY FARENTHOLD served two terms as a legislator in the Texas House, representing Nueces and Kleberg counties (near and including Corpus Christi) from 1968 to 1972. She went on to run for Governor of Texas in 1972, and received over four hundred votes at the 1972 National Democratic Convention as the first woman ever nominated for vice president. She has also served as a trustee of the philanthropic Foundation for a Compassionate Society, and in 1998 she received the Lyndon Baines Johnson Lifetime Achievement Award from the Texas Democratic Party.

Interviewed October 4, 1999, in Houston, Texas

Reel 2033; Time Code 00:28:51

Ms. Farenthold's concern for environmental issues began with an early experience of witnessing her mother's legal challenge to an oversized billboard near their property. At that time, it was a bold move for a group of women to undertake such measures, but they gathered strength with the aid of fellow Texan and former First Lady, Lady Bird Johnson. Ms. Farenthold recalls how those efforts dovetailed with the nascent environmental movement.

One of the real changes that came about was when Mrs. Lyndon Johnson came out for beautification. Up until that point, down in my region, we were a group of "meddlesome woman" that had "no business" being down at city council. It was Mrs. Johnson's work on eliminating billboards and beautification in general, which gave our local efforts a legitimacy that we didn't have before. And that made an enormous difference.

And then, in 1970 was the first Earth Day. I was in the Legislature at the time, and participated in it in Austin. We had a huge rally, more than several hundred people. Many of them were students. That was where the activism was at that time, what with the Vietnam business and the environment. The students turned out big time, so to speak, for that. Of course, their primary concern was Vietnam. But, outside of that, whatever the environment entails, they were interested enough to come to an Earth Day. I don't remember the specifics of what I said, though I remember doing my research and probably it was a very dull speech for them, because an open-air speech doesn't lend itself to data particularly. And I had picked up a lengthy article in the *New York Times* about the way our seashores were disappearing. And of course, it's still true. I mean I drive down to Corpus and what was once just a marsh now has apartment buildings on it. And we see that every place. But 1970 was a big Earth Day event in Austin, Texas and other towns and cities in Texas.

Ms. Farenthold graduated from Vassar College and then attended the University of Texas Law School as one of only three women in a student body of eight hundred. Her years working in the legal profession gave her a first-hand view of poverty and other social problems, which shaped her beliefs and compelled her to enter politics.

Reel 2033; Time Code 00:33:11

I had been Legal Aid Director for two years—that would have been 1965 to 1967. And I can only describe it as a soul-searing experience, because, it was also the time of the so-called, "war against poverty." As a young lawyer, the Bar Association guarded zealously what I could do. I was limited to civil actions and consulting, and I found that there was a whole underclass in my community that I was more or less oblivious to. They had what I call "cluster problems." Much of the system really worked against them. And many of the problems stem from state policy. I was repeatedly calling Austin, the Department of Public Welfare, and the regulatory agency for loan sharks. People had problems with what were "contract for sales," you know, rather than deeds. They were contracts where you never did develop any equity in the property and if you missed your payments you lose your house. Many of these problems went back to state policy. And the only state official that I found was of any help was a man who was head of the regulatory agency for the loan sharks. He was the *only* public official. And he actually sent an investigator down, because, by and large, my clients were Spanish-speaking. They had been intimidated into signing these contracts by being sometimes locked in a room until they signed them. I found that they would buy furniture from furniture stores in Corpus Christi that would come in big boxes and arrive broken. I ran into problems with the local Bar Association, because I found that some lawyers owned low rent houses that were in deplorable conditions. I found that we had a hospital for crippled and indigent children, and yet for mothers to get there

with their ailing children they had to change bus zones and therefore pay more fare.

I found so many things that either took place by neglect or indifference—I guess those are the kindest terms you could use for the things that I saw. I had studied the Texas Constitution, by the way, when I was an undergraduate at Vassar. I was concerned about the state and our government even back then. But those two years of Legal Aid gave me a picture of state government that I never, ever had before, of the lack of care, the lack of interest in human beings. So, the night of the candidacy filing deadline in 1968, a friend who had been in law school with me, and who had had been on the opposite side in some of these legal aid cases that I had tried down at the court house, asked me to run for the Legislature. And I said, "I'll have to ask my husband and I'll ask my cousin, Dudley Dougherty," who had served a term in the Legislature. And it was getting late in the evening of the deadline and so I talked to both of them and they encouraged me to run. They actually did. And I wouldn't have done it, at that time, without that support. And, so that's how I literally came to it. I later learned that I was to be a "stalking horse": I think I was put in the race to see that someone else *didn't* win. But I didn't know that until later. And by then, I was off on my own. During that election in 1968 I had all these men advisors, but the people that did the work were the women, and they were these women out of the League of Women Voters, primarily Jim Alice Scott and Ruth Gill. Both people very concerned about the environment in Corpus Christi and its environs. So that's how I came to the Legislature.

During her career in Texas state politics, Ms. Farenthold was an early critic of environmental abuses who challenged the barriers to public participation, conflicts of interest between government and industry, and the "loopholes" in the laws. Her strong support of campaign finance reform was no doubt influenced by an early encounter with the harsh realities of Texas politics.

Reel 2034; Time Code 00:03:55

". . . He wanted to give me some money . . ."

I didn't know until later that the statewide business lobby was such a major influence, but one incident made it clear to me. I had a very small office in a building, as I was still a practicing lawyer at the time I was in the Legislature. And this lobbyist came in to me and told me that he wanted to give me some money, though he wanted me to understand that "it was illegal." And I hit the ceiling. I think in part it was indignation, but it was fear too. It was something new to me and I asked him to leave.

Later, the head railroad lobbyist, who had been a grader of mine when I was in law school, laughed when I told him the story. He thought it was a big joke. And he took me to lunch one day, and he had a little black book with him and he said there were over two hundred bills that the railroads were concerned with. I never saw the interior of the little black book. But he told me then that the previously mentioned lobbyist had come back to him, and said that he wouldn't ever go see "that woman" again. I can still remember that first afternoon. I didn't know how to deal with it. I saw how it worked, how you're compromised before you ever get into office.

In another experience, I had a lobbyist come in and just start talking, and he told me he was from a shell dredging company. And, he assumed, since I was from the coast, that I supported that kind of activity. Actually, I found it abhorrent because I'd heard over the years what it had done. I could see those muddy bays that had been destroyed by the dredging. And, he said, in effect, you understand we don't ask you to carry our shell legislation, we give it to people in areas like in Fort Worth that won't be bothered by that kind of local coastal pressure.

I think it's a form of indoctrination that new legislators get. First, they get compromised by lobbyists, and I can understand that; you have to have money to run. And during that same period, those first two weeks or maybe even week, I was invited out by a committee chairman, and the chairmen were always part of what they call the "speaker's team." And, he told me how I would work as a team member, and be helpful to the speaker and to the team, and then I could get the legislation I needed and so forth. But that didn't last long. I went off the reservation very soon. But, I learned, I learned . . . I learned.

Politics, Private Property, and the Public Trust

A. R. "BABE" SCHWARTZ served in the Texas Legislature for many years, from 1955 to 1958 in the House and from 1961 to 1980 in the Senate. During his tenure in the Legislature, he chaired the Senate Natural Resource Committee and the Texas Coastal and Marine Council. While in the Legislature, among the most important concerns to Mr. Schwartz was the protection of Texas' "Open Beaches Act,"[1] a piece of legislation crafted by Texas legislator Bob Eckhardt. This Act guarantees the public "free and open access" to the beaches. The law sets the location of the "mean, high tide" as the demarcation of public and private property, but with beach erosion, coastal storms, and the potential for sea-level rise, this law has faced numerous challenges from private landowners and inspired a spirited defense by public servants.

Interviewed on January 20, 2006, in Austin, Texas by Jessica Schoenbaechler (Interview photos courtesy Jessica Schoenbaechler from the film *Beach Drive: Public Rights and Private Property* © 2006)

Reel 2389; Time Code 00:07:34

I first came to the Texas state House in 1955, and first came to the Senate in 1960, but 1961 was the legislative session in which I first served. My first session of the Senate, I was not too impressed with either the Senate or the senators, because I was the young, arrogant, minority Jewish member of the whole Legislature, and I was not well-liked by my enemies, and I didn't like them very much! So, there were tough times. It was very difficult to serve with people who you didn't respect and who gave you no respect in return. So that was a tough time. By 1969, I had become friends with a variety of these people who were friendly and who were on the same side of the battleground that I was. By that time, Barbara Jordan had arrived, and I can pick a few others here and there: Ronald Bridges, Chet Brooks, Joe Christie, Criss Cole. The minority began to carry some weight in the Senate. Before that it was a rock-ribbed, reactionary, right-winged, conservative organization. And by the time we were beginning to come up on eight or ten liberal members, the liberal or moderate minority came to be a controlling factor because of the rules. Once we got eleven votes in the Senate, we were making our own way and doing our own thing. And we were always a minority, but we prevailed more often than we failed.

About this time I began to use my nickname because it became a good political handle. More people were calling me "Babe." I had a bumper sticker about this time that I began to use that didn't have anything but the word "Babe" on it. It didn't have "Babe for the Senate" or "Re-elect Babe to the Senate," it just had "Babe." And people used to kid me about it and I told them, if they don't know who I am, if they don't know who Babe is, I can't get elected anyhow. But the nickname is a good vehicle, a good handle for politicians, if the nickname kind of fits the person. That was about this time I lost my hair, and by 1973, why, I'd lost a lot of it. And I think by then, we had fifteen or sixteen votes of liberal to moderate members of the Senate and we really began to take off and accomplish things that we wanted to accomplish. This was the beginning of a better Senate than we had experienced in the past. The majority of these members were really first-class people and easy to work with, dedicated to their work, by and large, and it was a good time to serve.

Reel 2387; Time Code 00:27:11

"When the hell did it become your beach?"

Fifty years ago, the beaches were really pristine by nature across the United States, except on the East and the West Coast, where the population growth had already overcome the ability of the states to manage their laws. And we began working on the projects that would preserve that state of the beaches and give us an opportunity for the public to have free access and complete use. It was 1959 before Bob Eckhardt[2] got to promoting this addition of this Natural Resource Code that became the Coastal Management Law, or the Open Beaches law. All the changes in the uses of the beaches—conflicts between recreation and development—brought about an awareness in the public that they had this "ownership." If anybody was going to protect that right, then it had to be done in the Legislature. Believe it or not, the Legislature will protect the public rights in that regard if they are aware of what they're doing. The problem is that all these inland members don't really understand this concept either. And you have to tell them, we have to tell them repeatedly, every legislative session, "Guess what? This is public land. Would you give them the Big Bend? Would you give them the river and its banks in your

home town? Would you give them the state park and let them call it private property?" All of these things have to be explained to every new member of the Legislature who's not from the coast. Somebody's got to tell them, "Those folks don't own that property at the mean high tide line, that's *your* property. And that twenty-two million people in Texas have a right to use it. And when you give it away to Joe Blow, because he had enough money to buy a beach house, you're violating the Constitution in the first place; in the second place, he's not entitled to the gift."

Reel 2387; Time Code 00:16:44

If the mean high tide line covers the property in and out over the year and it's determined that that is under the flow of the water and it is effectively "submerged land" some of the time of the year because of tidal influences, then that is no longer private property. They may have a deed to it, and they may proclaim they own it. And there may be part of it that's not subject to the mean high tide, and that is still absolutely their private property and they can go sit on it and enjoy it. But, the law has been the same since the second century: the *Annals* of a Roman named Gaius back in the second century became the *Justinian Code.* In the *Justinian Code,* the sovereign owned that submerged land, and the position of the mean high tide began to evolve as the distinction between sovereign soil and private ownership. It became English common law; it became Spanish civil law in the thirteenth century. It became the law of Mexico as Spanish civil law and it would've been the law of Texas. When Texas became a republic, it became the common law of the Republic of Texas. So, if a homeowner is going to damn the Open Beaches Act and if he's going to damn Bob Eckhardt, and if he's going to damn Babe Schwartz, then the truth is, he's got to damn Gaius, who recorded in his *Annals* that there was a distinction between sovereign soil and private property.

Murdoch's Bathhouse, Galveston Island shore, after Hurricane Ike—2008 (Courtesy Cody Austin)

The Open Beaches Act is under attack every day from every developer, every beachfront homeowner, who thinks they bought an exclusive piece of property from which they can prevent any other human being from using and enjoying. And it's the most ridiculous thing in the world for a person to believe, "I'm rich, I bought a beach house; I don't want anybody eating fried chicken and watermelon on my beach." And you can look them in the eye and tell them, "When the hell did it become your beach?" What has to be made clear is that nobody has the right, because they're rich, to buy and own public property unless the public property is for sale because the state decides to do so.

There's a doctrine called the Public Trust Doctrine,[3] which places a trust upon government to protect public rights to its property: real property, the air rights of that property, and the water rights for that property. And it's very, very restrictive, from the beginning of time through common law, that the state has no right to deny its citizens the use of public property except on rare circumstances. And it has no right to sell that public property to somebody who will deny those rights to citizens. So, it's basically an idea that if you're a human being and you're alive and you live in a state, then the state's got to protect your rights. And the developers don't understand that. The developers are born with a lump of avarice in their heart and nothing can persuade them that they don't have a right to buy everything, own it, and make it exclusive, because they can't make as much money off of something that might be utilized by both the public and the private sector. If they make it exclusive, then they can sell it to people just like them. And that's going on in Corpus Christi today.

Reel 2388; Time Code 00:57:55

The single thing that needs to be remembered in the passage of the Open Beaches Law is that the phrase, "the free and unrestricted ingress and egress to the beaches" is what is protected. And that phrase has never been altered. When I was in the Legislature, in the Senate, every session of the Senate, somebody tried to take out the word "free" or somebody tried to add or subtract from the "ingress and egress." But "free" is still in there. I have drawn a line through the elimination of the word "free" as many times as I've drawn any line through any phrase or word in a piece of legislation. Every time I saw someone take that "free" out, I'd write it back in and scratch out whatever they had removed. But it's only free for the public to access it, parking is provided and may be either free and paid. Again, using this overworked term of mine, that was the genius of Bob Eckhardt in wording the original act, and it was the basic right which I tried to protect for all these years.

1. Open Beaches Act, *Texas Natural Resources Code*, sec. 61.001 et seq.

2. Bob Eckhardt was a labor lawyer who served in the Texas Legislature from 1959 to 1965 and later represented the Houston area in the U.S. Congress from 1966 through 1980. He is often remembered for his constitutional scholarship and his particular interest in war powers, as well as his environmental work on the open beaches issue, Big Thicket protection, and toxic substances regulation. See Gary Keith. *Eckhardt: There Once Was a Congressman from Texas* (Austin: University of Texas Press, 2007).

3. The Open Beaches Act is an expression and codification of the Public Trust Doctrine, as Mr. Schwartz points out. The doctrine can be traced back to language in sixth century Roman law, itself only a recodification of second century B.C.E Greek principles. The *Roman Institutes of Justinian* 2.1.1

read, "by the law of nature these things are common to all mankind—the air, running water, the sea, and consequently the shores of the sea. No one, therefore is forbidden to approach the seashore." This precedent followed down into English common law: "In England, from the time of Lord Hale, it has been treated as settled that the title in the soil of the sea, or of arms of the sea, below ordinary high-water mark is in the king . . . [and] is held subject to the public right, *jus publicum*, of navigation and fishing." *Shirley v. Bowlby*, 152 U.S. 1, 13 (1894). In the United States, the Public Trust Doctrine is upheld in an early Supreme Court decision, "For when the [American] Revolution took place, the people of each state became themselves sovereign; and in that character hold the absolute right to all their navigable waters, and the soils under them, for their common use." *Martin v. Waddell's Lessee*, 41 U.S. 367, 410 (1842). The duty to enforce the Public Trust Doctrine is laid out in a later Supreme Court ruling, *Illinois Central RR Co. v. Illinois*, 146 U.S. 387, 453 (1892): "the state can no more abdicate its trust over property in which the whole people are interested, like navigable waters and the soils under them, so as to leave them entirely under the use and control of private parties . . . than it can abdicate its police powers in the administration of government and the preservation of the peace. See Joe Sax, *The Public Trust Doctrine in Natural Resources Law: Effective Judicial Intervention*, 68 Mich. L. Rev. 473 (1970).

The idea of open access to the beach was not just an abstract legal concept, but had practical roots. Seamen and fishermen had long needed to use beaches to land their boats, to dry their nets, and to harvest shellfish. In the roadless areas of nineteenth century Texas, the smooth, hard-packed beaches were also used for transport along their length, and, much like a cattle trail, could not be blocked by private landowners. Gary Keith. *Eckhardt: There Once Was a Congressman from Texas*. (Austin: University of Texas Press, 2007), 157–58.

By an October 19, 2009 vote of 77% to 23%, Proposition 9 enshrined common law and statutory public rights to the beach, amending the Texas Constitution to "protect the right of the public, individually and collectively to access and use beaches bordering the seaward shore of the Gulf of Mexico." Kevin Lewis, "Area Voters go against Props. 1, 3, & 5; Silverton OKs Tax," *Plainview* [Texas] *Daily Herald*, November 4, 2009, http://myplainview.com/articles/2009/11/10/breaking_news/doc4 af1b1697f890322592427.txt (accessed November 11, 2009).

The Edwards Aquifer and the Applewhite Reservoir

MARIA BERRIOZABÁL has been involved in San Antonio politics and environmental protection for a number of years. She was the first Mexican American elected to the San Antonio City Council, serving from 1981 through 1990, and also worked on appointed boards, such as the Mayor's Citizens' Water Committee.

Known for her outspoken opinions on the role of government in the everyday lives of its citizens, Berriozabál frequently clashed with her city council colleagues, as well as with powerful business interests within the city. On important economic development projects, such as the Alamodome, subsidies for PGA Village, and tax abatements for large corporations relocating to San Antonio, she often cast the lone dissenting vote.

Much of her opposition is rooted in environmental concerns, and her passion for the quality of water can be traced to one of her childhood experiences.

Interviewed on February 14, 2006, in San Antonio, Texas

Reel 2330; Time Code 00:06:55

"I remember that water, how it tasted."

In recent years, I've been trying to go back and literally write the stories that I was told when I was little, because I want to know, "what is this *thing* I have with water?" When I got elected to the city council, I didn't say to myself, "water is going to be the number one issue that I'm going to deal with." I was dealing with housing and jobs and transportation and garbage and potholes and the neighbor next door and the dog. . . . And then, water came up, and what I remembered was that when I was little we used to go to my grandfather's farm. They had a well, and my uncle would take us to the well. He would take the pail that was made out of wood, drop it down the well, and you could hear when it hit the water. And it was so deep . . . the water was so deep. And I remember that "splash," and then he would haul it up. He had a dipper we used to call "la dipa." And he would give us water. I remember that water, how it tasted. It was cold and it was so good and it's almost like the only water that tasted that good was water from that well.

When I was elected to the city council the first time, and citizens started coming, talking about the aquifer and the water and pollution, I don't think I ever stopped to think that I had a frame of reference for clean water. And yet, you have to appreciate what something is before you have a responsibility for taking care of it, so it won't get dirty. I can't explain it but it's almost like, to me, I have a picture of and a taste for water. So when I hear that there's benzene in the aquifer, when I hear that they have to close some wells because the children were getting sick, it's so immediate. It's an emotional response and even a physical one.

Ms. Berriozábal was often outvoted on economic development issues, but she was successful in her fight against the Applewhite Reservoir Project. She, along with a broad coalition of activists, twice defeated referenda in 1991 and 1994. She was concerned the costly reservoir would flood historic communities and farmland, and undermine efforts to protect the Edwards Aquifer.

Reel 2230; Time Code 00:25:27

This is where the environmental water wars begin to happen: in San Antonio, north is high terrain, and south is low. The San Antonio River drains from tributaries and goes into the Gulf of Mexico. The city is born around the downtown, around the river. The water that we're getting in the San Antonio River and the water we drink comes from the aquifer, comes from the north, from up high where there's a lot of rock. In the south, there's good, beautiful lowland, and this is where settlement started. This is where the city was born—downtown. Then the Mexicans start building their houses, humble houses, in what we call the West Side. Then there are farms in the whole southern area of the city where white people, but also Mexicans, have their land. And then the Germans come to downtown, in the early 1900s, where we are right now, which is called Beacon Hill. It was the "Queen of the Suburbs" in 1901. It's a stone's throw, five minutes from downtown.

In any city, what you have is shaped like a doughnut. You have where the city is born—the "hole"—and then you have the suburbs and they're all around the outside. Eventually, the inner city starts to decay. In San Antonio, we're unique because our whole tourism was born in the downtown . . . the Alamo, the Spanish Governor's Palace, the San Antonio River . . . we can't move them. We can't build another city, because we've got something that anchors us there—the downtown has been alive for tourism, which is one of the biggest industries.

Then the city began to suburbanize, started moving north, towards Austin and Kerrville. And the government, hand-in-hand with big developers, started buying land, speculating, to generate the growth to the north side of the city. So San Antonio, instead of growing like a doughnut, started growing like a pretzel—just to one side. And we underutilized and disinvested in the inner city and the south side because we were moving the investment, the interest, the economy, to the north of the city.

Lo and behold, in the 1960s, you begin to hear people saying that we're running out of water, and we have to figure out a way to solve this. Well, why don't we build a reservoir to supplement our aquifer? And let's build it in the south side, downstream. So when I get elected, in 1980, one of the issues that I dealt with was whether I supported a reservoir called Applewhite, which would be built downstream where all these little rivers, like Leon Creek, go into Medina Lake. Toxins in the water from Kelly Air Force Base would have flowed into it. It is the worst place that you could've built a reservoir. There were carcinogens underneath it, and still, the city administration, hand in hand with the developers, wanted to build it downstream. So I got elected because I was against the surface water project. Once I became an elected official, I had women and men, but mostly women—older women—who mentored me and taught me about the aquifer. It didn't make sense that we had an existing aquifer on the north side of the city that has been giving us water since the Franciscans came, and that has—everybody agrees—over two hundred million acre-feet of water, and yet we were going to build a reservoir downstream on Applewhite Road, deep in the south side of San Antonio and inundate it with water; build dams and destroy the land, because we were going to cover up all these artifacts and all these historic structures for a lake that will only have, at its highest, forty-five thousand acre-feet of water. But it passed. I was on the City Council that passed this two hundred million dollar reservoir in the south side in a place where there were carcinogens.

"Every time you have given people the opportunity to vote, they vote for their water."

Well, there were some tenacious people who I call "the water people" who started getting signatures to have an election. We had an election, and that election was held in May of 1990, concurrent to when I was running for mayor, and the people won. They said "get us out of Applewhite" even though we had already spent sixty million dollars. So Applewhite is dead. But then the developers come back again, and Nelson Wolf is elected mayor instead of me, and instead of paying attention to the wishes of the people who said "no" to Applewhite, he brings it back. Well, we go to work again, and we defeat it again, with only a ridiculously small amount like three hundred thirty thousand dollars that we raised against the seven hundred thousand dollars of the developers. And we win. That's why we like to say that in San Antonio, every time you have given people the opportunity to vote, they vote for their water.

Ms. Berriozábal's greater environmental concern marked her as an outsider on the council, which often neglected the issues she brought to the table. Not to be deterred, she found success in empowering the citizens she represented to speak for themselves.

Reel 2331; Time Code 00:07:15

The people have their own values, and people value their water. People don't want to be "taken" by their government. They don't want to be lied to. They want to be given information they need. All you have to do is just give them that information and make sure that you give it in enough places and to enough different people. That's what I was doing. I was working along with other people—mostly women—in a coalition. There was a woman who was a state representative, Karen Connelly, and she was very involved in getting African American people to work actively. There were some women who are very active in the LULAC [League of United Latin American Citizens] organization, which is a mostly Hispanic group—very active in civil rights issues and human rights issues—and they saw this as a human right issue. And then there were the environmentalists who are already present. The pure environmentalists essentially end up being middle class—upper middle-class whites. You can't win just with them. You need a swell of people in the Mexican American community and then you need the African American community—you need that because the word goes out with the ministers that something is wrong and we're going to vote "no." And then you have to find a catchy phrase, too. We had one: "No means no."

Reel 2331; Time Code 00:01:43

For the ten years that I was on city council, I never once voted for a zoning case to permit building over the aquifer, because at that time, developers were coming almost every week with zoning cases that would build over the water. It's wrong, and I'm just going to keep on voting my conscience. In fact, the clerk sometimes would remind me, "Hey, you haven't voted yet. Are you going to vote 'no'?" Sometimes I forgot to cast my vote, because it became such a routine thing—every week or every other week—of voting "no."

You have to have a lot of inner strength because you don't get "benefits" for voting "no." What I think one needs in order to do that, kind of to go against the grain, is to understand the way I see the political arena and getting involved with the community on these issues. One has to see the struggle for the long haul. It's not just something "for now." Maybe *now* what has to happen is somebody, particularly if you're an elected official, has to use that podium to say "it's wrong" and this is why it is wrong: this is who's going to get the raw end of the deal, and this is who's going to suffer. Truth has its own value even if nobody listens or nobody cares for it—it has to be put out there. And one has to have a lot of confidence in one's truth and in one's voice, to know that even if you're not going to win, it's still worth it because that little piece will go together with other pieces towards a greater good.

Blackland Prairie, Texas Parks and Wildlife, and Shell Dredging

BOB BURLESON was an attorney based in Temple, Texas, whose passion for exploration and conservation has taken him from early float and canoe trips down the Big Bend canyons, to efforts to create a national park in the Guadalupe Mountains, to service on the Texas Parks and Wildlife Commission, and to work on restoring native tallgrass prairie. For all his love of the mountains and prairies, though, one of his most significant accomplishments was his work in protecting the coastal bays and estuaries from the ravages of shell dredging.

Interviewed June 19, 1999, in Temple, Texas

Reel 2009; Time Code 00:05:05

I was born and raised on a ranch so I have grown up with the natural world and frankly, I've been a hunter since childhood. I always had an intense curiosity about the natural world. That was fostered partly by my mother, who was an educated lady and she taught me to read long before I was old enough to go to school—to the little country schools. She bought me, as a very young child, a *Britannica Junior,* a small encyclopedia, and I had read that thing, every single volume in it, from cover-to-cover before I went to the first grade. I learned a whole lot about the natural world just from reading that. And, then my grandfather on my father's side, R. C. Burleson, was a farmer who lived very close to the land and was very observant about the land and just trotting around behind him and working with him as a child also gave me appreciation for life. He would show me everything from the tracks made by insects to the eggs they lay. That was before the days of really widespread pesticides so you had to deal with, in your crops, everything from the boll weevil to the budworm. We looked at the way mice lived, the way the cotton rats lived, the plain old Norway rats in the barn, everything was interesting to him. We hunted squirrels on the creeks and fished in the ponds and the little creeks near his place, which was near Mark, Texas, on the Blackland Prairie, north of here, probably forty-five miles. He was a cotton farmer all his life and worked basically till he died. He gave me a real reverence for life, so to speak, along with my mother.

As far as conservation itself, I have to trace my real interest in it to the publication of Rachel Carson's *Silent Spring.* As far as I'm concerned, that was the first awakening in my life, in terms of getting me and my wife, Mickey, active in the conservation movement. I read every book she wrote—*The Edge of the Sea* and *Under the Sea Wind,* and things of that nature. They just sort of awakened in us an awareness that there were globally things going on we needed to be concerned about. In fact, I think nearly all the conservation movement in Texas probably ultimately traces its roots to Rachel Carson's book.

Reel 2010; Time Code 00:01:02

When Governor Preston Smith appointed me to the Parks and Wildlife Commission, my appointment was seriously opposed because of my conservation leanings. In Texas, the Senate must confirm a gubernatorial appointee to the Parks and Wildlife Commission by a certain majority. My appointment was opposed by the shell dredging industry out of the Houston area. Most people today don't really know what shell dredging was. Well, for nearly a hundred years, dredges—large floating dredges—had been digging oyster reefs out of the bays and estuaries of Texas[1] and using them for two things: one is a raw ingredient for Portland cement. There were large cement factories down on the coast near Houston, for example. And secondly, they were using them for road gravel and fill material on county roads and city roads and subdivisions.

"The truth is they would dig through anything that was in their path, including living reefs."

Dredging not only destroyed things by simply rolling a huge wheel that dug up the buried or fossilized oyster reefs—which causes tremendous damage in itself—but damage was done by siltation. With siltation, all of the sediment that was stirred up off the bottom of the bay or the estuary by these dredges then floated in a dredge plume. From the air you could see a plume sometimes three and four miles long of suspended sediments that would go behind these dredgers and they would drift wherever the current took them. And as they settled out, they settled on the very underwater environment that produced the life of the bay and estuary, the small oysters, the small shrimp, the small crabs, the juvenile fish. It smothered them. These dredges, for every oyster reef that they dug up, probably destroyed dozens of others by siltation. Additionally, channel dredging created what's called "spoil." Spoil is essentially mud that's been dug up from the bottom of a canal. Gradually it filters back in and begins to make the canal shallow again. So they re-dredge it and the spoil is dumped in a pile. That spoil is gradually carried out by currents, and it covers up the grass flats that are the livelihood of the bays and estuaries. And, of course, without the bays and estuaries, you've got no life in the Gulf at all. I mean, nearly all of these larval forms of sea life develop in the brackish or saline waters of our bays and estuaries.

As it happens, there was one particular, very powerful group called Parker Brothers in Houston. Parker Brothers was a major shell dredging industry and had, I think at that time, perhaps three dredges running. Parker Brothers had a very strong lobbyist, a former representative. And the Parker Brothers spent a good bit of money opposing my nomination and my confirmation as a commissioner on the Parks and Wildlife Commission. They had state senator Bill Moore—he's recently deceased—the "bull of the Brazos" in their hip pocket. And another senator named Jim Bates from down at Batesville, I think he's deceased as well. They had him in their hip pocket. The people that were working *for* me were Barbara Jordan and state senator Don Kennard and then my own senator, Murray Watson from Waco. None of these people are, of course, in the Senate any more. Barbara is deceased and Don is working in Washington. It came down to a very close vote but, thank goodness, Barbara Jordan and Don Kennard and some others got me confirmed.

Dredge "Roy Miller" (Photo by Doc MacGregor, Corpus Christi Public Libraries)

Well before long, the shell dredging issue came before the Commission. And obviously I was just one of six commissioners at that time—back then, the Commission had six people on it. But we did studies that showed the tremendous amount of damage that was being done. And even more importantly, although the dredgers always claimed that they were digging only "fossil," or "dead" oyster reefs that no longer would serve as a substrate for the growth of new oysters, the truth is they would dig through anything that was in their path, including living reefs. And they oftentimes lied about their position. When a vessel is on the water dredging, you can't tell just by eye whether they are in a permitted section of bay floor that's been surveyed and found to have no living oyster reefs, or whether they're over in a non-permitted area. We started triangulating on them with our Parks and Wildlife personnel down there and found out that they were, at night, oftentimes moving their position, getting into non-permitted areas, dredging live reefs and things like that. Well eventually the sum and substance of it was that we made it so hard on them to operate in the bays that they shifted to an alternative supply. What they did is they bought a lot of land up in the Texas Hill Country around New Braunfels and places like that and started excavating limestone, shipping it by rail to the coast and using that

material, which was environmentally far better for the bays and estuaries. Unfortunately, like all trade-offs, there's some awful big holes dug around New Braunfels for quarrying. But the trade-off, we felt, was a fair one in that the bays and estuaries were in serious trouble. There was a definite threat to the sport fishing industry and even the commercial fishing industry along the coast from shell dredging. And so it was the end of the shell dredging and then we later put constraints on commercial netting and even non-commercial netting.[2] We started putting in some real good regulations that pretty well put an end to indiscriminate netting on the coast. It still goes on illegally and you have to fight it all the time but those regulations were put in place. In the late 1960s and early 1970s, the Texas Parks and Wildlife Department became much more conservation and enforcement oriented in terms of preventing damage to the natural resources. I was proud that—of the commissioners that I worked with and the staff members of the department that did such a yeoman job on pointing out what the dredging industry was doing to our natural resources on the coast.

1. It is estimated that over 270 million cubic meters of oyster reef materials were taken out of Texas bays between 1922 and 1983. In 1953, shell dredging was banned within 457.2 meters of living reef, but in 1963, the buffer was decreased to 91.4 meters. Sahotra Sarkar, "A Year in Texas: Oyster Reef Restoration in Lavaca Bay," *Sarkar Lab, Biodiversity and Biocultural Conservation Laboratory, University of Texas at Austin,* http://sarkar.typepad.com/sarkarlab/2006/05/a_year_in_texas_2.html (accessed November 11, 2009).

2. Use of single-strand monofilament nets was outlawed in Texas in 1979. In 1980, gill net use in Texas bays was prohibited. Trammel nets and drag seines were banned in the state in 1988. In 1989, the State prohibited possession of illegal fishing devices on or near Texas waters. Shawn Bengston, Randy Blankinship, Craig Bonds, *Texas Parks and Wildlife Department History, 1963–2003,* (Austin: Texas Parks and Wildlife, 2003) 5, 8, 25, http://www.tpwd.state.tx.us/publications/pwdpubs/media/pwd_rp_e0100_1144.pdf (accessed November 11, 2009); Coastal Conservation Association, "What is CCA—Accomplishments," http://www.joincca.org/Accomplishments.html (accessed November 11, 2009).

Nature, Recreation, and the Land

ANDY SANSOM has been involved in a number of non-profit and government conservation efforts, ranging from his early work in land protection at the Department of Interior, to his later roles as executive director at the Texas chapter of the Nature Conservancy, the Texas Parks and Wildlife Department, and the River Systems Institute at Texas State University. A lifelong conservationist, among his chief goals were to encourage private landowners to accept stewardship of their property, while at the same time pushing, often against great resistance, for greater acquisition of public lands in a state that is rapidly urbanizing.

Interviewed on April 13, 2002, in Stonewall, Texas

Reel 2186; Time Code 00:02:24

I grew up in Lake Jackson, which is on the Texas coast, near the mouth of the Brazos River. Although neither of my parents were outdoors people, they were both very, very intelligent and they were very, very aware of everything around them, particularly my father. My father would take us almost every weekend to some interesting place, whether it was a natural place or some historic site around Texas. From the earliest age that I can remember, my parents were constantly making us aware of the things that were around us that were interesting, and part of the Texas heritage. I grew up on Oyster Creek, which flows on the east side of the Brazos, and my father and I built a boat for me to use in the creek when I was probably in the ninth grade or something like that. And I spent every day after that on the creek. I had a grandmother who lived on a farm in Alabama, and who in her later years, fished every day. My grandmother would take a cane pole and a can of worms that she dug up in the chicken yard and she would go down to this farm pond on the place and fish every single day. She taught me to fish, and I spent many, many hours both there and on that creek fishing, and so, that's probably where I first began to be really aware of the out-of-doors. On that creek, I learned firsthand what outdoor recreation and experience in the environment means to a young person growing up.

Brazos River (Courtesy Carol Von Canon)

". . . We all felt that we were part of something that was extremely important . . ."

I always worked in parks as a young person. Probably the first job I had was as a swimming instructor: I'm talking about when I was fourteen or fifteen years old. I was also a lifeguard, and through that experience in a community parks and recreation system, I became interested in parks and recreation. It never occurred to me in all those many summer afternoons that I sat in a lifeguard chair or spent in the pool with those children, that you could make a living at this, but at some point in time, I discovered a program at Texas Technological College at the time, now Texas Tech University, in Parks and Recreation. I went there after my junior year in college. I started out at a place called Austin College in Sherman, and I graduated from Tech with a degree in Parks and Recreation. While I was at Tech, I had the opportunity to interact with professionals from conservation organizations like the Sierra Club, the Defenders

of Wildlife, and others, and I became conscious that there was an avenue to professionally pursue what had become for me a way of life: an interest and concern for the out-of-doors. And so in 1969, I became the first intern at the National Recreation and Park Association [NRPA] in Washington, D.C.

NRPA was an organization that had been formed from a number of different kindred recreation and park organizations, like a federation. And it had been formed within a few years of when I joined them. And so I moved, with my wife, to Washington in 1969 to become an intern with NRPA and that's sort of how I really got started. That time was, of course, right in the middle of the Vietnam War and a tremendous emerging interest among young people in the environment, which was occurring at the same time. NRPA allowed me to become sort of the liaison, if you will, with young people. And so, I organized the first National Society of Students in Parks and Recreation and was the first executive secretary. I had a real interesting experience in dealing with young people at a time when there was this tremendous consciousness emerging. I played a small part in the organization and conduct of the first Earth Day. I think of myself as a part of a conservation movement, and I never felt it stronger than in those days. It was an emerging consciousness that was overwhelming. I mean, we all felt that we were part of something that was extremely important, that was—what's the word I'm looking for? Insurgent? And it was exciting and we felt that we were going to make a difference. I spent the first Earth Day traveling around the country, made something like six speeches during that day in different parts of the United States on college campuses. And that's really kind of where I got started.

Reel 187; Time Code 00:23:30

I believe that we are on the cusp of moving to the next level in private land conservation in Texas. That level will be reached when permanent commitments of stewardship begin to occur on private property through easements and purchase of development rights in ways that landowners actually make a commitment that, even beyond their own lifetime, the preservation of their property in private hands will continue.[1] It has always been my belief that you're much more likely to cause that type of effort to occur if you're not dealing with the government, if the landowner does not have to deal with an agency of government, but can deal with an institution which is much more user-friendly. And, to me, the best opportunity for that is a local land trust, which, in fact, may be composed of the peers of landowners. If they look and they see on that board someone who may own a ranch right down the road, or someone whom they trust, then they're going to be more likely to enter into a transaction which not only binds them, but their children and their grandchildren. And so that's why we worked so hard to get this movement of local land trusts established in Texas, and I believe today there are about thirty or so. And in the years to come, you know, there will be hundreds. And they'll be in places

like South Texas, below Corpus Christi; they'll be in the Panhandle; they'll be in the area around Brenham and Washington County; and you'll see them springing up in places where people are motivated to try to find a way to preserve their property beyond their own lifetimes, but they need a vehicle to do it.

However, let me say that, having said what I've said about private land stewardship, which I believe is as important an initiative as can be occurring in conservation in Texas today, it is not an excuse not to do public land acquisition. As hard as we need to continue to work to encourage conservation on private lands, we've got to redouble our efforts to make sure that we are continuing to acquire public land. And that's the hardest one. Really, the notion of getting private landowners into conservation was almost like a no-brainer. And it was widely supported. On the other hand, bringing land into the public inventory was extremely difficult. First, every time you spend a dollar to buy a piece of land, that's a dollar that you can't spend on something else. So, from an institutional standpoint, that meant maybe we didn't get to buy as many cars for the game wardens or, raise the salaries of the employees or any of the other things that would be competing for the use of those initial capital dollars. And so, there's an institutional resistance to investing in capital assets when we need money right now for day-to-day operating needs. Another built-in institutional resistance comes from the fact that when you acquire a piece of land, you have to take care of it. And so there's an attendant liability, if you will, for the management of the property. Which is why, in the middle of the 1990s, we began to try to figure out ways to endow properties that we acquired so that there was some stewardship support going in. There's a resistance to the acquisition of property that comes from the fact that most local government in Texas is financed by property taxes. And so every time you take a piece of property off the tax rolls, that causes a hit in the local school district's budget, the local county's budget, and in some cases, the local city budget. So, there is an institutional resistance from that standpoint.

"You've always got to try to keep everybody's eye on the future."

All of those obstacles and many more required a lot of effort to overcome whenever an acquisition was made. But, you've always got to try to keep everybody's eye on the future and never let yourself be deterred from that. It's probably a little presumptuous to make the comparison, but I think sometimes we should look at acquisitions like Big Bend Ranch, which has been controversial since the day it was acquired. There are people today who would sell it if they had the opportunity to. Look at it in the context of Alaska. When Seward bought Alaska for the United States, he bought it from the Russians for eight million dollars. What is now the entire state of Alaska! And it was considered to be the most asinine, foolish things that the U.S. government ever did. And in fact, Seward was ridiculed for it. It was called "Seward's Folly!" Imagine today, from a conservation standpoint, what it would have been like if we had not acquired Alaska? Although people in our time look at places like Big Bend Ranch, and ask, "Why would they want to do that?" in fifty or a hundred years from now people will say, "I can't believe they did that." And you have to always keep everybody's attention focused on that point: we not only have a responsibility to the children of today, but we have a responsibility to the children of tomorrow. And it's equal. Our responsibility to the present generation is no greater than our responsibility to the future generation if we're going to be true to ourselves as conservationists.

1. Due in part to generous grants of land made during the 1800s for serving in the military, building roads and railroads, digging canals, constructing shipbuilding facilities, and manufacturing firearms and munitions, Texas is unusual in having a very large proportion of its lands in private hands, with estimates ranging from 87 percent to as much as 95 percent. Aldon Lang, *Financial History of the Public Lands in Texas*, Baylor Bulletin, v. 35, no. 3 (Waco, TX: Baylor University, 1932), 23–24, 40, 45, 46, 48, 58, 62; Texas Center for Policy Studies and the Environmental Defense Fund, "Texas Environmental Profiles: Wildlife and Biodiversity: The Loss of Texas Wildlife Habitat," http://www.texasep.org/html/wld/wld_4hab.html (accessed November 11, 2009). As a consequence, habitat protection is subject to a variety of private sector stresses, including residential or commercial development, and estate or ad valorem taxes. Often, these private lands are subdivided in the face of these financial incentives and pressures, and in Texas, the pace is fast. From 1982 to 1992, the U.S. Department of Agriculture calculated that Texas lost 1.4 million acres of farm and ranchland to development, close to double the rate of the previous ten years. Texas Center for Policy Studies and the Environmental Defense Fund, "Texas Environmental Profile: Land: Agriculture and Urban Sprawl," http://www.texasep.org/html/lnd/lnd_2agr_sprawl.html (accessed November 11, 2009). The American Farmland Trust estimated that Texas lost 332,800 acres of quality farmland to development during the 1992–97 period, a 42 percent increase in the loss rate over the prior five years, and the greatest amount lost among the fifty states. American Farmland Trust, "Farming on the Edge," http://www.farmland.org/resources/fote/states/allStates.asp (accessed March 6, 2009); Lynette James, ed., *Fragmented Lands: Changing Land Ownership in Texas* (College Station: Texas A&M University, 2000), 2. http://www.texaslandtrends.org/Briefings/Previous/2000_Fragmented_Lands.pdf (accessed November 11, 2009). As a result of this fragmentation problem, conservation easements have been advanced as a way to give or sell the development rights of a tract to a government or non-profit group, lowering taxable values, and protecting against conversion to urban uses.

Filibusters, Public Interest, and the Environment

CARLOS TRUAN represented Corpus Christi in the Texas House from 1968 through 1976 and subsequently in the State Senate through 2001. He has been a staunch proponent of open government, and has also been a consistent environmental and public health advocate. He has helped enact laws to organize a birth defects registry,[1] to establish the Texas Coastal Management Program,[2] to enact the Coastal Dune Protection Act,[3] the Oil Spill Prevention and Response Act[4], the Water Saving Plumbing Fixtures Act,[5] a lead abatement program,[6] and a variety of other laws. As the Legislature has become less sympathetic to environmental concerns in recent years, some of his most noted contributions have been in stopping short-sighted legislation, such as bills that would have reduced landfill standards, abridged local control of habitat conservation plans, or harmed the ability of citizens to participate in the state's regulatory process.

Interviewed February 21, 2000, in Corpus Christi, Texas

Reel 2072; Time Code 00:01:58

". . . We have a responsibility to protect our neighbors."

I think my interest in protecting the environment—the air we breathe, the water we drink—really comes from a desire on my part to try to do what I can. And I don't know when it originated. It's just a concern I've had practically all my life. And I can't attribute that to my association with any organization or any individual. I think it's just a personal desire. It's a genuine, honest desire on my part to do what I can in my role now as a state senator to protect the environment that we take for granted. I have been astounded at how we have contributed, as a society, to the deterioration of our rivers, of the air, of the environment. I am concerned about people that couldn't care less about what the end result will be to the environment as long as they make a profit financially. I believe in economic development. I believe in bringing business. I'm a product of the private sector. I've been in the private sector for forty years. But I just don't buy the response that you sacrifice the environment because you want to create jobs, or you want to bring industry. I don't buy that. It's not good for us. It's not good for our children and for generations to come. It might be a well-worn saying, but to me it's a very simple thing. And I think I've always had a desire to enjoy the outdoors, to enjoy Mother Nature's contribution. I love the Texas coast. I like to see people catching fish and people hunting, even though I'm not a hunter and I'm not really a fisherman either. I try to just do what I can to promote people being concerned about protecting what we have here. I can't, you know, solve the problems of the world. But as long as I'm able to do my own little thing, I feel that I don't have to make excuses to anybody.

I've had a lot of people mad at me because I've participated in debates and filibusters where I had nothing to gain, not politically, obviously, because the people in favor of legislation that would pollute our environment are people that have the financial wherewithal to support or oppose people running for office, like myself. I've just done it because I think it's the right thing to do, as corny as that might sound. And I think that the general public can't be fooled. In every poll that I've seen about what people care about, they care about the environment.[7] They care about educating our young people about how to protect our natural environment. I realize not everybody thinks the same way, but I think the vast majority of people want to be sure we don't pollute the water that we drink and the air that we breathe.

Reel 2072; Time Code 00:25:17

Let me tell you, it never ceases to amaze me how people will attempt to do things that are ridiculous, such as denying the general public a right to participate at public hearings, allowing companies to do what they want to without any concern for the impact on the people in our state. There are those that are probably only concerned about the bottom line and satisfying their stockholders who live in another area of the country, and not being concerned about their own families. I'd like to think that if I was working in that atmosphere, I'd be concerned about the air that I was breathing, the water I was drinking and be concerned about my children, and the children of all. You know, we can't just be concerned about our children, and not be concerned about your children and others. There's no line that is drawn: the air that one breathes on one side of town is the same air that is being breathed by people on the other side of town. But there are people that have tried, through leg-

islation, because of their influence on certain legislators, to promote legislation that is simply not in the public's interest.

And it seems to me that the voters need to hold all of us accountable. They need to look at how we vote on what pieces of legislation and not be misled by stump speeches that miss out on the real crux of the matter on key legislation. I think people need to be more informed. We need more organizations, like the League of Women Voters, for example; like the Sierra Club, the Audubon Society, and others that are actively working on protecting the environment. I'd like to think that those times when people from the private sector were accusing everybody who was trying to protect the environment of being "weirdos" and being out of touch are gone. We need to understand that these environmental organizations have stood the test of time. They have promoted awareness, education, and have been there in Austin at a great expense and with very little in return for them. They were saying what needed to be said in an arena where, unfortunately, too many times very selfish and powerful special interests take advantage of legislation that has ultimately passed. I'd like to think that we need more vigilantes going after politicians' hides and proving that their voting record is such that they don't care about the best interests of the people that they represent, much less the people of the state as a whole. I think we need to do everything we can to be aware of what is being proposed. You know, there's an old saying: "figures don't lie, but liars figure." And there are those want to promote jobs and industry at a much greater expense, and we need to be careful of that. I don't think that we need to work at compromising on the air we breathe, or the water we drink. Industries need to know that if they're going to pollute the atmosphere, they're not welcome in Texas. But it's going to take the people in general to do this. And it's not going to take people that are just Democrats, or Republicans, or Independents. It's going to take an awareness across the board. Whether you're a member of one party or the other, whether you have one philosophy or the other.

Reel 2072; Time Code 00:39:11

Frankly, it is very difficult to push strong environmental legislation in the Texas Legislature, but one or more members can help to block bad legislation, utilizing the floor of the Senate where you have unlimited time to speak. And it's been in that role that I have been more effective in preventing bad legislation from becoming law. And you're not a very popular person when you do that. But I never went to the Legislature to be popular. To begin with, I defeated a member of the Senate who was a member of "the club," so to speak. And I was considered a persona non grata when I went to the Senate. And I was taught some very valuable lessons. And perhaps it was a blessing in disguise that I knew that if it had been up to a lot of the members in the Senate, I wouldn't be a senator. And so I felt that I owed it to the people that supported me, notwithstanding special interests that opposed me, to do the best I could. And so one of the things has been my working with people concerned about the environment, the environmental organizations, like the Sierra Club, the Audubon Society, Friends of the Earth, and other people interested and concerned about the environment.

In my work in the Senate, there've been a lot of efforts to try to undo whatever good legislation we had in place. There've been efforts to undo the Open Beaches Act, for example.[8] Some years back there was some good legislation that was put on the books, and over the years that, little by little, we have lost the protections. But my thinking is that you need to learn the rules. You need to know where you can come in and make a difference. A lot of people, under the guise of property rights, for example, will sometimes deter and prevent the state from doing its job in investigating issues. For example, people that want to have the right to dump waste and create whatever aroma arises from pigpens that affects their neighbors. I think that we need to understand that we have a responsibility to protect our neighbors. And you can take these property rights to such limits where you are literally stepping on other

people's rights. My role in the Senate has been to hopefully prevent bad legislation from passing. It's not very popular to be one or two of those on a committee voting consistently against the majority. It's not very popular. It's easier to go along, to get along. If people want you, as a member of the Legislature, to be popular, you're not going to accomplish much, because you'll just be going along with the majority. You've got to stand up for your constituents. You've got to stand up for what you believe is right. But you pay a price.

1. Surveillance of Birth Defects: Central Registry, *Texas Administrative Code,* sec. 37.301 et seq.

2. Coastal Coordination Act, *Texas Natural Resources Code,* sec. 33.201 et seq.

3. Coastal Dune Protection Act, *Texas Natural Resources Code,* sec. 63.001 et seq.

4. Oil Spill Prevention and Response Act, *Texas Natural Resources Code,* sec. 40.001 et seq.

5. Water Saving Performance Standards for Plumbing Fixtures Act, *Texas Health and Safety Code ,* sec. 372.002 et seq.

6. Lead-Based Paint Abatement, *Texas Occupations Code,* sec. 1955.001 et seq.

7. The Tarrance Group, under contract to the League of Conservation Voters, conducted a statewide poll in 2000, close to the time that Senator Truan was speaking. The poll found that, "Seventy-four percent of Texans believe that the laws protecting the environment are either not strong enough and we need stronger laws, or that the laws are tough enough but are not strictly enforced and should be." League of Conservation Voters Education Fund, Texas Field Office, "Texas Voters See No Conflict Between Having a Healthy Environment and a Strong Economy,"press release, June 12, 2000. This Texas survey is in line with long-series U.S.-wide data: an annual Gallup poll conducted nationwide from 1985 through 2006 shows that Americans have consistently placed a higher priority on environmental protection than on economic growth. Dennis Jacobe, "Half of Public Favors the Environment Over Growth," *Gallup, Inc.* (March 26, 2008) http://www.gallup.com/poll/105715/half-public-favors-environment-over-growth.aspx (accessed November 11, 2009).

8. Some of the harm to the Open Beaches Act has come indirectly. For example, government insurance subsidies, such as the Texas Windstorm Insurance Association and federal disaster relief, have created a moral hazard for risky construction on Texas barrier islands, covering structures that often come to be within the protected beach as erosion proceeds. See Erwann Michel-Kerjan, Howard Kunreuther. "Improving Homeland Security in the Wake of Large-scale Disaster: Would Risk-Based All-Hazard Disaster Insurance Help in the Post-Katrina World? (paper presented at the CREATE Symposium, University of Southern California, Los Angeles, August 18–19, 2006), http://create.usc.edu/assets/pdf/51953.pdf (accessed January 28, 2009).

Rod, Gun, & Lens

"Leading the mean, lean lives we do, we little know how much wildness there is in us. Only a few centuries separate us from great-grandfathers that were savage as wolves; this is the secret of our love for the hunt."[1]

JOHN MUIR

BE IT THE BOUNTY of the range or of the sea; be it for sustenance or for sport, the Texas tradition of hunting and fishing has strong historic roots. Men and women who hardened their mettle against storm-tossed bays and rugged terrain faced new and very different challenges in modern times: game laws, the Endangered Species Act, private property rights, and the burgeoning environmental movement. "Locking horns" would be an apt description for the early days of contentious conflict.

Today, these seemingly intractable opponents have come to understand that their goals are more similar than different. Without a healthy ecosystem, the game they seek will not flourish; without management of game, wilderness may become overgrazed to the detriment of the native fauna. A balance between humans and animals was needed, and the Texans portrayed herein have made achieving it their life's work.

Add to this mix a decidedly twenty-first century hunter; armed with a camera, this new breed seeks to shoot only pictures. By capturing and sharing the colors and forms of the state's flora and fauna, these ecotourists are creating a new model for linking economic development and wildlife conservation.

1. Robert Engberg, ed., *John Muir Summering in the Sierra*, (Madison: University of Wisconsin Press, 1984), 48

White-tailed Deer and the Hunting Experience

AL BROTHERS lives in Berclair, Texas. He holds a degree in wildlife management, has worked for Texas Parks and Wildlife Department, and has managed ranches in Webb, Zapata, and Jim Hogg counties in Texas as well as Grand and San Juan counties in Utah. In subsequent years, Mr. Brothers has operated his own ranch and served as a consultant to other landowners on land, livestock, and wildlife issues. Seeing hunting as part of conservation and wildlife management, Mr. Brothers uses the example of white-tailed deer to explain the difference between "preservation" and "conservation," and the role of hunting in supporting those activities.

Interviewed on February 22, 2000, in Berclair, Texas

Reel 2076; Time Code 00:01:24

Preservation is when you don't do anything and let nature take its course. And nature can be pretty cruel. I'm experienced in white-tailed deer, so let me give you a prime example. The preservationists are going to say, "We're not going to let man take any deer" and leave nature on its own. And here's what would happen: the population would build up and the deer would actually eat themselves out of house and home, destroy the habitat or degrade it to the point where there would be a die-off. They would die off back to a small num-

ber of animals and then, as the habitat started recuperating, they would come back along with it and you'd have these ups and downs—extreme ups and downs in population and habitat quality. However, due to development, land uses, and habitat fragmentation, you can't say that we have a "natural setting" anymore where the predators, accidents, disease, or parasites would affect the natural mortality of the deer population.

We've changed all that and we can't change it back, so you have to go in there and manage it. And to me, management is part of a conservation effort. When we start talking about that we also talk about what we call additive mortality and compensatory mortality. I want to try to explain it to you. Let's take, for instance, birds, like quail or turkey, as a good example. Each year they have very high reproduction. One pair of quail will, say, have eighteen young ones; a turkey will have a lot of young ones. And the reason they have a lot of young ones is because there's a high turnover rate in the population. In compensatory mortality, we know in quail populations that a very high percentage of quail are not going to live until next year, they're going to be gone before next summer or next breeding season. Whatever that percentage is, it could be sixty percent, seventy percent, there's a big turnover rate in quail whether you hunt them or not. So, they try to set the hunting seasons where you can go in and you take these birds before a lot of this other naturally occurring loss happens, and that's called compensatory mortality. But let's say that the dates for the hunting seasons or the bag limits are set wrong and you start getting into taking what we call the brood stock. In other words, what would be left to breed next year? That's called additive mortality and it's something you don't want.

And this concept applies in big game species. They are a renewable resource, and they have young each year. You're going to lose a certain amount naturally, and instead of losing them through attrition, you can harvest them before they degrade the habitat. In other words, a whitetail deer eats approximately five or six pounds of forage a day. If we don't hunt them at all—and we're already at saturation on carrying capacity, and this year's farm crop or recruitment is going to put us above that— they're going to eat five pounds of forage per animal, per day. If we don't hunt them, they're going to eat until there's nothing left to eat and then you start losing them. First you're going to lose young and old, and then you start losing the others because they're going to eat anything they can until they die. When they do that, they degrade the habitat.

Why not go in and take this surplus animal out of the population—since it's a renewable resource and won't hurt the herd—and provide this hunting revenue to the landowner, revenue to the state, revenue to the agency that helps manage them—all without hurting the resource? And that's what the system is set up for—not hurting the habitat and, yet, providing recreation, and supporting the economy. Hunting is a big business.

You've got to remember that hunters, since the passing of the Pittman-Robinson Act,[1] are the ones that have funded most of the conservation programs you have in all the states now. The Pittman-Robinson Act passed many years ago as an excise tax on sporting arms, sporting ammunition, and other things that go toward hunting activities. That money is collected, put into a central fund by the federal government, and then redistributed to the states for approved programs through the Fish and Wildlife Service. And it's been a very successful program. It allowed management of species that were of economic value, that hunters were willing to pay for, and it also supported the other fringe and non-game species along the way.

Unfortunately, here in Texas, the most monumental flop of all was a "non-game stamp." They came out with a non-game stamp, and it was supposed to be purchased by these guys that didn't hunt, but that went out and bird-watched and were photographers. They were supposed to buy that stamp and that would help fund the wildlife programs for Texas Parks and Wildlife. It was a monumental flop. And yet, in the last few years we're beginning to see problems in the states for non-game animals and non-game birds. They deserve support, but we found out that the people that really cry for the aid have not been stepping forward to fund it. We hunters always funded it for them. And that's changing because they now have an excise tax on binoculars, photography equipment, and fishing equipment. It's beginning to become more balanced. If a person is interested in something, he should be willing to help fund the preservation or the management of it.

Reel 2075; Time Code 00:30:08

"A 'trophy animal' is basically a byproduct of maintaining a good healthy herd."

There's been a tremendous change from say forty, fifty years ago to now regarding what we call "subsistence hunting" or hunting for meat. You would be far better off to go buy your meat at the local grocery store compared to what it would cost today to harvest venison.

So, basically, I look at hunting as an outdoor experience—not necessarily the taking of the game animal— but all of the experience you feel and get from the hunt itself. And, if there's an opportunity to harvest a quality animal, fine, that makes it even better. But the whole idea of quality deer management is: let's maintain a healthy herd. What you would term as a "trophy animal" is basically a byproduct of maintaining a good healthy herd. An unhealthy herd normally has no quality animals in it. In a herd with a poor buck-to-doe ratio, poor age structure, poor recruitment or too

White-tailed deer (Courtesy Texas Parks and Wildlife Department)

much recruitment, you very seldom find quality animals in that type of herd. When you have a good herd and have good buck-to-doe ratios, good age structure, good recruitment, and the numbers are in tune with the habitat, then you have quality animals out there.

You are not necessarily going to get them, and that shouldn't be your primary objective, although it is for a lot of people. To me, the outdoor experience—the actual experience of going out—camping out or being with your friends in hunting camp, the camaraderie, is what's important. Learning or knowing what plants the deer prefer and looking for that, or knowing how to track, or how to read signs and deciding where the best place for you to hunt is . . . all of those things go into the hunting experience to me.

You have people now who don't know anything about deer food habits or deer as livestock, but they're out there hunting deer, and they're hunting deer strictly for the trophy, for the head. And to me they're cheat-ing themselves of the very finest part of the hunting experience.

To me it's all a quality experience, and then the chance to harvest a quality animal just adds to the mix. The best way to say it, in a nutshell, is that I have a quality experience every time I go out and occasionally I fire a shot.

1. The Pittman-Robertson Act (formally known as the Federal Aid in Wildlife Restoration Act) was passed in 1937 and imposes an 11 percent excise tax on sales of handgun, rifle, shotgun, and archery equipment and ammunition, directed towards conservation and education. 16 U.S.C. sec. 669 et seq. Together with related federal legislation (the Federal Aid in Sport Fish Restoration Act of 1950, also known as the Dingell-Johnson Act, amended by the Wallop-Breaux Act of 1984), these sporting goods taxes contribute more than 478 million dollars annually into U.S. conservation programs. 16 U.S.C. sec. 777 et seq.; David Adams, *Renewable Resource Policy* (Washington, D.C.: Island Press, 1993), 416–17; International Foundation for the Conservation of Natural Resources, "Sportsmen Pony Up Half Billion for State Wildlife Agencies," http://wildecology.ifcnr.com/article.cfm?NewsID=287 (article posted June 2003, accessed November 11, 2009).

Shrimp, Snapper, and Shipwrecks

FELIX COX is a fisherman from Aransas Pass who has, for many years, shrimped the Texas coast and worked the Gulf's offshore reefs, particularly for red snapper. Born and raised in the Carolinas, he first developed a love for fishing as a youngster, and made it a life-long career that has weathered both natural and man-made hardships.

Interviewed on February 23, 2000, in Aransas Pass, Texas

Reel 2077; Time Code 00:02:10

My brother was shrimping in the Gulf of Mexico, then over working off of Campeche, Mexico. And I begged him to take me along because I had fishing in my blood since being a child. He finally agreed, but he was reluctant at first because it's a dangerous business and you have to travel long distances in rough weather. Finally, reluctantly, he took me. When we were trawling for shrimp, we'd stay gone from fifty to sixty days at a stint.

And we'd have provisions brought in occasionally by other boats—and we'd ship our shrimp back by way of the boats coming in—there were boats coming and going most all the time. I guess maybe a year and a half or two years into the Campeche fishery, they gave me a boat to run. They thought I was probably qualified to run a boat of my own as captain. And being only nineteen or twenty years old, I think that was a dire mistake on the part of the owners because ultimately what happened was I lost that boat in the Yucatan Straits between the Yucatan and Cuba. That was my first casualty in the business, and afterwards, we went back to Florida and shrimped over there a little while longer. Then my brother and I came to Texas to make the Texas summer season. After we'd been here maybe two or three months, I met my first wife, and elected to stay here in Texas. And I've been in Texas ever since. I stayed in the shrimping business for maybe another twenty years or so, and then eventually gravitated over into the reef fish fishery, which are red snapper and grouper and such fish as that. I think I love fishing better than shrimping because it's a little more titillating. I'm still doing it, still fishing.

Reel 2077; Time Code 00:22:39

"Son, we're going to lose this boat."

I had a brand new boat that I had built in 1985. It was a nice little thirty-five foot Lafitte-style skiff and, it was maybe only five months old at the time. I was using it for shrimping and sometimes for reef fish fishing, and we got caught in a norther in the first days of November 1985.[1] It was late in the evening and I had my son on the boat with me, and we were aware that a front was coming in. The captain of the *Mattie Grace*—the boat that I now have—he was up closer to the jetties than I was, and came on in the jetties and radioed me that this norther was hitting a little harder than we had anticipated. So we got our nets up and started steaming toward Aransas Pass.

We were about two hours normal steam from Aransas Pass and it was late in the evening, and it got darker and got rougher and, sure enough, the front hit real hard. It was blowing probably thirty or forty, maybe forty-five miles an hour and this small boat is not capable of handling much of that. So I elected to head over inside towards what we call "the gullies," which is right up close to the beach. It's a deep trough of water up close to our Gulf beaches and I figured I'd get some protection from the swell, from the seas. And I did. But as it got darker, I couldn't see as well, and I had my son shining the spotlight out, and I would zigzag out to the offshore bar, and then back in to the inshore gully, and back out until I'd feel the seas coming over the boat. At some point, my son opened the back door and said, "Dad, there's a awful lot of water in this boat, I think we're in trouble." And I said, "Well, hold the wheel just a minute," and I slowed the engine down and I opened the back door and looked out myself and we were half full of water. I said, "Son, we're going to lose this boat. . . . hang on, I'm going to try to drive it up on the beach if I can." My intention was to get it straight on in, up on the beach, as fast as we could.

Shrimp (Courtesy Texas Parks and Wildlife Department)

We were probably three or four hundred foot offshore, running up along the beach, and I hit the throttle and goosed it, and when I did, seas came over the stern of it and buried it right there, and we were sunk. There was enough air in the fuel tank that it held the bow afloat, but the stern was sunk and the seas were piling over the stern. We tried to leave the boat through the rear door and we couldn't because the seas just kept knocking the door back in on us. I told my son, "We're going to have to go out these front windows" so we opened the front windows. They lifted up on a hinge assembly. I told him, "Put on a life jacket now and crawl out of one of these windows and I'll be right behind you." And he tried to argue with me like he usually does, and I said, "For once, son, don't argue with me. Put on a life jacket," and he says, "Dad, I can make it without the life jacket." And I tell him, "Put a life jacket on and get the hell out of here and I'll be right behind you." He finally did, and he scooted out the window. I put on a life jacket and I scooted out behind him and we hauled boogie to the beach. I was hollering at him. I said, "Son, wait on me," and he just dug in a little deeper. He looked back and I think he said, "Every man for himself." We made it to the beach and lost that boat.

I knew that I was not ready to leave the fishing business and yet there we were, with no boat—and we had just paid sixty-five thousand dollars for that sunken boat—and didn't have one cent of insurance on it. My wife almost went into a shock over this, and it affected me quite heavily too. Two days later we had to charter a plane and found the boat up in the surf. We tried to raise it but couldn't, and I ended up selling the boat for a dollar just to relieve myself of the liability.

A friend of mine was running the *Mattie Grace* at the time, and he had come down from Waco and was interested in being a fisherman. However, after about a year of having the *Mattie Grace,* he found that he was, in fact, not a fisherman. And he agreed to sell the *Mattie Grace* to me on time. And so I started making a thousand dollar a month payments on the *Mattie Grace.* Gave him a five thousand dollar down payment and I still have a note outstanding on the boat that I lost at the bank, of some eight hundred dollars a month. So from the proceeds from fishing with the *Mattie Grace,* I ended up paying off the *Mattie Grace* and the boat that I lost in about seven years. It took a while but finally I'm starting making some money. So we were back up on our feet. It has ups and downs. This fishing business can be great at times, and it can certainly have some down sides to it. It's a roller coaster ride.

In addition to the forces of nature, fishermen like Mr. Cox also must deal with the implications of politics and economics on the Gulf's fisheries, which involve the decline in fish populations and attempts at regulatory control. Mr. Cox is working with regulators and with non-profits such as Environmental Defense to develop better schemes for managing the reef fishery. One of the more promising solutions is called the ITQ (Individual Transferable Quotas) system, which would apportion marketable rights to the harvest, and discourage the dangerous and wasteful derby system.

Reel 2078; Time Code 00:13:40

Unfortunately we don't have a strong voice in Congress for our Gulf of Mexico fishing concerns. Other fishing regions, like in the Northwest, have strong ties to their Congressional people, like in Alaska and the State of Washington. In Louisiana, their fishing industry has a relatively strong tie to Senator John Breaux and, as a matter of fact, I attended a field hearing just recently on the reauthorization of the Magnuson Act and Senator Breaux and Senator Olympia Snow were conducting these hearings. I gave a little testimony to them along with several other fishermen, specifically in regards to the individual transferable quota[2] programs that we might eventually enjoy. That was ninety percent of the debate at this particular hearing. I feel like it is *the* tool of the future for managing fisheries—privatization through individual quotas. When you speak of "privatization," lots of people cringe at that thought, because they have been capable of going out there and catching the fish any time they want to, seemingly forever, and this program is new and it's contentious. It's something to be dealt with though, because I think it's on the horizon. I certainly hope it is.[3]

I really and truly believe that there will come a time, maybe in several years, when the public, in general,

Red snapper (Courtesy Daniel Iggers, Creative Commons)

rises up and realizes that they need good, conscientious, commercial fishermen just like we need all different professional people. I strongly believe in commercial fishing because I've been in it all my life and I know that there's a need for it because people want to eat fish. Somebody is going to furnish it to them somehow, and if it's not the traditional way, it'll be some other way. I feel that wild caught fish is some of the best protein that a person can encounter. My private feeling is that when I'm sixty-five years old and hopefully retired and getting Social Security and probably nothing else, I would still like to be able to go down to the fish market or a restaurant and buy a fish. And if commercial fishing is extinguished, I won't be able to do that and I think that will be a great loss to the whole nation. So I have some optimism. I feel like somewhere in the future, there'll be a turnaround for commercial fishing.

1. Fishermen have sometimes been forced to take risks with the weather, where they might not otherwise have been so bold, to catch their limited share of a capped harvest. This has been the situation for red snapper fishermen, such as Mr. Cox, where a quota of a permissible take is calculated, and then the season is closed once the quota is filled. This kind of pressure creates a risky, weather-be-damned "derby" race to take the last fish. Kristen M. Fletcher and Elizabeth B. Speaker, "Red Snapper Fishery Tests License Limitation System," *Water Log: A Legal Reporter of the Mississippi-Alabama Sea Grant Consortium* 18, no. 3 (1998): 1, 10. http://masglp.olemiss.edu/Water%20Log%20PDF/18-3.pdf (accessed November 11, 2009).

2. Individual Transferable Quotas allow the estimation of a total sustainable harvest from a given fishery, and then assign shares to the industry's local fishermen, in proportion to their historical catch. These fishermen can buy or sell these shares, encouraging the industry to approach an economically efficient size, commensurate with a profitable harvest. This helps stabilize the industry at a financially sustainable level. Ecologically, ITQs are believed to help stop fishery collapse and restore those in decline. Christopher Costello, Steven D. Gaines, and John Lynham, "Can Catch Shares Prevent Fisheries Collapse?" *Science* 321, no. 5896 (2008): 1678-81. As Mr. Cox points out, some criticize ITQs on the basis of its privatization of wild fisheries, and others condemn the costly barriers raised to new fishermen's entry to the industry.

3. The ITQ program that Mr. Cox hoped for was adopted in March 2006 for the Gulf red snapper fishery. *Final Amendment 26 to the Gulf of Mexico Reef Fishery Management Plan to Establish a Red Snapper Individual Fishing Quota Program,* (Tampa, Florida: Gulf of Mexico Fishery Management Council, National Oceanic and Atmospheric Administration, 2006) 104-167. http://www.gulfcouncil.org/Beta/GMFMCWeb/downloads/Amend26031606FINAL.pdf (accessed November 11, 2009).

Robins, Binoculars, and Piping Plovers

JESSE GRANTHAM has lived in Corpus Christi and Rockport, Texas, during assignments with the National Audubon Society. He is a field botanist and ornithologist who has worked since 1971 in Pennsylvania, California, Mississippi, Puerto Rico, Texas, and elsewhere conducting field research and natural inventories, managing endangered species restoration programs, and acquiring and operating sanctuary lands. Most of his career however, was with the Audubon Society, where he served as Texas director of bird conservation and Texas sanctuaries manager. His interest in birds and the natural world started at an early age, and Mr. Grantham recalls how this fledgling interest developed into a lifelong passion.

Interviewed October 25, 2003, in Rockport, Texas

Reel 2289; Time Code 00:02:04

". . . I remember playing sick from kindergarten so that I could sit and watch that nest."

I can tell you first of how I got interested, and that was when I was five years old. It was April Fools' Day. My father came in and said, "There's a robin building a nest outside my bedroom window and you might want to come look at it." I remember getting up out of bed and walking into his room and looking out the window and watching this robin building its nest. I was absolutely mesmerized by that activity of that bird going back and forth and building this nest. And I could see, every once in a while, the bird would look up at the window and see me and then it would go about its business. So I really had this tremendous opportunity to be right there, looking in this bird's eye, and probably watching the wheels turning up there as it went through thousands of years of evolutionary process in building this nest. And I became so enamored of that thing that I watched it every spare moment that I could, to the point where, I remember playing sick from kindergarten so that I could sit and watch that nest. And I watched it so much that the bird eventually abandoned the nest. I mean, I watched her lay eggs, I watched her incubate the eggs and then, at some point, she just couldn't handle it anymore with me being there, watching her, so she left. And I think it's that time I discovered my father's seven-by-thirty-five binoculars and I was able to put those on the nest, too. I had the window open and the binoculars sitting on the windowsill, focused on this nest. And after she abandoned the nest, I remember I spent days and days sort of watching, waiting for her to come back, and then climbing up the tree and feeling that the eggs were cold and eventually the nest fell down and the eggs were taken by predators and that was the end of that. But that was for me, the real beginning. I specifically remember that instance, and from then on, I had this real interest in birds. I think it was focused on bird behavior and reproduction, you know, building nests and sustainability and all of that. Maybe that's where all of that came from, in those first few weeks, sitting and watching that bird build the nest.

From then on I met people, older people, retired folks, who would occasionally take me to see birds or to go on a bird watching trip somewhere, and I'd bring my father's big seven-by-thirty-five binoculars, which were a third the size that I was, so they hung down probably to my knees. Then I went through a stage in my life where I kind of got away from birds, and when I was in high school, you wouldn't get caught dead with a pair of binoculars around your neck. I remember getting to that stage of where I put them away, of having to hide the binoculars if I saw any of my friends coming because that would've been a serious infraction of boyhood or manhood to have a pair of binoculars, to be watching birds. It wasn't until really about my senior year in high school that I suddenly realized this was silly. This is really what I love to do, and I got back into it and joined some clubs and met some great people. From then on, I just spent a lot of time, a lot more time, out in the field. Now, to say that I got away from birds when I was in my high school years doesn't mean that I didn't ever go out. I lived out in the country so, of course, every spare moment that I had at home was out in the field, but by myself. So for those early years, I really didn't have any mentors, anybody who was sort of pushing me in the direction of a conservation agenda or ethic with birds. I was more into just watching birds when I would go with people. But when I was out there by myself, I would usually spend many, many hours just watching a particular bird or watching a particular nest and not knowing it at the time, but certainly, I was learning a lot about their behavior and their survivability tactics and the kinds of things that would impact bird populations.

Audubon staff members, like Mr. Grantham, have worked to protect Texas' 620-plus resident and migratory bird species since 1899, through conservation education, management of thirteen thousand acres of leased rookery islands, and coordination of habitat protection on private lands.[1] One of Mr. Grantham's concerns, an outgrowth of his early studies of birds and their nesting habits, is the plight of endangered species like the piping plover, which makes its home on the Texas coast. Since Texas beaches are also open to vehicle and human traffic, these impacts, often unrecognized by the general public, can severely affect the lives of the tiny birds dotting the shoreline.

Reel 2290; Time Code 00:03:55

"They can't change their biology. They can't change ten thousand years of evolution. We can change"

To you and I, driving down the beach, it looks like a piping plover, sitting on the beach, taking a rest, but to somebody who's doing research on this, they're beginning to realize the critical importance of these beach habitats for this small shorebird. It wasn't too long before they began to realize the impacts of people on this little shorebird, particularly on weekends when people are driving up and down the beach. It's a twenty-five mile per hour beach, and people are doing fifty, sixty miles an hour down the beach. They're bringing their dogs and coolers and volleyball sets and all this stuff and they're putting it right in, or alongside, the territories of these small piping plovers, which then flushes these birds off.

The birds can't use their territory so they can't feed there, which means they have to find some other place to go. And they can't just move over, because then they're in another bird's territory, which is defending that territory because it has to in order to survive. It can't just let all the other piping plovers come in there because there's not enough food. Obviously, if you have too many sitting at the table, there's not going to be enough food to go around if there's only a finite amount of food to begin with. What happens is they all get bumped down the beach and they end up in marginal

Piping Plover (Courtesy Texas Parks and Wildlife Department)

habitats, or habitats that don't have any food at all and they just can't do anything but sit all day. So they're not actually putting on fat reserves for the winter months, or for when something in the environment changes and maybe the food availability is not as accessible or not as prevalent as it would be at other times. They've always got to be way ahead of the game. They can't be skating on the razor's edge. They've always got to be putting on fat and being prepared for that time when things are not going to be optimum. And, obviously, if they didn't do that, they wouldn't survive. But now they're being forced down to where there are maybe two days out of the week where they can't defend their territories and they can't find the amount of food that they need. Some birds are disappearing and new birds are coming in, and what does that mean?

I think what it meant for me was how little we know and understand and appreciate the niche that these birds fill on our coastal beaches; that we just accept them for granted as, "It's just another little piping plover on the beach. Isn't it great? It's entertaining." We look at it and get pleasure from it, recreational pleasure, aesthetic pleasure. But, for that individual animal, it's a life and death struggle on a daily basis. And so, being run off of your territory means that you're going to be skating on the razor's edge. If the amount of traffic and the conditions on the beach increase so that the amount of time that these birds can spend on their territories is less and less, it's pushing that bird toward that endangered species listing. Now, *we* have a direct impact on that. I ask, "How do we deal with that?"

Here's just one example: how do you deal with these piping plovers that are setting up territories? They're heading toward endangered species status. There's no way they can get out of it. They can't change their feeding behavior. They can't change their biology. They can't change ten thousand years of evolution. *We* can change, by encouraging people not to drive sixty miles an hour down the beach and swerve over into the surf and flush these birds off. Or, there are areas maybe where you put people to have volleyball courts and picnics and that sort of thing so that you're not right on the beach disturbing the birds. The question is, how do we deal with just that one issue? That's just one bird and one set of issues, and are we willing to put the time and effort into changing *our* behavior so that this bird is not then put on the endangered species list and then, who knows what will become of it? Obviously, more time, money, and effort is going to have to be put into studying that bird.

1. Nongame bird protection, and Audubon's role in that effort, can be traced back to the late 1800s. Early roots can be found in an 1886 report by ornithologist Frank Chapman of the American Museum of Natural History. Mr. Chapman found that three-quarters of women's hats were decorated with feathers, most often from snowy and great egrets, but also including terns, orioles, tanagers, and warblers. The trade was valuable and large. Nuptial egret plumes sold for thirty-two dollars per ounce, nearly twice the price of gold at the time. One auction house sold 1,608 packets of heron plumes in a single year, with a lone packet holding 48,240 ounces of feathers, representing nearly two hundred thousand birds killed. As a result, by 1899, citizens in fifteen states had organized Audubon Societies which shared a common goal: "to discourage the buying and wearing for ornamental purposes of the feathers of any wild birds." In 1905, these Societies formed the National Associations of Audubon, the predecessor of the National Audubon Society. In 1923, to protect the populations of the wading birds that had been decimated for the millinery trade, the Audubon group established a network of island sanctuaries along the Texas coast. Some sanctuaries were bought outright, others were leased from governmental agencies, principally the Texas General Land Office. The preserves now include more than thirteen thousand acres and thirty-three islands that are home to over twenty species of colonial waterbirds, such as the reddish egret, brown pelican and roseate spoonbill. Richard Moore, "Green Island . . . Lower Laguna Madre Sanctuary, Home to World's Largest Colony of Reddish Egrets," *Richard Moore Outdoors*. www.richardmoorenature.com/Article/968305 (accessed January 28, 2009); Audubon Texas, "Coastal Stewardship Program," http://www.tx.audubon.org/Coastal.html (accessed January 28, 2009).

Galveston, Ecotourism, and Birds

TED EUBANKS is founder and president of Fermata, Inc., a cause-oriented business involved in researching and developing nature and historical tourism throughout the United States and abroad. His interest in eco- or experiential travel grew out of his interest in birding (he has served on the boards of the Houston, Texas and National Audubon Societies), his efforts to secure bird sanctuaries (including High Island, Smith Woods, Bolivar Flats, and other bird preserves), his advocacy to protect habitat (such as the fights against the West Side Houston airport and Wallisville Reservoir), and his study of the broad economic impact of birding and other non-consumptive natural resource uses in Texas. His landmark essay, "The Culture of Conservation," is considered a cornerstone in the ecotourism field.

Interviewed on April 15, 2002, in Austin, Texas

I think, for many people, there is some sort an epiphanic moment: you know, lightning bolt out of the sky type stuff. For me, it was part of the fabric of my life. Both of my parents, now in their late seventies, are still involved in the outdoors. I'll be birding with them a couple of weeks from now, on the Texas coast, which is sort of a ritual for our family. I grew up from the first possible cognizant moment, being aware of the natural world. My mother, several years ago, gave me some first or second grade drawings that I had done. Every drawing has flying birds in the background, so it's obvious to me that this was always part of who I was.

In terms of recreation, I sort of remember this montage of trips our family took. We always had sort of a traditional trip down to Galveston in the summer; we had a "vacation every year," as we used to say, and we did the *same* vacation every year. We always went down to Galveston! I can remember a real fascination with shorebirds at a very early age. They were accessible

Seagulls, Galveston, Texas (Courtesy Ed Schipul, Creative Commons)

and they're visible—animated—so I have pretty vivid memories of seeing sanderlings and things like that. I can remember a goldfinch in the yard when I was a little kid and being fascinated by those birds coming into a sweet gum tree. There are many, many moments in my young childhood, when I was exposed to birding, and then, of course, by the time I was in high school, it was more formal. I fed birds, but I don't remember building many birdhouses. You know, all those sorts of artificial accoutrements never interested me at all. I always thought these sorts of structures got in between me and

what I was looking at. I like a more intimate experience between myself and the outdoors, so, it wasn't as much of a home-based activity as something outside.

"He picked up this road kill—it was an opossum— and brought it in to class and we stuffed it!"

I'd walk to school, and I can remember, being fascinated by, not only the birds, but soft-shelled turtles and all those other sorts of things that were around. I was very lucky when I was in fifth grade at Spring Branch

Elementary School, that my science teacher was Robert Vines, who wrote the guide to all of the woody shrubs and trees of Texas.[1] And we were his little minions. We would go out and collect leaves and specimens for him. He was a cool guy and did some pretty interesting stuff. I remember one instance quite vividly: he picked up this road kill—it was an opossum—and brought it in to class and we stuffed it! That was a great mentor to have when you're in fifth grade. Later in life, even when I was out of school altogether, I continued my contact with him, up until he died. For all those other sorts of interests, say, the viewing aspect, watching birds, my mentor would've been my father. He was a hunter. I hunted, too, and then we both sort of evolved out of it, simultaneously. To this day, he's still fascinated by birds and astronomy. So, I think that ethic was instilled at a very young age.

Reel 2191; Time Code 00:51:11

"We conserve what we use."

Promoting ecotourism has really been the focus of my efforts for at least the last decade, maybe the last fifteen years. That's what we built this company on. We're a strange company: this is a "cause-based corporation." It's a for-profit that works on issues that are as much ethical as they are financial. There's an interesting mix here, and though I'm not sure how many cause-based corporations there are, we certainly call ourselves one. One of the things that became clear—and why I ultimately sold off my other business and created this one—was that it was obvious to me that *people conserve what they use.* That's a fundamental, cardinal rule: we conserve what we use. And we conserve those things that we value, and that value comes through that use.

So, if people were using these resources for recreation, then I should be able to tie conservation into that equation. Okay, we care about this because we use it. We conserve it because we use it. That's really what all of this is about. And one of the things we started off

with, is, my God, if we have all these people looking at birds, and they care about this sort of thing, what about those people that may not use it but would derive economic value from having people visit—travel and tourism.

I started looking at that, and I did an early paper on the ecotourism potential for Galveston Bay, which I presented at the very first Galveston Bay Estuary Program annual meeting. That's over a decade ago. I did some of the first studies: what birders were spending, where they went, where the dollars went, and so forth. And now I don't know exactly, but our body of work is nationally probably the most significant in this field regarding this sort of recreation.

Then we started taking those numbers and going to Mission, Texas or Hidalgo or Grand Island, Nebraska or wherever and saying, look, you need to understand what this means: the Platte River is not just a lot of migrating cranes, it's also about forty million dollars a year in economic impact coming from people who want to see those cranes. By recognizing that relationship, we've been able to open doors that would've never been opened before. I was in Bottineau, North Dakota last week, as a keynote speaker at their annual economic development conference to discuss the potential for North Dakota. Both of their U.S. Senators were there, and both of them are very much involved in what's possible. We're about to look at a major statewide effort. This is North Dakota! The initial interest, what opened the door, was the fact that here is an opportunity for an agrarian economy, which has really suffered in the last twenty or thirty years, to diversify. It's why I've developed really splendid working relationships with private landowners and their groups in this state, Texas. We have ranchers and farmers that need to diversify out of a commodity-based economy into a service-based, or even as I call it, an "experience-based" economic strategy.

Beneath that, or overlaying this economic impact, is the fact that, there is this mass of the American public that finds its way to nature through birds. Seventy million! Seventy million Americans find their way to nature through birds. They don't have to be birders. They don't have to call themselves birders. But that is their vehicle for entering in the outdoors, into the natural world. If I can develop programs and opportunities, whether it's a trail like the Great Texas Coastal Birding Trail,[2] or the trail we just finished in Virginia, or the ones we're doing in Connecticut and Wisconsin, if we can bring these people into the outdoors and show them the value of those natural resources *and* show them the need to conserve those resources because they *do* value them—that could have a major effect on public policy. Seventy million people? How many of those would I have needed to swing the last election? That's where I want to work: with that potential, amorphous mass. They're not birders, they haven't defined themselves in that way, their interests haven't crystallized, they just realize that there's a very important way to connect, to become rooted in nature. Let's go back to that increasingly urban population that is increasingly disconnected from nature. What, particularly in the post-9/11 world, is out there that's safe, real, authentic, trustworthy? Well, it's the outdoors; it's nature. We've seen that in increased park visitation post-9/11, we've seen that in visitors to wildlife sanctuaries. That will be my life's work, working in that field and trying to swing that mass.

1. Vines, Robert, *Trees, Shrubs, and Woody Vines of the Southwest, a Guide for the States of Arkansas, Louisiana, New Mexico, Oklahoma, and Texas* (Austin: University of Texas Press, 1969).

2. Begun by Texas Parks and Wildlife in 1993, the Texas Coastal Birding Trail now allows visitors to spot as many as 450 bird species on over five hundred miles of routes and more than three hundred wildlife-viewing sites strung along the coast, stretching from Brownsville to Orange. Madge Lindsay, "The Great Texas Coastal Birding Trail: A Tool for Avitourism," in *Strategies for Bird Conservation: The Partners in Flight Planning Process*, ed. Rick Bonney, David N. Pashley, Robert J. Cooper, and Larry Niles (Ithaca, NY: Cornell Lab of Ornithology, 1995). http://birds.cornell.edu/pifcapemay/lindsay.htm (accessed November 11, 2009).

Pulpit & Lectern

"The sun shines not on us but in us."[1]

JOHN MUIR

"WHY BOTHER?" It's a simple enough question, and whether asked with irony or naïveté, it innocently begs a bigger question, "why not?" Faced today with the overwhelming ecological crisis, from climate change to environmental injustice, many people have thrown up their hands in seeming helplessness.

But there are some who have not. Drawing their motivation from sources both secular and religious, they seek to inspire in others a passion to care, to participate, and to realize their inherent capacity for good. However, this is not merely another form of self-help therapy, but a zealous call to action. Rooted in historical movements for social change such as trade unionism, civil rights, and feminism, these influential thinkers offer bold ideas for community engagement and economic reassessment.

1. Graham White, ed., *Sacred Summits: John Muir's Greatest Climbs*, (Edinburgh, UK: Canongate, 1999), 80.

Refineries, Churches, and Environmental Justice

ROY MALVEAUX is a Baptist minister who has served congregations in both Corpus Christi and Beaumont. He has also led the statewide public interest group People Against a Contaminated Environment (PACE), which grew out of his concern that air and water emissions from powerful petrochemical facilities abutting these communities were affecting the health and livelihoods of his neighbors and congregants.

In addition to challenging corporate polluters and state regulatory agencies, Reverend Malveaux also found himself at odds with some members of the religious community, who felt that his advocacy was stretching the boundaries of the church's purview. In response, he evokes the struggles of the civil rights movement as analogous to the environmental justice movement.

Interviewed on October 8, 1999, in Beaumont, Texas

Reel 2048; Time Code 00:06:13

As a trade, I'm a machinist. I was in the Navy for thirteen years, and I worked for the Department of Defense for ten years. I often came in contact with chemicals and even machined some exotic metals that let off fumes when they came in contact with the cutting tools. I often used acetone to machine magnesium or aluminum or many of the other exotic metals. And at that time I was not aware that I was really coming in contact with some toxic chemicals. But it wasn't that, so much, that got me involved in understanding my environment. It was a lot of things that lead to my awakening. . . .

My children were going to Crossley Elementary School in Corpus Christi, Texas. And the way I got involved in understanding the environment I live in is one night they came home from school and said, "Daddy, the refinery blew up." Of course, I said, "Yeah." You know how parents are, "Yeah, um-hum." "And, Daddy, they put us underneath the desk. It was fun!" Now I'm really listening. What is my child doing underneath the desk? If the refinery is blowing up, that's not the safest place to be. And I learned later this was called a "Shelter In Place" program. Needless

Industrial neighborhood, Corpus Christi—1994 (Copyright 1994 Corpus Christi Caller-Times. *Photographer: George Tuley)*

to say, it was a *suicide in place program.* I started to listen very carefully after that incident because I never saw anything in the newspaper. I didn't see anything on television. It wasn't two or three weeks later they came home and told me the same thing. And this time, it showed up on the ten o'clock news. I was outraged. And so a group of concerned people got together to say, "You know, there's something wrong with the fact that our children are being put in danger and we have to find out about it on the ten o'clock news."

"I just know that politics is tied to pollution. Or else it would be solved by now."

So we had a meeting at some local churches and as a result of those meetings, we formed a group called People Against Contaminated Environments, which is PACE. I am the state Executive Director of that group. There were a series of explosions and fires from '89 all the way to '94. And that led to me getting involved to the point where I had to read everything I could read. I had to educate myself. I had to find books. I read a book called, *Dumping in Dixie* by Robert Bullard.[1] I read everything I could get my hands on, and I interacted with other groups and went to seminars. I was really outraged at the things that I found out that I had no knowledge of. I had never known that there was a group called TNRCC, Texas Natural Resources and Conservation Commission, who were supposed to be "protecting and serving." And after I got that initial shock, through my children, then I had to get busy.

We didn't all agree, at first, that the church had a role to play in the environmental justice movement. I believe the church has a large role to play. As a matter of fact, the church ought to lead it. Now, the polluters would like us to think that, "my product never leaves my fence line." And that's just not so. . . . Unfortunately, politics and pollution go together. To me, the issue has already been solved. The Clean Air Act has already solved a lot of our problems with air emissions. The Clean Water Act has solved a lot of our problems. However, the Legislature does things that open up loopholes, that allow factories to continue breaking these laws. If I broke a law, well, three times, *and you're out.* That's criminality. That's a repeat offender. But some environmental criminals break these laws three and four times a month. As a matter of fact, some of them have broken the law three or four times a week. And they are never prosecuted. The reason I say that politics is tied to pollution is because we have a governor that says he's tough on crime. But he just means street crime. White-collar crime never enters the picture. As a matter of fact,

Playground, Texas City—1990 (© Sam Kittner/kittner.com)

he's being supported by a lot of environmental criminals and I hope I'm not making anyone feel uncomfortable by what I'm saying, but I just know that politics is tied to pollution. Or else it would be solved by now.

The neighborhoods that are overburdened with pollution shouldn't still exist today. If I had something that caused me a liability, I would either buy it out or try to find a way to remove it. That's just good business. And so the reason I say it's tied to politics is because if we wanted to solve it, we could. America's a great country. We have intelligent men all over the United States. There's no reason why it should keep on going. I had to convince my clergy friends that this, in fact, was the problem. Then I had to convince them it was a religious problem also.

Reel 2048; Time Code 00:40:03

There's a great reluctance on the part of the church to become involved in the environmental justice movement as a whole. Especially because the petrochemical plants have a lot of money and they have a long reach. Let me put it to you this way: I like to tell the story of David and Goliath. David was supposed to be home taking care of the father's sheep. His brothers were at the battle line, facing the Philistine giant Goliath, who was shouting out insult after insult at them. They were at an impasse until David stepped up to challenge Goliath. Even David's brothers told him, "You need to go back home, you ought to be taking care of the sheep." Yes, even among family, jealousy is a problem. When a man does step up, he gets ridiculed. And not only ridicule, there is also fear. Goliath was big. His spear was probably about nine feet. His shield was probably five or six feet. He was big, like the petrochemical industry. This industry has some deep pockets. They can reach deep. They can touch people and that gives people fear. And so, when you step out, the first thing they're going to say is, "We'll get you." And they don't tell you that straight on. For instance, since I've been in this movement, I've gotten a lot of calls from funeral parlors—several since I've been here. "We want to sell you a funeral plot." And I tell them, "No thank you." Because I'm not going to be in that body. That body's going to the ground, and my spirit's going to the Lord. And I'm not going to need a funeral plot.

"If you have faith, you can't have fear."

Those are the type of things that intimidate you. I worked for the Department of Defense and while I was leading the Corpus Christi group, I got many calls from my supervisor telling me that I need to come to work and stay away from the kind of stuff that makes "trouble." And so, a lot of people are afraid of the giant. But the story doesn't stop there, and I thank God it doesn't. Because no matter how big the giant is, and no matter how much he roars, he can be beat. Recall that there are two men in any military battle that are stronger than anybody. One is the private, because he doesn't have anything to lose. And the other is the general, because he has *everything* to loose. And those are the two most dangerous men that you ever want to come in contact

with. Well, I think I represent one of them, but I'm not sure which. But I did face this giant, and on many occasions I didn't have any money. And I still don't. I thank God I have what I have. But the giants will not rest until they have expended all that they can. Ask yourself a question: Why would an industry who has billions of dollars, makes twenty-five million in profits each day, spend millions of dollars to fight a case when they can just remove the liability? Arrogance? Perhaps. Or not. You can't make it easy for people to sue you, so I can understand their business side. Pastor friends of mine tell me, "Man, I don't know how you do it. You've had to move three times, and you still haven't gotten it through your head who is pulling the strings." And I always tell them, "God has the last word." And that's just the kind of faith that you need in this environmental movement. If you have fear, you don't have faith. And if you have faith, you can't have fear.

1. Robert D. Bullard, *Dumping in Dixie: Race, Class and Environmental Quality,* (Jackson, TN: Westview Press, 1990).

A Just and Decent Society

ERNIE CORTES is a community organizer and protégé of Saul Alinsky, and has served as director of the Southwest Industrial Areas Foundation in Austin. He was also a founder of Communities Organized for Public Service (COPS) in San Antonio, and Valley Interfaith in South Texas, and a leader in many other multi-ethnic efforts to help bring drinking water, sewer and flood management to poor communities in South Texas, as well as improved education, training and job opportunities. He has used the social justice teachings from the Judeo-Christian faiths as a philosophical basis for institutional and non-denominational grassroots development.

Interviewed on April 12, 2002, in Austin, Texas

Reel 2185; Time Code 00:02:14

Growing up in San Antonio, you saw a lot of things that didn't seem to be quite the way they were supposed to be. The environmental concerns came to me, frankly, out of concern for public health: questions about toxicity of water, concern about lack of sewage, impact on health from air quality. This whole analogy that I like to use—which is not mine originally—is of the "coal miner's canary." The environment is like the coal miner's canary. And so we have to be concerned about the environment, not only for its own sake, but because of its impact on the quality of human life, or even the viability and the sustainability of human life. It comes for me from all kinds of places, like the Book of Genesis: believing early on that we have dominion or responsibility, stewardship, over the Earth. And that means we have to be concerned about quality of life for *all* living creatures.

I learned an incredible amount about issues relating to public health in organizing and working with farm workers in the Rio Grande Valley and learning about the impact of pesticides on human beings, and on farm workers, in particular. And, also, on us, from the impact of eating foods which have been laced with pesticides, and the dangers and the carcinogenic impact that they have. There were a lot of other things that were going on, in the sixties when I grew up and was going to school, which affected how I saw the world. There're a lot of people I've read: Barry Commoner, Rachel Carson's *Silent Spring.* When I eventually went to the Industrial Areas Foundation, to become involved as an organizer, it was to learn *how* to do something about those concerns, not to understand those concerns.

Reel 2185; Time Code 00:14:17

Justice takes on many different dimensions and many different understandings. For instance, there is the kind of justice that comes out of the biblical traditions. The word *mishpot* comes to mind, which has to do with the concrete realization of certain ideals—in certain municipal institutions—which state that no one should be left out, no one should be deprived of the means to participate in the prosperity of the community. This notion of *mishpot* meant that no matter who you were, that no one could take away from you the tools that were necessary—your house, your farm implements—in order to be able to participate in the shared prosperity of the community. Even if you owed money to a moneylender, if you owed money to a landlord—and even though that debt was legitimate—if it meant that in order to pay the debt you'd lose your home or capacity to earn a living—justice would not allow that to happen. So therefore it was incumbent upon the people who ran these municipal courts to not deprive you of that, and to rule in your favor—even against the powerful interest of people who

were the economic power players of that particular lot and community.

And so, that understanding—*that tradition*—is something that animates us, and frankly, it is reflected in the populist tradition in Texas. The Homestead Exemption[1] comes out of that understanding, and the notion of a safety net comes out of that understanding: that there's a level below which people should not ever fall. You may have an enterprise economy with risk taking and dynamism and "winners and losers," but there's a level below which people never fall, and therefore we never deprive people of certain basic things, which are important for their humanity. Adam Smith in *The Wealth of Nations* said that a just society is one where a working person can appear in public without shame, without being humiliated. That meant, in his time, being able to have a decent shirt, pair of shoes, and that was important for the people who ran that society to understand that everyone should have the access to those things which are necessary to appear in public without feeling humiliated.

"They have a right to be heard, a right to participate, a right to deliberate."

So, the question for us, in the year 2002, is what is necessary for a person to be in public without shame? And I always argue, it's more than just clothes, it's also access to health care, it's access to education, it's access to running water, to shelter. In 1949, the Republican-controlled Congress, led by Senator Robert Taft, passed a Housing Act.[2] And that Housing Act of 1949 said that every American, no matter who he or she is, should be provided with a decent home and a suitable living environment. I think that's something, which is frankly a part of our tradition, and something which we should be accountable to. So there is this kind of understanding of justice which means that we have access to the prosperity, to the *shalom,* if you will, in the Biblical tradition of the community.

There's an Israeli scholar by the name of Avishai

Colonia near Reynosa, Rio Grande Valley, Mexico (Courtesy Alan Pogue, Texas Center for Documentary Photography)

Margalit, who wrote a book called *A Decent Society,*[3] and he said that there's a difference between a "civilized" society and a "decent" society and a "just" society. A "civilized" society is where the people of that society are "nice" to each other—kind and sensitive. But you can have a "civilized" society that is not a decent society because a "decent" society requires that the institutions of that society do not humiliate adults. So you could have a society where the institutions humiliate adults and which treat adults as second-class citizens, even though people are "nice" to each other. What comes to mind is the American South before the Civil Rights movement, where you had people who were nice to African Americans, nice to the black people, warm and sensitive to them, but nonetheless, the institutions, the schools, the courthouses, the public institutions treated African American people as second-class citizens. The same thing was also true in South Texas, with Mexicans, and in San Antonio, where you had institutions that denied people the right to participate. You had institutions that treated adults as second-class citizens; to be seen and not heard. That was *not* a

decent society. So, in order for there to be a "decent" society, those institutions—whether it be the schools, the workplace, the universities—have got to make it possible for people to feel that they are first-class citizens. They have a right to be heard, a right to participate, a right to deliberate. Now, in order for it to be a "just" society, it means that they have to have access to the resources of that society which are necessary in order for them to maintain a decent standard of living—health care, education, full employment—which enables them to participate, again, in, what we call the shared prosperity, or what the Hebrew community would call the *shalom* of the community.

San Antonio was not a decent society—and it certainly was not a just society—because you had whole communities that were left out of access to public facilities, that did not have flood control in their communities. When it rained, people couldn't go out. Their homes were flooded and therefore, it was, ipso facto, an unjust society. It was not a decent society because when they tried to participate, there was a resistance to their participation. And it took the organizing of

Communities Organized for Public Service, the COPS, in order to open up the institutions, the political institutions, to enable them to participate. The same thing is true in the Rio Grande Valley, where you have people who live in whole *colonias* and hovels, who don't have water, who don't have access to sewers. Clearly, you know, that community is not just. If, when you pay people less than a decent standard of living, when you pay people poverty wages and then you subsidize and give corporate welfare to developers who sustain poverty wages, then it's clear you have an unjust system. And in order to change that unjust system, you're going to, oftentimes, have to create or enable institutions to develop capacity, and that means, in the process of making it just, you make it decent as well.

1. The Texas Homestead Exemption includes protection of productive assets, including "farming or ranching vehicles and implements," "tools, equipment," "two firearms," "two horses, mules, or donkeys and a saddle, blanket, and bridle for each," "12 head of cattle," "120 fowl," and two hundred acres of rural land and its structures or ten acres of urban land and the home on that land. Texas Constitution, art. 16.

2. *Housing Act of 1949*, 42 U.S.C. sec. 1471 et seq.

3. Avishai Margalit, *The Decent Society*, trans. Naomi Goldblum, (Cambridge, MA: Harvard University Press, 1996).

Nature—Spirits, Commodities, and Gifts

GENEVIEVE VAUGHAN is an Austin-based philosopher, activist and philanthropist who has been involved in many efforts for peace, feminism, and environmental protection. Through her book, *For-Giving: A Feminist Criticism of Exchange,*[1] she explains her views on oppression and exploitation as an essential part of the profit-oriented market economy and in relations among producers and consumers, and offers the idea of a needs-based gift economy, such as that in the love between a parent and child, as a more sustainable alternative.

Interviewed on April 10, 2002, in Austin, Texas

Reel 2177; Time Code 00:01:52

". . . Every blade of grass can be a whole world . . ."

I was born in Corpus Christi, Texas in 1939, and lived right on the bay. My father was a hunter and liked to take us hunting and fishing with him, which I hated. My first political action was to *not* go hunting or fishing with my father because I felt really bad about the animals being killed. But he had a lot of knowledge of nature and he transmitted that to us. On the other hand, my mother's side of the family was Irish and there was a kind of "fairy story" atmosphere about things. They talked to us about fairies and Daddy told us stories about fairies so I believed in fairies a lot as a child. Of course, fairies are nature's spirits, and living there near the bay in Corpus Christi, I had a real sense of nature right there. I found out later, as I was growing up, that that area had been a Native American graveyard, so the spirits of the ancestors really were there.

Now, here's something I hadn't thought about before. When I was a kid, they showed us a movie in elementary school called *Nature's Half Acre,* and it showed all of the tiny little things that were part of nature in that half acre, how every blade of grass and every little insect were doing, growing, and interacting all at the same time. That influenced me so much. Thinking back, what I learned from that was: every blade of grass can be a whole world, and you can sit in front of the grass and look at it up close and it will fill your whole perspective. As a result, you can find nature anywhere you are, because you can find that blade of grass or that weed that grew in the cement, or look at the sky and see the clouds. Right now you can hear those doves calling outside. And I actually do have a place in the country where I go, which is really beautiful. There's a little sunken grotto and I'm sure some nature spirits live there. I'm sure they live in other places there where there are lots of wonderful Texas wildflowers and other beautiful deer and animals. The nature spirits live in the blades of grass and in the weeds and in the sky and in the wood that was used to make this house and even in the carpet that women wove. Nature and culture go together and we're all connected and there's not a distinction between humans and nature.

"We need to lead according to these gift-giving values . . ."

Now, as I grew up and grew older, I started wondering why we had money and other people didn't. And I worried about that a lot, and nobody could answer that question for a long time. I went away to school in Dallas and then Pennsylvania and there was still no answer to that question until I met this Italian philosopher, who I eventually married and then later divorced. He explained to me that poor people were poor because rich people were rich, that there was a transfer of wealth going on from one group of people to the other. It was not a happy explanation, but I began to wonder what could I do because I was obviously on the wrong side of this equation. My husband and I got married and moved to Italy, where I lived from 1963 to 1983. Early on when I was in Italy, I went with him to a meeting of some professors who were talking about applying Marxist theory of commodities and money to language. And I was so blown away by this idea, the way they explained it, that it really changed my perspective and I started working on it, and so did he. Finally, he made a theory in which language was like "exchange," like mar-

ket exchange. And I made a theory in which language was like "gift-giving," not like exchange. In exchange, something goes "over there" in order to "come back here," so the gift, or the relation, is cancelled because it has to come back for my good—it's not "other oriented" anymore. So there's not a transfer of humanity, let's say, from one person to the other. My idea is that what we need to do is create a society that's based on gift-giving instead of on exchange. And I believe also that we have washed gift-giving out of our understanding of society. And that's why, for example, I think it's very important to see language as a "gift," which is what I have worked on for all of these years. I see words as "verbal gifts" that take the place of the material gifts, verbal communication that takes the place of material communication.

Reel 2177; Time Code 00:29:02

I have practiced this theory since 1981, when I first started the funding.[2] I have tried to find women, because I believe these values are closer to the surface in women than they are in a lot of men. We need to lead according to these gift-giving values and we need to do it at a conscious level, in which you stand back and say, this is about moving society from "here" to *here,* and not just about taking care of this one person or doing this act of charity or even fixing this one particular social problem—be it housing the homeless in Austin, or even stopping nuclear proliferation. And so all of the social change work that I've funded I did as a gift to society, and funded people who could pass that gift to others.

Reel 2178; Time Code 00:23:41

"We sang them their own song."

One of the first places that I did go when I came back to the U.S. was Pantex. Pantex is a place near Amarillo where they were assembling all the nuclear weapons,

Mourning Dove (Courtesy Texas Parks and Wildlife Department)

and now they have been disassembling them. A very heroic woman named Mavis Belisle runs the Peace Farm out there, of which she has been one of the mainstays now for quite a long time. She, and the other people before her, have just lived there like a tick on the dog's ear and not let go. For years and years she's been able to have quite an effect on the community in Amarillo itself. There have been many demonstrations out there. Some of them I went to. And I think it's a very inspiring sort of thing that she's done. I remember one right now that we went to, I can't remember the year it was, but I had made a "peace tent," like the peace tent that we had

used at events in Nairobi. It was blue and white striped. And so everybody that did demonstrations liked to have our tent with them. People would line up along the side of the road outside of the Pantex weapons complex, and there wasn't a lot of space there. It was more like a drainage ditch and the peace tent just barely fit in there.

And there were, for some reason, a bunch of fundamentalists out there who were really mad at us. So, while we were demonstrating against the nuclear assembly plant, the fundamentalists were there in favor of them. And they were yelling and screaming at us all along side the road. I was supposed to give a speech or something, I can't remember quite what, and instead I started singing *Amazing Grace.* That quieted everything down and we won the day through *Amazing Grace,* through moral superiority! We sang them *their* own song. It's a beautiful song, anyway. I suppose that the opponents think that you're like bleeding-heart liberals and you're not part of reality, you don't understand the way things really are, and you're Commies and that kind of thing. I've recently encountered a little bit of this doing "Women In Black" demonstrations in front of the state capitol. Every once in a while somebody will come up and say, "You're for Saddam and you're for Bin Laden," and, "What are you gonna do and how are you gonna do it?" There're some real macho fellows that like to come up there and berate people. It's interesting, isn't it? It's mainly the macho fellows that have an issue with us, but they do. You can try to talk gently to them, you can ignore them, you can sing a song, or you can argue with them, but that doesn't usually work too well.

Sometimes, when dealing with people and issues, people really need to see things like statistics and so forth. And so back in the early 1990s, I hired Susan Lee Solar and Betty Brink from Dallas, to try to do some health surveys, which they did. Later I got Rosalie Bertell, who is a doctor and a nun from Canada, to come and teach the women here how to do health surveys around Kelly Air Force Base, where there's a lot of toxic waste. And I asked Rosalie also to go to the Philippines to a project there called the People's Task Force For Base Cleanup, that I have supported over the years, which has tried to bring up the issue of the U.S. responsibility for the toxic waste it left at Clark and Subic bases, which have caused numerous health problems for so many people living there. I think that Rosalie Bertell's health survey did really help a lot in bringing that issue up. I went seven years ago the first time and then again two years ago. I saw so many deformed children with their mothers having to take care of them all the time. It's totally tragic when your government does that and there's so many tragic things that the U.S. does.

1. Genevieve Vaughan, *For-Giving: A Feminist Criticism of Exchange* (Austin, TX: Plain View Press, 1997).

2. Ms. Vaughan funded and helped direct the Foundation for a Compassionate Society, which underwrote a variety of efforts including opposition to the nuclear industry and support for peace, art, communication and spirituality. The Gift Economy, "Foundation for a Compassionate Society," http://www.gift-economy.com/foundationsummary_found.html (accessed January 28, 2009).

Caprock, Cicadas, and the Promised Land

BISHOP LEROY MATTHIESEN, EMERITUS was ordained to the priesthood in 1946. Following ordination, Matthiesen became an editor and columnist for the *West Texas Register* in 1948, and from the 1940s through 1980, served as pastor to the St. Mary's, St. Laurence, and St. Francis congregations in Amarillo as well as rector to St. Lucien's Minor Seminary and principal of Alamo Catholic High School. In 1980, he was named Bishop of the Diocese of Amarillo, a twenty-six county area of the Texas Panhandle, where he continued until his retirement in 1997.

Bishop Matthiesen has been outspoken in his ministry for peace and in his public opposition to nuclear arms for their threat to humans and all life. At the same time, his roots on a humble family farm have also given him an appreciation for the land, and for stewardship of the bounty it produces.

Interviewed on October 3, 2002, in Amarillo, Texas

Reel 2210; Time Code 00:03:12

". . . I often wondered what was beyond that farm."

I'm sure that my boyhood days on a farm in central West Texas, thirty miles northeast of San Angelo, had much to do with the way I think about these issues.

There were eight children, so there were a total of ten within the family. We lived on a one hundred twenty acre cotton farm and we produced almost everything on the farm that we needed, particularly for food. Mom had a wonderful garden, and we would share that in early spring, all summer long, and into late autumn. And then she would can those vegetables for winter use. We had our own chickens, and they produced eggs. We had our own cows, we milked them and made butter and clabber and all those wonderful kinds of things out of that. We had our own hogs and our own cattle, we had horses too. I grew up in that kind of situation where I saw the bounty of God's creation, and we were able to live a very wonderful life.

Looking back on it in hindsight, I often wondered what was beyond that farm. I used to read a lot, and in time, I decided that even though I loved the farm, I was going to leave that farm; leave it to someone else. In fact, it is finally now in the hands of one of my brothers. And he continues to live on that family farm. I was born in 1921, so I'm now eighty-one years of age at this particular taping, and I remember during those days, we lived between the Concha and the Colorado rivers. It was seven miles from the Concha, nine miles from the Colorado, and they came together south of us and formed the Colorado River that flows through Austin and on down to the Gulf of Mexico. And we would go swimming and we would go fishing in the Concha River, "concha" meaning a shell. And it was a clear stream. We did not swim or fish in the Colorado because it was a red river, that's how it gets its name, Colorado. That river flowed up through Colorado City and saw its beginnings off the Caprock, where I live at the present time. We were just part of nature and we knew that we lived by the seasons of the years. We saw the planting, we saw the growth, we saw the harvesting, and we saw the renewal of life. And my dad always cautioned us to love nature. He taught us even to love snakes. I remember he told us about bull snakes, that they're very gentle creatures, that they protect the environment. But rattlesnakes—be careful of them, and the copperheads in the water! So we learned to be cautious, but we also learned to appreciate all of that. I remember many an evening, being out on the porch and looking at the stars, watching the falling stars, hearing the bull bats [nighthawks], as we called them in those days, swooping down as they were hunting for insects in the evening, and hearing the cry of the cicadas, we called them "hitch criers." I grew up in this German ethnic folk island, and Mom and Dad talked German.

Then I went to the seminary and studied Greek, Hebrew, and Latin, of course. I began to realize that there was a much bigger world out there than I was experiencing. And I think I was driven to try to extend what I had experienced to that other world. My primary focus, of course, was in pastoral ministry, ministering to our Catholic people, in parishes later on. But I remember during World War II, we were classified as divinity students, classified as 4D, right next to 4F. And the government, thank God, allowed us to continue in the ministry while others went off to fight the war. And we went to school in the summertime, and I was ordained in 1946 and came back to Amarillo and experienced a new kind of life here on the High Plains of Texas. We're up on the Caprock; we're almost four thousand feet above sea level. The skies are so beautiful here, one writer has described this area as "three-quarters sky." And I experienced a new beauty, a new kind of fascination, here, on the Caprock of Texas. And I just love this area as I love the place where I grew up.

Cicada or "Hitch Crier" (Courtesy OakleyOriginals, Creative Commons)

Reel 2210; Time Code 00:19:57

"You won't grow any money."

In the early 1980's, I resumed an interest in environmental projects and that came about through two of our priests, Father Darryl Birkenfeld, and another priest, Father Jerry Stein, who approached me and suggested a new vision for this area of the Texas Panhandle. Now, Amarillo seems to be doing quite well economically and otherwise, including most of the arts and culture. There's a big medical center here. At the same time, the little towns in the Texas Panhandle are drying up; I think that process has maybe almost stopped. But the little towns have lost a lot. So Birkenfeld and Stein approached me with a project of reviving those small communities through sustainable agriculture. This area up here has gone now into big agribusiness, with huge, huge expenses for the equipment and all of that. So, I endorsed that concept. Now, there is already a National Catholic Rural Life conference that's based in Iowa, I believe, that has been on this issue for a long, long time. So we developed a Diocese in Catholic Rural Life conference here, and we would bring the farmers, the big producers, and the workers together. We had a lot of migrant workers up here at the time; they were constantly calling strikes, to which we said, "That's not the answer." You know, we've got to come together. So, we did.

We took on some patron saints, Saint Isidore and Saint Maria. They were born in Spain and they were farmers and they're kind of our patron saints now. And so we would go around the diocese in the spring of the year and have "rural life days," and bring farmers and producers together again, to make farmers proud again of what they're doing. But we didn't want to encourage them to overreach themselves. You know, this is a semi-arid region and I get a little bit amused when we're always asked to pray for rain. And I say, you're asking God to change his order of creation. He made this a semi-arid region, so we need to live in that kind of atmosphere. Don't try to squeeze out of the land more than what God has put there for us to live on. After that, Darryl Birkenfeld and Jerry Stein developed the Promised Land Network and began to have annual urban-rural conferences in January, which were quite successful. Darryl had a master's degree from the American College in Louvain, Belgium, on this issue of environmental preservation and then later achieved a doctorate in moral theology, but with an emphasis on sustainable agriculture, organic farming, and family farms. That involves getting away from the use of pesticides and herbicides and all these kinds of chemicals that do bring about a higher level of production but at the same time we seem to be poisoning ourselves. So there's progress being made and I'm very hopeful about this for the future. And this is what the Promised Land Network is about. It is about educating people into what's really important in our lives, and that is that we just simply sustain our land, we sustain our families, but we don't make the almighty dollar our God.

That's a real problem in our society today. When you grow something in a field, you're thrilled when the seed comes up and you see the plant growing, whether that's cotton or corn or tomatoes or whatever it might be. And it produces more and we have some wealth. And we should have the wealth in the form of edible food, which we then share with others, particularly with the poor of the world. Now, the emphasis and the focus seems to be on growing money, you know, as if that's something that you can eat and you can wear. You can't. It can *buy* those things, but then you see around us, societal difference, like in Mexico, where you have the wealthy and you have the poor. There's a middle group developing in Mexico at the present time. But in many countries of the world you see very wealthy people there, and you see the poverty.

It reminds me of the story that Jesus tells about this farmer who filled his barn up with crops; then he had more produce, so he built another barn, and then he built another barn. And in the story that Jesus told, God says, "You fool. Tonight you're going to die. What are you going to do with all those barns?" And it seems to me this is the problem with our economy at the present time, it's what makes money seem important, and so we "grow money" and we pocket that money, we put it into our barns, into our banks, or into the stock market and then we get nervous about the stock market going up and down and all this kind of thing. We need to get back to a common sense way of life, and the environment is absolutely crucial to it. You won't grow any money, you won't grow anything else if we destroy the land and the air and the water. Those are elements that are absolutely essential, and we can't live without them.

Slide Rules & Specimens

"In drying plants, botanists often dry themselves. Dry words and dry facts will not fire hearts."[1]

JOHN MUIR

WHEN THE SUBJECT is our natural world, the challenge of motivating students and citizens grows tougher amidst a myriad of electronic distractions and "virtual" realities. How best then to engage students in a manner that places the fragile elegance of a butterfly's wing or the tenacious wriggling of an earthworm into the grander context of our biological heritage? It takes extraordinary teachers, whose insight, ethics, and dedication draw in their students. It needs teachers who understand that classroom learning is not enough to kindle the spark of inquiry, and that dirty fingers and soggy socks are as much a part of the learning experience as trig tables and chalk. Further, it requires teachers who realize that frogs and birds are worth examining not only for their biological characteristics, but also as the indicator species who hold the clues to the fate of our entire living world.

1. Enos Abijah Mills and Laurence Frederick Schmockebier, *Your National Parks*, (New York: Houghton Mifflin, 1917), 363.

Red Ants, Tamaulipas, and the Rio Grande

CAROL CULLAR moved to Eagle Pass in 1979. Ms. Cullar has been involved there in a number of ways in educating and conserving the Rio Grande Corridor and Trans-Pecos area. She has written and edited poetry and prose with a natural bent, and has served on the Historical Commission of the City of Eagle Pass. Her most rewarding and challenging work, however, has been in teaching children about the natural world through her work at the Lehman Research Foundation, Rio Bravo Nature Center and Rio Grande/Rio Bravo Basin Coalition.

Interviewed on February 22, 2006, in Eagle Pass, Texas

Reel 2359; Time Code 00:02:26

"We chased the roosters and they chased us."

I grew up on a small farm in western Oklahoma that's right on the Texas border. We spent every moment barefooted and outdoors and drowning out crickets and playing in the dirt and harvesting apricot trees and helping in the garden. My dad had honeybees, we helped take care of the baby pigs, and we chased the roosters and they chased us. So if the weather were clement then, I was outside and generally barefooted for the first six years of my life. And then my parents began to move from small school to larger school to larger school in their teaching careers. And then in the summer my dad got his master's degree, and he did that in western Colorado in Gunnison. And rather than taking afternoon classes, he took trout fishing. And so we had a big food box all packed up with our cornmeal and our flour and whatever else we were going to take with us that day. He took architectural drafting and industrial arts teaching classes in the morning, and then every afternoon we would hit a different trout stream somewhere on the Gunnison River or up Grasshopper Creek. And my mother would take a paperback book and her folding chair and she would sit and read a book. My dad would get down into the stream and be fly casting and they forgot they had us. So my sister and I just ran loose up and down the canyons there in Colorado. We were tasting things that we had no idea whether they were

Cattail Springs, Chihuahuan Desert (Photograph by Jim Kennedy)

edible or not, and discovering gooseberries and currants and animals and plants and it was really a wonderfully idyllic way to grow up.

And I think what has gotten me into all of this conservation movement is the fact that children today simply don't have that opportunity. They play in organized sports, and if they're outside, they're on a sports field where there is a single monoculture grass that has been mowed to oblivion. All the weeds have been sprayed with poison and removed, the trees have all been trimmed and we put cotton wool around all our children nowadays. And I lived in a tree! When I grew up, there wasn't a day that I didn't climb a tree and jump

from branch to branch and swing off of the treetops and drop down on the chicken house roof. Kids today are all protected and they're sheltered and they don't get out[1] and they don't play in the mud and they don't play in the dirt and they don't play with the wild creatures like the horny toads. I used to put a chair down over the ant bed when I was a child and I lay there for hours—literally hours—watching the harvesters, the red ants, watching them making trails, removing rocks and bringing in food. It was so much fun and it truly made me a part of the earth, it connected me to what I felt like was some of the most important, joyful, parts of my life. I really think it's incredibly important that if we hope to protect the earth today, if we are going to do anything about conserving aspects of natural places for our progeny, then we have to do it through interesting the children because they're the conservators of the future. And if we don't get them out there and having fun playing with bugs and enjoying being out in nature and canoeing or wading or all these things, then we're not going to have anyone who has a vested interest in protecting the natural places on the earth.

Reel 2359; Time Code 00:15:42

"Kids really are not familiar with what we have here and because of that, they simply don't value it."

What I do now is to carry a science program around to the various elementary or middle schools, even the high school here in town. And what I invariably run into when you begin to talk about wildlife, you hear without fail some student saying something about tigers or kangaroos: animals that simply are never going to exist in this part of the country, but it's what they've seen on TV. And they love animals. Children always want to relate to animals. They're excited by that, but they are starved for and simply not exposed to what we have right here. They have no interest in it simply because they don't know what we have. And if they have seen a skunk, it's because it was run over on the road, the same if they've seen an armadillo killed on the road—do you know that joke? "Oh, look at the armadillos, they're all taking naps by the side of the road."[1]

So the kids don't have any kind of grounding in the wildlife of our region, and we're actually a part of the Tamaulipan Biotic Province. It is the most diverse as far as the number of species of plants, the variety in species of animals and insects on earth. The Tamaulipan Biotic Province is just about the size of the state of Illinois, and extends from right about here in Eagle Pass all the way to the Gulf of Mexico, and down into Mexico and all the way into the mountains around Monterrey, Mexico.

Picture an area the size of Illinois that runs from the coastal marshes, which would involve our shrimp and all the variety of the rich Intracoastal Waterway animals and species, and then all the way up into this part of the country, right along the edges of the Chihuahuan Desert, and then over into the mountains. You would have wildlife that's marine, you have fresh water aquatics and then you have the elevation changes that makes for incredibly diverse plant life as well. And they're not exposed to that. The kids really are not familiar with what we have here and because of that, they simply don't value it.

And this lack of awareness spreads over into adulthood, so that when you do come in with all the growth and the development of people moving in to the Rio Grande and the basin here, you get developers who come in with the bulldozer and they blade off every square inch down below the level of the top soil. And yet they will call it Vista Heights after they've wiped out the vista, or they'll call it Cenizo Acres—which is the purple sage—and then they come in and bulldoze out all the cenizo. If we want to change that, if we hope to have any spirit of cherishing of what is natural, we have to do it through an educational approach. You're not going to get it through the politicians; you're not going to necessarily get it through the adults because their habits are all set when they're four to seven years of age. So my focus and my hope and intent then is to develop an appreciation and awareness in youth here in the community for what we have here. I don't want them to yearn for beautiful green lawns and lush bushes and brilliant, brilliant, brilliant flowers that have to be watered at least once a day when they are living here in Eagle Pass. It's nonproductive.

This brings us then to the Rio Grande, and the fact that this basin, this part of Texas, is one of the fastest growing areas in the entire United States. The Rio Grande is not growing. It has exactly the same number of drops of water in it that it had a hundred years ago or fifty years ago or is going to have a hundred years from now. So the reality that we're faced with is that there is even already talk of turning it into a concrete lined water ditch. And it serves now as one of the longest sewer systems on earth. Piedras Negras as a city, dumps eleven million gallons of semi-raw, semi-processed human sewage into the Rio Grande every day. Eleven million gallons. Now, it is semi-processed at this point but, you do not want to swim in it or fish south of town, okay? The irony of that is that from just south of Del Rio to the middle of Eagle Pass, about where the international bridge is, we have some of the most beautiful and least contaminated section of the river for the whole eighteen hundred miles that it runs. And so, on the north side of town we can wade and fish and swim and even eat the fresh water clams if we wanted to. But south of town it's not recommended simply because of the pollution. We have to focus on what's going to happen to the Rio Grande, what is going to happen to the people who live here, how will people living here forty years from now supply their drinking water? I hope that the people who live here, who understand the problems, will be the ones that are solving the problems. We don't want the problems solved by someone in Washington, or even someone in Austin. It's too far away. We've got to have people who cherish and understand and respect that this ecosystem is really a very brittle, very fragile one. It all rises and falls on what care we take of the environment and the Rio Grande.

1. The range of independent mobility for North American twelve-year-olds is estimated to have shrunk from one mile thirty years ago, to 550 yards today. Elizabeth Goodenough, "Secret Spaces of Childhood and the Pedagogy of Place," *Green Money Journal*, (Winter 08/09): 22.

The Sabine River, the Rio Grande, and Water Conservation

JIM EARHART is a retired professor of biology who taught at the Laredo Community College. He has also worked as a co-founder and executive director of the Rio Grande International Study Center, and as a board member of Laredo's Citizens' Environmental Advisory Committee. In each of these posts, Dr. Earhart has worked to protect the Rio Grande and the contributing creeks, wetlands and watersheds from the booming growth and development in the Laredo area.

Interviewed February 23, 2006, in Laredo, Texas

Reel 2366; Time Code 00:02:15

". . . I'm thinking about bug juice right now."

Back then, we didn't think about nature in the term of being "environmentalists" or "activists." I just went hunting and fishing with my dad in those rolling sandy hills and in the piney and hardwood complex of East Texas, and we enjoyed it tremendously. I learned to love nature that way without even thinking of being an environmentalist. We used to go out and squirrel hunt. We liked to eat, and when we killed something, we ate it. We ate the squirrels. And I remember my dad and I would come up to some friends' house in the woods, and they'd invite us in, and we'd sit around the fireplace (this would be wintertime or fall of the year, when it was cool) and they would have some baked potatoes and parched peanuts, and we'd sit there and eat and talk. And then we'd get back out in the woods and look for the squirrels again. And of course, we went duck hunting, fishing, those kind of things. It was tremendously enjoyable. You couldn't say my dad was an "environmentalist" in the modern sense of the word, but he greatly appreciated the out-of-doors. He enjoyed it and I think if we had a whole world with his attitude right now, we'd have a lot better environment. He had a deep sense of love for it. When there's a reverence, even when you go kill an animal, a deer that you're going to be using for your livelihood, you kill it in reverence and with thanks. And I think my dad had that kind of attitude.

Sabine River (Creative Commons)

There was no trophy hunting. I never thought about it at the time, but if my dad had thought about it, he would probably have figured it was kind of expensive to get the heads mounted, but we just never considered trophy hunting. It was hunting for animals, fish, and so on that could be used for food, plus the fact it was enjoyable just to go and be outdoors. We used to have big family picnics, for example, down on the Sandy Creek, which was one of the creeks that passes nearby Hawkins and is a tributary of the Sabine River. And so we'd gather together sometimes on holidays and Sundays and somebody would've been down there the night before with trotlines, catching fish. There was a big black wash pot with a fire cooking fish in deep fat and then having fish and hush puppies and coleslaw, and iced tea or coffee. And then we'd be sitting around in the out-of-doors and talking. Those kinds of things made a tremendous impression upon me as a kid. . . .

I think being in scouting was probably one of the things that really gave me a deep appreciation for nature and for wildlife. We used to spend time out camping, sometimes just a Friday evening meeting around the campfire, but other times, we would be out for extended trips. We went to Camp Tonkawa, which was down close to Henderson or Mount Enterprise, Texas, in that area, kind of deep East Texas. Those were great times. "Bug juice"—I'm thinking about bug juice right now. Bug juice was the Kool-Aid that was in a big container, a big barrel down by the mess hall. And of course, at lunchtime, we'd all have the detail to go down and pick up the food and bring it back to the campsite. We'd go down with containers and bring back the

Kool-Aid, and when you would reach down to get the Kool-Aid out of the barrel, you got all these yellow jackets and wasps and stuff flying around in there. That's why we called it bug juice!

Reel 2367; Time Code 00:39:49

"We need to be at the table with them."

Our local political leaders keep riding the political hobbyhorse of saying, "Hey, we've got to have a secondary water source for Laredo. We're going to have to raise our water rates in the city so we'll have this money to go get the water from the Carrizo-Wilcox Aquifer in northwest Webb County. My opinion, after fifteen years or so of studying this, is that the Rio Grande provided water for this area for two hundred fifty years and, if properly managed, can provide it for another two hundred fifty years. *If properly managed*—that's the key point—because right now, eighty-five gallons out of every hundred gallons of water that is taken from the river goes for agricultural irrigation. Agricultural irrigation along the Rio Grande is a highly wasteful process. The delivery systems to the fields or orchards for irrigation are very leaky. Some of them are uncovered and so there's chance for evaporation, there's a chance for water seeping into the subsoil. The irrigation practices themselves sometimes flood a whole orchard.

In fact, when Jim Hightower was Agricultural Commissioner of the State of Texas, we had the Texas-Israeli Exchange Forum on the Laredo Community College campus. We had a group of people at the College from Israel, and they raised various crops using drip irrigation. The drip irrigation was controlled by computers. This is back in the 1980s. With drip irrigation, the Israeli experience has shown that you can, depending upon the different kinds of crops, probably save anywhere from forty to sixty percent of the water used by irrigation, and I think that doesn't even count what's lost in the delivery systems. So I think we could save far more than half of the water that's being taken from the river. Today eighty-five percent out of every hundred gallons goes for irrigation, for agricultural irrigation. So that means that cities such as Laredo and other cities along the river are taking their water out of the other fifteen gallons. Now, if cities could work with the irrigators and somehow help provide the financial backing, basically purchase water from those irrigators so that they could put in modern, water-conserving delivery and irrigation technologies, they could save a tremendous amount of water.[1] Just think: if you use eighty-five percent, and you save ten percent of that, you saved almost as much as municipalities are using. And if you save twice that, you'll have more than what you're using for cities right now. This is what I'm trying to get the local politicians to see, because they sort of have their head in the sand. They're saying, "Oh, no, no, no. We can't deal with the people down in the lower Valley, there are too many of them." But that's the whole reason that *we should* be dealing with them, because there are so many[2] and they're using so much water. We need to be at the table with them. I went to a water summit down in the lower Valley here in the fall. I saw *one* person from the City of Laredo, who was an underling, and nobody from the top level that could be negotiating. I didn't see anybody from the county. We need to be negotiating with those folks, we need to get our representatives in the Legislature to get involved, and it's going to take the passage of one or more bills to get that kind of interaction going.

A gallon of water is worth a whole lot more in the city than it is in agriculture. You stop and think about that: a gallon of water coming into a doctor's office can bring a lot more money than a gallon of water going to irrigate a crop. If, by saving ten or twenty percent of the water that's used for agriculture, you would more than double the amount of water that's being used by municipalities right now! And you could save probably forty percent or maybe fifty percent with time. And you could have room for a tremendous amount of municipal growth by saving the agricultural water. That's the biggest area to save.

But there's another important area for saving, and we're also trying to get our local politicians to see this. This would also need involvement from the Legislature. And that would be to allow cities like Laredo to "bank" water that is saved through conservation. Right now, the City of Laredo has a two hundred gallon per capita usage per day. For each citizen, two hundred gallons of water are used per day. San Antonio is, the last I heard, one hundred forty-seven. Years ago, San Antonio was using two hundred thirteen gallons per day. Some of our local politicians have said in the past, "Oh well, we can't save water like San Antonio because if we save it, then we just lose it. We don't have a place to store it. They've got the Edwards Aquifer." I'm not sure how sound an argument that is, but just to satisfy that argument, we need to be interacting with our representatives in the Legislature. We need a bill in the Legislature that would allow municipalities along the Rio Grande who develop a water conservation program and save water to be able to bank that water for future use. And that water for us is stored in Amistad Reservoir. True, we're talking about a water bank account that is not like your checking account at a regular bank, because it is subject to climatic change, be it drought or lots of rainfall. And so your balance might fluctuate from year to year. So it would have to be done on some kind of percentage basis: you save so much, and when the times get lean, at least you'll have a certain percentage out of what's left there. Or, maybe you're growing and you expand a lot and you need a lot more water. Then you could start drawing more water against what you've banked. We need that kind of thing and then, you know, the incentives will be there for the city to conserve.

A few years ago, Laredo implemented a water savings program and very significantly reduced the amount of water that was used for watering lawns and so on in the summer. When the council looked at that, they said, "Wow, we got a million dollars less this time than we normally get. We can't have this. We can't have water conservation." They only saw conservation as lost utility revenue. That's the kind of mentality that we need to get rid of.

1. As one example, the City of Roma paid 2.8 million dollars for irrigation canal improvements and used forty-one hundred acre-feet in saved agricultural flows as new municipal supplies. Jan Gerston, Mark MacLeod, C. Allan Jones, *Efficient Water Use for Texas: Policies, Tools, and Management Strategies* (College Station: Texas Agricultural Experiment Station, Texas A&M University, 2002), 30.

2. The entire Rio Grande Valley is showing high rates of growth: the four counties there recorded a 30.9 percent growth in population from 1990 to 1997. More recent population increases are still high, with McAllen-Edinburg-Mission ranked second and third in the entire state with 24.8 percent and 20.7 percent growth, respectively, in the 2000–2007 period. U.S. Census, "B-02 Metropolitan Areas," http://www.census.gov/compendia/smadb/TableB-02.xls (accessed November 12, 2009); University of Texas Pan American, Division of Community Engagement, "Profile of the Rio Grande Valley," http://www.coserve.org/disc/lmi/section_1/section1.html (accessed November 12, 2009). Future projections are high too, with a 391 percent growth rate above 1990 expected for Laredo by 2030, 397 percent for McAllen-Edinburg-Mission, and a 202 percent rise for Brownsville during that same period. Rio Grande Valley Texas. Rio Grande Valley of Texas, "Valley Information," http://www.rgvtexas.com/ValleyInformation.htm (accessed January 27, 2009).

Science and Weapons, Nature and Education

RUTH LOFGREN was trained as a microbiologist, receiving her Ph.D., and later teaching in a medical school and helping pioneer electron microscopy. From 1956 to 1976, she taught ecology and science education at the City University of New York (CUNY). Her philosophical approach to science and her deep commitment to the ethics of scientific research are evidenced in this early anecdote from her career, which occurred while she was doing post-graduate work at the University of Michigan.

Interviewed on February 14, 2006, in San Antonio, Texas

Reel 2328; Time Code 00:36:22

"I think this is unethical and I can't be a party to it."

One of the great tragedies of this world is that the human race doesn't get its act together, and so war is one of the most wasteful and yet prevalent practices of human beings. Following World War II, the chairman of the department died and was replaced with another individual who really believed that research in bacteriological warfare was going to be the U.S.'s best protec-

tion against World War III. And so he had set up a very strong mood in the department that we should emphasize bacteriological warfare research. Well, I think that it's extremely dangerous for beginning students to be working with such virulent organisms. But more than that, it's very immoral because I can't think of anything worse than the diabolical business of trying to kill off your enemy with epidemics or microorganisms. I saw this as intolerable for me personally and I knew that weapons of mass destruction have been popular for as long as we can think back. As we know, many of the American Indians were killed off with blankets that had smallpox virus and set up smallpox epidemics with the American Indians. It's a great tragedy in this world. I told the chairman that I was not comfortable with this, and that I would resign from the department. And he said, "Oh, no, just take a sabbatical." And I said, "I'm not going to change my attitude, my beliefs. I think this is unethical and I can't be a party to it." So I resigned as soon as I'd finished advising my last two doctoral students, because it's an awful problem if you're a doctoral student and your chairman takes off. So I finished the two doctoral students that I still had pending and I resigned.

I then went to New York City to work in a research institute where I could try to broaden ideas about teaching. The one thing I really wanted to do was to see if students couldn't understand a functioning, living organism very quickly when they're beginning in physiology.

So rather than have them sit and memorize the names of enzymes and bones and muscles and so on, I wanted them to get a sense of how an organism functions. So we start off with a chicken foot, or a chicken leg with the foot attached, so that they can see how the tendons pull the foot forward and how many different kinds of tissues there are all working together. Then they see first the organ, then the organ system that it's connected with, and then all the parts right down to the toenails that make up a functioning part of a living organism. And sure enough, I think that's a very valid way to approach understanding physiology.

Very often students had questions that didn't get answered, and they just settled on not understanding. And one young woman student that I remember had a husband and a couple of sons who had convinced her that, as "the little woman," she didn't need to understand "complicated" things; she could just call them and they could change the fuse plug or do whatever is needed. And so, she had thought of herself as a sweet, lovely, gracious, intelligent lady. But was always puzzled because, in the summertime, she could drive in and out of the garage and the door opened with no problem. But in the wintertime, the door often wouldn't open and she couldn't figure out why. One night, though, she came into class just thrilled. She said that this time, when the door was stuck and it wouldn't open she got out of the car and took a look. "Well, what was it?" I asked her. She had found that during the day, the snow melted and the water ran down, and then at night it froze and so the door was stuck in the ice along the edge of the doorsill. And as soon as she cracked the ice, the door would open. You could see from the twinkle in her eye that she knew she had a brain that could handle this. She didn't have to ask her husband or her boys to go out and open the garage because she now understood what happened as a force of Mother Nature, and that it was a perfectly normal process. She said, "I always thought that things expanded when it got warm, so I thought the door would be bigger and it would bind in the summertime and then contract in the winter. She now realized

that things don't have to contract in the winter, they may contract, but the ice was the thing that had held the door from opening.

The scientific method is a very natural kind of process, and so the kinds of questions that children ask are the ones that the scientist asks, too. If you don't get to the place where you forget what it was like to be a child, and you learn how to memorize and you learn how to dish back what was dished out to you so that you get straight A's on your transcript, then the chances are that you need to go back to that childlike inquisitiveness of actually looking to see what the situation is. And from there you have a natural process of moving into the scientific exploration, of being disciplined about keeping a narrow focus on what your question is, and then being honest about the results that you're seeing. And if you find that you can't get any results, your question is too complicated. You need to break it down and find a smaller part that you can ask. And so you get more and more specialized in science. And often, if we're not careful, we can lose our focus on the place that specialty plays in the whole picture.

In 1976, Dr. Lofgren retired from CUNY and moved to San Antonio, becoming involved there in environmental education and policy. In the classroom, she taught science enrichment in a Quaker school for emotionally disturbed students. With these children, she recognized the value of touching and learning from the outdoors. She also served as the Water Chair for the San Antonio chapter of the League of Women Voters, speaking out on ways to protect the plentiful and clean flows of the Edwards Aquifer.

She also became a long-time volunteer and guide with the Mitchell Lake Wetlands Society, a non-profit group dedicated to the refuge at the six hundred acre lake and seven hundred acre buffer lands located south of San Antonio. Initially a sewage sludge pond for San Antonio from 1901 until its replacement with the Dos Rios wastewater treatment plant in 1987, the Lake is one of only two large freshwater bodies in south central Texas and so forms a critical stop on migration routes for over 270 species of waterfowl, raptors, shorebirds, and song birds. Dr. Lofgren shares her story of helping to bring public awareness to the restoration of Mitchell Lake by using her educational expertise and experience.

Reel 2329; Time Code 00:31:04

"We'll invent a project!"

The first real program was in 1990, when the Junior League sent a notice around to various organizations stating that they thought the environment was an impor-

tant issue and they should add environmental projects as one of the choices that their girls could volunteer for. Even though they were working in various activities around the city, they didn't have anything that was "environmental." When the notice came to the League of Women Voters, I said, "We'll invent a project!"

So we invented the Mitchell Lake Wetlands Project, and I presented it to the Junior League, and five or six girls signed up for the project. I had assumed that we could then just go out and plant aquatic plants and start making it into a *real* wetlands, and was rather shocked when I discovered that it *wasn't* a wetlands. The diked areas had so much sludge deposited in them that the algae loved growing there, and the algae decomposing made the water more alkaline. San Antonio water is already alkaline, and so in some of the areas the pH was

Snowy Egrets, Mitchell Lake, San Antonio, Texas (Courtesy Howard Eskin)

as high as 8 or 9, so it was not appropriate for the girls to go out and plant aquatic plants. They took one look at it and said that with the reputation Mitchell Lake has as a "stinking sewage lagoon," we needed a public education campaign to convert it from that image to one that says "wildlife refuge."

The first thing they did was to learn more about wastewater treatment: what was involved and how it was polluted. And then they developed a charming brochure that told the story of the dream of a Mitchell Lake Wildlife Refuge. The first printing disappeared almost immediately because people were delighted to find out that there was an alternative to the image that they'd had in the past. Our first educational process was working with the Junior League girls, and the second year, they put on a photo contest. The theme was "Focus on Wildlife" and "Focus on the Wetlands" and it was co-sponsored with the *San Antonio Express News*. And they rounded up enough money to offer some really good prizes in a whole series of areas so that professional photographers from far and wide came for the photographic sessions there. The fourth year of the project, the Junior League pulled back to encourage more community activity. At that point, we developed the Mitchell Lake Wetland Society as the basis for a 501(c)3 organization where we took the people who were dedicated supporters of Mitchell Lake as a wildlife refuge.

We are now in our twelfth year at this point and membership is drawn from the San Antonio Audubon Society, the Bexar Audubon Society, the League of Women Voters and the Junior League. There have been people coming to Mitchell Lake to do birding over the years from all over the world. Just recently a lady was visiting our Quaker meeting and she mentioned that she was an avid birder and she was on her way down to the coast to see the whooping cranes. Someone brought her over during coffee hour and told her she needed to know about Mitchell Lake. The following day, one of the really outstanding birders in the area met us at Mitchell Lake and we took her birding and then back to her hotel. And I told her, the important thing for you to remember when you go back to New Jersey, because there are a lot of avid birders in New Jersey, is to please tell everybody that, before they go down to see the whooping cranes, stop at Mitchell Lake. This is easy because they'll usually fly into San Antonio before they go down to the coast. We still have a wide variety of people that come through, but we need the core support in local residents so that our local politicians understand that this is very precious. It may be city property, but it really belongs to the community.

Chemists, Bureaucrats, and Citizens

MARVIN LEGATOR was a toxicologist and professor of Preventive Medicine and Community Health at the University of Texas Medical Branch in Galveston, and earlier served as chief of the genetic toxicology branch of the U.S. Food and Drug Administration. He was a critic of the weaknesses in the toxicological testing, risk assessment and epidemiological review of many commonly used and discharged chemicals. Dr. Legator was an author of *Chemical Alert!* and the *Health Detectives Handbook,* and worked in other ways to testify for, consult with and assist those affected by environmental releases of toxic chemicals.

Interviewed on October 23, 2003, in Galveston, Texas

Reel 2283; Time Code 00:02:20

What really intrigued me about the area of toxicology is that it is one of the few areas where you can combine good science with the goal of trying to help people. In other words, you're almost a public health advocate if you're a toxicologist because we are very aware of our environment and the way people are exposed to hazardous substances. The whole issue is: how can we modify or remove some of the substances that can play a major role as far as people's health is concerned? From my early days, even in high school and through college and my doctorate degree, my emphasis really was on toxicology. However, I found in those days there really wasn't such a thing as a curriculum for toxicology. In fact, most of my colleagues have come into toxicology from other areas, whether it be genetics or physiology or pharmacology. And I basically came into this area from genetics and microbiology and that's quite opposed to what we have now where we do have really good structured programs in toxicology.

I was very intrigued by a figure in Sinclair Lewis's book *Arrowsmith* by the name of Gottleib. He was a cancer researcher and I thought that was really the kind of person I would like to imitate. And then there are a series of books during my particular time of growth and in high school by Dr. Paul Lecruth, and he also was a writer, scientist, and microbiologist and he played a real influence on my life too as I read through his various books. Then right after college, when I had my Ph.D. degree, I worked for Shell Oil Company in Modesto, California. While there I had an extremely good experience with toxicology in industry, and from that point I went to the Food and Drug Administration where I felt that we were covering almost all of the areas in toxicology. We had the tools, but the one area that we had completely overlooked and had no way of even determining if there were effects, was the field of genetic toxicology. That is the area where chemicals interact with our genetic material and cause various aberrations. So I went from Shell Oil in industry to the Food and Drug

Administration where I headed the branch of genetic toxicology.

I came to Galveston because of an extremely knowledgeable clinician who worked for Dow Chemical, which is just down the road here at Freeport. His name was Dr. Jack Killian, and together we had this great ideal concept. What if we could look at all the workers, examine their pre-employment physical, and see what their chromosomal analysis looked like? That's when we look at all their genetic materials in this packed area of a chromosome. And we felt that if we did that and then moved sequentially with the workers over time, we could see how indeed, or *if* indeed his cytogenetics would change at all, as far as aberrations occurring. We felt that this would be an extremely good method of making sure the workers were not exposed to hazardous chemicals.

"If you look at industrial chemicals it's exactly the reverse. Seventy-two percent had never been tested."

I moved to Texas because I wanted to be a part of the enterprise that was going on at Dow Chemical in Freeport and I thought this was the wave of the future—and I still do, by the way. And it's interesting because we did that for many years. And what occurred was fascinating. After using some of the most sophisticated instruments and working with a really good group in toxicology who were looking for mutations, we found what we were looking for. We found that benzene caused chromosome breaks. Now, the interesting thing about this is that we were probably one of the most well-advertised groups in Dow Chemical as far as TV and radio exposure, the latest state of the art application of genetic toxicology in the workplace. But when we found that benzene caused chromosomal aberrations in workers, then we found the going was a little tough. In fact, I think I can say, in terms of the timing, that shortly after our findings were presented, there no longer existed a toxicology group at Dow Chemical. It was simply phased out. My interest, of course, had

simply been in looking at populations using various procedures that would be the way of determining if we had hazardous substances in the workplace that had yet to be identified.

This is kind of a sad story, but a few years back there was a National Academy of Sciences meeting on what classes of chemical agents have been tested sufficiently to determine whether they were either a threat or were safe, whatever "safe" means. This was called the Upton Committee. It was the former director of the National Cancer Institute, Charlie Upton, who headed this committee, and what they found was rather interesting if not frightening. When you look at drugs, about twenty-five percent of the drugs available had not been fully tested for hazardous effects. If you look at industrial chemicals it's exactly the reverse. Seventy-two percent had never been tested.[1] That means that we have been exposed to many, many chemicals that have never been evaluated for toxicity in any great detail.

This has an extremely important meaning to us today. As I go around the country and interact with certain individuals who are exposed to toxic chemicals, I notice that the one thing that they all tell me is that they had a federal or state official addressing them at a meeting and telling them that there is "no evidence that this chemical is dangerous." They're exactly right! The only part of it is they never say what the flip side of the statement is: there is no evidence that this chemical is *safe* either. In fact, it has never been tested. There's a tremendous difference between a negative result in a well-conducted experiment and something that's never been tested at all. The problem we now have is that a chemical that has not been tested is considered safe just as if it had been tested. And this is probably one of the major, major mistakes I think that is made continually by lay individuals: they are hearing correctly from the state and federal officials, but they're not understanding that when he or she says that there is "no evidence" that it is harmful, it doesn't mean the chemical was ever tested to see if it was harmful. This is the biggest myth I think we have to explode. It's easy for somebody from EPA to

Dal-Tile waste site, Wilmer, Texas (Courtesy Sharon Stewart)

say that there's "no evidence that this compound will cause you a danger." And they usually will not be asked, "But has it been tested?" So if I do anything else, what I'd like to accomplish is to ask people to never take this concept that, "There is no danger from this chemical," and to ask, where it has been tested, how it has been tested, and to see the data.

Reel 2284; Time Code 00:01:23

". . . These people know they're having a problem."

I'd like to see our regulatory agencies become more closely aligned with the populations that they are supposedly monitoring. There is often a disconnect between the community and the regulators. And many times if you go into a community and you ask who the villain is, believe it or not, it's *not* the toxic waste generator. It's the officials from the state and federal agencies who they think are there to protect them, and very quickly learn that they don't. That's where the greatest animosity comes in almost every community I've been to. And again, the reason is because of this deception about there being "no problem" when these people *know* they're having a problem. So I'd like to see the government agencies do a better job of interacting with communities than we're doing really right now. I mean, if you were a government official sitting in North Carolina and just putting pins on a map to mark toxic sites, you're not going to be nearly as excited about the pins on a map as if you were down there actually talking to these people and listening to them. So there's a tremendous disconnect between regulators and citizens.

The second thing I think, and I hate to say it, but I think it plays a very key role, is that if you look at a government employee, of which I was one, and you look at these poor people down here without many resources, you know that if you say anything that'll antagonize the large toxic waste generator, there may be hell to pay from your superiors. We see this happening with whistle-blowers all the time. And, you know, we often talk about the "revolving door," and this is operating beautifully now. Usually, if you're in government and do the "right" thing you will get a job in one of the industries that you had regulated. We see this going on all the time. So there are many reasons, not appropriate ones, but many reasons why the individuals who are exposed to toxins do not get the attention and do not get the programs that they really need.

I would obviously like to see something we call the "precautionary principle" come into use.[2] The precau-

tionary principle says that if indeed you don't have the safety data, then you don't get to market that product. In other words, we get the data before people are exposed. I'm afraid that'll be a long time in coming. The good news is we have some extremely good tools that have developed because of molecular biology that allow us to have more information than we ever would dream possible five or ten years ago.

1. *Full* testing may need yet more review: "complete health-hazard assessments appear to require further testing of 82 percent of the drugs and excipients in drug formulations, 90 percent of the pesticides and inert ingredients of pesticide formulations, 95 percent of the food additives, 98 percent of the cosmetic ingredients and essentially all the substances in the three production categories of chemicals in commerce." National Research Council, *Toxicity Testing: Strategies to Determine Needs and Priorities* (Washington, D.C.: National Academies Press, 1984), 126. Further, the vast majority of this limited chemical testing is done by industry: the EPA has assessed the risks of only about 2 percent of the chemicals in use. General Accounting Office, *Toxic Substances Control Act: EPA's Limited Progress in Regulating Toxic Chemicals* (GAO/T-RCED-94–212, May 17, 1994), 11. http://archive.gao.gov/t2pbat3/151661.pdf (accessed November 12, 2009).

2. The precautionary principle is not a new or abstract idea. It appears throughout U.S. common law, statutes, and treaties. For example, the age-old judicial principle of "duty of care," requiring attention, caution and prudence, has much in common with the precautionary principle. One major environmental statute, the Clean Air Act, requires that hazardous air pollutant emission standards be calculated "with an ample margin of safety." 42 USC sec. 4112(d)(4). The international treaty, the Montreal Protocol of 1987, applied the precautionary principle to the control of chlorofluorocarbons for protection of the ozone layer by imposing regulations on CFC production before irrefutable evidence of the causal link between the ozone hole and CFC emissions. Paul Harremoes and others, eds., *The Precautionary Principle in the 20th Century: Late Lessons from Early Warnings* (London: Earthscan Publications, 2002), 1, 85–86. Unfortunately, many environmental laws with precautionary intentions became hostage to the costs of monitoring and analysis, the delays of administrative and judicial review, and the philosophical debates about acceptable risk.

DDT and Birds, Yellowcake and Workers

PAT SUTER is a retired professor of chemistry who taught at Del Mar College in Corpus Christi. Ms. Suter has been involved in many regional conservation organizations, and has worked to integrate these concerns into her teaching. The following anecdotes illustrate how she was able to make the power of chemistry—and its real-world implications—more meaningful to her students.

Interviewed on March 2, 1997, in Corpus Christi, Texas

Reel 1006; Time Code 00:08:00

". . . The birds have come back"

The Audubon Outdoor Club, which is our bird-watching club, was organized in 1962, and we began, through that club, strenuous conservation efforts on the brown pelican. The demise of the brown pelican along the entire Gulf of Mexico coast was due to pesticides.[1] And it's DDT that caused the thinning of the eggs. You see, the pelicans eat primarily menhaden, and menhaden eat primarily little phytoplankton and, it's a long, involved tale with pesticides, but we became concerned about the peregrine falcon and concerned about hawks in general. At that time we also were worried about the eagle, American eagle. And on the King Ranch, which is just

south of here, they were using herbicides and pesticides like mad. We became very concerned about all of that. And so, working strenuously with groups around the country, ultimately in 1972, DDT was outlawed in this country, and since that time the birds have come back. The peregrine is coming back. You can now see brown pelicans on a regular basis as you drive along the shorelines in Corpus Christi or over at Port Aransas. And so they have made a comeback.[2] DDT mimics the female hormone in birds and causes thinning of egg shells, and this seems to be the problem. And it affected many other birds and animals as well, but those were the ones that were mostly in the news.

Reel 1006; Time Code 01:21:00

". . . that Geiger counter went berserk."

At Del Mar College, I had taught radiation among other things. We have a number of uranium mines, in situ uranium mines,[3] around Karnes City and here and there. They're shipped out of Corpus Christi, yellowcake, or used to be, it's not shipped here anymore. But I had the son of a very prominent, very wealthy family here in my class. And Richard was trying to prove himself to his family. You know, he'd been brought up with not only a silver, but a gold spoon in his mouth. He was trying to prove that he can do it on his own, and so he got a job in the labor pool. And he walked into my class and it was fortuitous that I just happened to be teaching radiation that afternoon, and I had a Geiger counter on my desk-

Brown Pelican (Courtesy Texas Parks and Wildlife Department)

top. And he walked in to take his customary seat over there and as he walked in, that Geiger counter went berserk. And I said, "Richard, where have you been?" And he said, "Oh, I was working down at the harbor." And I said, "What were you doing?" and I knew he was in the labor pool, and he said they'd been sent in to clean out a tanker. And I said, "What'd the stuff look like?" and he replied, "Oh, it was some yellow powder, it was terrible stuff."

And I said, "Did they give you any protective devices?" and he said, "No, what should they have given us? It was just a yellow powder." And I said, "Richard, that was yellowcake! Do you know what yellowcake is?" And he said, "No," and I had him empty his pockets. He had a little powder, not much, but he had powder in all his pockets, and I sent him home. And I said, "You go home and you get rid of every stitch of clothing you got on. Don't put them in the wash or anything, get rid of them, because you'll never get this stuff out of your clothes." And I told him, "You take not one shower, but you take six or seven between now and six P.M. You wash your hair, you wash your fingernails, you wash everything you have on you. And then you come back and then you let me test you." He came back the next morning and he was still radioactive a little bit. The boy had gone home scared. He didn't know what he was doing, and his father called me. And his father said, "What is this and why were you so upset?" And I said, "You should have seen my Geiger counter go off." And so I said, "You do something about what they are doing over there in the Port of Corpus Christi." Well, he had the clout to do it. And they never did do that again. But that doesn't mean that they don't do it in other fields. They send those labor pools in to work anywhere out here. They say they are trained, but I don't believe it because the labor people tell me they are not.

Uranium mine, Karnes County, Texas (Courtesy Sharon Stewart)

1. The historical, pre-settlement brown pelican population in Texas is estimated to have been roughly five thousand. Yet, in 1964 and 1966, none was reported to have successfully nested, and during the entire 1967–74 period, only two to seven pairs attempted to breed. K. A. King and E. L. Flickinger, "The Decline of Brown Pelicans on the Louisiana and Texas Gulf Coast," *Southwestern Naturalist,* 21 (1977): 419, 422; L. J. Blus and others, "Brown Pelican: Population Status, Reproductive Success and Organochlorine Residues in Louisiana, 1971–76," *Bulletin of Environmental Contaminant Toxicology,* 22 (1979): 128–35.

2. U.S. Department of Interior, Fish and Wildlife Service, "12-Month Petition Finding and Proposed Rule to Remove the Brown Pelican (*Pelecanus occidentalis*) from the Federal List of Endangered and Threatened Wildlife." *Federal Register* 73, no. 34 (February 20, 2008): 9407–33.

3. Yellowcake being shipped out of Corpus Christi likely came from strip mines or in situ mines near Karnes City or in other areas of South Texas, including Live Oak, Duval, Bee or Jim Hogg counties. Aside from risks with transport, uranium strip mines leave behind tailings, which can leak into soils and underlying aquifers, or off-gas radioactive substances, while in situ or solution mines can cause problems with spills of leached-out uranium and process fluids, along with releases of radium, arsenic, molybdenum, and selenium freed from the substrate by the mining solution. As well, contamination from tailings and waste associated with facilities used for extracting and milling uranium has been a problem in Texas. Texas Environmental Profiles, "Uranium Mining," www.texasep.org/html/wst/wst_6ird_mnng.html (accessed January 28, 2009); A. J. Kuhaida, Jr. and M. J. Kelly, *Solution (In Situ Leach) Mining of Uranium: An Overview,* (Oak Ridge, TN: Oak Ridge National Laboratory, Energy Division, 1978). http://www.osti.gov/bridge/servlets/purl/6566581-mAm2ve/6566581.pdf (accessed November 12, 2009).

Bottomlands, Bulldozers, and Ethics

CARL FRENTRESS grew up in an old Texas family with farming traditions, earned a BS in Wildlife Science from Texas A&M University, and in 1972 joined Texas Parks and Wildlife as a wildlife biologist, serving as one of the first nongame staff in the department. He is noted for his pioneering work on aerial photo interpretation, his expertise in bottomland hardwood systems, and his knowledge of waterfowl. Mr. Frentress's early life experiences on his family's farm made a deep impression on what would evolve into his professional conservation ethic.

Interviewed on October 25, 2000, in Athens, Texas

Reel 2127; Time Code 00:02:18
_____

There's no doubt that my family and the land had a lot to do with how and where I wound up with a profession. Both sides of my family for quite some time back have been in Texas and, in fact, the Frentress family was in Texas before it was Texas. We have a relative, Dr. James Frentress, and Dr. Frentress was with Sam Houston at San Jacinto and we know that he was in

Texas about 1830. Noah Smithwick wrote about him and the little town of Frentress near Lockhart is named after him. The other side of my family, they were old settlers in Texas also, so this land and the people who are on the land had a lot to do with my attitude. And today we're here on a piece of land that I own and it's been in the family since the 1870s, belonged to my great-great grandfather on the maternal side and he was a Civil War veteran and came back here to settle.

Being reared in what I call a kind of a pastoral or farming and land-oriented ethic really influenced me. And I was brought up with a lot of love and caring and respect—I guess those old core values that we talk about were much a part of my life. We were always on the land, every day. And a lot of the land was still wild. What wasn't wild was in a farming operation and it required constant care.

I guess I'm kind of predisposed for this profession. I can remember being in high school and thinking that forestry was where I was going to go because I didn't know anything about wildlife management, it was not a widely discussed profession in those days. And then ultimately when I went on to college, I tried to get into chemistry and that didn't suit me. I began to get information about wildlife management and I knew that was the way I wanted to go, and so I did. But I've always had an interest in natural history and all the activities that go with the land. Certainly hunting and fishing were a big part of my recreational pursuits and adventures, and they still are.

Mr. Frentress's childhood experiences exploring the lush, bottomland hardwoods of his family's land ended abruptly with the construction of Lake Athens, a reservoir in northeast Texas. After the crippling drought of the 1950s, an ambitious plan to impound rivers and ensure a more reliable water supply was rolled out across the state. In an era before the birth of the environmental movement, there was little room for the type of public input and criticism of these projects that is more commonplace today.

Reel 2127; Time Code 00:16:36

"We saw the bulldozers absolutely lay bare the ground."

This was a period of intense unrest in this community that probably has colored my intensity about bottomland hardwoods and reservoir construction[1] in my job today. I don't want to imply here that there is passion beyond objectivity, but it made me quite aware of what goes on, and I had first-hand knowledge of what happened. I was a teenager in the early sixties when Lake Athens was proposed and then built. And we've talked about how East Texas was full of people on the land, relating to the land, and often there were many, many places like my grandfather's and later with my father and the property that he came to own, that had been in the family for quite some time. They'd lived on it, flourished or gone through adversity on the land, either way, but they were there. And there was a lot of intense devotion to it, and then here comes something totally unexpected and they were told, "We're taking your land, you don't have any choice." And therefore you had to negotiate a sale. There was one woman who had inher-

Carl Frentress, with his grandfather (Courtesy Carl Frentress)

ited some land that did not do that and she was given a dollar and her land was taken by eminent domain. And probably that was used as an example. But, in those days, there was no mitigation[2] for losses and so a lot of the bottomland hardwood system, which was still fairly intact and in pretty good shape, was lost and there was no compensation for that. Those were wetlands. And we got nothing for that kind of destruction.

The other impact was, after my father was forced off the land and had to move to town, he didn't live long after that because that was not his kind of lifestyle. Then this lake was cleared and we saw that. We saw the bulldozers absolutely lay bare the ground and the creek itself. Flat Creek was just a ditch going down through this big, couple thousand acre bare cleared area, and all those trees were just burned. It was a very shocking experience for everybody who had some sense of connection to that land and never realized that the city would move into the countryside and affect it in that way. Now that's just one side of the story, but it's a personal side that I saw.

Athens definitely has benefited from the water supply, but I'm not sure we've balanced this well. And maybe that's a point that I should mention about a credo or a philosophy. There needs to be a harmonious and balanced approach to land use so that there's some conservation on one hand, either de facto or by intent, and there's land use to produce things, either economic or direct immediate needs, on the other hand. And I see a lot of that getting out of kilter in my career. Things are done that make you wonder why they were done when the option is there to maybe have a little bit more harmony, have a little bit more balance, in the full approach to land use. And that's probably a driving force in my subconscious as I deal with people in my work trying to offer recommendations on how they could do things. So, undoubtedly, I'm affected by this whole era of invigorating experiences on the land and suddenly there's this big shock that yanked from us a substantial part of our heritage. The land would have stayed in the family and we would have access to it now if it hadn't been taken. Now there's only nine-tenths of an acre and we keep it sort of as an icon of that farm.

I guess for the record it would be important to comment that not all of the reservoir projects have this high noble cause of water supply associated with them. There are advocates for reservoirs who stand to gain substantially financially by getting the project done. I do know that when land acquisition started here for the reservoir, at the same time, there was a real estate boom for people to purchase surrounding land. And those were people who were able to buy the land and they offered good prices to those people who had land that would be adjacent to the lake and then that became lakeshore real estate and it's quite high. Lakeside lots at Lake Athens are bringing lots of money right now and I'm sure that's been repeated wherever there's lakeside development. And so that's an issue or component of reservoir construction that sometimes gets swept under the rug because it's kind of an ugly scene and it's not always thoroughly explained. Well I saw it happen here, and things might be a little bit dif-

ferent, it might have been a little bit more tolerable if we had had mitigation and no lakeshore development, there would have been something saved.

Reel 2128; Time Code 00:30:51

"We should ask our children to learn to love the land before we ask them to protect it."

What's happening in these river basins is, as floodwaters go down through river basins, the waters are held up and the water is cleansed. Cities like Houston or Beaumont are not aware of that. The forest in East Texas moderates our climate, has something to do with our air quality, and most people are unaware of that. That's why I say youth education and making it real (it doesn't take much to connect young people with the outdoors) is important. David Sobel in his book, *Beyond Ecophobia*[3] says, "We should ask our children to learn to love the land before we ask them to protect it." And the best way to do that is just to get them into their backyard. If you learn to love your vacant lot or backyard or park, you can make that jump to rainforests in South America. If you don't make that connection, then talking about rainforests in South America and the loss of those in a classroom is meaningless to the child because there's no connection. It doesn't make any real sense to them. Once they learn to love the land deeply and fulfill themselves in their own development, I think that's a very powerful part of education.

My grandfather's farm was such a place for me. Unfortunately, I can't see it anymore. It lives in my mind and I'm thankful for having spent a lot of time around it. That tract of land is about a couple miles away from here and it's in the bottom of Lake Athens. I can remember a lot of places on my grandfather's farm in that bottom that were a lot of fun and I still think about it. So I guess a favorite place for me is any good, high quality bottomland hardwood forest. I like being there.

1. There are currently 209 major reservoirs in Texas, according to Texas Water Development Board records. Texas Water Development Board, "Texas Major Reservoirs," http://wiid.twdb.state.tx.us/ims/resinfo/viewer.htm (accessed November 14, 2009). At the turn of the twentieth century, there was only one major lake in Texas, Caddo Lake. Most Texas dams were built in the years following the severe drought of the 1950s, during the 1960s and 1970s. Construction slowed as fewer good reservoir sites remained, as federal cost-share moneys declined under the Water Resources Development Act of 1986, and as a 1985 state law required freshwater releases from new impoundments within two hundred miles of the coast. *Water Resources Development Act*, 33 U.S.C. sec. 2215; National Research Council, Commission on Geosciences, Environment and Resources, *New Directions in Water Resources Planning for the U.S. Army Corps of Engineers*, (Washington, D.C., National Research Council 1999), 26–27, Table 2.3. http://books.nap.edu/openbook.php?record_id=6128&page=R1 (accessed November 13, 2009); Texas Water Code sec. 16.1331.

2. The evolution of mitigation requirements for reservoirs has been gradual. In 1977, the Corps of Engineers, operating under its dredge-and-fill permitting authority of Section 404 of the Clean Water Act, was required to *urge* a permit applicant to "modify his proposal to eliminate or mitigate any damage to such [fish and wildlife resources]." In 1986, the Corps' mitigation policy was strengthened to ensure that a project was not contrary to the public interest. Rather than only *urging* the permit applicant to mitigate damage to fish and wildlife resources, the district engineer was required to *deny* the permit if the permit applicant refused to provide compensatory mitigation.

Attention to historic wetland losses brought greater support for environmental mitigation in general. Draining and filling for development, mosquito control, and water supplies have caused wetlands to decline dramatically in the United States. By the 1980s, wetlands covered only 53 percent of the original area found in the United States in the 1780s. With the reduction in wetlands came harm to natural flood control, water quality protection, groundwater recharge, shoreline stabilization, wildlife habitat, and fishery support. National Research Council, Committee on Mitigating Wetland Losses, Board of Environmental Studies and Toxicology, Water Science and Technology Board, Division of Earth and Life Studies, *Compensating for Wetland Losses under the Clean Water Act* (Washington D.C.: National Academies Press, 2001), 1. In 1989, President George H. W. Bush set a goal of "no net loss of wetlands" for the country and in 1990 the U.S. Congress reiterated this goal (*Water Resources Development Act*, sec. 307). As a consequence, in 1990, the EPA and Army Corps of Engineers entered a Memorandum of Agreement on mitigating wetland losses, emphasizing on-site, in-kind mitigation. This was followed in 1993 by a Corps/EPA Joint Memorandum on Mitigation Banking, arguing for larger, more collaborative protection schemes. This mitigation bank approach became increasingly strong and explicit in language from the Intermodal Surface Transportation Equity Act of 1993 and the National Wetlands Mitigation Action Plan of December 26, 2002 issued by the Corps, EPA, and Departments of Agriculture, Commerce, Interior, and Transportation. Mitigation, particularly through banking efforts, has grown in the years since. In 2005, the Corps' Institute for Water Resources calculated that there were 450 approved mitigation banks in the United States, with fifty-nine sold out of credits, and an additional 198 banks in the proposal stage. Critics charge, however, that wetlands, and other natural resources, are unique, and their loss cannot be mitigated by protecting other resources in other locations. Further, there is concern that the mitigation strategies are more political than ecological, allowing public opinion to be assuaged, while yielding less environmental value. Ikuko Matsumoto, "Mitigation or Manipulation?," *Tropical Resources Bulletin* 25 (2006): 77 .

3. David Sobel, *Beyond Ecophobia: Reclaiming the Heart in Nature Education* (Great Barrington, MA: Orion Society, 1996).

Alphabet Soup

"Not blind opposition to progress,

but opposition to blind progress . . ."[1]

JOHN MUIR

EPA FDA NRC SEC USFS CAA ESHA HUD NOAA GAO BLM

A cryptic code? A word puzzle? An unsolvable anagram?

In reality, these are the ABCs of environmental activism—the alphabet soup of acronyms representing a myriad of federal agencies responsible for regulating everything from air and water pollution to drug safety, finances, and wildlife. This incomprehensible cipher would, however, be instantly recognizable to those who have spent their lives monitoring not just the industries and developers that capitalize and consume resources shared by the public commons, but to those who scrutinize the oversight bureaus as well. In short, they are the stock and trade of the watchdogs *of the* watchdogs.

This is a risky calling. The advocates who choose to tackle corporations and government institutions know that a great deal of money and power is at risk, and neither side is timid. At the same time, they also know that speaking truth to power is perhaps the highest calling and ultimate duty of a citizen.

1. From its founding in 1892, the Sierra Club has used this phrase as its motto. It is generally attributed to John Muir.

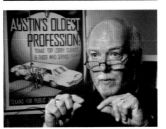

Dirty Air, Dirty Money

CRAIG MCDONALD has been involved in civic life at the local, federal, and state level. His career began as a local community organizer in the Saul Alinsky model and progressed in the 1980s as Director of Public Citizen's Congress Watch, arguing on the national stage for stronger health, safety, and environmental protection, an end to corporate subsidies, and improved access to the courts. In 1997, Mr. McDonald came to Austin to found and direct Texans for Public Justice, a non-partisan, non-profit group focusing on corporate and governmental responsibility in the state. Of particular interest was their work documenting the influence of campaign contributions on clean air legislation, and the attempt by industries to "grandfather," or exempt, older, non-complying pollution sources from the new more stringent requirements.

Interviewed on March 6, 2008, in Austin, Texas

Reel 2445; Time Code 00:28:14

I've always been a political junkie, so this work fits me perfectly. I think I was watching the Huntley-Brinkley Report on TV back in the fifties when I was five years old. So I've always had an interest in politics and actually ran my first political campaign when I was ten years old at Kent Hills Elementary School. We did a mock presidential campaign and I was a surrogate Dick Nixon—and we kicked JFK's ass at Kent Hills, even though JFK became the president eventually. So I've always been involved in and fascinated by politics, and had a growing sense that you could commit yourself to justice and get by. You could do good work, and that was the highest calling. I grew up during the civil rights movement and I always felt bad that I might've been a little too old, or too young, for it. There wasn't much of a role for me then, but I certainly observed it and saw the power and the change you could bring to the political system through individual action. Years later, even in Grand Rapids, I actually ended up knowing a couple of Freedom Riders and people who have been in the civil rights movement, so that inspired me.

I was "politicized" by the Vietnam War. I was a high school dropout, and I was a draftee. In 1969 I'd lost the lottery, and so I had to go to the war. There wasn't much of a support system back there. This wasn't Amherst, this was Grand Rapids, Michigan, a conservative factory town. I felt I had no other alternative but to go, so I went. And when I came back, I actually took a GED and went to college and got an education. But I think that experience spoke to me and said, "I'm never going to be their fool again." I'm never going to get fooled like this, and I'm going to try to have the courage to do what's right because that was a major regret of mine: that I went and served in a war that I certainly thought was unjust. I just didn't know what to do about it or how to articulate it at the time. So I think I dedicated myself to learn how to make political change.

And I went to work for Ralph Nader. I had to carry the books around for years to all the speeches, and you hear them day in and day out and some are just beautiful and marvelous. But one thing you learn from Ralph, if you follow him around long enough, and some people only have to hear one speech to learn it, but if you follow him around long enough, it's that the highest calling in a democracy is citizenship. It's about being active citizens that make political change and dedicate themselves to trying to make the country a better place, to make the world a better place. And there's not enough people to do it, but I think that helped inspire me to get up every day and work for justice. It's a wonderful thing, most people don't get to do that, but I do.

Reel 2443; Time Code 00:57:49

"Money drives the political process in this state."

I came to Austin in 1997 to found Texans for Public Justice. And a lot of the issues that I saw Smitty Smith at Public Citizen and the other groups working on in Texas over the years were not successful because they came up against big money. You know, big money runs Texas, maybe more so than other states, and big money plays a role in the outcome of public policy debates in

Texas. We have a lobby here that is extremely active and well-funded. There's a campaign finance system with virtually no limits. There's a campaign finance system that allows even our courts, the civil courts, to receive campaign contributions from the very people they're judging that day in their courtroom. In short, it's not very well hidden corruption; money drives the political process in this state. And unless you have a very dramatic issue, an issue that's getting lots of attention, it's very difficult for the good guys, the environmentalists, the health and safety reformers, the campaign finance reformers, to get something through this Legislature. You come up against entrenched interests every time you turn around. I felt there was kind of a void in that no one was really documenting the money and how it flows to members of the Legislature. In Texas, we thought that Public Citizen, Consumers Union, and the Sierra Club often talked about the role that money played in defeating their agenda, but they very seldom documented it. I think it was because they didn't have the time or the resources. You know, they're busy working on the substance of their issue. They're busy working for cleaner water, for breathable air. They didn't have time to do this. Well, I had some expertise in doing it as the director of Congress Watch. We knew how to set up a model and how to document the flow of money and who it flows to in the political system, and to draw the lines between public policy, campaign contributions, and politicians. And we thought there was certainly a void here.

Reel 2444; Time Code 00:17:25

In 1998 we issued our first environmental report. Again, we're not strictly environmental advocates but we do care about the environment, and many of our colleagues are in the environmental community. They had been trying for years to get some legislation through to cap the grandfathered air pollution that was coming from the major stationary air polluting sources around the

Texas state capitol, Austin, Texas (Courtesy Ville Miettinen, Creative Commons.)

state. We did a study called *Dirty Air, Dirty Money* because the environmental community came to us, as communities sometimes do, and said, "We know there's a connection between the money that comes from these polluters and our inability to get reforms through the committee. Could you use your databases, your resources, and your expertise to document that because that will help us in our fight." So that's the role we play. I believe that *Dirty Air, Dirty Money* took a look at the largest grandfathered facilities[1] and the owners of those facilities around the state and then tracked how much they had given in campaign contributions to members of the Legislature. And lo and behold, and not surprising, if I remember the results of that study, the chairperson of the Regulated Industries Committee, which

oversees this particular legislation, received the most money from the polluting industry. It happens time and time again, case by case, involving the people in power to regulate an industry or to do some consumer protection that would affect an industry. The industries and the lobbyists are not naïve. They know that those are the people to give their money to, and that money promotes their agenda[2] at the expense of those on the other side who don't have the money, the resources, or the economic self-interest to give money.

"The 'breathers' of the state weren't organized . . ."

In the case of *Dirty Air,* it was the "breathers" who lacked clout. The "breathers" of the state weren't organized into a very effective political action committee. Yes, they were members of the Sierra Club and the Sierra Club did all it could, but again, I take you back to that statistic where you are looking at sixteen hundred paid lobbyists in Texas and only thirty-three of them work for the environmentalists. And when it comes to campaign contributions, the environmental community, the labor community, and the consumer community aren't even a blip. So we would document that the largest emitters of grandfathered air pollution, I forget the exact number, gave X millions of dollars to the Legislature.[3] And the environmentalists took that report and used it with the media to make their case on why nothing is getting done about grandfathered air pollution. The major polluters, which are primarily made up of the utility companies in this state, were also huge donors to Governor Bush. Governor Bush, as you might recall, had his clean air program that he announced to take care of grandfathered pollution. And lo and behold, whom did it benefit? It was called the CARE Program, it was an acronym for something [Clean Air Responsibility Enterprise], but the secret to it, and the beauty of it, was that he *said* he was doing something, but it was an absolutely voluntary program that took not one gram of CO_2 or grandfathered pollution out of the skies.[4] So it was beautiful for his donors. And it's not a partisan thing. The Democrats were, to a large extent, beholden to the business interests as well. But in that report, *Dirty Air, Dirty Money,* we tried to make the direct connections between the polluting industries who had been grandfathered and the politicians who received the money and their role in making sure that the industries were not adversely regulated.

1. The Texas Legislature provided a "grandfathered" exemption from the state's Clean Air Act for industrial facilities that were in existence when the Act went into effect in 1971. The reasoning was that it would have been prohibitively expensive to retrofit these older plants to bring them up to modern standards, and that these plants would likely be retired soon anyway. However, many of these plants survived, with significant impact on state air quality. State figures from 1995 showed this long-lived impact of grandfathering, indicating that 1,070 of Texas' largest industrial facilities were grandfathered and emitting close to one million tons of "criteria" pollutants, amounting to 36 percent of all industrial emissions in the state. Galveston-Houston Association for Smog Prevention and Lone Star Chapter of the Sierra Club, *Grandfathered Air Pollution: The Dirty Secrets of Texas Industries* (Austin: Lone Star Sierra Club, April 1998), 24.; David Groberg, "Grandfather's Last Days? Voluntary Permits and Economically Sustainable Air Quality in Texas," *Texas Business Review* (February 2000): 2, http://www.ic2.utexas.edu/bbr/publications/2000-texas-business-review/february-2000-texas-business-review/view.html (accessed November 14, 2009).

2. In the case of the voluntary compliance program for grandfathered air polluters, the "agenda" was quite expressly written by industry. Texas Open Records Act requests by the Sustainable Energy and Economic Development Coalition revealed that the SB 766 bill creating the voluntary compliance plan had been drafted and submitted to legislators by R. Kinnan Golemon, general counsel to the Texas Chemical Council. Louis Dubose, "The Greening of George W. Bush: The Governor's 'Clean Air' Bill Hasn't Cleaned up Texas' Air, *The Austin Chronicle,* October 27, 2000.

3. Political action committees affiliated with the "Dirty 30," the most egregious grandfathered corporate polluters, spent 2.5 million dollars to influence Texas politicians between December 1995 and March 1998. Seventy-eight of the largest grandfathered air polluters in Texas hired 359 different lobbyists in 1997, paying them between 9.7 and 20.6 million dollars to sway Texas elected officials. Texans For Public Justice, *Dirty Air, Dirty Money: Grandfathered Pollution Pays Dividends Downwind in Austin* (Austin: 1998). http://info.tpj.org/docs/1998/06/reports/grandfather/ToC.html (accessed November 14, 2009).

4. A study found that two years after implementation of the CARE program created by SB 766, only 12.5 percent of the 828 eligible grandfathered plants had volunteered to reduce their emissions. Lone Star Sierra Club, "New Report: 87% of Grandfathered Plants Not Signed Up for Emissions Reductions under Bush 'Voluntary Plan,'" http://lonestar.sierraclub.org/press/newsreleases/report.html (accessed January 28, 2009); Control of Air Pollution by Permits for New Construction or Modification, Permits for Grandfathered Facilities, *Texas Administrative Code,* title 30, subchapter 116(H), February 1, 2007.

Shareholders and Workers, Profits and Health

SISTER SUSAN MIKA is a Benedictine nun who lives in San Antonio and who has served as a schoolteacher and a public advocate. Practicing social justice theology for people and encouraging stewardship of the earth, her advocacy work has focused on showing corporations the need to be more responsible in their care of workers and the environment. Using the proxy votes of shareholders, Sister Mika, along with other religious orders, has successfully pressed for change in corporate policies. In this instance, she relates a story about a challenge the nuns faced against the Alcoa Corporation.

Interviewed on April 17, 2002, in San Antonio, Texas

Reel 2198; Time Code 00:03:49

In 1982 I had the opportunity to interview for a job with what at that time was called The Texas Coalition for Responsible Investment. Now it has changed its focus, not just on Texas, but for our whole region, so it is today called the Socially Responsible Investment Coalition. I was expected to start up the organization, but it would be a regional branch of the Interfaith Center on Corporate Responsibility based in New York. And when I heard the type of work that it was, I said, "Well, that would be a challenge to me and I

would like to try it." So, I took that position in 1982 as the Executive Director of the Texas Coalition for Responsible Investment. And immediately people said, "Go to the border and try to find out what is going on at the U.S./Mexico border." Some did not know exactly what was going on, but there were reports coming out at that time about problems with the factories, which were called the maquiladoras.[1] And so as part of that ministry, then, I began traveling to the border to try to meet with groups, with workers, with activists that were along the U.S./Mexico border and to see what was really happening. And I did that for about eight years.

Reel 2199; Time Code 00:02:08

"It was really a chance for workers to speak truth to power. It was just an amazing conversation."

We've been involved with Alcoa since 1995. And at that time, the Benedictine Sisters filed a shareholder resolution with Alcoa asking them about their wages in Mexico. Alcoa wanted to meet with me. They wanted me to come to Pittsburgh, and I said, "Well, why don't you come to the border and let's meet with some of the workers." So we did. We had a meeting and some of the people from the corporate headquarters got to hear first-hand what was going on in the factories. The workers made a little chart from their "Market Basket Survey." They were receiving twenty-one to twenty-six dollars a week for working forty-five to forty-eight hours. And they showed that, with that money, they were able to buy about fifteen or sixteen items, things like onions, tomatoes, rice and beans, deodorant, toilet paper, and some basics. We had three babies in the meeting and they were crying and had to be fed. It was just a wonderful taste of the reality that these workers face. How are you going to buy diapers? How are you going to buy formula for a small child? After the meeting, I sent a letter to Paul O'Neill, who was the CEO of Alcoa, listing all of the concerns that the workers had. We also sent some articles from the local newspaper because some of the workers had been "intoxicated" which in Spanish means being "overcome." And so the headlines were that a number of the workers from different plants were in the hospital getting checked out because of this "intoxication." And I could tell right away that the corporate secretary from Pittsburgh had no idea what really had gone on. Anyway, I didn't hear anything back from Paul O'Neill. It was getting near the time for the shareholder meeting in May of that year, and I was planning on taking some of the workers to the annual meeting because we wanted to find out what had happened. Then I got a phone call from Paul O'Neill, and he had found out that we were coming. And, oh, he was very, very angry with me, really screaming at me on the phone. And those are my words because he doesn't remember that he did that. But he was very, very forceful on the phone, and wanted to know if I was coming. And I said, "Yes, that I was." And he wanted to know if I was bringing workers. And I said, "Well, I'm trying to get them across the border, and it's no easy task to get the paperwork and to get visas and all of that." He was just so angry and upset; he finally calmed down and said, "Well, do you want to meet with me?" in a very strong voice, which was interesting because, on TV he doesn't always come across like that. And so I said, "Well, I'll have to ask the workers and then see what they would want to do and then we'll get back with you." I still remember coming out from my office and I was in total shock.

We did go to the annual meeting. At the door, the corporate secretary actually tried to keep us out. They wanted to only let myself and the two workers inside, and not the two other people that were part of our delegation. I said to him, "We're a delegation, we're all representing the Benedictine Sisters, and we are going in." And he says, "Well, you're a shareholder, those two are workers, they can go in, but not these other two." The other two were Martha Ojeda from the Coalition for Justice in the Maquiladoras, and Julia Quiñonas, who is a promotora [an Hispanic community educator and liaison involved in raising awareness of health and educational issues] for these workers with Alcoa. I said, "No. We're all together as a delegation," and we literally had to move him aside. I could hear that the meeting had already started, and sometimes these meetings are very short. And I was really worried that this was a stalling tactic; that we might not be able to get into the meeting and have the workers actually tell their story.

So we went in and we had to sit in the back because it was full and the meeting had already started. But we did have the workers tell their stories in Spanish and a translator translated what had happened to them and you could have heard a pin drop in the room. They were talking about their salaries and what they couldn't buy. The day before they left Mexico, a woman had gotten her leg caught in some of the machinery. They took her out to the clinic, she stayed there for a little while, and then they brought her back out to the production line so that there were no lost work days or work hours. Things like that are really horrifying. After the workers stopped speaking, I got up to the microphone and just thanked everyone for listening. Then Paul O'Neill said, "I want you to stay up here because I have questions for you." He grilled me for about fifteen to twenty minutes in front of all the stockholders. And I just answered every question that he asked and gave challenges back to him. He wanted to know if we wanted all of the plants that they had out of Mexico, out of Poland, out of any place they were in the world. I told him, "I never said that to you. I said on the phone to you that you needed to pay sustainable wages and you needed to look at environmental conditions wherever you were having those plants. I never said to you that we were trying to get those plants to leave. We're trying to get you to be responsible." I said, "You're an important person. You're a CEO of a major company. You talk to a lot of CEOs everyday." Then I added, "But I'm an important person, too. I'm a shareholder in this company. I talk to a lot of people about all these conditions. And, I expect something of you."

After that meeting, we did meet with him at the Alcoa headquarters. He brought in a couple of other people to listen to the workers and he spent about an hour and forty-five minutes with us. He asked us for six weeks after that. And we said, "Well, that's fine." So he went down there himself. He's the only CEO that I know of that actually went down there to do the investigating. And he made changes, big changes. Even though he said at the shareholders meeting to me and to all of the two or three hundred shareholders present that he would not raise those wages, he raised the wages five dollars and thirty cents a week for each worker. We figured out that put about a million to a million and a half dollars into that economy, because those are small-scale economies. And Alcoa has eight to ten thousand workers in Ciudad Acuña and Piedras Negras, just in those two little areas. He finally paid profit sharing, which they had not previously paid. Alcoa, that year, had seven hundred ninety million dollars in profit. When the workers had asked Paul O'Neill, "Why didn't you pay us profit sharing? It's an arrangement under Mexican law that is mandated," he answered, "There was no profit in your company." And so they said, "We just heard in the big meeting where there was a lot of profit in our company," because, of course, Alcoa was bragging about their profit. So it was really a chance for workers to speak truth to power. It was just an amazing conversation.

1. Maquiladoras are plants owned by multinational corporations, typically assembly facilities where televisions, toys, clothes, lenses, washing machines, keyboards, batteries, cassettes, and other consumer items are put together for export. They are sited within one hundred kilometers south of the U.S./Mexico border, employing some million Mexican nationals, and enjoying duty-free imports from the United States, and tariff-free value-added exports to the U.S. market. While the maquila program has attracted foreign investment and higher-paying jobs to Mexico, there are concerns that the maquiladoras undercut unionized wages in the United States and Mexico, host unsafe working conditions, spawn unregulated colonia development, and emit poorly controlled pollution. Patricia Wilson, *Exports and Local Development: Mexico's New Maquiladoras* (Austin, Texas: University of Texas Press, 1992), 2–3; Khoshrow Fatemi, *The Maquiladora Industry: Economic Solution or Problem?* (New York: Praeger Publishers, 1990); Vicky Funari and Sergio De La Torre, "Maquilapolis," www.maquilapolis.com/project2.html (accessed January 28, 2009). The maquiladora plants grew out of the Border Industrialization Program (BIP), which began in 1965, and spread rapidly from 448 maquilas and 74,500 workers in 1976, to 865 plants and 227,900 workers in 1986, and finally peaked at 3,051 factories and 1,035,957 laborers in 1998. Avery Wear, "Class and Poverty in the Maquila Zone," *International Socialist Review,* May and June 2002. http://www.isreview.org/issues/23/23.shtml. (accessed November 14, 2009). In turn, the BIP replaced the earlier "Bracero" program that had brought inexpensive Mexican labor to U.S. agriculture and railroads during the American labor shortages of WWII. "Official Bracero Agreement," August 4, 1942, revised April 26, 1943; *Extension of the Bracero Program,* Public Law 82–78, *U.S. Statutes at Large* 65 (1951): 119.

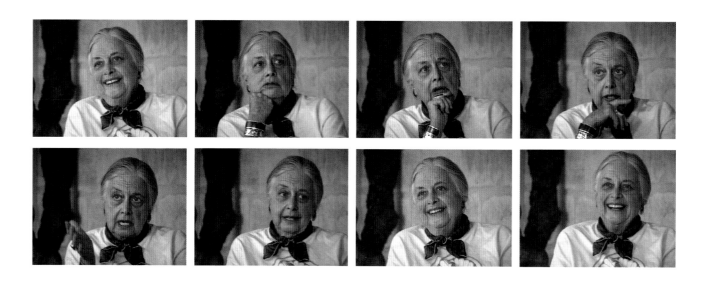

Bayous, Channels, and Floods

TERRY HERSHEY is known as a catalyst in Texas conservation circles, having had a role in forming numerous non-profit groups in Houston and statewide, including stream protection groups, the Bayou Preservation Association and Harris County Flood Control Task Force, a networking organization, Citizens' Environmental Coalition, and a park advocacy group, The Park People.

Houston's proximity to the Gulf of Mexico has subjected it to fierce rains and hurricanes, which were allayed in earlier times by the natural drainage of the wetlands and bayous that ring the city. But, as the city became a megalopolis after World War II, nature's systems were "improved" for the sake of development, often with unanticipated consequences. The widening, straightening and paving of these bayous caught Ms. Hershey's attention, and took her before the Army Corps of Engineers and the Harris County Flood Control District.

Interviewed on April 13, 2002 in Stonewall, Texas

Reel 2188; Time Code 00:00:07:28

"We had no credentials, except common sense . . ."

It was '66 and I came back to Houston and Ernie Fay was picking me up—my husband Jake was out of town that weekend—and Ernie said, "Well, they've started." And I said, "Who's started what?" And he said, "They've started clearing Buffalo Bayou." And I asked him why. I didn't live on it, but I knew it. He said, "I don't know, they're just clearing it." And so the next day, Mary Kelsey and Isabelle Steenland and I got in the car to go up and see what was going on, and found nine acres being cleared and they were layering the trees with rubber tires and burning them. Very stinky, you know, in a residential area. I went back and called my County Commissioner the next day, which was Squatty Lyons. Now, I didn't know about County Commissioners. And he said, "Oh, Miss Hershey, some big government people are coming in and telling us little folks what to do." And I asked, "What big government people?" And he said, "Oh, that Army Corps of Engineers." And I said, "Well, then why does it say *Harris County* Flood Control all over the trucks?" And he said, "I'm busy, I don't have time to talk to you," and hung up. And it made me mad and I stayed mad for thirty years. Checked into it and found out, yes, that they had concreted Brays Bayou and they were working on White Oak and this was the Corps' plans, but as my friends in the Corps said later on, "Terry, we do not go uninvited. We presume that it's your elected officials who ask us to come do these things as the will of the people." I said, "Wrong, but we'll take that up at a later date."

"Changing a river into a concrete ditch!"

They were starting the channelizing of Buffalo Bayou. They had the plans. There was a group of men who had loosely formed themselves into a group that planned to do something about it. But they just hadn't really gotten themselves totally organized although most of those did live close along the Bayou. So we got them sort of organized and George Mitchell was the first president. I thought it was going to be very simple, you write the Corps and say this is not a good thing to do, this is not ecological and they would say, "Oh, my!" and go away.

But that's not the way it worked. And so, then we tried with pictures, and the Garden Club was very helpful. We took pictures and I had volunteer photographers that took pictures all up and down the Bayou and we showed the concrete bayous. And from there, we kind of mobilized a set of folks and finally, we ended up meeting George Bush Sr. He was our Congressman. He looked at the pictures and said, "Oh, what a terrible thing to do to a river." And I said, "Yeah, I think so."

The Army Corps was planning on straightening it, stripping it, "improving it," they called it. Concreting it. Like Brays Bayou. Like White Oak Bayou. Changing a river into a concrete ditch! Their philosophy was that the water would run faster. We asked, "Isn't that just flood transference? Isn't just moving it downstream faster onto somebody else?" They said, "Well, you're not an engineer." And I said, "No, but I've played with a hose and a sand pile and I kind of know what water does." But we had no credentials except common sense, which sometimes is fairly important. Anyway, George [H. W. Bush] looked at it and *he* had common sense, and he said, it was a terrible thing to do. So the next thing, he went up to D.C. and set up a

Rectification of Brays Bayou, Houston, Texas—1957 (Courtesy Harris County Flood Control District)

Houston flood—December 1935 (Courtesy Harris County Flood Control District)

meeting with the Subcommittee on Appropriations. And all these guys—Strauss, Steenland, Fay, Mitchell—they were all busy, so they put me on a plane, sent me up there. So George met me, and we made our presentation, and this was sort of a somnambulant group. They didn't look very interested in anything. And so I started talking and he was running up and down showing them the pictures, running up and down in front of them, you know, showing the pictures. He was great. So, they finally said, "Congressman, do we understand you're asking us *not* to spend money in your district?" And he gulped, and he said, "Yes, sir," he said, "I think there's a better way to deal with storm water and I would like a re-study." And they said, "OK," and walked out. And I said, "What happened?" And he said, "I think we won." He took me back and put me on a plane and I went home and I said to my husband, Jake, "It wasn't hard, you know. Why is governing so hard?"

We did get their study, but a funny sidebar on that was Bush asked for a study of Buffalo Bayou. Well, now, "Buffalo Bayou" is the whole thing: It's the Ship Channel, the Turning Basin, and everything else on down. And we were actually talking about *upper* Buffalo Bayou, from the city of Houston up. And they cut off the funding for the whole Buffalo Bayou. Well, the Army Corps Colonel, he was the maddest man I ever saw, he had steam coming out of his ears. He said, "What have you done?" I said, "We've finally caught your attention, that's what we've done." But George changed the wording in it and said, "I meant, *upper* Buffalo Bayou," so they could go back to dredging the Ship Channel, which may or may not be a good idea but anyway, but that's another story.[1]

Reel 2188; Time Code 00:13:41

Some of these engineers thought it was a great thing to do. They were terribly wrong, but they didn't know they were wrong. They thought they were right, and they thought we were wrong. I thought they were stupid because it was flood transference. It was dumping it downstream. The city of Houston was downstream, nobody ever sort of looked. We have twenty-two watersheds in Harris County, and we haven't had the big rain on the Buffalo Bayou watershed since '35, when the water was up to the second floor downtown in Houston. You can see the pictures. And that's before the Katy Prairie was area was developed; it was before Memorial was developed. And, so that's when they went to the Army Corps, the city fathers at that time, and said, "Save us," thinking the Corps was the preeminent engineering group, which in a sense it was. Have any of you ever read that wonderful book about the '26 flood on the Mississippi and the Corps' really big fight about whether they were going to build levies or let the river flow? It's a fascinating book. The Corps, in its wisdom, thought that they could alter the watersheds. The community asked them to do that after the '35 flood. The Corps came in with a plan to build the two "retentions:" the Addicks and Barker dams, and to straighten and strip all the rivers that went from there on down to the bay.

Reel 2188; Time Code 00:17:09

Now when it's flooded downstream, downtown at the confluence of Buffalo and White Oak Bayou, it's because White Oak is channelized and the water just dashes down. In fact, in the '72 flood, it was pouring water into downtown so fast that it pushed Buffalo in reverse. Buffalo was actually flowing the other way because of the force of the White Oak Bayou. So, when we've had big rains, the confluence of all those bayous causes it to flood in that area downtown. But, as any idiot knows, when you're living at the confluence of two rivers, you shouldn't be putting stuff in the basement.

And it's flooded since then. The Medical Center's flooded at least five times since then. This last one was just unconscionable when you think of the thousands of animals that were drowned in their basement. They talk about it setting back their research program! I think of the animals: you're swimming higher and higher and the water's rising and you can't get out. Four thousand of them perished in the Medical Center basement.

1. The twenty-three mile segment of Buffalo Bayou below Houston, the Houston Ship Channel, has been repeatedly cleared and dredged for navigation for over 160 years, but strong controversy remains. In 1843, the Republic of Texas first granted the City of Houston the right to remove obstructions and otherwise improve the Bayou to allow shipping. After 1845, when Texas joined the Union, free wharf space was granted to shippers who volunteered to keep the stream clear of obstacles. Seeking to bypass Galveston's control of sea-going traffic, the Bayou Ship Channel Company dredged a channel in 1874–76 from Galveston Bay to just downstream of Houston. Title to these private channel improvements was transferred to the federal government in 1890, and with federal appropriations the channel was dredged to 18.5 feet by 1909. County bonds paid for dredging to a twenty-five foot depth in 1914. Local and federal funding helped bring the Channel to a four hundred foot width and forty foot depth by the 1990s. However, with the growth of shipping traffic and the petrochemical industry along the Channel's edge, concern grew that the Channel was too shallow and too narrow for commerce and for safety. The Port of Houston was consistently ranked as the second or third busiest in the nation. Further, much of the traffic carried toxic and flammable chemical products. Between 1969 and 1972 alone, seven hundred vessel casualties were reported, some with catastrophic results (such as the 1947 fire on board the ammonium nitrate freighter, *Grancamp*, and the 1979 explosion of the tanker, *Hawaii*). To cope with this heavy traffic and risk, the Army Corps of Engineers has been working on dredging the Channel to a width of 530 feet and a depth of 45 feet. Ironically, dredging the Channel to avoid the kinds of accidents mentioned above has raised separate environmental concerns about saline intrusion into Galveston Bay and regarding disturbance and disposal of contaminated sediments. R. M. Farrar, *The Story of Buffalo Bayou and the Houston Ship Channel* (Houston: Houston Chamber of Commerce, 1926), 9–26; Marilyn Sibley, *The Port of Houston* (Austin: University of Texas Press, 1968), 69, 95, 105–107, 130.

Osage Hills, Clear-cuts, and Pine Plantations

NED FRITZ carried on a full private practice as a consumer credit attorney, while also managing to participate in a variety of early Texas conservation efforts. He helped build several of the key environmental groups in the Texas, such as the Dallas Audubon Society, the Texas Land Conservancy (formerly the Natural Area Preservation Association), and the Texas Conservation Alliance (once called the Texas Committee on Natural Resources). Throughout, Mr. Fritz was also active as an environmental attorney: he filed the first lawsuit under the National Environmental Policy Act, and was diligent in using the Endangered Species Act and National Forest Management Reform Act as tools to protect the Texas National Forests from clear-cutting.[1]

Interviewed on May 17, 1997, in Dallas, Texas

"The sidewalks were paved to the street, and the back yard was closed in with practically no vegetation."

Reel 1008; Time Code 00:00:45

Growing up, I remember that my mother had little interest in the outdoors or nature per se, though she'd liked our backyards, very civilized, that we lived in. I was born in the busy part of Philadelphia, Fifty-second and Walnut Street, where there were no trees, except they still had a couple of walnuts scattered down the street maybe. But the sidewalks were paved to the street, and the backyard was closed in with practically no vegetation. So, my first sight of nature, other than walking to a park in Philadelphia, was when we moved to Tulsa, Oklahoma, where I saw plenty. My father had a natural interest in the out-of-doors. But he satisfied that by fishing, and he took us boys, that is, my friends and I when I got to Tulsa, on weekend fishing trips. We could get right there in the water, throwing the bait and soon the flies 'cause we learned to flyfish out into the stream and under the trees, and that was when I began to get the feel of it.

We had a little bit of "nature" education in school, but in those days, there was very little in biology except the parts of the body, and sometimes, the relationships of plants and animals: mostly I guess the basic biological facts. But, I really got into it as a Boy Scout and pre-Boy Scout, going to camps: the YMCA Camp, High Y, and the Boy Scout camp outside of Tulsa, Oklahoma. We had a young man there who knew about nature and they showed us some of the aspects of nature. Mostly I learned it myself by passing merit badges, and the Boy Scouts had instructions and had books with the different species in them, and I would learn them out in the woods close to home. I lived on the edge of Tulsa, Oklahoma, from the age seven to age twenty-four. And, I could walk down the hill a couple of blocks and be in the woods. It was also on the edge of Osage County, where the Osage Hills at that time, and even up to today, were mainly a wild, rugged, Post Oak/Cross Timbers area, almost the way Washington Irving[2] described them! And he went through right where I lived. His route came, according to maps, within a few blocks at most of where I lived. So, he describes it in the wild back in 1832. And, it was still about like that, outside of the edge of Tulsa, when I lived and would walk into the woods, and learn the trees and plants, for my Boy Scout merit badges.

Reel 1001; Time Code 01:14:00

"They bulldozed it down and planted a crop"

The history of clear-cutting[3] for timber in Texas has two distinct periods, and the difference is significant. In the 1890s,[4] when they clear-cut, they left most of the vegetation to grow back, and ultimately obtain a native balance of biological diversity. In the current clear-cutting process, they only grow back *one* species of tree. Both forms of clear-cutting are the most destructive forms of logging ever devised by human beings, but modern clear-cutting is worse than clear-cutting used to be, and

only now has "selection management" come into it. In many places in Texas, as a more modern approach, they maintain a canopy of trees at all times but take a tree out here and a tree out there, leaving room for natural regeneration in the sunlight that the cut tree formerly occupied. In Europe, selection management originally went way back. It was one of the earliest forms of logging in some places, and was very successful. But the clear-cutters replaced it, because they could make a quicker profit by selling everything, all the good commercial timber, and wiping out whatever was left. They bulldozed it down and planted a crop of one type of tree, what's called even-age management, where they grow all one or two sets of trees on each stand of the same age, and this became predominant.

This form of monoculture pine plantation[5] brings about lots of ecological problems. In the first place, from the soil to the water usage to the recreation, in every way, a naturally diverse forest is superior to a plantation of one or two species. Beginning with the soil: in the South, for example, where they plant pine trees, they are eradicating hardwoods by burning too frequently, or by herbicides that killed the hardwoods and not the pines.[6]

They are reducing the hardwoods to a disastrous extent, and that disaster includes in the soil, because

Clear-cut, FM 1818, Angelina County, Texas (Courtesy Richard Donovan)

Girdling hardwoods, Sam Houston National Forest—1950 (Courtesy Larry Shelton)

the hardwood roots actually participate in a nutrient-building process, and in a water-storing process that the pine roots do not participate in. And furthermore, fungi come into it because fungi, particularly on the roots of hardwoods, sustain a great many species. These fungi provide certain nutrients to the trees that the tree roots cannot actually produce, but the trees in turn sustain the fungi because they have chlorophyll in their leaves; then they are able to produce certain sugars that go over to the fungi that the fungi cannot produce. So there is a natural symbiosis. You can go beyond that into the relationship between certain birds and certain insects in the trees. They're depending upon each other, and

once you get rid of a part of a certain plant community in order to boil it down to commercially profitable trees, you begin to lose the health of that community.

The current talk of the timber industry that wants to have the government produce more commercial timber for it to make a profit out of, is that the health of government forests[7] is maintained by more drastic management processes, such as more prescribed burning or even *more* logging. They say this will maintain the health of the forest, whereas what they're doing is reducing the health by all these management processes. Their prescribed burning, for example, changes the ecosystem from one that is accustomed to a certain fire

Loblolly pine plantation, Angelina National Forest—2002 (Courtesy Larry Shelton)

thereby vastly reduce all the animal species of the inner forest, which includes many of the birds that require a deep, shaded forest to survive, and that includes several species of warblers. It includes hurting several species of animals: lizards, salamanders, and vireos. In addition, many species of plants are threatened that need a fairly dense, shaded forest for survival. It also has the indirect effect, when you open areas up, of allowing more cowbirds to come in. And the cowbirds lay their eggs in the nests of warblers and other smaller birds, which they predate, and the net result is to vastly reduce the warblers. This in turn vastly reduces the checks and balances of certain insects that can be very deleterious to the hardwoods and so forth. Your overall effect is to ruin the existing ecosystem, the native ecosystem, and to replace it with a man-made ecosystem that, beginning with the soil, is poorer. These fungi and these hardwood groups and so forth enrich the soil. They hold carbon and other nutrients, and the soil is the basis for the rest of the vegetation.

1. Mr. Fritz was a lead attorney in two important cases which directly limited timbering in Texas national forests, and that indirectly influenced forestry policy nationwide. A 1988 judgment enjoined the Forest Service from clear-cutting within twelve hundred meters of colonies of the endangered red-cockaded woodpecker, affecting some two hundred thousand acres of habitat. *Sierra Club v. Yeutter,* 926 F.2d 429 (5th Cir. 1991). While limited on appeal, the case did lead the Service to restrict timber sales. Mr. Fritz also led the plaintiffs in winning a 1993 ruling under the National Forest Management Act, a law that he had helped draft and support. Janice Bezanson, phone conversation with author, March 3, 2009; 16 U.S.C. sec. 1600. The ruling ultimately required inventories and monitoring of resources and impacts. *Sierra Club v. Espy,* 822 F. Supp. 356, 364 (E.D. Tex. 1993), vacated and remanded, 38 F.3d 792 (5th Cir. 1994). Robert W. McFarlane, *A Stillness in the Pines: The Ecology of the Red-cockaded Woodpecker* (New York: W.W. Norton & Company, 1994), 226–43. The protections achieved through litigation were bolstered by legislation that Mr. Fritz helped mobilize, setting aside thirty-seven thousand acres of wilderness areas in five national forests in Texas. *Texas Wilderness Act of 1984,* Public Law 98–574, *U.S. Statutes at Large* 98 (1984): 3051–54; John Bryant interview transcript, October 26, 2000, Texas Legacy Project, www.texaslegacy.org/bb/transcripts/bryantjohntxt.html.

2. Washington Irving, *A Tour on the Prairies* (London: John Murray, 1835).

3. Regarding clear-cutting, even-aged management, selection management, shelterwood cutting, and other forestry management methods, please see Edward C. Fritz, *Sterile Forest: The Case Against Clear Cutting* (Waco,

frequency to one that can survive a more intensive fire frequency,[8] such as they're creating, which means pine trees instead of hardwood trees. Pine trees can survive the more intensive fire frequency, and that's what they want for money.

There is also an effect on species, from insects to large mammals. The effect of these forestry practices is to help temporarily those mammals that can survive in the pine monoculture, and to reduce or eliminate those species that depend upon a native biodiversity for survival. For example, they think they can help deer by throwing more grasses under the pine trees, and they

TX: Eakin Press, 1983) and Edward C. Fritz, , *Clearcutting: A Crime Against Nature* (San Antonio, TX: Marion Koogler McNay Art Museum, 1989).

4. Following extensive cutting in the Midwest and eastern states, timber harvests in East Texas began in earnest in the last quarter of the nineteenth century. In 1880 alone, it was estimated that 146 million board feet of timber were cut. By 1915, most of the old-growth forest in Texas had fallen. Texas Environmental Profile, "3. Forestland in Texas," www.texasep.org/html/Ind/Ind_3for.html (accessed March 5, 2009). Between 1880 and 1930, it is estimated that fifty-nine billion board feet of lumber were cut in East Texas. University of Texas, College of Liberal Arts. Texas Beyond History, "Aldridge Sawmill and the East Texas Logging Bonanza," www.texasbeyondhistory.net/aldridge/index.html (accessed April 18, 2010). By 1932, Texas timber yield had troughed, dropping to 350 million board feet, only 15 percent of its 1907 peak.

5. Originally, the East Texas woods were made up of shortleaf pines in the north, longleaf pines in the south central area, and loblolly pines in the west and south. Hardwoods, such as oak, ash, hickory, gum, and cottonwood were found in the bottomlands of rivers draining East Texas: the Trinity, Red, Sulphur, Sabine, Angelina, and Neches. As lumbering proceeded, the hardwoods were often cut to allow space for the more commercially profitable pine species. As early as 1935, the Forest Service newsletter, "The Houstonian," reported that hardwoods on 24,194 acres in all four Texas national forests had been removed, with remarkable precision and diligence: "this work was done by eight crews which averaged 20 men per crew . . . an average of 3.6 acres per man day was attained, with a removal of about 35 trees to the acre." Larry Shelton, e-mail message to author, March 1, 2009. As hardwoods were reduced, pine plantations were also spreading rapidly: in 1975, East Texas had 550 thousand acres of pine plantation, in 1986, it had 1.2 million acres, and in 1992, it had 4.2 million acres. Now, it is estimated that 22 percent of all Texas timberland is in loblolly pine plantation, with the majority (72 percent) on forest industry lands. In addition to being a monoculture, these plantations are typically young (a 1992 survey estimated that 71 percent were less than twenty years old) and do not have the range in age and stature of a natural forest. Texas Parks and Wildlife, "Pineywoods Wildlife Management: Historical Perspective," http://www.tpwd.state.tx.us/landwater/land/habitats/pineywood/ (accessed January 29, 2009).

6. Hardwoods have been controlled through a variety of methods, under an approach the U.S. Forest Service termed "Timber Stand Improvement." Beginning in the mid-1930s, the Service would girdle larger trees with an axe, and "hinge" saplings (cutting three-fourths through the trunk and bending them over, reducing the chance that they would resprout, as a full severing might allow). Later, the Service began treating girdled trees with an herbicide, ammate. In the 1950s, the girdling process was mechanized with a tool called the "power beaver," a motorized backpack unit with a flexible shaft and a rotary cutter at the end that would quickly ring a tree with a one inch girdle cut. In the 1960s, the hypo-ax was introduced. It was a hollow-tipped hatchet connected by a hose to a backpack tank of herbicide; striking a tree several times would inject the herbicide into the tree, killing it in short order. Larry Shelton, e-mail message to author, March 1, 2009; Robert G. Wagner and others, "The Role of Herbicides for Enhancing Forest Productivity and Conserving Land for Biodiversity in North America," *Wildlife Society Bulletin* 32, no. 4, (2004): 1028–41.

7. The history of modern-day public forests dates back to the 1930s in Texas. In 1934, the Texas Legislature approved resolution SCR-73 authorizing the United States to purchase cut-out private timberlands to create national forests in the state. In 1935, an initial ninety thousand acre parcel was purchased from the Houston County Lumber Company at a price of $8.90 per acre. Subsequent purchases secured land for the Davy Crockett (160,000 acres), Sam Houston (163,037 acres), Angelina (153,179 acres) and Sabine (160,656 acres) national forests. State Parks.com, "Sabine National Forest," www.stateparks.com/sabine.html (accessed January 28, 2009). Reforestation of the public lands by Civilian Conservation Corps members began in 1935, with thirty-six thousand acres planted by 1940. Texas Society of American Foresters, "Highlights of Texas Forestry," www.tsaf.org/highlights/highlites3.htm (accessed January 28, 2009).

8. Natural fire intervals may have been as infrequent as every thirty to sixty years, while prescribed burn regimes can bring fire to southern U.S. forests as often as every two to three years. These frequent fires favor adapted trees, such as mature pines, but harm younger pines, hardwoods such as oaks and hickories, and understory trees, such as dogwoods, hawthorns, and plums. Intense and regular fires can also volatilize organic matter in the soil. John Stanturf and others, "Fire in Southern Forest Landscapes," in *Southern Forest Research Assessment,* ed. D. M. Wear and D. Greis, Gen. Tech. Report SRS-53 (Asheville, NC: U.S. Department of Agriculture, Southern Research Station, Forest Service, 2005), 607–30. http://www.srs.fs.usda.gov/sustain/report/fire/fire.htm (accessed November 14, 2009).

Smelters, Mines, and Neighbors

BILLIE WOODS is a classically trained musician living in Elgin, who has been active in organizing and leading a non-profit citizens group, Neighbors for Neighbors. She and the group have worked to improve the environmental performance of the Alcoa smelter near Rockdale, which has been fed annually by six million tons of lignite from its fourteen thousand acre strip mine. A recent settlement led by Neighbors for Neighbors exposed a multi-year pattern of Clean Air Act violations at Alcoa, and succeeded in securing major emissions improvements. Ms. Woods and Neighbors for Neighbors continue to work with Alcoa on groundwater issues.

Interviewed on October 17, 2003, in Rosanky, Texas

Reel 2263; Time Code 00:06:20

". . . It ended up on my doorstep."

Well, I'm ashamed to say that my involvement in this issue is because it ended up on my doorstep. I wish I could say that I just really kept up on the issues and was environmentally active all along. I did pay my dues to the Sierra Club, Environmental Defense and World Wildlife Fund. I would send them money and I recycled and all of that, but I was not an activist. I did not go out and talk to people. I did not try to participate in any kind of protest or anything like that anywhere. So it literally wasn't until it ended up on my doorstep that there's the epiphany. It has to hit you in the face, I guess, for most people; which is kind of sad, but I think that's probably a reality. And that's what happened.

Lignite is a very soft, brown coal. It is just in between the stage of peat and what you would think of as hard coal. So it's very soft. It's very crumbly. It's not real stable. It takes a whole lot of it to get a sufficient number of Btus to produce a good amount of electricity for

Lignite strip mining, Lee County, Texas (Courtesy Alan Pogue, Texas Center for Documentary Photography)

them to operate with. And that's all Alcoa uses it for. They have three power units over there, and this was how they generated their electricity in order to power the smelter where they smelt aluminum and make atomized aluminum that fuels the space shuttle, for example. That used to be the largest smelter in North America. It is now the second, I think, and will be even less than that within the next few years. They're cutting back.[1]

The lignite strip mine is many hundreds of yards wide. I've seen it and it's just mind-boggling. They have something like eighty pieces of heavy equipment in addition to those drag lines that actually remove the lignite and dump it onto a conveyer belt. It goes to a facility called a crusher and then it goes onto the conveyer belt right to the plant where they then have some stockpiles of it. They have to use it fairly quickly, because

when it sits outside it degrades and it just takes more and more and more of it to burn. It is the dirtiest source of fuel available—lignite. It burns about as well as burning dirt. They'd be better off burning cow patties.

Reel 2263; Time Code 00:29:02

The air pollution from Alcoa's three boilers were and are emitting over a hundred thousand tons of criteria air pollutants each year. That includes sulfur dioxide, nitrogen oxide, volatile organic compounds which people refer to as VOCs [Volatile Organic Compounds], particulate matter, and carbon monoxide. There are heavy metals, but those are not criteria air pollutants. Those are toxins, so they're classified differently. About one hundred four thousand tons of these criteria air pollut-ants are emitted annually. Particulate matter, especially the very fine particulates, goes into the lungs. They have been associated with all kinds of lung disease: asthma, chronic obstructive pulmonary disease, emphysema. Particulate matter has also been associated with heart disease, particularly fibrillations and that kind of thing, or just heart failure. Sulfur dioxide is also just horrible for asthma and triggering all kinds of lung diseases. And of course, VOCs and nitrogen oxide are what form ozone when it gets up into the atmosphere, and every-body knows how horrible ozone is. Alcoa's pollution is the equivalent of over a million cars. That's one way that you can sort of get a handle on how bad that is.

We discovered this because of the mining and the water issues and trying to convince people that the right thing for them to do would be to not burn lignite because it was so dirty, and so we needed to understand how dirty it was when it was burned and what effects that would have. And as it turns out, Alcoa engages in some pretty bad habits, and their bad habits tend to include skirting around the law at times. The Clean Air Act has a piece to it called NSR, New Source Review, which was a way to allow older polluting facilities to have some time to come up to modern day pollution standards to reduce their emissions. Unfortunately, many of these companies, including Alcoa, took advan-tage of that.[2] The idea was that as long as they were operating as they had been and they didn't make any major enhancements to the facility, that all they were doing was just some routine maintenance to just keep it going, the older standards applied. They really expected that by attrition these old plants would shut down and when new ones were built they would be cleaner. Well, Alcoa claimed that they were doing rou-tine maintenance when in fact they were rebuilding their boilers. We have documentation from folks who were in management positions over there at the time who were quoted as saying, "We've done everything but build it new from the ground up," and, "We've replaced every-thing." They did in fact spend over sixty million dollars in the mid-1980s to pretty much rebuild all three of those units. They should have gone and gotten permits and installed the appropriate pollution controls at that time. They did not because they claimed that it was rou-tine maintenance. So that's what we found. We found all the documentation that supported the notion that they broke the law, the Clean Air Act, and that's when we filed our citizen's suit. . . .

Unfortunately, the deck is stacked. Everything is geared much more in favor of the industry than as a policing situation to protect the people, and that again goes back to politics. We were fortunate in that after we filed suit on December twenty-six, on January ninth of 2002 both the Texas Commission on Environmental Quality (TCEQ) and the EPA issued Notices of Violation to Alcoa for these exact same violations. And so it definitely gave us the credibility, which was really a good thing. Alcoa had all along been saying that we were just this little fly-by-night group, that we didn't really have any members to speak of, and essentially tried to say that we were lying about our base of sup-port. Suddenly they couldn't really say that anymore. They couldn't say that we were not credible, that we were a bunch of environmental "wackos" out here in the middle of nowhere just trying to go out and hug every tree, which was certainly not the case. We are by and large a group of farmers, ranchers, teachers, execu-tives, data processing folks, lawyers, doctors, scientists.[3] We're not at all the tie-dyed T-shirt types—not to say that I don't have a tie-dyed T-shirt—certainly I do. But we're not at all the kind of group that they were con-stantly trying to make us out to be. And in fact we've never considered ourselves an environmental group because, frankly, a lot of our farmers and ranchers are not environmentalists at all. And if they thought that we were going to team up with some group like the Sierra Club, they would just be appalled at this. But you know, when it's in your backyard, even when you've been against environmental issues, suddenly you become environmentalists. It's a very interesting dynamic, what has happened in the community as a result of this.

We were fortunate in that we were validated by government agencies even during a political time when normally, this probably would have never occurred. We went through months and months and months and months of depositions, discovery, going into court, having continuances. You know, the whole bureaucratic game that you play once you get into court. And once EPA and TCEQ came along behind us with support, suddenly Alcoa wanted to negotiate with them. Their attorney said it would be "a cold day in hell before they would sit across the table from Neighbors for Neighbors," and that we were not to be allowed in any discussions. And now to EPA's credit, not to TCEQ's credit, but to EPA's credit, they pushed very hard to have us included from the get-go. They didn't have much backbone in enforcing it from the get-go. They waited until they had an agreement in principal before they really put their foot down. And they came down here to meet with us and pretty much issued Alcoa an ultimatum that they would be at this meeting and they would talk to us and we would be included from that point forward. And we were.

So we have now a settlement that has been executed. Alcoa had to pay a civil penalty to the government of 1.5 million dollars, which is puny considering we've figured out that they probably profited by as much as seven hundred and fifty million dollars. But they also had to invest two and a half million in environmental mitigation projects. That directly affects the County of Bastrop, the County of Lee and the County of Milam. So that's a good thing. I think that it is reprehensible

that they were not penalized more because it certainly sends a message of, "Well, it's more profitable to break the law by far than to comply." I don't really think that's a message the government should be sending but that's definitely the message.[4]

1. In November 2008, Alcoa announced that it was closing its Rockdale aluminum smelter, on account of declining aluminum prices. Jeanne Williams. "Life After Alcoa: Rockdale Must Learn to Promote Itself," *Temple Daily News.* November 25, 2008. http://www.tdtnews.com/story/2008/11/25/53938 (accessed January 28, 2009). The power plants that drove the smelter will, however, turn to supplying electricity to the grid, and will continue to operate and discharge. Martha Boethel, phone conversation with the author, March 4, 2009.

2. New Source Review (NSR) is triggered when existing plants expand capacity or significantly modify their facilities, with the intention of bringing older plants gradually into compliance with current pollution rules and treatment technology. Some firms, however, have styled significant changes to their plants as "routine maintenance," thus skirting the NSR process. In the 1990s, the EPA took note that coal consumption at power plants had significantly increased since the late 1970s, yet virtually no power plants had applied for NSR permits. A subsequent investigation determined that 70 percent of coal-fired power plants were in violation of NSR. U.S. Environmental Protection Agency, "Coal Fired Power Plant Enforcement Initiative," www.epa.gov/compliance/resources/cases/civil/caa/coal/index.html (accessed January 28, 2009).

3. Ms Woods and Neighbors for Neighbors' opposition to the Alcoa operation was also based on the mine dewatering process of the firm, and its proposals to sell and export fifty-five thousand acre-feet of the drained groundwater to San Antonio and other users. Robert Glennon, *Water Follies: Groundwater Pumping and the Fate of America's Fresh Waters* (Washington, D.C.: Island Press, 2004), 94. Local landowners of various political stripes feared that private and municipal wells in the vicinity of the mine might go dry due to such large-scale pumpage and export.

4. See Mary Kelly. *Environmental Enforcement in Texas: A Review of Trends and Issues* (Austin: Alliance for a Clean Texas, 2003).

The Brazos and Water Pollution, the Gulf and Incineration

SHARRON STEWART is a coastal advocate and educator based in Lake Jackson, working as principal consultant for Quintana Environmental Services. On the federal level, she has served on the National Advisory Committee on Oceans and Atmosphere, the Coastal Management Advisory Committee, the Galveston Bay National Estuary Program and the EPA Gulf of Mexico Program. Her interests and advocacy on behalf of protecting the heavily industrialized coastline near her home combine grassroots and legislative work. The skills she has acquired in both fields came to the fore in her battle to prevent the incineration of hazardous wastes on ships in the Gulf of Mexico.

Interviewed on October 23, 2003, in Lake Jackson, Texas

Reel 2285; Time Code 00:01:57

As an environmental activist, air pollution was the first thing that interested me. After I moved here I realized that chemical companies were emitting things that did not smell very good and one of my daughters and I were quite sick as a result. But there was not much information, so I spent about a year and a half reading everything on the reading list of the American Association of University Women's "Beleaguered Earth Study Group" list. Then I got involved with a local organization involving labor unions. They had issues with Dow Chemical, the largest employer in the area, regarding labor issues, but they were also fighting over environmental issues. The first issue was the Brazos River, which, as you know, is red and muddy. But the lower reaches, from Lake Jackson through Freeport and on to the Gulf of Mexico, were bottle green. That was back in about 1970. And the union leaders had formed a separate organization called Citizen's Survival Committee. It was a terrible name, but they had four thousand members, which does make a difference. And they went to the Legislature and asked them to do something and to get someone down here and check out the lower Brazos

River. So the Legislature directed that such a study be done because State Senator Babe Schwartz was on the Senate Finance Committee and Neil Caldwell, our state representative, was on House Appropriations. A study did get completed by Texas Parks and Wildlife and the old Water Board, and it showed that the lower two miles of the Brazos River had flocculating solids on the bottom from glycol—which is antifreeze—and that there were no benthic organisms living there. This was the first attempt to look at anything "environmental" in this area.

As a result of that project, I also met Neil Caldwell and Babe Schwartz and became involved in working for their campaigns. The first time I heard Babe speak, it was on the first anniversary of Earth Day. He gave a speech at the Methodist Church by the Capitol to over a thousand people who were there on environmental issues. And he said, "You cannot beat the big guys with all their money, but you can make a difference." You do that by getting involved in people's campaigns and letting them know that you are involved, and that that really can mean a lot. Well, Babe had a very tough campaign at that time and I got involved. And the next thing I knew, he had me working in the Legislature as the first environmental aide. This was back in the early 1970s. He put me on the Senate Finance Committee and I learned another lesson. That lesson is: your budget *is* your policy statement. Doesn't matter what pretty words you write on policy, your policy is where you put the bucks. I learned that one well. Sissy Farenthold was in the Legislature at the time and my husband ran her campaign for governor. And so, when there was an environmental issue in the House, Sissy would come over and ask me to brief her. I loved it. I spent lots of time lobbying both Senate members and House members for what I thought were good environmental choices. We seldom won, but it's amazing how many times, even if people can't vote with you, they do things to help, or they will abstain and not vote against you. Doing that work for a couple of legislative sessions helped me gain contacts. For somebody in a small town down on the Texas coast, it was a good way of getting to know who the players were in Austin.

Reel 2286; Time Code 00:18:27

". . . It was the largest public hearing the EPA ever held."

The *Vulcanus I* was an old oil tanker that had been converted into an incineration ship.[1] And in the early seventies, they did a series of test burns off the Texas coast. It was the summer of 1974, because I had a SeaGrant fellowship and I was going over to Galveston every day of the week and taking courses in estuarine management and water quality testing. In fact, on Tuesdays and Thursdays, we went up the Houston Ship Channel and did the water quality testing for the state. But some of the people I was taking this special course with worked for EPA [Environmental Protection Agency], and they were called out to do the monitoring on the *Vulcanus.* And it never worked right. Incineration of hazardous waste is a very difficult thing to do on a stable platform. You put it on a rolling platform, which is what you have if you're on a ship offshore, and it's even more unstable.

In the 1980s, Waste Management Incorporated bought *Vulcanus I,* although it had never gotten a permit to burn in the United States. They had been burning naval waste in the South Pacific, where they didn't need a permit. And they commissioned *Vulcanus II,* which was built like *Vulcanus I,* only bigger. Now, they commissioned it with incineration technology that was out of date even then, and had never completed a successful burn. All their burns were compounded by what are called PICs, Products of Incomplete Combustion. And they did another series of burns, but unlike the first ones, which were off of Galveston and Brazoria County, these were down off of Brownsville. And a group of women in Brownsville got really upset about it and started organizing the local communities along with the group that's still down in the Valley that organizes through the churches, Valley Interfaith. Well, there was a hearing in the Rio Grande Valley and it was the largest public hearing the EPA ever held. They started at nine o'clock in the morning and it went on until almost mid-

Vulcanus II *incinerator ship (© Greenpeace/van der Veer)*

night. Over four thousand people attended and hundreds testified.

I testified right after the elected officials because the hearing examiner knew me from the studies I was participating in as a member of the National Advisory Committee on Oceans and Atmosphere. He wrongly assumed that I would be for the incinerator and had no idea I would be totally opposed. My testimony in opposition early in the proceedings really energized the crowd, and I became involved with the women from the Brownsville area in fighting against this. And it *was* fought, believe me, in Congress and in the EPA. At some point, they finally held a second hearing in Brownsville. They turned out another four thousand people and EPA lied about the numbers. It was really interesting. Jack Ravan, who was head of the EPA

Office of Water, convened a two-part seminar on regulations in Washington. And I wasn't at the first part; I was at the second part, which was for all of the interested parties, to draft the regulations. And somehow or other, I had acquired a set of the draft regulations the night before, and somehow or other, a whistle-blower at EPA just happened to walk into the seminar with copies of it. The Attorney General's Office from Louisiana and Texas, Greenpeace, the women from Brownsville and myself, we were all very organized. We literally destroyed that meeting. They made the press leave. There was a local Potomac news service video crew present, and they got thrown out. The next day, the women from Texas were meeting with Jack Ravan, and it suddenly dawned on me, we did this great takeover of the meeting and exposed that they had been lying, and there was no recording! They had one woman taking minutes and once all this fracas happened, she threw her hands up and didn't take minutes anymore. Ravan had been out of the country for our seminar, and so we met with him and told him what had happened. And no one inside EPA had told him what happened. Not one word.

It turns out that Steve Shatsall of the EPA was best of friends with one of the chief lawyer lobbyists for Chemwaste Management [Chemical Waste Management was a subsidiary of Waste Management, Inc.]. Shatsall was in charge of the EPA Ocean Incineration Program, and he was determined that there *was* going to be a program. And the women from Brownsville were determined that there *wasn't* going to be a program. One of those women was Deyaun Boudreaux, whose husband was a shrimper. I knew her from work I had done with shrimpers to save habitat. Other than union people around here, the only people who would ever help me were the shrimpers and they did so time and time again. Deyaun and I kept pushing EPA and pushing in Washington. And Jack Ravan came up with the idea for the creation of the Gulf of Mexico Program. He looked at the Great Lakes program; he looked at the Chesapeake Bay program and said we need something to address all these things happening in the Gulf. And he went back to Atlanta and took a job as EPA Regional Administrator there and pushed for the Gulf of Mexico program. Deyaun and I got letters of support from the governors of Texas and Louisiana, as well as Congressional agreement. Ravan already had the sup-port from EPA Region 4, because he was the administrator. He really did this just to get the program going, so there would be some way of addressing issues in a way that is non-regulatory, but involves all of the agencies, the public, industry, and the fishing interests, both commercial and recreational. In the end, the possibility of an incinerator burn site in the Gulf of Mexico was "de-listed" by the EPA and so those ships never operated here.

1. Ocean incineration dates to 1969 with the launching of the German ship, *Malthias I,* a modified chemical tanker. Following a 1973 EPA ban of ocean dumping, use of ocean incineration in the United States was first proposed in 1974. Shell Chemical requested permission to burn organochlorine wastes on the Dutch ship, *Vulcanus I,* 190 miles from shore in the Gulf of Mexico. Burns of eight shiploads, or thirty-two thousand metric tons in total, were conducted in December 1974 and January 1975, and again in 1977. Seven thousand metric tons of PCBs were burned onboard the *Vulcanus I* in late 1981 and summer of 1982. Tests of emissions, nearby waters, and sediments suggested minimal effects. In October 1983, EPA proposed issuing two, three-year special permits and one, six-month research permit to Chemical Waste Management to incinerate three hundred thousand metric tons of PCB wastes, and nine hundred metric tons of DDT-containing material. Public opposition to the permits grew quickly, culminating in a November 21, 1983 hearing before sixty-four hundred citizens, the largest to date of any EPA hearing. The EPA denied the permits in May 1984. In December 1985, the EPA announced tentative approval for a research permit for the *Vulcanus II* to burn seven hundred thousand gallons of fuel oil contaminated with 10–30 percent PCBs in the North Atlantic. In May 1986, and after opposition from the states of New Jersey and Maryland, and the National Oceanic and Atmospheric Administration, the EPA decided to deny these permits as well. D.G. Ackerman, J.F. McGaughey, D.E. Wagoner, *At-Sea Incineration of PCB-Containing Wastes Onboard the M/T Vulcanus,* EPA-600/S7–83–024 (Research Triangle Park, NC: U.S. Environmental Protection Agency, 1983), 2; United States Congress, Office of Technology Assessment, *Ocean Incineration: Its Role in Managing Hazardous Waste,* OTA-O313 (Washington, D.C.:U.S. Government Printing Office, 1986), 108, 179–83.

Cancer Alley and CAFOs, Toxics and Pathogens

REGGIE JAMES is a Navy veteran, attorney, and Director of the Southwest Regional Office of Consumers Union in Austin. He has worked on legislative and regulatory advocacy for improved public and environmental health and safety, and for better low-income legal representation. He has focused much of his effort on alleviating food safety problems, including reducing pesticide exposure, regulating confined animal feeding operations, and questioning genetically-engineered products. He has also been involved in standardizing and promoting organic food production as a safer alternative to conventional agriculture.

Interviewed on October 15, 2003, in Austin, Texas

Reel 0255; Time Code: 00:03:48

My parents are from Louisiana. My dad's from New Orleans, he's a city boy. My mother is from a rural area outside of Baton Rouge. I used to spend summers with my mother's parents, and they had a farm outside of Baton Rouge. There are a lot of bayous out there and I used to love it. It's like stepping into another century. . . . I mean, it's like a rain forest. It's very green; things grow there very readily. One incident in particular I remember from when I was probably about twelve or thirteen. I was spending the summer there, and I was pumping water from the well (they had well water) and I noticed that there was sort of a shimmering rainbow aspect to the water. And my grandmother said that that's because of all these chemical plants out here,[1] and that they're just messing up everybody's water. She was just convinced that it was bad. The water there had a natural sulfur smell, sort of a rotten egg smell, and that was the natural smell and you'd have to get used to it. But this was different, and she knew that it was different. She had an ongoing argument with the people that were the next generation, that would've been my parents' generation: they were all happy with the plants being there because they were providing some jobs, although a lot of the jobs were not that good. There were still a lot of vestiges of racism there so a lot of the people that had the good jobs typically weren't even from Louisiana, they were from somewhere else, and a lot of the menial labor were the African Americans in that general community.

Well, my grandmother's belief was that the piddly jobs these plants were providing were not worth what they were doing to all of our property. And at the same time, people were having problems with calves being born deformed, and she made the connection immediately. There were women having miscarriages, and my grandmother again made the connection immediately, she blamed everything on the plants. But nobody else did. I think most of the other people didn't think that there was a connection. Their thought was that this is modernization and they would have arguments: "Well, did you complain when they brought electricity out here? Did you complain when they brought the sewer lines out here?" And she answered, "No, those were good things . . . but this is not a good thing. We're not really getting anything out of all these plants being here." And I would listen to these arguments, and I was very strongly influenced by my grandmother and my grandfather who was a minister in that little community. And then fast forward to the time when the environmental justice movements started, probably about fourteen, fifteen years ago, and it was the same issue. And this area is really one of the easternmost extremities of cancer alley, which runs all the way through to Texas, and it's just strung with chemical plants, which have had next to no controls. And I remember my grandmother talking about how bad these plants were. And nobody cared about the farms that were there, about the people that were there.

His childhood interest in water quality, and his worries about the health and safety of farms and agriculture, be-

came part of Mr. James's career. In his work at Consumers Union, he has raised concerns about the environmental and human health impacts of confined animal feedlot operations, or CAFOs, which can be found in great number throughout the Texas Panhandle.

Reel 0256; Time Code 00:35:47

"It's a little late. We've already created all these new diseases."

The nature of the pathogens in large-scale food production has changed. And this is one where there are so many different things related to food safety that it just becomes dizzying. The one factor that seems to be the strongest is that if you increase the size of the operation, you're cramming a whole bunch of animals all together, then you're going to increase the pathogens that are associated with those animals. And in some respects, it makes perfect sense. If you had a mad scientist that wanted to create new diseases, the way you do it is, you'd get a whole bunch of the same species and cram them all together as closely as you can and they're going to pass all these germs back and forth.

Historically, we've had small operations, small cow operations, relatively small chicken operations, and we've always had some food-borne pathogens. These have been with us forever because a lot of these things are inherent to mammals. We've always had to cook our meat well, but what's different now is the nature of the pathogens. One of the things that they have to have in large-scale agricultural operations is the use of antibiotics. Because you cram all these animals together, you create much more stress on the animals, diseases start passing through, and they use antibiotics to control these diseases. Well, as it turns out, they don't just use antibiotics to control the diseases. They also use antibiotics to increase growth. Well, the down side of that is that if you take antibiotics, over time then you're going to start a selection process for the microorganisms that

Cattle feedlot (Courtesy Sharon Stewart)

naturally occur to be resistant to those antibiotics. It's a classic example of survival of the fittest. Only the ones that are immune or resistant to the antibiotic are going to survive and all the other ones are going to die. So over time, of course, you're going to continue selecting for bacteria that's resistant to whatever antibiotic you're using. We've wound up breeding all these different pathogens in these animal feeding operations that were resistant to the antibiotics that we have. So we've got all these new bugs that we've created in our food supply system and if a person contracts these diseases they're going to have to use a different antibiotic for it. Now, people pretty much understand this phenomenon, but it's a little late. We've already created all these new diseases.

So the antibiotics are one aspect of that, but the other one is just the population pressure. And some of these operations have just gotten ridiculous. You have millions of chickens in an operation, hundreds of thousands, tens of thousands of pigs and cows and especially with an animal like pigs that are a little biologically more similar to humans, you create some really dangerous situations. And if you start looking at some of the reports of food-borne illness,[2] it's bearing that out. We're getting more virulent strains of different pathogens[3] that are being bred in these operations and we're having a harder time dealing with them when people get sick because we've restricted the number of antibiotics that can be used to deal with them. It's not just restricted to the food supply. Something that we've been learning is that people in agricultural areas are now contracting some of these pathogens, just from being in the area, because of the background level of these bacteria (and almost all these bacteria that we find in animal guts are things that are naturally occurring in the soil, that were originally naturally occurring). What we've changed by introducing them into a large population, is that they're mutating, and the more virulent strains are the ones that seem to survive better, developing a resistance to the antibiotics. But these don't just stay in the animals. The animals defecate and the manure contains these pathogens, which are going back into the earth. They're either going in water, or they're being applied to land.

So we're introducing this whole new pathogen load that can have disastrous consequences for us and for other mammalian species, although some, like salmonella, affect birds and affect reptiles. Now add to that one more thing: for example, I get sick and I go to the hospital. We've got a new breeding ground for more virulent strains of pathogens in a hospital because of the rampant antibiotic use in the hospital. Bad hospital procedures occur where people are getting infections in hospitals, and they're typically getting more virulent strains of pathogens in that hospital for the same reason that we're getting more virulent strains in an animal factory. You've got a bunch of people in an area and you're using lots of antibiotics so you're selecting for resistant strains, and also resistance to other anti-microbials. We've got some strains of staph infection that we can't figure out how to kill right now. Those are not just staying in the hospital though. If I leave the hospital with that pathogen, I can spread that pathogen somewhere else and it makes its way into the ground, into the soil, and it can make its way into a cow. . . . starting the cycle all over again.

I think people are getting it now. There's a very strong movement and lots of people in the medical community that are trying to intervene at least in the use of antibiotics exacerbating this, but there doesn't seem to be any one entity that's grasping the entire picture and developing a plan to do something about it. This scares me far more than pesticides did, plus I think we're winning the pesticide battle. We're phasing out the worst pesticides, the practices are changing, public attitudes are changing, the industry is changing. With the food production and this whole cycle of making more virulent pathogens, I don't see us getting a handle on it.

1. These chemical plants are part of an industrial corridor of eighty-seven plants and refineries that produces about a quarter of the nation's petrochemicals. They run along a one hundred mile segment of the Mississippi River from Baton Rouge to New Orleans, familiarly known as "Cancer Alley." Epidemiological results are rough, but the region's rates for male lung cancer, female kidney cancer and rare childhood brain cancers are above expected levels. John McQuaid, "'Cancer Alley': Myth or Fact?," *The Times-Picayune*, May 23, 2000; Frederic T. Billings, "Cancer Corridors and Toxic Terrors—Is it Safe to Eat and Drink?, *American Clinical and Climatological Association* 116 (2005): 115–25; *Green*, DVD, directed by Laura Dunn (Austin, TX: Two Birds Films: 2000).

2. In 2003, there were twenty-one beef recalls in the United States for possible *E. coli* contamination, the most in five years, and the amount of beef involved, 33.4 million pounds, was the most ever. Kent Garber, "Beef Recall Latest in a Bad Year," *U.S. News and World Report,* February 20, 2008.

3. Food-borne pathogens, including salmonella, *E. coli,* and staphylococci, are increasingly showing antibiotic resistance. For instance, resistance in *Salmonella typhimurium* to the common broad-spectrum antibiotic, tetracycline, has risen from zero in 1948 to 98 percent fifty years later. Birkhäuser Basel, "Spread of Antibiotic Resistance with Food-Borne Pathogens," *Cellular and Molecular Life Sciences* 56, (1999): 755–63.

Sierra Blanca, Sludge, and Citizenship

SUSAN CURRY is a graphic manager and editor who lives in Alpine, and has been involved in various conservation efforts in that area, ranging from managing the Chinati Hot Springs to challenging various questionable projects proposed for West Texas, including the Entrada Al Pacifico road and the Sierra Blanca radioactive waste disposal site.

Interviewed on April 5, 2001, in Alpine, Texas

Reel 2156; Time Code 00:02:36

I grew up in Colorado and my dad was quite an outdoorsman. We spent a lot of time staying in my grandfather's cabin up in Buena Vista, Colorado and just learned to love being outdoors. As little children, my sister and brother and I ran around an awful lot; we just made fort and Indian encampments and just learned to really enjoy the beauty of nature.

We grew up in a suburb of Denver, called Westminster. If you look at a map, in one direction to the northwest you're going to find the Rocky Flats nuclear weapons plant,[1] and to the northeast you're going to find the Rocky Mountain Arsenal.[2] We were in an area that had wheat fields all around us. It *looked* pristine—although it was all very secretive—but later

in life, we've all learned that there are probably a lot of complications to a lot of people who lived in that area. As it is now, they're trying to figure out what to do with all the massive amounts of toxic waste that are in both of those locations. I'm not real sure exactly because it's all been confidential, what was going on in those areas. At the time, of course, we just played in the wheat fields. We didn't know that there might be contamination, but there were large releases that happened. I do remember reading about it in the newspapers as a teenager, it's just that they were far enough removed from us—they weren't in our immediate backyard. But, growing up in Colorado, I think there were a lot of people that are a bit concerned about what was going on in locations that they didn't know about.

As an adolescent, I did a lot of debate in high school. I just picked up a few elements of what was going on, learned about it there, and went off to college in Wisconsin. I started a family after getting married and continued in school with children under my arm. There was not a lot of time to take for the environment, for conservation issues at that time. And it really wasn't until we moved out to Alpine that I truly got involved with the environment and trying to protect it more. And it does happen that my introduction into the movement, so to speak, happened on my birthday. Hal Flanders came to us and said, "We're going to be going to Sierra Blanca to the public hearings, because they're thinking about putting a radioactive waste dump in Sierra Blanca." And so a group of us from Alpine went.

"We really are here! There are people living here and we are not expendable commodities."

It was about one hundred six degrees in a school gymnasium that was stifling, there were flies everywhere, and an unusual smell. When we asked about it, we realized it was because of the way the wind was blowing: We were actually smelling New York City sewage sludge that was being hauled to Sierra Blanca.[3] So, that didn't sit real well on my birthday. My birthday is August sixth, which is the anniversary of the atomic bombing of Hiroshima. I was born in Japan—my mother is Japanese, and my dad was a serviceman who was stationed in occupied Japan right after World War II. It started to bring home the importance of what that day meant and how insulting it was for our state to begin hearings where they were going to dump radioactive waste in a largely Hispanic community, where the people basically didn't have a voice, and even if they did have a voice, it would be spoken in a different language. It seemed to me that the legislators who were doing this did not care, and in fact, it was easier for them to get it done because of those obstacles. I just felt that there was an importance to all of the people out here in West Texas to get involved. My husband, Tom, and I talked

about it and we realized what a hardship it would be, because we didn't know how long the hearings would last, but we knew that they were going to go on for a while. And if one of us was to step in and say, "I want to be a party to these contested hearings," that it would take a lot of dedication and it would take time away from our own business. And yet we made the decision that "yes," we were going to do that. And I was the principal person I think mainly because of my tenacity and big mouth. I was the one that stepped to the plate and said, "I want to be a party in these hearings."

And that began a four-year period of learning an awful lot more than I wanted to about radioactive waste. And since getting involved in radioactive waste issues, I've also realized that the issue for West Texans and our environment is far greater than that one problem, that there are many problems that this area is inundated with mainly because of our lack of voice, our lack of ability to go to where the decisions are being made and say "We really are here!" There *are* people living here and we are not expendable commodities. Those issues beyond radioactive waste have to do with the very air we breathe and the water we drink. Those issues reach into a lot of areas: whether it's pollution from NAFTA [North American Free Trade Agreement] truck traffic or from

Sierra Blanca, Texas (Courtesy Alan Pogue, Texas Center for Documentary Photography)

the maquiladora factories on the border, or whether it's New York sludge that is being dumped. We need to work on all of those issues and to continue to let people know that "we are here."

Reel 2156; Time Code 00:46:21

All the issues are interrelated with each other, but keeping standards so that our health and safety and that of our children are not hurt is where the primary emphasis needs to be. And it may be that one week it is going to be stopping the Carbon One coal plant in Mexico, and we're going to have to put our emphasis on that; but it may be in the next month we're going to be having to deal with what the Legislature is going to do to us if they allow Department of Energy waste to come to West Texas. When you look at the big picture, you can see it as clean air, clean water; but on a day-to-day basis, it's individual issues that we're going to have to tackle on an individual basis.

This last summer I went and spoke at hearings, the first hearings on the effectiveness of the Texas Natural Resources and Conservation Commission. I actually went to visit my mother in Alabama, and I took my granddaughter with me on a road trip. We ended up in Austin and we met my husband Tom, and we stayed for the hearings. There were twenty hours of hearings, by the way, over a three-day period. And my granddaughter is eight years old. Throughout the first day of sitting there, she was actually reading *A Wrinkle in Time,* which I thought was very appropriate. She was sitting and listening to the politicos go on and on, and after the first day, she asked me "Ma, would it be okay if—would they let me speak?" And I said, "Let's sign you up." And so she did. She signed up and she walked around out in the hallway practicing what she had to say. I think there may have been two or three speakers after us, but we were there at the end of a very long third day, at ten-thirty at night and they finally called those of us from Brewster and Presidio County up to

speak. And there was Gary Oliver, Tom, my granddaughter, and I. She was the one that got written up in the national news because of what she said. Her statement was very simple, and basically she said, "You know, grownups put you here to be our leaders and our leaders should be here to listen to what the people say and do what the people ask them to do. And I know that when I grow up and I'm able to vote, I'm going to vote for people, for leaders, who actually listen to the people." She got an ovation and even the chair of that committee was actually clapping. And she did get a commendation from one of the senators who was at that hearing and a very nice letter stating how what she said made so much sense. And I think that that's what we need to do, to teach our children from a very young age that it is nobody's responsibility but their own to take care of what is happening. If we can teach them that their voices are important, but even more so when spoken collectively with other voices saying the same thing, then we can make change.[4] I think that's what we have to do.

1. The Rocky Flats plant was a nuclear weapons production facility in Denver run by Dow Chemical, Rockwell International, and EG&G, with oversight by the U.S. Atomic Energy Commission and the Department of Energy from 1952 to its closure in 1992. Following closure, efforts have been made to treat spills and plumes of plutonium, tritium, carbon tetrachloride, and beryllium. Plant lands have also been set aside as national wildlife refuges. Len Ackland, *Making a Real Killing: Rocky Flats and the Nuclear West* (Albuquerque: University of New Mexico Press, 2002), 3, 106, 138–40, 167, 172. Jeff Brown, "Nuclear Weapons Facility Dismantled, Decontaminated," *Civil Engineering* 76, no. 5 (2006): 32–33.

2. The Rocky Mountain Arsenal was created by the U.S. Army in 1942, and operated by the Julius Hyman, Shell Chemical, and Colorado Fuel and Iron companies on seventeen thousand acres outside of Denver as a site for the manufacture of chemical weapons, including mustard gas, white phosphorus, and napalm until 1969. Commercial pesticide production continued there until 1982. The site was used through 1985 for munitions destruction. In subsequent years, the site has undergone remediation for its contamination with pesticides, insecticides, solvents, heavy metals, asbestos, PCBs and chemical warfare agents. Parts of the site have since been protected as a national wildlife refuge, and also used for development. Stephen Gascoyne, "Slipcovering a Superfund Site," *Bulletin of the Atomic Scientist,* 49, no. 7 (1993): 33; Wikipedia contributors, "Rocky Mountain Arsenal." *Wikipedia,* http://en.wikipedia.org/wiki/Rocky_Mountain_Arsenal (accessed January

29, 2009). Kirk Johnson, "Weapons Moving Out, Wildlife Moving In," *New York Times,* April 19, 2004, 15.

3. Following publicity over floating debris, shellfish bed closures, and high pathogen levels along New York and New Jersey beaches, Congress passed the Ocean Dumping Ban Act of 1988. The Act prohibited disposal of sewage sludge and industrial wastes at sea after 1991. *Ocean Dumping Ban Act of 1988,* Public Law 100–688, *U.S. Statutes at Large* 102 (1988): 4153. As an alternative to ocean dumping, the City of New York pursued landfilling, awarding a six-year, 168 million dollar contract to the Merco firm for disposal of roughly a fifth of its sewage sludge. Stymied in its original plans for disposal in Oklahoma and Arizona, Merco turned to the Sierra Blanca site in West Texas. In 1992, weekly application of 250 tons of wet sludge to a 78,500-acre site at the Merco lands began; in 1997, disposal rates increased to four hundred tons per week. The disposal contract was terminated in 2001. *Peter Scalamandre & Sons v. Hugh B. Kaufman,* 5th Circuit Court of Appeals, 113 F.3d 556, No. 96–50253, (5th Cir. 1997).

4. An epilogue: the effort by the Curry family and others was indeed successful in blocking the proposal for a low-level nuclear waste repository in Hudspeth County. However, HB 1567/SB 824, passed by the Texas Legislature in 2003, has allowed for two privately-operated radioactive waste sites in Andrews County. One facility would accept as much as 2.3 million cubic feet of compact, low-level waste, and the second would accommodate up to twenty-six million cubic feet of Department of Energy nuclear weapons manufacturing waste from all fifty states. Ken Kramer, personal communication, December 3, 2008; Michael King, "Texas Wants Nuke Waste," *Austin Chronicle,* May 16, 2003. http://www.austinchronicle.com/gyrobase/Issue/story?oid=oid%3A159811 (accessed January 28, 2009); Lone Star Chapter of the Sierra Club, "Texas: Ground Zero for the Nation's Nuclear Power and Nuclear Weapons Waste?," *Sierra Club.* http://lonestar.sierraclub.org/radwaste/eis.asp (accessed January 28, 2009).

Farmstands
& Feedlots

"Bread without butter or coffee without milk is an awful calamity, as if everything before being put in our mouth must first be held under a cow."[1]

JOHN MUIR

EVERYTHING GROWS BIGGER in Texas! A Texas-sized boast? Perhaps. But when the fabled "Cattle Kingdom" once produced BIG JIM—a steer raised by Will Rogers and weighing in at thirty-one hundred pounds, even that cowboy sage might have been left speechless. And in the fabled "Winter Garden" growing region, the Texas-trademarked Rio Star grapefruit claims to be seven to ten times redder than the ordinary Ruby Red! Yes, the Texas cornucopia overflows with superlatives.

But what has this cost the land? The once verdant plains, the fields and prairies—many are now vanished; their fertility dissipated. Voices have arisen to address this crisis; a new breed of cattlemen seeks to mimic the natural grazing of the ancient buffalo herds while others work to mitigate the adverse consequences of industrialized agriculture. Today's Texas farmers are turning "tradition" on its head by embracing organic growing techniques. Bigger may no longer be their sole claim to fame, but rather *better*; better for the land and the people.

1. Linnie Margh Wolfe, ed., *John of the Mountains: The Unpublished Journals of John Muir*, (Madison: University of Wisconsin Press, 1938), 97.

Citrus, Chemicals, Soil, and Water

DENNIS HOLBROOK is a commercial-scale organic citrus grower based in Mission, Texas, within the Rio Grande Valley. He also has served as chairman of the board of the Texas Organic Farmers and Gardeners Association, and worked on the Organic Standards Advisory Board for the Texas Department of Agriculture. He has found that organic methods have drastically lowered his off-farm chemical costs, reduced his water use, restored soil tilth, produced safer, more nutritious products for his customers, and created a better price niche for his business.

Interviewed March 1, 2000, Mission, Texas

Reel 2093; Time Code 00:02:10

My family moved here in 1955. My father was a farmer from another area in the county and moved here and began farming citrus and some vegetables: a dry land farming operation, primarily. As a kid growing up, I had the opportunity to work on the farm from the time I was big enough to be of some use. I enjoyed being on the farm and being involved in agriculture. My father had a grove management company that managed citrus properties, our own citrus and for absentee owners, people who were investing in citrus who perhaps didn't live in

the area. We had a grove management company and a dry land farming operation. I grew up in the business, all through high school, then went off to college for a while, and then came back and went into business with my dad. I bought him out of the business in 1977.

". . . how to get off the chemical merry-go-round."

It wasn't until the early eighties that I began to really start to look at conventional growing methods and question whether we were going the right direction. I'll give you some background as to why I got to feeling that way. When I was a kid, probably eight, nine, or ten years old, the first job you have on the farm is to irrigate because it's a pretty simple, straightforward type of a job. And at that particular time, we weren't using any kind of chemical weed control in our orchards. They were all done under mechanical cultivation. So you would irrigate and then the weeds would sprout, and the grass and so forth, and then you would just disk them and till them back into the ground. That was probably during the early and maybe mid 1960s. By the time that the early 1980s came about, after I had bought the business, I began to notice changes in irrigation patterns. Back in the sixties, three to five yearly irrigations were pretty much the norm. Very seldom did you ever irrigate more than four times. It had to be a serious drought condition to go into five irrigations. But by the early eighties, we were up to eight to ten irrigations just to make a crop. It didn't really matter whether it was a drought condition or not.

I began to evaluate that. The cost factor alone got to be substantial. Your normal irrigation water allocation is usually only three to five irrigations a year. Once you exceed that, then you have to start buying additional allotments.[1] So the cost got more expensive, and I got to looking at that real seriously. I had a soil agronomist that I had conferred with. He had a soil lab here in the Valley for a number of years and he said, "Well, let me pull some samples that I had documented back in the early fifties and let's just do some comparisons to see what we find." The bottom line that came down was that because of the cultural practices that were used in the late forties and early fifties—where they were planting cover crops in the wintertime, such as clover and other things like that—they had built up a much higher organic matter content in the soil at that time. They were anywhere from two to three percent organic matter. Well, my analysis in 1981 showed the highest organic matter content of any of my orchards, which had been under chemical weed control for probably ten to fifteen years, was less than a half of a percent. And the lowest that I had was a point two-two-five [0.225 percent].

That began to tell me something about what we were doing: that by eliminating the competitive plant life, which happens when you use chemical weed control, you also eliminate the input of organic matter back into your soil. And there's a conversion that organic matter goes through by virtue of its decaying process that converts it from organic matter to humus. And humus in the soil is nothing more than microscopic sponges. They hold the water in suspension in the soil, and they're also a food source for the microbial activity in the soil—earthworms and so forth. We had found that we had depleted that to such a low level that we had shut down a lot of the natural life cycle in the soil by virtue of starving it out, not having enough there for it to feed on. So the next question for me was, once I determined the problem, was to how to get off the chemical merry-go-round.

Well, in December of 1983 we incurred a major

freeze, and that created the opportunity. I decided that I would take my own orchards organic, and also those of one of my tenant clients who would align himself with this way of thinking. I approached him, told him what I was thinking about doing, and he said, "You know, I trust you enough that I will go with you on that." So, in 1984, I created South Texas Organics. And we began to rehabilitate those orchards that were frozen by the freeze and replanted the trees that were killed by the freeze. And we started out with sixty-five acres of organic production. I kept very close tabs as to the costs of organic growing versus my conventional growing method, because I was still doing both. And the reason I was still doing both is because when you're in a grove management company, like any other type of management business, your client is only interested in the bottom line. Not knowing what organics were going to do, and what direction it would take us, I didn't feel comfortable in trying to sell anybody else on it before I could prove to myself that it was a viable way of producing citrus.

I started producing citrus organically in 1986. It took that many years after the '83 freeze before we actually had any commercial production available. In 1989 we incurred our second one hundred-year freeze, just six years apart. We had kept meticulous accounting records of production costs and yields, and by that point in time, I had determined which was the right direction to go. I just kind of laid it out on the table for the remainder of my customers and told them, "I'm going to go all organic. If you want to go with me to continue to manage your grove under that type of growing methods, I will be glad to do that. If not, I need to recommend some other companies and you can go your separate way." And after having two major freezes, six years apart, you don't have a whole lot of investors left. To give you an idea, in 1983, prior to the freeze, there was approximately seventy thousand acres of citrus in the Rio Grande Valley. Now, after going through the both freezes, having a lot of acreage bulldozed out, replanted and so forth, we have probably somewhere between twenty and twenty-five thousand acres remaining in citrus in the Valley. So you can see there's been a lot of people who have gotten out of the industry. The customers who felt like that they could go organic and still have a return in their investment, joined forces with me. The rest of them went with different companies.

Reel 2094; Time Code 00:05:41

"Organics are more mainstream everyday and will continue to be so."

I consider myself fortunate that I was inspired to look at organics as an alternative. It has been a struggle for the conventional growers over the years. They've had more lean years than they've had good years. And so I got into the organics by virtue of thinking that there had to be a better way. It was better for the environment, better for the long term viability of my land, and I would have something that, when I passed it on to my kids, would be healthy to work from. The organic industry, as far as agriculture, has probably been the only bright star for the last ten years. Since 1990, organic production dollar-volume sales have increased a minimum of twenty percent a year, for the last ten years. It was originally looked upon as a specialty market, you know, a niche. But I can honestly say that with passing time, as I've seen it go by, that organics are more mainstream everyday and will continue to be so. It offers the buying public a choice. And when there is as much concern as there is about what's being consumed, it's something that people pay more attention to and become more interested in. And I honestly believe, though it's not something that I can probably prove to you scientifically, but I've done this experiment with many different people: I can take an organically grown grapefruit or orange or piece of fruit and have them compare it to a conventional one, and there is somewhat of a taste difference. I consider the truck drivers to be the connoisseurs of produce. And the reason I say that is because

they don't go anywhere, to any packing shed, where they don't get given a little sample of what's being packaged. And I've had more truck drivers tell me on return trips that they were really glad they got my order here because I have the best tasting oranges and the best tasting grapefruit of any other packing shed in the Valley. And that's all subjective but that's what they're telling me. And I believe it.

1. Due to shortages, irrigation water may be costly, as much as sixty dollars per acre-foot. Melissa Jupe, and others, "Water Conservation and Water Pricing in the Lower Rio Grande Valley," Texas Cooperative Extension Service, Texas A&M University. http://farmassistance.tamu.edu/publications/Posters/Water%20Conservation%20and%20Water%20Pricing%20in%20the%20Lower%20Rio%20Grande%20Valley.pdf (accessed November 14, 2009). Or, purchases may be barred: irrigation districts in the Lower Rio Grande Valley typically restrict water rights transfers, unless they are required by a municipality. Andrew Sansom, Emily Armitano, Tom Wassenich, *Water in Texas: An Introduction* (Austin, Texas: University of Texas, 2008), 257. Or the water may simply be unavailable. Water shortfalls in the Rio Grande have grown acute, with the once-mighty 1,885 mile river actually failing to reach the Gulf of Mexico in 2002. Part of the problem is an arid climate (less than twenty inches of rain per year) and periodic drought, particularly serious in the lower Valley during 1995 and 1996. Another part of the problem is rapid population growth in Brownsville and Matamoros, Laredo and Nuevo Laredo, with Valley population doubling from 1.1 million to 2.2 million from 1970 to 2008. International political dynamics form still another problem: the 1944 Rio Grande Treaty requires Mexico to send 350 thousand acre-feet annually into the Rio Grande, in exchange for the release of 1.5 million acre-feet of Colorado River water by the United States to Mexico. However, at times, Mexico has fallen as much as 1.5 million acre-feet in arrears on their pledged water deliveries. Texas Natural Resources Conservation Commission, *2002 State of the Rio Grande and the Environment for the Border Region, TNRCC Strategic Plan, Fiscal Years 2003–7*, Vol. 3, (Austin: Texas Natural Resources Conservation Commission, 2002), 3; Jim Yardley, "Water Rights War Rages on Faltering Rio Grande," *New York Times*, April 19, 2002.

Panhandle Cotton, Dust Storms, and Hogs

JEANNE GRAMSTORFF is a farmer and banker in the north Panhandle town of Farnsworth, Texas, who has helped organize and operate the non-profit group, ACCORD (Active Citizens Concerned Over Resource Development). ACCORD has been seeking to improve operations among the region's confined animal feeding operations (CAFOs), chiefly hog facilities. Mrs. Gramstorff and other ACCORD members are concerned about wastewater runoff, aquifer contamination, nuisance-level odors, increased flies, and airborne diseases emanating from these facilities and the threat large facilities pose to many family-run, locally-based businesses. Finally, Mrs. Gramstorff and others within ACCORD are concerned about the erosion of due process rights under recently streamlined administrative procedures, which largely eliminated CAFO permit hearings.

Interviewed on October 5, 2002, in Farnsworth, Texas

Reel 2219; Time Code 00:02:15

"They wanted it to be loved."

I was born and grew up on a farm in Floyd County near Lubbock. My father was a cotton farmer and my mother grew broad-breasted bronze turkeys. They went through the Depression and the Dust Bowl and had some tough times. But they held in there and paid for that farm. And mother always had a great big garden and we always had chickens and hogs and cows. And so I was always active in some part of the fieldwork or the farm work. And I grew to love the farm as my family did. They took good care of the farm. They wanted it to be in good shape. When I finished high school I went to Texas Tech, and there I met the man who became my husband. He had come from Boston to Perryton because his aunt was a daughter of Judge Perry, and they didn't have any children, so they'd offered him the opportunity to come to Texas to farm. Living in Boston, he thought that sounded great, but he decided he needed to learn how to farm and so he went to Texas Tech. We met there and married and moved to Perryton. My family always cared about the land. And they wanted it to be taken care of. They wanted it to be loved. My dad was a real farmer. It wasn't that he was only trying to make money, this was what he really enjoyed doing. So we've always been a family of farmers. My husband Jack and I farmed up here since 1951 and enjoyed it and loved it.

"Once you've seen one of those dust storms, you don't want to see any more"

On my parent's farm, I can still remember when my dad had mules instead of a tractor. I remember when we got the first tractor. He was a row crop farmer and mostly raised cotton. Later on he did start to irrigate that cotton farm because it became pretty important to keep it going. He had several brothers who were farmers too and they were all very careful to take care of the farmland and to keep it from blowing. Once you've seen one of those dust storms, you don't want to see any more. I remember one Sunday afternoon we were coming home from my grandmother's in Matador and we got nearly home and it was so bad that we couldn't see. Dad couldn't see to drive the car anymore! We had to just stop. We were just totally engulfed in a sand storm and had to wait until the wind went down before we could go on home. We had a few like that up here during the early fifties when we had a drought and the dirt was blowing. See, the farmers up here at that time farmed by using a disk plow. When they did that they put all of the upturned "trash" plant life under the ground so that the dirt was just lying there on top. Well, when that wind starts blowing and it gets that dry, I can guarantee you're going to have a dirt storm. And I can remember a few even after we moved out here in 1956 that were absolutely horrible. The farmers finally got smart, or a little smarter anyway, and decided that they would use a sweep plow that left the plant life on top of the ground so that it held the dirt down.

Reel 2219; Time Code 00:17:46

Some years ago we had a neighbor in this area, western Ochiltree County, who decided that he would go with the Seaboard Corporation and put in two confined hog operations. In a confined hog operation the hog is always kept inside, never has his feet on the ground, never sees the real world, never does anything but turn around and eat and turn around and eat. That's all he can do. Sometimes he can't even turn around very well. This is the latest method of raising hogs in this part of the world. They grow about eight thousand hogs in each one of these two confined animal operations, which are small actually. We have one in Ochiltree County now that has three hundred twenty-five to three hundred fifty thousand. For each one of these hog operations, they have to have an enormous "lagoon" system. They call it a lagoon system but what it actually is a cesspool. All of the waste is piped out into this pool that is open and it causes a tremendous amount of odor, a lot of nitrates rise into the air. I have had more flies in around here than you can imagine because, of course, the flies go to these places. If they close down these operations and just leave those lagoons, then somebody has to go in and clean them out and fix them up after it's all been left. And that's what happens so often with these confined animal operations.

"The rules are just nonexistent."

I think these plants come to Texas because Texas said, "Oh, come on in, our regulations are so terribly weak."[1] They have said, "We want you, we want the business, we want the economic development." And the rules are just nonexistent. At one time, when ACCORD started in 1995, we had the right to a public hearing. We could appeal for a public hearing. They have since denied that.[2] You don't have any right for a public hearing; you don't have any right to appeal. We took them to court one time and won. The only problem was, we really lost. We didn't get anything out of it. It just cost us money. We won the case, and that was the end of that. It was in a district court in Texas. So that's the way life has gone for ACCORD members.

We started out as a group of neighbors because we were so very concerned. It has grown. When Nippon Pork came into Ochiltree County and started their Texas Farm, which consists of about five hundred thousand to seven hundred fifty thousand animals, we

"No Hog Factories" (Creative Commons)

had a lot of other people besides just us neighbors who wanted to join. We became a pretty good-sized operation. Then when Gray County had Premium Standard Farm coming in there, those folks called us and asked us what we were doing, and we told them, and they said, "Well, we want to start a group too." So they are a group of ACCORD.

There aren't too many small family hog operators up here, but there are a lot of farmers. What they're planning to do over in Hutchinson County is, where they have the center pivot irrigation farm operations, they are selling the corners of the lots off to Seaboard and they're going to build their hog operations on the corner of every farm. Well if you live close to one of those things, I can guarantee you are not going to like that because it doesn't smell very good. That was one of the reasons that there has been so much opposition. Probably as

much because of the odor as anything else, and there are lots of other reasons. I don't like the confined animal's situation. I think it's hideous to do that to an animal, what they do to the hogs. There have been some people around who've had hogs and chickens and of course a lot of people raise cattle and graze them on their farms. But we don't have very many sole hog operations except for these confined ones.

Reel 2219; Time Code 00:23:27

". . . I guarantee you that they accept more than my nose does!"

One year Rick Costa from Amarillo, who was with the state environmental agency—the Texas Natural Resources and Conservation Commission [TNRCC]—he came up with his monitoring system after we'd filed so many complaints. And he monitored around these hog operations and he actually found some places that were not acceptable. Now, I guarantee you that they accept more than my nose does! But they did allow that there are places, especially around Texas Farm Number 3 and Number 4, which have such huge numbers of hogs, that their operations were not in compliance. But nothing was ever done. Mr. Costa was with the TNRCC. And I think they asked him if he didn't want to leave.

I went down and testified before the Texas Natural Resources Committee. The Texas legislator Warren Chisum is the chair of that so I can tell you how much Warren Chisum was involved. He didn't really want to hear what I had to say. And when they got through with reviewing that at TNRCC, they actually made it *easier* for corporations to get the permits for the facilities and dismiss the odor complaints without anybody getting anything done. They think it's all about economic development, and since there aren't very many of us up here in the Panhandle anyway, we can't cast many votes. They think if they talk economic development, well, we'll go along with it.

1. CAFO rules in other states were tightening in the 1990s. For example, in 1997, North Carolina strengthened CAFO regulations (*Clean Water Responsibility and Environmentally Sound Policy Act* H. B. 515), followed by Mississippi in 1998 (S. B. 2895) and Georgia in 1999 (Georgia Board of Natural Resources, "Resolution Regarding Large Hog Producing Operations in Georgia," January 27, 1999). Legislators and agency officials in these states were becoming concerned that waste from these operations released hydrogen sulfide, ammonia, and methane, and that spills and infiltration from CAFO lagoons contaminated area waters with bacteria, viruses, and high nutrient loading.

2. In 1995, the Texas Natural Resources Conservation Commission (TNRCC) issued its Subchapter K rules, streamlining the permit process for animal facilities, and limiting the basis for contesting permit applications. Invalidated by court order, the TNRCC replaced the Subchapter K rules with Subchapter B rules in 1999, which critics continue to feel are too lax, particularly in tandem with monitoring efforts which they view as half-hearted. Consumer Union, *Animal Factories: Pollution and Health Threats to Rural Texas* (Austin, TX: Consumer Union, Southwest Regional Office, 2000), 14, 21. http://www.consumersunion.org/pdf/CAFOforweb.pdf (accessed November 14, 2009); D.H. Constance and A. Bonanno, "CAFO Controversy in the Texas Panhandle Region: The Environmental Crisis of Hog Production." *Culture and Agriculture* 21 (1999): 14–26.

Native Plants, Health, and Habitat

BENITO TREVINO lives on a ranch in Starr County, north of Rio Grande City, a part of a land grant that can be traced back in his family to Spanish times. He manages the Rancho Lomitas Native Plant Nursery, which has provided close to two hundred thousand native plant seedlings for habitat restoration at the Lower Rio Grande Valley National Wildlife Refuge, various Texas Nature Conservancy sanctuaries, and on private lands throughout south Texas. In addition, Mr. Trevino is well known as an expert in the biochemical makeup of native plants, and in their traditional uses, which he has shared with high school students, gardening groups, birders, and others through lectures and in tours of his ranch. His keen interest in the native plants of this region can be traced to his childhood experiences, when his informal education began at the hands of his elders.

Interviewed on March 1, 2000, in Rio Grande City, Texas

Reel 2095; Time Code 00:02:21

". . . I always had an interest in what was around us."

I came from a family of thirteen and even though there were so many of us and we lived in a two-room house, there was enough time for each one of us to develop our own interests apart from the whole. And I can think back when I was a youngster, five, six, seven years old, that I always had an interest in what was around us. We really didn't have any toys or bicycles, none of the typical things that somebody my age might have had in other areas. So I would be making observations on grasshoppers, or birds feeding, or looking at a plant bloom, those little things. In this area, conditions are pretty harsh. There really isn't much work. I come from a migrant worker family background and we would migrate all the time. And I'd spend almost a hundred percent of the working time in the fields and with plants. Somehow, associating with plants when I was trying to entertain myself and then when I was working, I started developing an interest in the plants themselves.

And I recall as a child that my mother would say, "Benito, your sister doesn't feel well, could you go to the river and get me the outer bark of a willow tree, and then on the way back get me the inner bark of a mesquite tree and then get me some cactus root?" I knew the plants that were all around us, so I would take one of my brothers or sisters and we would take a machete or an ax and we'd collect the ingredients and we would give them to her and then we'd go on our way. And this happened a lot throughout my childhood. When I became an adult I began to wonder what my mother was doing with all of these plants, because I knew all of the individual things I collected, but I really didn't understand what she was using them for. And later, at the University of Texas in Austin, I studied the morphology of plants, the nervous system, the transportation system, how plants transport minerals and such. And that was pretty fascinating but I couldn't make a connection with my childhood experience. But now I have the technical knowledge, and after graduating I returned and I spent a great deal of my adult life making those connections.

". . . How did she learn all these little things?"

What my mother was doing, even though she only went through eleventh grade in school, was like a Ph.D. chemist. She was taking salicylic acid from the *Salix nigra* or the river willow, and then she was taking the bark of the mesquite as a flavoring agent, and then she was taking the root of the cactus as a buffer. So she was making Bufferin, a buffered aspirin, from all of these things. And it became a fascinating question for me: how can my mother, way out there in the woods where she really doesn't read that many books, how did she learn all these little things? If we had hurt ourselves real bad, there were plants that she could use. Now, as an adult, I could do research and ask, what characteristics does that plant have that? Does it have an anti-inflammatory agent or what mechanisms does it use? And it's amazing to me to find out that maybe they learned by trial and error and the information kept on passing from generation to generation. There were very specific plants used for very specific ailments, and they all worked and it made sense. If you were to use that plant for a different ailment, it wouldn't work and it's just fascinating to me. Every opportunity I have to find a senior person, in their eighties or nineties that's still

around, I just try to extract that information from them because the knowledge itself, it's not there—even in all the research I've done. It's handed down and it has stayed that way.

Reel 2095; Time Code 00:29:38

". . . Can people today actually make a living without destroying the habitat that we have?"

It just boggles my mind how people could survive here. And they did for centuries. I find arrowheads here that have been dated to, you know, five thousand, six thousand, sixteen thousand years old. Obviously they lived and survived here. When my wife and I moved here, I knew I could make a living working in other fields. It doesn't bother me to be a janitor or to pump gasoline; I've done it before—I've had really bad jobs and I've had some good jobs. But I wanted to know: can people today actually make a living without destroying the habitat that we have? Because of my interest in plants, I started a small native plant nursery. And it was basically more for a research purpose than anything else. I really wasn't growing for sales. I was just kind of exploring the possibilities of what things can be marketed and how can we produce them. It's one thing to buy a tomato seed and mix the soil mix and put the seed in water and a tomato comes up. Well that's a tomato that's been under cultivation and worked on genetically for many, many generations. Native plants are extremely difficult to germinate. With some of them you could take a thousand seeds and plant them, you'd be lucky if you got fifty seedlings to come up! So when I first set up I was kind of exploring one of the possibilities of what I might be able to do to make a living right here without destroying anything. Just be part of the woods rather than destroying it. And I worked on that for about two years and I tried many different techniques of germinating different things and then finally I decided "I think I can do it. It might be hard at first, but I think I can find enough people that have interest in landscaping with native plants that are the best choice around." You have color, you have texture, and you have blooms for attracting birds and butterflies.

A problem today is that if a person gets married, they buy a new house, they have a nice little lot, they want to landscape it, they go to the nursery and they buy what the nursery offers. Mainly exotic plants, so that's what they use. And I figured that they needed to have an alternative, so when they go to the nursery, they have more choice. When they think about low maintenance, hardiness, along with color, maybe they'll start thinking, "Hey, I'm going to try native plants." And in my first two years I would grow and give plants away because I ran out of space. So whoever would come and say, "What is that?" I would say "Oh, that is a scarlet sage. God, it's got a beautiful red bloom. You want it? Take it, I need more space for the other stuff." It took about twelve years before things started to happen. And now I have trouble keeping up with demand for native plants. The demand has just skyrocketed.[1] Thankful to the Texas Nature Conservancy, Texas Parks and Wildlife, the Department of Interior, the Sierra Club, the Frontera Audubon Society, all those organizations that have pushed the use of native plants, have educated people, have had seminars where people are learning all the advantages that they have. They're starting to appreciate birds and they realize that if I plant lots of exotics in my yard, I'm not going to have the birds because birds are like people. It's like this: I recall going with my wife and in-laws to a restaurant and they would order shrimp and oysters and I would be thinking, what can I order to eat? I mean, those foods are foreign to me. I don't know how to eat it. I didn't develop the taste for it. Birds and animals are the same way: there might be plenty of food here in an exotic plant and they simply do not recognize it; they don't recognize the smell, they don't recognize the taste. So even though we might think, "I'll plant this plant and it's good food, it'll bring birds," it won't bring birds. They don't recognize the plant for nesting material. So if people are interested in

Scarlet sage (Courtesy Texas Parks and Wildlife Department)

the wildlife then they'll develop interest for the natives, and those interests have sky-rocketed.

1. The demand for native plants is coming from non-profit, private, and government groups that are involved in habitat restoration in the Valley and throughout South Texas. The restoration is driven by the loss of some 95 percent of the native Tamaulipan thornbrush scrub to agricultural development and urban sprawl in the lower Valley, by the interest in restoring habitat for deer, dove and quail hunting, and by the urge to protect the endangered ocelot and jaguarundi native to the border zone. For example, Environmental Defense, with the U.S. Fish and Wildlife Service and U.S. Department of Agriculture, is working to restore privately-held sorghum cropfields to ocelot habitat in Cameron County. Karen Chapman, Margaret McMillan, Linda Laack, "Texas Landowners Making New Homes for Rare Ocelots," *Environmental Defense Fund,* http://www.edf.org/article.cfm?contentID=5923 (accessed January 28, 2009). Meanwhile, the U.S. Fish and Wildlife Service is working on federal lands, such as the Lower Rio Grande Valley National Wildlife Refuge, where it has reforested some ten thousand acres within its eighty-five thousand acre boundaries, with species such as tepeguaje, palo blanco, anacua, tenaza, jaboncillo, and Vasey's adelia. Karen Fedor, "South Texas Eco-Wonderland," *American Forests,* http://www.americanforests.org/productsandpubs/magazine/archives/2004winter/feature2_1.php (accessed January 28, 2009).

Aphids, Ladybugs, and Compost

MALCOLM BECK began his career in sustainable agriculture as a family farmer in the 1950s, raising and selling organic produce near San Antonio, Texas. Later, he turned to helping others find alternatives to conventional agricultural methods and materials through his business, Garden-Ville. Garden-Ville mines bat guano, chips mulch, digests municipal sludge, and prepares compost for sale as non-chemical ways to build the organic matter content of soil. Mr. Beck has also been a prolific author explaining and promoting sustainable horticulture and agriculture, through his books, *Garden-Ville Method: Lessons in Nature, The Secret Life of Compost, Texas Organic Gardening, Texas Bug Book,* and other titles.

Interviewed on April 18, 2002, in San Antonio, Texas

Reel 2200; Time Code 00:02:02

"Those are good bugs!"

I grew up on a farm. Luckily I married a girl that grew up on a farm, so we both liked the outdoors. We got married in '57 and bought us a little farm out southeast of San Antonio. I wanted to be a modern farmer and I didn't want to do that old stuff like my grandpa and my dad did. So, I got myself a copy of the *Progressive Farmer* magazine. And in there was an article about the Colorado potato beetle and how it had migrated down into Texas and told about all the damage it was doing. So, I got to thinking, "I'd better go look at my garden and see if I got potato beetles." Sure enough, beetles all over my potato plants. So I went to the store and I got the recommended insecticide. I think it was malathion. The next morning I was out there dusting all these plants, when a buddy of mine walked up and said, "Beck, stop, you're killing lady bugs." I said, "Lady bugs? I thought these were tater bugs." He said, "No, those are good bugs!" Well, so what? I killed some good bugs. That was my only thought. But about ten days later, my potato plants didn't look good. When I looked close under the leaves, they were full of some type of little lice. I went into the house and I called this buddy and he said, "Yeah, those are aphids." He said, "The lady bugs are out there feeding on the aphid eggs, keeping them in check. You killed the good ladybugs, and they reproduce real slowly. The aphids reproduce about a generation per week. Now you're going to need more poisons."

Well, my feelings were a little hurt. I had a city boy telling a country boy something about nature. I asked him, "How do you know about good bugs and bad bugs?" He said, "Well, I've been reading a little magazine called *Organic Gardening and Farming.*" He gave me several copies of that magazine, and all through that magazine the editor, J. I. Rodale, was trying to sell a philosophy: if you planted adaptive plants in their proper season and the soil was balanced with minerals and enriched in organic matter, they grow naturally and you wouldn't need a bunch of chemicals to keep them propped up. Then I went back and I read through my *Progressive Farmer* magazine. Every page was advertising some chemical you needed to be a farmer. And I got to weighing these two philosophies and thinking surely nature wasn't designed so we'd have to use all these chemicals to grow the food we eat. Why can't we just work in harmony with nature and do it her way?

My wife and I decided that we were going to take our little farm all natural—organic—whatever you want to call it. And after a few years it was beautiful. We had this little place manicured. It was just a little eleven-acre place, and we started getting all types of publicity. People were calling us backwards, old-fashioned. Some even have called us hippies. I didn't smoke pot, so I guess I wasn't a hippie. Anyway, the Agricultural Extension Service agent came out and looked around, and this gentleman said, "Beck, this is beautiful. You sure you're not using any of our modern chemicals?" I said, "No, I'm being a purist here." He said, "Well, this is nice, but this is not practical on large acreage. We have to feed the world." Well, here was a new challenge. My wife and I decided to sell this farm and buy us a bigger farm. We moved out to here and said, "Boy, this place was worn out." I mean, it had been farmed to death for eighty-two years.

It so happened that Robert Rodale, the son of the man that published *Organic Gardening and Farming*, came down to visit me. In fact, I had a bunch of stories in his magazine, got on the front cover one time. Anyway, Robert Rodale was out here and I showed him around this old farm and I said, "Robert, this farm is so wore out Johnson grass won't even grow knee high in a good year. What can I do to build it up?" He stood there a minute and he looked around and he said, "Malcolm, your land is level. It hasn't washed away." He says, "It's clay, it hasn't leached away." He says, "It's alkaline." "Everything is just tied up." He said, "What you need in the soil is energy." I thought about that for a moment and I said, "Thank you. Now where does soil energy come from?" The energy comes from the sun and, and it's collected by the plant. So, the best adaptive

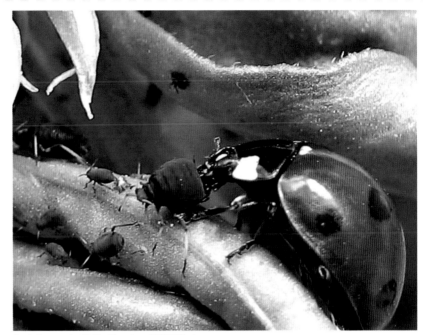
Lady bug and aphids (Courtesy Neil Kelley)

plants here were the weeds. So, I just let the weeds grow for two years and I kept mowing them off with a sickle bar mowing machine and pretty soon I had a thick mulch laying on top of the ground.

From then on, the soil started becoming alive. That was so simple, yet it costs so little. I pretty well stayed with that philosophy and we started truck farming out here with one hundred percent organically grown vegetables. We were selling them everywhere and people were coming out to the farm to buy our produce. I had two sons at that time and they were just learning to drive. I bought each of them a pickup and I let them go all over the neighborhood and gather up manure from all the farmers and the dairymen. Well, they worked like the devil just to get the chance to drive, and I was paying them two dollars. Pretty soon I had a big pile of manure out here, and whenever the crops were out, then the boys and I would haul it out into the field and we'd spread it out in the field.

Well, this one family was out here all the time. The son was in a lawn care business and he kept asking to buy some of my "compost"—they call that manure compost. They were such good people, so, I said, "Why don't I sell you a load?" He put sideboards on his pickup and we loaded about four yards worth. I didn't know what to charge him so he gave me forty dollars. Boy, I got to looking at that forty dollars and I said, "That was easy money. Why am I taking this manure out there to the field and planting—preparing a seedbed, cultivating, harvesting—and then taking the vegetables to the store and letting somebody else dictate the price? Why don't I just sell the manure?" Well, his mother then came along and wanted some of that manure or that compost mixed with sand. I did that for her and she paid me for it and then his uncle wanted some mixed with sand and topsoil. Well, word got around the landscape industry that you could go out to this farm and buy manure, topsoil and sand mix and here they came. They just flooded out here. Pretty soon I ran out of the old rotted manure and I was mixing it fresh.

I delivered to this one family that had a nursery. They were growing plants in big containers in their backyard. I was visiting with the lady that owned it and I looked over all of her shrubs in those big containers and I complimented her. I said, "Elaine, you sure do a good job of weeding. There are no weeds in any of your pots. In other nurseries I go around they have weeds in their pots." She says, "Oh Malcolm, your soil never has any weed seeds in it, ever." And I got to thinking about it. When you mix this raw manure with topsoil and sand, the fermenting and composting activity kills the weed seeds. Well, word got around in the neighborhood you could go out to this farm and buy weed-free topsoil sand and compost mix. And then somebody said, "Beck, why don't you handle railroad ties so we don't have to stop somewhere else." And another guy said, "Why don't you handle fertilizer?" There's another one wanting me to handle the tools, and after a few years I had a four million dollar a year business. All accidental. I never planned any of it and of course we didn't know anything about bookkeeping. I kept the money in a cigar box and then I'd take it to the bank. At the end of the year if there was money left and all the bills were paid, I made money. I mean it's pretty simple. At one point, I sold the business to a lady and they put it all on computers along with the bookkeeping and everything, but they couldn't make a go of it. Finally some old friends of mine bought into this company—they're a couple of country boys you might say from up in San Angelo—and they know how to run a business and we're going straight up. Anyway, that's kind of the history of Garden-Ville. It more or less accidentally happened.

Stewardship, Cooperatives, and Cotton

LARHEA PEPPER and her husband, Terry Pepper, farm 960 acres in dryland organic cotton near the Panhandle town of O'Donnell, Texas. As the third generation in a line of family farmers, her decision to farm organically follows a tradition that had been informally practiced by her predecessors.

Interviewed on October 12, 2002, in O'Donnell, Texas

Reel 2242; Time Code 00:07:27

"It's not our land. We're simply there as caretakers."

Part of why I'm involved in organic agriculture is based on my family legacy. As a child we still had some of that farm diversity: we had some chickens, dairy cows, and part of our land was in a crop rotation system. So, my family land has never used the synthetic chemicals or fertilizers because granddaddy felt like we're simply stewards of the land. It's not our land. We're simply here as caretakers. That concept and that philosophy and those stewardship principles were a huge part of our family. So even though granddaddy and daddy didn't necessarily preach that in a direct way, it was done indirectly.

I was the oldest grandchild on the farm, and I was sent to ride along with my granddaddy or dad, so I was with them a lot as a young child before I went to school, and even after school or in the summers. I remember driving by a place where a new farmer was putting up tanks for chemicals and starting to use the fertilizers and a lot of the synthetic chemicals that came along in the late fifties and early sixties. And there would just be comments from my father and grandfather like "they're poisoning their land," and "we don't do that, we're not going to do that, it's not respecting the land, it's not right." There were strong opinions in my family growing up as to what "stewardship" for the land meant.

As a young girl, I played in the dirt! When Daddy was plowing there's nothing better then running behind the tractor and smelling the dirt just so fresh and turned and alive with life and earthworms. You can smell it— the soil smells good and healthy. You know, on a lot of the conventional farms right now their land is almost played out. It's nothing more then a sponge, and they have to apply so many fertilizers and so many other things to the land in order to have any kind of soil fertility. Whereas our land is balanced and healthy and it still smells good and it feels good to walk in it. It's not like this hard pan of concrete. So part of my childhood is the legacy that was passed on from my father and my grandfather directly has to do with my respect for the land.

Mrs. Pepper has also been active in helping create the processing, distribution, and markets to support organic cotton farmers. In the early 1990s, she co-founded the Texas Organic Cotton Marketing Co-op, to ensure an adequate supply of raw fiber to the industry, and organized two firms to convert this fiber into finished products ready for sale: Cotton Plus and Organic Essentials. Cotton Plus exists to buy back ginned cotton and to contract spinning and weaving into prints, plaids, flannels and other fabrics. Organic Essentials sells organic cotton personal care products, such as cotton balls and swabs.

Reel 2242; Time Code 00:20:01

"Nobody called wanting a five hundred pound bale of cotton."

When my husband and I started farming in 1979, the reality of the economics of the farm really hit us. As a young family (we have two boys), we started looking at the future of the family farm, and came to the realization that it was not working. The inputs are going up, diesel costs more, labor costs more, and the price for the cotton is simply not there. So we looked at what we'd need to do to diversify. A lot of families "diversify" initially by having the wife get an off-farm job and in order to support the family on the farm. We looked at that, and over the years I've taught school and done different things, depending upon what the crop year was looking like. But that's not a long-term answer for what was going on at the "farm gate" level. We just did some serious talking, and in the back of my mind was the first degree that I have from college, in fashion design and textiles. And when my husband Terry and I were dating, that was before we decided to farm, I always had dreamt of something involving fabric and textiles. I've just always loved that. And then, Terry decided to farm with my granddaddy and I could not believe that I was moving back to the farm! It's a mixed blessing kind of thing. And I'm like, "Boy, this degree in fashion design's going to do me a whole lot of good in the middle of the cotton patch!"

But when we started looking at it, we realized that two things happened kind of at once. In 1990, the enabling legislation for certified organic products came into being and a lot of public and private certifying groups started developing standards for organics.[1] Those were words that had been floating around out there for a number of years, but there wasn't a set of standards or methods that you could use here and apply those to your land. The other thing that happened was we saw a need to diversify our farm base. Out here we get about seventeen inches of rain, and that's on a good year! So, we don't have a lot of cash crop alternatives. We've had three years of droughts right now, and we haven't averaged over about seven or eight inches of rain. This is a very tough climate in regards to rainfall, and there're just a limited number of crops that can grow in this area on a limited amount of rainfall. When we looked at diversifying, other cash crops didn't come to the top of the list. There just wasn't anything out there that you consistently grow on an annual basis in some kind of a crop rotation basis that could be the cash crop that cotton is for us.

The other thing that happened involved the organic standards. I found out that we needed to change a little bit of our farming dynamics as far as how we did crop rotation, and fill out a stack of paper about this deep to become certified organic farmers. And then, another whole dynamic opened up. It's one thing if you're a strawberry grower or a green bean grower. You can take your crop to a farm stand at the edge of your farm, or in town to a community farmers market, and you can sell your organic crop to the people that know you or who come by your farm stand. You can be an organic farmer, the customers trust you, and everything's great and wonderful. But no one, no one, wants to buy a five hundred pound bale of cotton! No one. People were calling us wanting organic cotton tee shirts or tote bags or sheets, all kinds of different things. Nobody called wanting a five hundred pound bale of cotton. The market simply wasn't there.

Cotton bolls and fields (Courtesy Martin LaBar/Flickr)

This situation presented us with both some opportunities and with some challenges. When we started looking into the fabric side of it, which is my love, we found out that the finishing mills required a four thousand yard minimum of fabric to make a production run. There were many different manufacturers interested in making jeans, tee shirts, tote bags, baby clothes, sheets and linens, but they didn't have or couldn't acquire enough organic cotton to meet the four thousand yard minimum for the manufacturing mills.

From a marketing standpoint, we expanded from just *growing* the cotton to getting involved in the product manufacturing process. From our 1991 crop that had been certified organic, we took some of our bales down to New Braunfels, Texas and had four thousand yards of denim fabric made, and that was just a riot. I remember Terry and I driving back thinking, "What have we done?" When we got home, I started calling back all those people who had previously expressed an interest in some organic fabric and I said, "I'm making some denim, and are you guys interested?" And they were! Well, three months later, by the time it got spun and woven and finished, we had four thousand yards of denim in our family room. And I had all that denim sold before it was delivered. So then we ordered another round of denim, added a chambray, a twill, a flannel, and now Cotton Plus has celebrated its tenth birthday.

We have about forty different fabrics in our inventory and we service between six and seven hundred accounts, so, people are interested. You've just got to get the product. Nobody wants the five hundred pound bale, but they certainly want all the different products that are available to be made from organic cotton. And from that came the formation of our farmer's cooperative, because it's so important when you're growing a market that you have stability and consistency and sup-

ply. Since it's really difficult for one farmer to do that, we had other farmers in our area who were interested to join. The co-op also celebrated its tenth birthday this year. We have thirty families involved. About ten thousand acres in our geographic area are organic, and about half of that is in cotton. So we've got a strong rotation program going, strong families, strong commitment, and that provides a stable foundation for the organic industry.

1. *Organic Food Production Act of 1990,* 7 U.S.C. sec. 6501.

Conventional and Sustainable Ranching

WALT DAVIS is a cattleman who operated a family ranch—the "country" as he refers to it—in the Red River valley north of Paris for many years. He came to believe that the kind of industrial agriculture that is widely taught today in land-grant colleges has been ecologically damaging and financially risky. He practiced a more conservative, low-input operation that used rotational grazing, high stock densities, and late calving seasons, as options to the more traditional methods of continuous grazing, chemical weed control, parasiticide use, and ammonia nitrogen fertilization. He found that both the soil microbes and the cattle have benefited, as well as his own pocketbook, from this alternative approach based on concepts of Holistic Resource Management.[1]

Interviewed on October 19, 2000, in Albany, Oklahoma

Reel 2115; Time Code 0:01:59

We came here from Nolan County in West Texas in the early 1950s, looking for grass and water, to escape the great drought. We started putting this country together and we made all of the mistakes that most people make when they change countries. We were under the impression that if we could ever get to somewhere it rained forty inches a year, that would solve all of our problems.

And I don't mind telling you we nearly went broke the first four or five years we were here, because we didn't know how to operate in this country. We couldn't understand how a cow could stand knee-deep in grass and starve to death. So, it entailed a learning process on our part. Here's a brief history of what we did: we made the transition from a range operation in West Texas with no hay, and a winter program of maybe a pound of cake a day for ninety days, to a country where we wound up literally farming for the cattle. We came here intending to produce year-round grazing, and we started clean-tilling wheat, over-seeding Bermuda grass, inter-planting various crops. And before we knew it, we were farming twelve hundred acres and losing money every year. We had an extremely high-tech operation. We produced a tremendous amount of beef. But we weren't making any money. Our production was very high but our costs were higher. We realized that we had to make a change if we were going to survive.

In 1974, we had a beef market crash that woke us up. But we also didn't like what was happening to our country: we didn't like the materials we were handling. At one time we were using at least one hundred pounds [per acre] of actual nitrogen on all of our country, and a high rate of herbicides. We were spraying for horn flies every twenty-eight days. We were worming everything with chemical wormers twice a year. There were tremendous inputs, tremendous technology use, tremendous production—but no profitability and definitely no sustainability. One of the things that happened about this time is that I got sick and went to the doctor here. He was no help and I wound up going to a clinic. And one of the doctors, after they had poked and prodded and looked, said, "What chemicals have you used in the last year?" I took his notepad off his desk and wrote down a list of fifteen or twenty chemicals that I'd handled in the last year. He looked at it, read it, and just pitched it back to me. He said, "I can't help you." Well it turned out that I wasn't chemically poisoned, I had brucellosis. We finally diagnosed the problem, and they treated it, and that was the end of it. But it started me thinking; here I was handling and asking my help to handle material that was very virulent. For instance, methyl parathion, which we used routinely, is so dangerous, that if you dip a matchstick in it, then touch it to the skin of the back of your hand, you're dead before they can help you. At the time I had three little girls, and my wife washing the clothes that I was bringing in from the field. We decided there has to be a better way.

"What we're doing basically is mimicking nature's method of grazing."

The first thing we did was to replace our nitrogen fertilizer with forage legumes. All plants have to have nitrogen to grow. But it doesn't have to come out of chemical feedstocks. We began to subdivide our paddocks and pastures, to have better control of what the animals were allowed to eat, and to get better utilization out of it. It was a long learning process. We started out thinking that four or five paddocks per herd was plenty. We know now that the minimum in this country is twenty to twenty-five paddocks per cow herd. Thirty to forty is better for a stocker herd. We began to get a handle on being able to control our animals, and thus control the land.

What we're doing basically is mimicking nature's method of grazing. All of the great grasslands of the world evolved in exactly the same way. They evolved in areas of erratic rainfall, under the influence of herding animals, whether it was the Pampas of Argentina,

the Plains of Africa, or the High Plains of Texas, large herds of grazing animals that were kept in a herd mode by predators. This was the secret that we hadn't understood for so long. There's absolutely no difference in the way a buffalo grazes and a cow grazes. They're both mass grazers that come out over the top, they take one bite, they take the second bite and if there's something left, they come back and take the third bite. But they graze in exactly the same way. The difference between what happened when the buffalo was grazing this country and what happened when the cows were grazing this country, is that the buffalo were kept in a compact mass by predators like wolves, so that the herd had to stay together. If the herd has to stay together, the herd has to go to graze where there is sufficient density and height of forage that all members of the herd can fill up with a reasonable expenditure of energy. Grazing is the "work" that grazing animals do. If they don't get a living wage for their work they die. So under nature's method, the herd goes to graze where the forage has recovered from the last grazing. They don't go to the area where it burned last week and it's only two inches tall, even though that tastes quite good to them. They don't go down in the creek where it's six feet tall and hasn't been grazed all year. They go where the forage is growing and is of high quality. It's exactly what we're trying to mimic now with fencing or with herding. That's the basis of what we're trying to do.

Reel 2116; Time Code 00:08:02

"There are no quick fixes in agriculture."

Agriculture is an extremely hard way to make a living today. It's one of the most rewarding careers that I can imagine—but it's almost like the priesthood now—because you'd better have a calling if you're going to do it. I would not even advise anyone, any young person, to take up a career in conventional agriculture. If you want to go out and farm in the manner that is "conventional"

Buffalo herd (Courtesy Amber MacPherson/Flickr)

today, then I'd say go get a job selling shoes. If you want to make the complete shift to sustainable agriculture, then I would encourage you to get with people who are trying to develop the knowledge base that's being developed at this time. We don't have all the answers yet, and part of the reason is that a lot of the knowledge that was common seventy and eighty and a hundred years ago has been lost. Some of the best information that I find is in books that were published literally eighty and one hundred years ago, when we didn't have the option to use a "quick fix" chemical solution. We didn't have the opportunity to get a bigger plow, a more potent herbicide. We had to work within nature's cycles. On the other hand, toxic agriculture uses all these materials that are poisonous. They're deleterious in any way that you want to look at them. But perhaps the most insidious thing about them is that they bring the mindset that says, "I can solve this problem by spraying. I can solve this problem by using this quick fix." There are no quick fixes in agriculture, when you're dealing with an extremely complex biological system. And when you impose an economic system on top of a complex biological system, then top that with a sociological system, the complexity reaches points you can hardly imagine. And every time we try to make a quick fix, we wind up creating more problems than we've solved.

I am convinced that the work that's going to save

American agriculture is not being done in the labs today with genetic modification of organisms, or with new chemistry techniques. It's being done on family farms and ranches all over the country where we are rediscovering the techniques that allowed our grandfathers and great-grandfathers to produce year after year on the same land without tremendous inputs. It can be done, but not with today's mindset. It all comes back to managing the water cycle of the land, the nutrient cycle of the land, the energy flow of the land. If we manage these three ecological blocks—water cycle, nutrient cycle, and mineral flow—then we will advance biological succession and we'll have a strong energy flow. The whole system will become more productive and more stable. If we shortchange any one of those, then biological succession will either stop or regress. I'm speaking primarily of holistic resource management and the sustainable agriculture movement.

I farmed this piece of ground for twelve or fifteen years with row crops. And putting this piece of ground back to grassland has given me as much pleasure as anything I ever did in my life. I'm constantly bombarded with people saying, "That's fine, you can do that. But I've got to pay the mortgage." I tell them, "We make our living on this land. So if it doesn't pay, we can't do it. It has to be profitable for us to do it." My family has been on this piece of ground since 1950. We were never consistently profitable until we began to make the changes toward what we're doing now.

1. The idea of Holistic Resource Management, HRM, is generally thought to have been brought to the United States by Stan Parsons and Allan Savory, natives of Zimbabwe. They have urged that agriculture and businesses integrate ecological, social, and economic concerns, and that lands be managed in a way that balances mineral, energy, and water cycles. In the case of grazing lands, HRM is particularly associated with the idea of intensive rotation, where cattle, sheep, goats, or other animals are brought into a pasture at high densities, but for short periods and with long intervening rests, to approximate the pressures of the wild, migratory herds with which grasslands evolved. Allan Savory and Jody Butterfield, *Holistic Management: A New Framework for Decision Making* (Washington, D.C.: Island Press, 1999), 222–23, 402–406; Allan Savory and Stan Parsons, "The Savory Grazing Method," *Rangelands* 2, (1980): 234–37.

Corn Kernels and Prairie Seeds

BILL NEIMAN is the founder and operator of Native American Seed, a business based in Junction, Texas that finds, propagates, harvests, and sells seed for a variety of native grasses, forbs, and other plants, as a tool for restoring ecosystems. In running his business, he has developed a number of essential reaping, planting, and cultivating tools and methods for working with native plants. His interest and skills find some of their origins in his early family life.

Interviewed on April 20, 2002, in Junction, Texas

Reel 0207; Time Code 00:01:53

I'm of the belief we're all kind of an accumulation of our experiences, and it's what makes every person unique, different. And so, of course, I have a long list of experiences that leads up to here and now. There's two or three things that stand out in my mind that might be noteworthy: I've always had an interest in land and water, as a kid we had a pretty spacious place to live and grow up even though we were on the edge of Dallas. And I had about a two or three hundred-year-old tree to play underneath in our backyard. The yard was kind of bare dirt, and I could build and sculpt and then add water and make little rivers and streams and little hills and mountains and lakes—and I learned a little bit about erosion and landscaping!

Also, I remember being a kid in Sunday school, and they'd give you this kernel of corn to sprout: you wrapped it in a paper towel and then you see if it sprouts, and then they'd put it in a little cup, and after weeks and weeks, you finally take it home and plant it. So I took mine home and planted it and it grew through the spring, and by the end of May, around my birthday, we had a birthday party. You know how rowdy a bunch of seven or eight year old boys playing around can get, and someone broke my corn stalk, and I cried. It was an important thing to me to have watched this thing start from a dry grain.

My dad was raised in a farm-type setting and had lots of rural connections, with family members in the Blacklands around Elgin and Taylor and Denison and Sherman and Terrell. His mom and dad had actually lost their farm in the Dustbowl Depression time

Blackland Prairie (Ed Nottingham, courtesy Texas Parks and Wildlife Department)

and moved into town and ended up doing like a lot of people did: got a job with a big giant corporation that would allegedly take care of their employees. He was quite a craftsman and an outdoors naturalist himself. I was taught to shoot, hunt, and fish real early, real early. The first time I ever went rabbit hunting in the wintertime with a double barrel, four-ten [.410] shotgun was on the north shores of Grapevine Lake, which is now Flower Mound, Texas. All these areas are now totally overgrown with urbanization. It's hard to bring my own son to a place like that now. I can't bring him to the places where I used to play and hunt and fish. Today, the words "*taking* something, hunting to *take,* fishing to *take*" have a different meaning to most people. But my dad was pretty savvy about this, and it's not like we

really *took,* as much as we came to be *in the hunt* or *in the fish.* We came to be part of the life that's out there, and to begin to appreciate their movements and their needs; to become part of their habitat. And we never took anything that we didn't use, and we never used more than we needed.

Mr. Neiman had owned and operated a conventional landscaping business until a drought in the late 1970s. He noticed both that the non-native species were unable to withstand the drought, and that the native plants had adapted, over thousands of years, to survive the cycles of drought and flood. Coupled with the realization that scarce and precious potable water was being used for ornamental irrigation, Mr. Neiman found himself redirecting his business towards the propagation of native plants and the restoration of prairies.

Reel 2207; Time Code 00:20:43

After this drought happened I came to the realization that we should be looking at native landscaping. That was in 1980. And it was exceedingly difficult to find a source of native plants to be able to offer. That got me onto a new path of discovering how to produce the native plants. And so we became one of the first nurseries in North Texas to pioneer into this area, and it was difficult and not particularly profitable, but we felt very rewarded by our work. And eventually we altogether removed every non-native plant from our nursery, starting with African Bermudagrass, Asian jasmine, Chinese holly, Indian hawthorn, Japanese boxwood, I mean the list[1] is all very familiar to you. This has more or less been forcibly spoon-fed to us, and for some reason, we accepted it without even questioning. But the time has come to make this change.

"Why don't we fix our own backyards?"

I continued ahead for a stretch of eighteen years in the landscape and nursery operations until I realized that I could cover so much more ground, instead of working with live potted plants, but by working with seeds. In the palm of my hand, I could hold an acre's worth of seeds. But it's very difficult to put an acre's worth of live plants into a diesel truck. So the power of seeds kept growing within my mind, of thinking about what more I could be doing. I started trying to find where would I get these seeds, and I came to the understanding that in my own home place, the upper Blackland Prairie, point zero-zero-four [0.004] remains, four thousandths of a percent. Do you know what that means? Take a dollar bill out of your pocket, go to the 7–11 store and cash it in for one hundred pennies. Take ninety-nine of them out to the parking lot and cast them away. Take the one

penny you have left and go to your garage, or of your granddad who might still have a hacksaw, and cut into one thousand slivers. Take nine hundred and ninety-six of those and throw them out in parking lot with the others. Those four slivers that remain are what we have left of our native prairie in Texas. This prairie once covered twelve million acres on some of the richest soil probably on this side of the planet—up to three hundred feet deep, with no rock. With thirty to thirty-five inches of rainfall a year, the grasses grew up to the head of a horse. This was only one hundred to a hundred and fifty years ago, and we have, in a blink of an eye, effectively "extincted" them down to this small percentage.

That's when I found that instead of cleaning up behind the bulldozers, it would be smarter to get in front of them. I shifted my work out of the nursery and went into the business of finding out where that four thousandths of a percent remains, and finding ways to encourage the seeds and gather them, always leaving enough for the other life forms that may also be depending on these seeds . . . yet encouraging other people to now take these seeds and help re-grow them.

I became intensely interested in whatever information I could find about the species of plants that belonged in these prairies. What was their connection to the big picture? How did the people before us treat these plants, or utilize them without destroying them? How did it come to be that in only a short "three grandmas back," there was a whole society living here, long before the white people got here. Some of the oldest bones found in North America, in fact, came from that same drought where the lakes started drying down and due to the wave erosion over years and years. In some of the lakes around the Dallas area, some old Indian encampments were washed out. In 1980, in Lake Lewisville, they found bones of humans that were ten thousand years old. Yet, America and the United States . . . we're only two hundred and something years old. It seems difficult to imagine: how could we possibly live here for ten thousand years, given the way that we're living now?

It's one of those things I see like the madness of the American people and their concern for saving the rainforest, and to the degree that it is now taught in schools, that we *must* save the rainforest, the lungs of the Earth. And yet you go to a school and you ask a young person, have you ever been to Brazil? Can't find anyone that would raise their hand. Do you know anyone from Brazil? No? Can you just tell me five trees that live in the rainforest, the names? No. How are you going to save the rainforest, when you live in Texas? Wouldn't it be smarter to take a look and see if we didn't have our own rainforests around here? And maybe it wasn't a forest, but in fact, a prairie. And could it be that in fact, there are many "lungs" on this Earth? When you find a piece of this tall grass prairie that is up to your chest of solid green leaf biomass, it becomes easy to believe that these prairies had the ability to make a lot of oxygen, and convert carbon from the atmosphere and release clean oxygen, just as much as a rainforest. Why don't we fix our own backyards? And if everybody was fixing their own backyard, I'll bet the Brazilians would probably have the rainforest fixed up.

1. The exotic plant species that Mr. Neiman mentions have come to the United States both by chance and intentionally. Bermudagrass is an example. It is likely that Bermudagrass first came to the United States from Africa in hay used as bedding for slaves brought to this country. During the 1940s, Dr. Glenn Burton of the U.S. Department of Agriculture in Tifton, Georgia developed and distributed new Bermudagrass crosses for golf, lawns, and pastures. David M. Kopec, "The History of Bermudagrass," *Cactus Clippings* IX, no. 1, (2003), http://turf.arizona.edu/ccps103.htm; David A. Burney, "Historical Perspectives on Human-Assisted Biological Invasions," *Evolutionary Anthropology,* 4, (2005): 216–21; George W. Cox, *Alien Species in North America and Hawaii* (Washington, D.C.: Island Press, 1999), 25–36, 127–42.

Pen & Press

"This business of writing books is a long, tiresome, endless job."[1]

JOHN MUIR

HIS PROTESTS NOTWITHSTANDING, the legacy of printed words left by Mr. Muir is now enlightening readers into a third century, and can well be called the cornerstone of the environmental journalism movement. As Mr. Muir later mused, " . . . I never dreamed of writing a word for publication, and since the beginning of literary work it has never seemed possible that much good to others could come of it." But of course, he was wrong.

The twentieth century was rife with stories—well told—that exposed the insults to the earth: from Upton Sinclair's Chicago slaughterhouses to Aldo Leopold's sand hills; from Rachel Carson's *Silent Spring*, to Edward Abbey's *Monkey Wrench Gang*. These printed words have done much more than open the hearts of people; they have incited, outraged, and led to genuine reforms in the way humans interact with their environment. Their spirit finds a home in Texas, too, where writers have forged the brittle and ephemeral medium of paper and ink into the sturdiest of tools.

1. Terry Gifford, *John Muir: His Life and Letters and Other Writings* (Seattle: Mountaineer Books, 1996), 885.

Laredo and Austin: Ranching and Reporting

MARIA 'MEG" GUERRA is an editor and publisher of the newspaper, *LareDos,* which covers a variety of issues throughout the Texas/Mexico borderlands. The newspaper has been a traditional chronicle of local cultural, business, athletic and day-to-day lifecycle events, as well as a witness to nearby and international environmental problems. Ms. Guerra's interest in the long-term vitality and sustainability of the area is also shown in her deep local roots, which date back to 1750, and her stake in a family ranch near Zapata.

Interviewed on March 2, 2000, in San Ygnacio, Texas

Reel 2097; Time Code 00:02:36

". . . they've been the music of my whole life: the sounds of wildlife, the sounds of cattle, the coyotes serenading at night."

I grew up in Laredo, Texas, thirty-six miles north of here. The family ranch, however, was always the backdrop for weekends, Easter, holidays, things we would do with our family out on the ranch. When I grew up, in the late forties and fifties, Laredo was about a third of the size that it is now. I think the population is about one hundred eighty-five thousand right now. And it was a very different place: it was a clean place. The river was clean, and it had movement. And, the river figured largely in our thoughts. We spent a lot of time in both cities, Laredo and Nuevo Laredo. Commerce was conducted on both sides of the border. Our ties, culturally, and in many ways, are with Mexico. The place never felt like two cities. It felt like one place. As far as the ranch goes, I think this is where most of the environmental lessons in our life had been learned, from grandmothers, uncles, people who ran the ranch . . . What else can I tell you about those experiences? The noises that you hear on this place, they've been the music of my whole life: the sounds of wildlife, the sounds of cattle, the coyotes serenading at night. The way the wind blows through here. The way the stars look; everything in its natural setting. All of those things just figure into who you are, and at some point, you have to become the person that is made up of these life experiences. . . .

As with many peers of her generation, Ms. Guerra's experience and attitude were deeply influenced by the cultural upheavals of the 1960s, which she witnessed when she traveled to Austin to attend college.

Reel 2097; Time Code 00:08:14

In the late sixties and early seventies, Austin was a hotbed of political change, and with that, environmental change. It was a time for learning, responding, and finding your conscience, both politically and environmentally. In school, a number of ideas that seemed radical then, aren't now. In fact, they make perfect sense now. Culturally, so many things were happening. With music, so many things were happening. Politically, of course, it was just nirvana. And with that came changes in how people thought about the environment, at least in my generation. Reading Rachel Carson, I think, was just a huge moment of introducing good thoughts and good ideas in how you went about having a voice in the environment. All of a sudden, just getting a conscience about the environment was one of those moments. Reading Rachel Carson was just such an important piece of education, even though it wasn't presented to me in a biology class, or anywhere like that. And it made perfect sense. You kept parts of it for yourself that you would apply the whole rest of your life, to things you felt strongly about. The thing that reinforced what I read in Rachel Carson was a huge fish kill in Austin. . . . I do remember the sight and the smell of fish just on

the banks of Town Lake [now Lady Bird Lake] and the river.[1]

When I was married, my husband and I had a plant nursery in Austin called the Jungle Store. We didn't spray with chemical pesticides, or use chemical fertilizers. Our pesticides were ladybugs and praying mantis, which really seems primitive, but it worked. And consequently, we had beautiful plants, really beautiful foliage plants. It was an indoor plant nursery. We were organic farmers and had a little place out in Buda. It was during the tail end of that whole back-to-the-earth revolution. And it *was* a revolution for anybody my age that lived through those years in Austin. It was a revolution— politically, and certainly, environmentally. It was the peak of the Vietnam War. Those were really important years to people that are my age, baby boomers that were born in the late forties. Those were really important years for figuring out what you believe in and what you think about.

Ms. Guerra returned to Laredo years later, and began her career in print journalism. Infused with the sense of justice and ethics fostered during her student years, her newspaper has been a thorough investigator of and witness to political corruption, social inequity, and environmental negligence along the border.

Reel 2097; Time Code 00:21:37

"That oil change you let leak onto the ground, you'll be drinking sooner or later."

Laredo is a city that just doesn't want to hear bad news. The bad news is that this city has allowed business to be conducted in a way that keeps bad things moving into the river, from industry, from ranchers, from farmers, from all the lawns in Nuevo Laredo and Laredo that are highly fertilized, highly doctored with pesticides. All that stuff ends up in the river. This whole area is a watershed of the Rio Grande River, and that is our sole source of drinking water. I think everyone needs to understand that gravity always prevails. Whatever you throw on the ground, that oil change you let leak onto the ground, you'll be drinking sooner or later. It's going to be in your water.

I publish a newspaper called *LareDos*. It's a seventy-two-page news journal. And we devote a lot of it to environmental issues. And I've learned, late in life, that by "educating" you can actually change things. In our case, we're trying to educate our public leaders, our city council members, decision makers in city administration whose work concerns the environment, water, and those kinds of things. And in my newspaper, sometimes we do it with a lot of decorum, and other times we just sort of slap them around a little bit. Because they don't seem to really get the idea that we need to do something about the environment. This is a city that should be acting as an example to its citizens with the practices it conducts, like using xeriscape for water conservation. Why are they still planting oak trees? They should be planting cenizos and mesquites and things that grow well here on the desert. By example, they should be showing the citizens of this town how you can have greenery at no cost to the environment, at no cost to your water source. They should be building buildings that are energy-efficient. This is the desert, for goodness sake! We should be operating in that fashion. We shouldn't be wasting water. We shouldn't be wasting resources. But, this is a city that is big on ceremony. It's not what we do; it's what we say, and how we say it. But that doesn't translate to action; to having a conscience about the environment. I served on a committee, the Citizens' Environmental Advisory Committee, which was appointed by the city council. I served on it for about a year. But it became so clear to me that this is not a city that's acting like it has environmental concerns . . . because progress must occur at any cost.[2] That's the mindset of governance in Laredo, Texas: "It's infrastructure first, more roads, more public stuff. The environment has always been there. It will always be there. What's the big deal?" It's just a lack of regard for keeping the balance between the environment and infrastructure.

Reel 2097; Time Code 00:51:05

You know, by Laredo standards, *LareDos* is just radical, I mean, just radical. And actually, I think we temper things. You have to temper things when you publish a newspaper. We publish pictures of filthy things that need to be addressed on both sides of the river. Now, the City of Laredo hates to be embarrassed. So, if you run pictures of degradation downtown, with a headline, "You call this revitalization?," they'll call me and say, "Ms. Guerra, we cleaned up the parking lot at such and such on Lincoln Street, we're working on the one on . . ." They're very responsive that way. But it takes embarrassment to move them along. There are some things they won't respond to at all. Certainly they won't tell Mexico, "Stop putting your raw sewage in the river." They haven't found the protocol to do that.

In the beginning, that honesty cost us dearly to do investigative pieces. My guess is that we did lose advertising revenues in the beginning. One of our targets, early on, was the school district. And, of course, they employ a lot of people and buy a lot of products locally. So we were compromised when we would try to sell ads. Some advertisers had already been called and told, "I don't think it's in your best interest to advertise in that rag,"—they did call us a rag and yellow journalism and all that stuff—which I found sort of offensive. But, I think what we've done for five years is sustain our credibility. And how you sustain your credibility, is that you just tell the truth. Every time: tell the truth. Don't write from any place other than a truthful place. Don't write for any motive other than telling the truth. And so I think that we've gained respect that way. And maybe people who don't agree with us "environmentally" still advertise with us. A lot of people call us and thank us and tell us things they would never tell us in person. But they tell us, "We're real happy you're doing this. Thank you for doing this. Thank you for caring." We get a lot of feedback, more positive than negative at this point. And I think people feel like they have the right to say, "Hell no, I won't advertise with you. I don't like what you do." But more and more we feel like there's more support in the community for what we do.

1. Rachel Carson reported that a January 1961 release of insecticide to Colorado River caused a massive fish kill: "for 140 miles downstream from the lake [Town Lake, now Lady Bird Lake in Austin] the kill of fish must have been almost complete, for when seines were used later in an effort to discover whether any fish had escaped they came up empty. Dead fish of twenty-seven species were observed, totaling about 1000 pounds to a mile of riverbank." Rachel Carson, *Silent Spring* (New York: Houghton Mifflin, 1962), 145–46.

2. Federal Reserve research echoes what Ms. Guerra has seen in the local business growth. The Rio Grande's lower Valley, stretching from Laredo to Brownsville, has indeed registered rapid economic growth, seeing 70 percent job growth, greatly outpacing rates in Texas (33 percent) and in the United States (20 percent), from 1990 to 2005. José Joaquín López. "Dynamic Growth in the Rio Grande Valley," *Southwest Economy* 2 (March/April 2006), http://www.dallasfed.org/research/swe/2006/swe0602c.html (accessed January 28, 2009).

School and Work,
People and Things

DANIEL QUINN is a philosopher and author based in Houston who has written a number of fictional and factual books about the interrelationships among the human species and the rest of the community of life. Perhaps his best known books are those in the *Ishmael* trilogy, including *Ishmael, My Ishmael,* and *The Story of B,* which involve a kind of parable of sustainability, a Socratic dialogue between a wise gorilla and a human student regarding humans' place and responsibilities on the planet. His early career with the "professional" education industry changed his attitude about what life skills young students, and society, need.

Interviewed October 20, 2003, in Houston, Texas

Reel 2269; Time Code 00:02:30

My career began so long ago that if you used the word "environmentalist," no one would have known what you were talking about. If you used the word "sustainable,"

no one would have known what you were referring to. It actually started not with an issue about the environment or conservation or anything like that, but about what we teach our children in school. In about 1961, I went to work for Science Research Associates, and we were putting out a mathematics program beginning with kindergarten, first grade, second grade, third grade, and so on. Now, we all remember what college was like. Some of us remember what high school was like, but very few of us remember what kindergarten, first grade, and second grade were like. So I basically went to school all over again, and I was very struck by what I saw, and struck by the strangeness of it. Strange to me, of course, wasn't necessarily strange to other people. And I began to think about why we send children to school and how school came to be in the shape that it is right now.

This led me to many other things. One of the great mysteries to me at the time was my awareness that children in aboriginal societies by the age of thirteen or fourteen are fully competent adults with survival skills of one hundred percent, whereas in our own more advanced society, children graduate from school on average at age eighteen with virtually zero basic survival skills. I thought this was very peculiar and began to wonder why it was that we dismiss the first three million years of human history as "of no interest and no value," as if there is nothing from that time period for us to learn. I found that unacceptable. I began to look into this question and looked back into human history, and began to see that much of what we learn and teach our children is false. And I thought I would be able to begin to infiltrate some new ideas into the curriculum, but I soon realized that that was impossible because the educational publishers serve the schools, and the schools tell them what to put out, period.

Mr. Quinn's works often reflect on the dominant human paradigm of people as "takers" of resources, beginning with the notion that agriculture's excessive production and storage of food have allowed human population to grow beyond sustainable levels, and at the expense of the other organisms with whom we share the earth. And yet, grim as this prognosis for civilization is, he also espouses the belief that people—often a single enlightened individual—can cause ripples of positive change throughout society.

Reel 2270; Time Code 00:17:14

"People with changed minds are needed everywhere, and they're needed in the worst places."

At one time a group of people—high level business consultants who were great admirers of my work—had an annual get-together and I was invited. After two days they finally said, "What you've got to do is start an organization and we can help you do that." And I let myself be talked into that, and the organization was a complete flop because I'm *not* an organizer. What I can do is to write and create materials, and so that's what I do. And when people ask me what they should do I say, "You've got to use whatever resources you have because there is no twelve-step program. Is everybody doing what they can do?" People with "changed minds" are needed

everywhere and they're needed in the worst places. There are people who write to me and say, "I think I'll go and live on a mountaintop." And I answer, "Now leave that mountaintop alone, and do what you're good at because that's where you're going to have the greatest impact."

I was doing a television interview and the young man said, "I work in the film industry and you may not be aware of it but, the film industry is really a terrible polluter and destroyer of natural resources. Every time they build a set they cut down trees and then the sets are all thrown away. It's tremendously wasteful." And I said that I didn't know that. His question was, "Should I be in this industry?" I answered, "Of course. Now you're in a position to do something about it, why leave? Don't leave it to the bad guys; we need people with changed minds in the industry."

One of the most important changes that I know stemmed from my work has been in the commercial carpet industry. Ray Anderson, head of the Interface Corporation, one of the biggest global makers of industrial commercial carpeting for airports, hospitals, and so on, read Paul Hawken's book *The Ecology of Commerce* and then my book *Ishmael.* After reading those two books he realized that while he'd always been in compliance with regulations, simply being in compliance with government regulations was not nearly enough. He really had to shift the entire focus of his company, and he made up his mind that as soon as he possibly could, he would cease producing petroleum-based carpet. He would go to natural fibers. Secondly, he would aim to produce as quickly as possible carpeting made from one hundred percent recycled materials that were one hundred percent recyclable. He also offered the "green lease" as it is called: Interface Carpet will keep your floors covered the way you want them, and when you are tired of this carpeting or it's worn out, they'll come and get it, take it up, and recycle it. One man changed the entire industry, because after his innovation, everybody else had to do the same because he was the leader. They had to compete with him. One mind made a tremendous difference. All of his suppliers, DuPont and others—they now had to start coming up with new ideas for him and that's how change happens.

It's always been my position that this is not about "giving up things." We are not rich people giving up things that we really want. It's not about that. It's about poor people, needy people, desperate people, getting more of the things that they need. In my lifetime I've seen the most amazing changes in the way we live. Growing up in the fifties despite the expectation that any day a hydrogen bomb was going to go off and start the Third World War, we thought there was a future, an unlimited future, and we were lighthearted. We felt good about it. We felt good about ourselves and we didn't go to school armed. I mean, the idea that someone would come in with a submachine gun and start shooting down their classmates: it would have been laughed at. The idea of drive-by shootings, of people

massacring their families, massive parts of the population in a state of depression, suicides going up all the time—it's becoming a nightmare here. And it's not because people don't have a widescreen television set. It is because they're not getting the things that they need as human beings. I've said that we have a heaven here, but it's a heaven for *products,* because every year the products get better and better and better and better. If you were a product, you would think life was beautiful! It's getting worse and worse and worse for *people,* and it needs to start getting better for people. I was reading an undergraduate thesis about my work and she said that I had progressed from talking about saving the world in *Ishmael* to saving people, saving the takers, in *Beyond Civilization,* the last of these four books. Why? Because if we don't save the people, we're going to lose the earth. We need to find a better way for people to live.

Rivers, Dams, and Stories

JOHN GRAVES is a farmer, rancher and celebrated author, known for his books, *Goodbye to a River, Hard Scrabble,* and other titles. His works explore the often contentious relationship among people's follies and dreams and the natural world.

Interviewed on October 16, 2000 in Glen Rose, Texas

Reel 2107; Time Code 00:02:07

I grew up in a standard, middle-class neighborhood in Fort Worth, but within a mile or so of where I lived, there was the Trinity West Fork river bottom, which was pretty much wilderness: it wasn't being used or anything. And we spent an awful lot of time down there hunting and fishing. My father came from a town in South Texas, called Cuero, where I had some relatives and they were hunters and fishermen, too. And every year we'd go down there for a matter of weeks or so. I spent some summers down there that were all oriented toward hunting and fishing, which is a good entry point.

I think Thoreau said that if he had a son he would teach him to hunt and fish because that was a good entry point for the study of nature.

I can remember pretty clearly the feel of some fishing trips that I took with one of the uncles down to Rockport. Those were the days before big motors and fancy boats and so on. And he had a five-horse Johnson. We'd carry it in the trunk of his car and he'd rent a wooden rowboat down there and we'd chug out to Oyster Reef and catch all the fish in the world. I mean, they were thick with reds [red drum], yeah.

Mr. Graves's early career as a writer started with sales of articles to magazines like *Holiday,* to which he would submit occasional stories. He returned home in 1956 when his father became ill, but took the opportunity to use his free time to explore anew the countryside along the Brazos River that he remembered from his childhood. This led to the inspiration for his first major book, *Goodbye to a River.*

Reel 2107; Time Code 00:10:35

One of my mainstays back in the 1950s or so had been the old *Holiday* magazine. They would throw me things to do or I'd have ideas and submit them and so on. I figured maybe they would publish an article about a float down that part of the Brazos. And it just went on from there. By the time I got through with the article, there was so much left over that the book just kind of started writing itself, you know. That was *Goodbye to a River.*

> *"I wanted just to get it down as it was and as I had known it."*

It has no real story. It's got the trip down the river and the camping spots and the food I ate, and that kind of thing. It's got the old pioneer history associated with the regions I was passing through and it's got a lot of natural history in terms of birds observed, fish caught, and ducks shot. It just kind of flows along like the river. It has another real story. Ostensibly, though, the reason for my taking the trip was that, at that time, there were five new dams being planned between Possum Kingdom and Whitney, which would have just made the river a series of stair-step lakes, you know, much like the Colorado from Lake Buchanan down through Austin and so on. Partly for that reason, I wanted just to get it down as it was and as I had known it, more or less. As it turned out, only one of those dams was built, which was the one up at Granbury, because the Federal agencies had started backing off from cost participation in dam projects by that time, and also the Brazos water was too salty for most uses. Granbury, for instance, is using Brazos water municipally but they have a desalinization plant to make it usable. They did build that one, which turned out to be used for cooling water for a couple of power plants, including the local nuclear plant.

I made that trip in 1957, and that was before the Texas Water Plan and all that started revving up. These dams on the Brazos at that time were a proposal by the Brazos River Authority, not the Federal agency; it was a state agency. The Federals came in later on that Texas Water Plan and laid out proposed reservoirs all over the place and a system for diverting the water from east to west and all that kind of thing.

I can't remember the exact dates the Texas Water Plan was introduced. I was working in Washington for (Interior Secretary) Stewart Udall on the Potomac River from 1965 to '68. I was writing the reports and stuff for that big Potomac effort. It petered out when Lyndon Johnson decided not to run for president again in '68, and also Vietnam was eating up all the money. But, I think in the years after, a lot of studies and recommendations were made from that. I worked with some awful good people up there. Particularly like the scientists in the U.S. Geological Survey. So, later on some of the things got accomplished. I don't think it was all wasted effort.

At any rate, I wouldn't say I was "steamed up" about it, but I was full of information and interest in water matters after that work. A fellow named John Mitchell, who was then head of Sierra Club Books, wrote me proposing that I write one of three articles in a book to be called *The Water Hustlers.* The other two articles were on New York and California. I did it, and it was probably the most political thing I've ever written. I haven't looked at it in years so I don't know how accurate it would look at this point. But that proposal, the Texas Water Plan, considered as a single proposal, would have diverted enormous quantities of East Texas water, not only along the canal on the coast, which is known as "Burley's Ditch" after the Corps of Engineers officer who had conceived it, but clear down to the Rio Grande Valley. They were proposing a pipeline to take some of that water, even Mississippi water, clear across Texas to the High Plains. It was wild. They had to include West Texas because West Texas has voting strength, you know. At any rate, it was so overblown that it got defeated at the polls, when they held a vote on it. Now, that may have been before I wrote that thing. I think maybe it was 1968 it got defeated. But, like all of the other Corps of Engineers and Federal dam proposals, they're still on the books and some of those things have been built, some of those reservoirs and so on have been built since that time and they never go away.

Reel 2107; Time Code 00:35:10

I have always been suspicious of polemics. I talk about writing as "written expression," not as propaganda or anything else. And, to the extent that polemical intentions take over what you're writing, and despite how fine the expression may be, they limit the duration of its appeal. I think Rachel Carson was a wonderful, wonderful, wonderful person and she did have a huge effect. She really did . . . almost single-handed she got rid of the chlorinated hydrocarbons. But I don't think many people read her for the "written expression" involved any more, because it was accomplished, what she set out to do. That's wonderful, that's great. It's simply not my bag. Now, I do have feelings about those things and they get into your writing inevitably. But it's like me saying a little bit ago that I like the engineers. I can't help that. I'm of two minds about them. I disapprove of many of their projects but I find them good functional people and rather worth being around and talking to.

You don't have to look very far to get gloomy about the environment these days. I mean, there are successes but a lot of them are just within this country, they never get as much going on elsewhere. And the absolute biggest thing as far as I'm concerned is overpopulation. It's the real ogre out there because it's not only overpopulation, but overpopulation by people who want to live the way the richest ones do, which is us. And if everybody in the world were living that way right now, there just wouldn't be anything left. And then there's the problem with the ozone. Most of those things, if they can be dealt with at all, will take a century and a half, two centuries to do anything really important about it. So, I'm somewhat a pessimist. I do enjoy life though, and I'm glad to be here! I'll say that. I'm not a gloomy person.

Facts, Opinions, and Cartoons

BEN SARGENT is a widely syndicated, Pulitzer-winning editorial cartoonist. During much of his career, he drew for the daily *Austin American-Statesman*, but previously worked as a political reporter covering the Texas Capitol for the *Corpus Christi Caller-Times*, the Long News Service and the UPI. His cartoons lampoon many of our foibles and failings, but return to the themes of greed, sloth, and shortsightedness as found in the public's and politicians' views and actions regarding air pollution, climate change, flooding, energy resources, population, water quality, mass transit, roads and development.

Interviewed on October 15, 2003, in Austin, Texas

Reel 2257; Time Code 00:02:12

I was sort of born into the newspaper business. Both of my parents were newspaper people up in the Texas Panhandle. I learned the printing trade from my dad when I was about twelve years old and didn't ever know there was any other business to go into. I got a journalism degree from the University of Texas and started out as a reporter, and did that for about five years and sort of fell into doing political cartooning. I had been drawing all my life, I guess, but I never really thought about doing it for a living until I found myself doing it. I have

had a lifelong interest in politics and it was also an interest of my parents and frequent topic of dinner table conversation. They were two things that sort of naturally gravitated together.

I was working as a reporter for the *Statesman* and began doing some little drawings on the side to illustrate feature stories. I left the *Statesman*, went to work down at the state capitol for UPI. But I kept doing the drawings for the *Statesman*, and after a couple of years they came back and asked if I wanted to come over and draw full time. I thought, "Well, I'm kind of a mediocre reporter. I'll give this a shot." And my career is still stalled at that point nearly thirty years later.

"We can say what we really think."

I think that my time as a reporter was invaluable in terms of having seen the beast from the inside—particularly the Texas Legislature and Texas politics and government. That gave me a journalist's take on things and a journalist's way of processing and organizing the information. It was very valuable, I think, to have come to this from the journalism side because to my mind, as political cartoonists, we're editorialist first and cartoonist second. After all, what we are about is making opinions, and what we're doing is as serious as the guys out in the next room who are writing editorials or columns. We're all doing opinion journalism, just in different media. The distinction is fairly simple between our part on the editorial page and the rest of the newspaper, or the rest of journalism. All of us in journalism are obligated to be fair, complete, accurate, and when you're on the news side, objective. Well, when you get over into the editorial page you're still obligated to be fair, complete, and accurate, but you don't have to worry about being objective anymore. On the editorial pages, we can take one side of an issue. We can say what we *really* think are the merits of some question of the day, and it's an exhilarating thing to be involved in. You are at the center of the public debate and you sling out a lot of heat and you take a lot of heat and there's always something new. You think after you've been doing opinion journalism for thirty years that things would start to sort of repeat themselves, but it's astonishing what people in public life can come up with that's new.

Reel 2257; Time Code 00:13:40

The language of cartoons is symbolism, and that's why to me, cartoons are sort of talking to the reader's uncon-

"Mike Leavitt arrives at the EPA" (Courtesy Ben Sargent)

scious. "The language of the unconscious is symbolism," as Professor Jung would tell you. I think cartoons have a particular ability to sort of reach the reader on a real inner level, where his basic feelings, fears, prejudices, and principles live. A given cartoon is really a system of symbols that are carrying across the message that you're trying to convey. If that symbol is a person—because people relate to people—and if you make it the president or the governor rather than just some sort of faceless entity—that gives it punch and is certainly useful in a democratic political system. It helps put responsibility back on those people for their policies if they are made the center and the symbol of the policy that's being carried out.

Reel 2257; Time Code 00:36:25

As one example of that, I did a cartoon when Mike Leavitt, then Governor of Utah, was nominated to replace Governor Christie Todd Whitman as head of the Environmental Protection Agency. It's a fairly simple cartoon, but you take a kind of strong image and hope that it conveys what you're trying to say. In the parking lot outside the EPA headquarters, it says, "EPA Parking Only" here. And then "Mike Leavitt, Administrator." And then to symbolize his approach to the environment I just put a giant bulldozer parking in his space, because his policies in Utah have certainly been geared toward seeing that development occurs first before protecting the environment.[1] Also, occasionally a cartoonist gets to revert to being like a ten-year-old boy and gets to do stuff like draw this bulldozer.

Another cartoon related to a local issue in Austin. It was fairly controversial, and had to do with Barton Springs, a spring-fed swimming pool that's been in Zilker Park for nearly a hundred years, and which the environmental interests in Austin are very anxious to keep clean, both so that people can swim in it, and because it's kind of symbolic like a canary in the coal mine of how good a job we're doing in taking care of the central Texas environment.[2] Our newspaper had a series of stories saying that they discovered the sediment at the bottom of the water had significant contamination, probably from nineteenth century industrial activity upstream. And this was the cartoon they ran on the first day that that story ran: it shows a swimmer here saying, "This can't be good." And then the lifeguard is in a protective moon suit with the breathing device and air tank. As the story developed it became increasingly complicated and involved the city, the state, and national environmental people. Everybody had a different opinion of what was contaminated and how greatly it was contaminated, and I think it still hasn't been straightened out. But that's what that cartoon related to.

"This can't be good!" (Courtesy Ben Sargent)

Reel 2257; Time Code 00:24:38

". . . Tomorrow it's going to be wrapping garbage!"

The process of getting ideas for cartoons is still a mysterious process to me after thirty years. I'm not exactly sure where they come from. I guess it's a matter of trying to stay aware of the events that are going on and kind of measure them against your opinions and see what you come up with. Coming up with opinions is not really hard, but trying to express those opinions in a graphic form is sometimes tough. Occasionally cartoon ideas will just leap into your head full-blown, but all too rarely, and usually it's more a situation where you're really having to sit there and scribble and kind of grind it out. It's a process of deciding, first, what issue you're going to deal with that day; secondly, what you want to say about it; and then third, and maybe the hardest part, finding an image that will carry that opinion in a strong, clear, and readily understandable way. You kind of turn your brain loose on it and see what associations it may call up. I usually work best with just a yellow legal pad and a pencil and just sketch around and try

to find an image that will carry across that opinion in a symbolic way.

An editorial cartoonist is really like the producer of a play. He's got a little stage there in his space. He's got to put scenery in there. He's got to people it with characters. He's got to write dialogue. He's got to make it all flow like a play would on a stage. Sometimes they'll start with an idea for a picture, an image. And sometimes they'll start with an idea for the words. And sometimes you've just got an idea of kind of what opinion you want to express.

And I guess it's unlike most businesses in that every day you have a whole fresh clean chance to do something, because if you do a brilliant Pulitzer Prize winning cartoon today, you know, tomorrow it's going to be wrapping garbage! And if you do a piece of crap today, then you know that tomorrow you'll have a fresh chance. It's an interesting rhythm of work, but you've got those five spaces to fill every week and you just keep moving on.

1. Leavitt was criticized for his role as Utah's governor, prior to his appointment as the EPA Administrator, in opening public lands to mineral development and road building, and generally seeking more local discretion over environmental matters. While governor, he had sued the Bureau of Land Management for rejecting drilling and mining permits on three million acres of scenic lands that the Clinton Administration had given interim wilderness status: in the suit's settlement, six million acres were opened to development, and precedent was set for reduced executive powers over these wilderness designations. Leavitt also signed a Memorandum of Understanding (MOU) with the Department of Interior widening exemptions to the Federal Land Policy and Management Act of 1976 (43 U.S.C sec. 1701 et seq.) and the 1872 Mining Law (30 U.S.C. sec. 21 et seq.), opening public lands to road development. Brett Beaulieu, Ashley Smith, and Emily Lehr, "President Nominates Utah Governor Leavitt for EPA Administrator," *American Geological Institute, Government Affairs Program,* http://www. agiweb.org/gap/legis108/epa_admin.html (accessed January 28, 2009).

2. Barton Springs are four springs that contribute some thirty million gallons per day to a three-acre pool in a dammed creekbed in central Austin. The springs are fed by outflow from the northeastern portion of the Edwards Aquifer, a karst aquifer that is very porous and susceptible to non-point source pollution on the land surface, including nutrients, bacteria, oils, and pesticides that have contaminated the pool, caused algal blooms, and threatened the endangered Barton Springs salamander. In that way, the springs and pool have become an impetus and benchmark for the protection of the southwestern outskirts of Austin. Turk Pipkin, ed., *Barton Springs Eternal* (Austin, TX: Softshoe Press, 1993); Austin. Barton Springs/Edwards Aquifer Conservation District, "Homepage," http://www.bseacd.org (accessed January 28, 2009); Scott Swearingen, *Environmental City* (Austin: University of Texas Press, in press).

Watchdogs & Watersheds

"THE ANIMAL KINGDOM." "The Plant World." "The Community of Life." Broadly geographical and all encompassing, these are powerful, if metaphorical, descriptions of our living world. In a more pragmatic way, humans have attempted to further refine *their* map of the world, breaking it down into such abstractions as *districts, zones,* and *subdivisions*.

But for all the lines and fences that may be superimposed over our lands and waters, the physical world does not always follow these man-made borders. Pollutants, in the form of plumes and vapors, regularly cross these boundaries. Habitats overlay and spread far beyond these artificial divisions. Animals, plants, and people in shared communities migrate and commute back and forth across many of these false frontiers.

And therein lies the source of much confusion and conflict. Who is responsible in this crazy quilt of jurisdictions and decision-makers? Where does the proverbial buck stop? Sometimes it stops where and when a private citizen speaks up. Here is a collection of advocates who have volunteered to campaign for the air, water, and open space in our shared "backyard," wherever the lot lines and fences may be.

"Most people are on the world, not in it—having no conscious sympathy or relationship to anything about them—undiffused, separate, and rigidly alone like marbles of polished stone, touching but separate."[1]

JOHN MUIR

1. Linnie Margh Wolfe, ed., *John of the Mountains: The Unpublished Journals of John Muir,* (Madison: University of Wisconsin Press, 1938), 320.

Volunteers, Gifts, and Communities

ANN HAMILTON lives in Houston, where she worked from 1991 through 2009 as a grant officer focusing on environmental programs for the Houston Endowment, the largest foundation in Texas. She has also served as a trustee for the Jacob W. and Terese Hershey Foundation, a Texas family foundation which supports land conservation, parks and open space, animal protection and human population initiatives. As well, she co-founded the Texas Environmental Grantmakers Group as an effort to explore and develop conservation funding opportunities and partnerships in the state.

Prior to her philanthropy work, she worked as executive director of the Park People, a non-profit advocating for increased open space protection in the Houston area, and as executive director of the Houston Parks Board, a vehicle for enabling public support and participation in the acquisitions and operations of the city's Parks and Recreation Department.

Interviewed on October 21, 2003 in Houston, Texas

"I felt like a modern-day Betsy Ross . . ."

Reel 2273; Time Code 00:05:03

I went to the University of Colorado in the early sixties—and there were many of us in Colorado at that point in time that were very involved in the "out-of-doors." We loved Colorado, we swam in the high mountain lakes and hiked and camped and drank beer in the woods and had a wonderful time and did a lot of laughing and just cared so much about the natural world because Colorado is so beautiful. And I got very involved, at one point, in Governor Lamm's campaign. He ran for office in the early seventies and he walked the state. And so there were a bunch of us that got behind him and he ran on an environmental platform. I guess that was a real turning point in my life as a young mother—I had married early and had a couple of children—and Governor Lamm was one of our heroes. And Earth Day was very important at that point in my life. I remember sitting on the banks of a bluff above my house on the first Earth Day. Dennis Hayes was there—in Colorado—running a solar energy organization. And

I sewed a green flag and flew that green flag for probably, I guess, a good ten years after that. Every Earth Day we'd fly the green flag and, of course, our neighbors wondered about that, but I felt like a modern day Betsy Ross, sewing a green flag.

Moving back to Houston to be near her family in 1985, Ms. Hamilton first took a job as the executive director of an open-space advocacy group for Houston. A year later, a position opened up for an executive director of the Houston Parks Board, for which she immediately applied.

Reel 2273; Time Code 00:25:01

When I told one of the Parks Board members that I was interviewing for the job, he looked at me and he said, "You'll never get that job. . . . You don't have the experience for that. You haven't been in Houston long enough, and you'll just never get that job." Well, that's what spurred me on to get that job. You have to challenge me like that and then I'm going to do what I have to do. I came up with some creative ways of interviewing for that job and interviewed a whole lot of the board members and ended up with that job for four years. It was an incredibly interesting job because it was very much like the job I had in Colorado. It's sort of public-private. It was connected to the government in that the board members were mayoral appointees who were not necessarily very interested in parks and open space. They were there because they had done something that the mayor wanted them to do and they got this plum of an appointment for it. I went and talked to every one of the people on the Parks Board and we started working on some campaigns and projects.

One of the first projects we did was a little park on the east end called Parkadalia Amistad, which is in Hidalgo Park. And we built a playground for the children of the east end with Robert Leathers. He's a wonderful man who is very creative and designs all his own playgrounds, and they're very distinctive: they're all wooden. He comes into the community and literally talks to the people in the community and goes into the schools and talks to the kids in the schools and asks them what they want. And in front of them, he then draws what they want. Well, this one had to do with cars and little castle-like houses and lots of little tunnels and little bridges that you could walk over and a teeter-totter. We built this playground on the east end, right out there at the Turning Basin. It overlooks Buffalo Bayou at the Turning Basin and we built it in five days with a team of volunteers. Hardest job I've ever done recruiting volunteers. It was really tough because this is a very, very poor neighborhood of Houston. Anyway, we got it done and that park is still there today and it's a wonderful, wonderful playground. And you can drive out there and see children playing on it and it was just a great exercise. And everybody's supposed to be involved in the actual construction, not just in the background. And one of the hardest things we had to do was to try and to get the women out of the kitchen, hammering, and the men into the kitchen, cleaning up. It was not easy; it's not a part of that culture. But we managed to do that and lots of people got out, hammered and nailed, and sawed and cut wood. It was just a wonderful, wonderful project.

"We ended up buying that seven hundred fifty acre park in the middle of, what they thought, was nowhere."

Then we bought a big park, a seven hundred fifty acre park out in Fort Bend County. At the time, we were criticized for that because it wasn't necessarily right in the city limits. It was in the ETJ, extraterritorial jurisdiction, of Houston. But some of our board members who were on the Land Acquisition Committee decided that that part of Houston really did need a park, a big park. And this piece of land became available. It had belonged to Doctor Cooley, then it ended up in bankruptcy and the Texas Commerce Bank owned it. We had some people on that Parks Board that were really very knowledgeable about land acquisition and they went after that piece of land and we got it. And thanks to the Brown Foundation, and a lady by the name of Nina Cullinan who had left us some money: we used some of her money for that. Several other foundations were involved and we ended up buying that seven hundred fifty acre park in the middle of, what they thought, was nowhere. It's out on Highway 6 now. Today it is surrounded by homes. Surrounded by homes! So the people out there now have a central park that they will always have, which is a huge piece of green space that wouldn't have happened had those Parks Board members not anticipated where the growth was going to happen. I was very proud of that project.

Reel 2273; Time Code 00:40:00

"We're beginning to see a new ethic . . ."

But why haven't we had park space? The ethic hasn't been there. We are a town of high diversity and it's a "can-do city" where we're going to do it, no matter what. And it's sort of a "transactional" city where we make a lot of money. And we haven't, up until the last four or five years, really cared about our quality of life.

And now, we're beginning to create a group of people, and I think that Mother Nature can take credit for it, of the young people that have moved into this city who have said they want a quality of life here so that we can raise our children to be healthy, contributing citizens. And the other issue is that a lot of young people aren't coming here. And I think the leaders of this community have seen that and said, "Wait a minute, we've got to do something about this." And so, I think we're beginning to see a new ethic of, not necessarily parks, but quality of life. We have beautiful amenities around the city of Houston. There's a lot to be attracted to here, if we can showcase them and if we let people know about them.

Hazardous Wastes and Volatile Reactions

PHYLLIS GLAZER ran a ranch in Winona, located about two hours east of Dallas. She became concerned about public health dangers from a hazardous waste recycling, blending and injection facility that had been constructed in the early 1980s near this low-income, African American community.[1] In 1992, she decided to start MOSES, Mothers Organized to Stop Environmental Sins. Following many complaints against the waste operation regarding releases, spills, upsets, fires and strong odors by the Winona community and MOSES, the facility was successfully shut down in the late 1990s. However, the experience left Ms. Glazer with a strong sense of the injustice and indifference that can mark government and industry in their dealings with poor and minority communities. She has carried on the efforts of MOSES to educate other disadvantaged communities, and to seek reforms in the state environmental agency, to make it more responsive and accountable.

Interviewed October 21, 2000, in Winona, Texas

Reel 2119; Time Code 00:20:30

"They say, 'There's nothing to worry about. It smells a little bit, but it's not going to hurt you.'"

Most of the people really just felt it smelled and they were very worried about their water, about water contamination. But you've got to understand that there are a lot of people here with very little education. And so it's very easy to believe government agencies and officials when they say, "There's nothing to worry about. It smells a little bit, but it's not going to hurt you." I remember the first time that I called the agency to ask them why there was a smell. They told me not to worry about it, that I was only "smelling solvents." Now, I have no education, but I said, "Do you know what solvents are?" I said, "Solvents are chemicals. Why wouldn't I have to worry? What kind of solvents?" Boy! There was a hush! I just heard a hush. And that was basically what was happening. I don't know if there were payoffs, which I have always suspected, I just don't know all that was involved. But there were very few officials with the Texas state agency that I believe were really on the up-and-up in trying to even do their jobs.

Sometimes they would tell us that *we* were the "nuisance," and not to bother them again: "Next time, just call the sheriff's department." Sometimes they'd really tell us off. They told off an elderly woman once, Mary Johnson. She was an asthmatic and the company was setting fires that burned our forests down. It's a long story but it was their "forest beautification project." They had put up a big sign and basically burned down the woods for miles all the way from the Interstate to Winona on both sides of the highway. And we would complain for months to the agency about this outdoor burning, day and night, where we had to actually turn our lights on to drive through here during the day. And the odors were unbelievable, they were chemical odors, it wasn't an odor of woods burning. So this old woman calls them up and said she needed help, she was an asthmatic and all that smoke was in her house. I still remember the man's name: Joe Burgess, of the Texas Natural Resources Conservation Commission, and he told her that she was the nuisance and not to bother him again. And she said, "Well, there's three fire engines out there right now and I think there's more on the way and everybody in town is trying to fight the blaze." And he said, "What?" And he hung up and she moved away. And there were other people that did the same.

We had a similar response from the health department: "The problems were all in our minds," "It was probably because of inbreeding in the community." And I want you to know that *new* people coming in would develop asthma or cancers. I knew a family that had moved here from Ireland that then had two sons born with birth defects, one of them has just died. Inbreeding? I mean, that's a racist remark. Of course it is. You know, the EPA [Environmental Protection Agency] is investigating Title 6 complaints, or environmental racism complaints, in communities with hazardous waste facilities.[2] And they just haven't found any yet. And I always say you have to look at the big picture. EPA tries to break it down and look at each case individually instead of looking at all of the cases together. There is not an affluent white community in this entire country that has children like Winona, but I can show you plenty of minority poor communities that have children like Winona: dead children, sick children, maimed children. So if you look at the big pic-

"Environmental Justice Now!" *Winona, Texas (Courtesy Tammy Cromer-Campbell)*

ture, I see racism. And I'm a white woman who had led a very sheltered life and was totally unaware that such a thing was going on in this country. I would have never believed it.

Reel 2120; Time Code 00:17:28

"We will defend our young against anything, anything."

Everybody knows about a mother bear. You never go near a baby cub if the mother is around! You never do, because a very peaceful bear that is an herbivore, that eats berries, will kill you. And humans are no different. We're an animal, and we will defend our young against anything, anything. A mother will try and save her child if a diesel truck or a locomotive was coming after her, she would try to save her child. And that's an instinct—that love, that instant love the moment you have that child. It's a gift. And I think that anyone who is that determined to do something can do it. I don't care who they are. I'm always talked about in industrial circles as having "used bad science" or not "being an expert." And if you look up the word science, it means "knowledge, especially through experience." Many of these scientists do not have their knowledge through experience. They have it through books. They haven't seen children like this. They haven't talked to people who have lived through a nightmare. They haven't even come here. In fact, many of the doctors involved in examining us would not come to Winona to do it. We had to go to other cities because anyone who knew what kinds of chemicals were being handled at the facility wouldn't come here to see us. And we had children to put to bed every night. We had children who were playing in the area and we couldn't defend them.

Mary Shelley wrote a book called *Frankenstein*. Frankenstein was not the name of the monster. The monster was never given a name. Frankenstein was the creator. The creator made a monster and abandoned it and the monster went wild. That's what happened in Winona. They unleashed a monster, would not claim him, abandoned it and left a community to fend for themselves. That's what happened here and no one came to our aid. Why did I come forward to do this? Because God put me here. How on God's earth could a Jewish, wealthy woman from Tucson, Arizona marry a Texan and come here to this God-forsaken place in the middle of nowhere, unless destiny brought me? So I knew that I had to do everything, everything humanly or inhumanly possible.

Reel 2119; Time Code 00:54:46

Some of the activism that we did was really new to all of us. I mean I had never been an activist, ever. One time we picketed the company's shareholders meeting and

we hired a very bright red crop duster to pull a banner that said, "Gibraltar pollutes, Mobley stock falls," which was true. Gibraltar Chemical was a division of Mobley Environmental Services. And we had the crop duster diving over the shareholders' meeting so that the whole building shook. It was a glorious day. May thirteenth, 1993. It was wonderful. And we found out that they had an ordinance in Kilgore, Texas that if you were going to picket you had to get a permit, which, of course, is unconstitutional. Our First Amendment right says we can assemble. So I went to try and get this permit and, of course, I was denied it. So I said, "Buckle your seatbelts, because we're coming." I remember that our law firm, which is a corporate law firm that did a lot of work for my husband, was trying to help me. And they were terrified. So, one of the owners of this huge firm was on standby all that night trying to talk me out of doing that protest. And we had about twenty people that were going to picket. All of them knew that it was very probable that we would be arrested. So those were twenty people ready to go to jail. But I had alerted the press and boy, the press was there. We had press from all over the state there. It was just incredible. And I heard that John Mobley, who was the owner of the facility, who was in the shareholders' meeting, was saying, "That damn plane," because the whole building was shaking. So it was just great. I told my lawyers to bail everybody out, but not me. I said, "Do you realize how bad I'll look after I've been in jail for a night?" I said, "Bring national press, I'm going to look pretty bad, so just leave me in there until I rot." But they never arrested us and I then sued the City of Kilgore for an unconstitutional ordinance and won.

Lawyers and courts cannot win a battle like this. My lawyers will tell you that what won was public opinion. What won was press. Our legislators hate press and I always say it's because it's a reflection of themselves. What they get from the press is what they are. All I know is that the press that has been involved with us has saved this community. The press has done that. So, I'm very grateful. I'll always be grateful to the press.

1. Founded in 1982 and based in Winona, Gibraltar Chemical Resources handled twenty-five million gallons of hazardous waste per year, blending chemicals for fuel in cement kilns, recycling solvents, and injecting liquid wastes in a mile-deep well. From 1982 to 1992, Texas agencies heard over one hundred complaints against Gibraltar and fined the company over ninety thousand dollars. In 1993, the Texas Natural Resources Conservation Commission shut Gibraltar's plant for several days to allow outside experts to improve the facility's operations. The publicity hurt business, with revenues dropping 40 percent. Will Nixon. "Texas Air Wars—Pollution Caused by Gibraltar Chemical Resources, Inc.," *E: The Environmental Magazine,* August 1994, http://findarticles.com/p/articles/mi_m1594/is_n4_v5/ai_15585566/ (accessed November 15, 2009). Gibraltar was bought in 1994 by American Ecology for a fifty-fifty share of cash and retirement of debt. In 1997, William Sanjour, the EPA Inspector General, advised EPA Administrator Carol Browner to close the Winona facility due to its poor record, and the plant was shuttered. William Sanjour to Carol Browner, EPA Administrator, May 8, 1997, Collected Papers of William Sanjour, http://pwp.lincs.net/sanjour/Winona.htm (accessed March 5, 2009); Skip Hollandsworth, "Phyllis Glazer" *Texas Monthly,* September 1997, 133; Tammy Cromer-Campbell, Roy Flukinger, and Phyllis Glazer, *Fruit of the Orchard: Environmental Justice in East Texas* (Denton, TX: University of North Texas Press, 2006), 2–4, 17–18.

2. A pattern of siting hazardous facilities in minority neighborhoods first gained wide public notice around opposition to a PCB landfill proposed in 1982 for an African American community in Warren County, North Carolina. Eldon Enger and Bradley Smith, *Environmental Science: A Study of Interrelationships,* 9th ed. (Boston: McGraw Hill, 2004), 28. Further research strengthened the concern. A 1983 federal study found that three out of every four landfills were located near predominantly minority communities. U.S. General Accounting Office, *Siting of Hazardous Waste Landfills and Their Correlation with Racial and Economic Status of Surrounding Communities,* GAO/RCED-83-168, (Washington, D.C.: General Accounting Office, 1983), 1, 4, App. I, 1, 3, 5, 7. http://archive.gao.gov/d48t13/121648.pdf (accessed November 15, 2009). In 1987, a report showed that the most significant factor in determining hazardous waste facility sites, nationwide, was race. The study also found that three out of every five African Americans and Hispanics lived in a community near unregulated toxic waste sites. United Church of Christ Commission on Racial Justice, *Toxic Waste and Race in the United States: A National Report on the Racial and Socioeconomic Characteristics of Communities with Hazardous Waste Sites* (New York: Public Access, 1987), xiii, xiv. http://www.ucc.org/about-us/archives/pdfs/toxwrace87.pdf (accessed November 15, 2009). In 1992, a report alleged EPA discrimination in enforcement, pointing out that federal fines were not as strict for industries operating in communities of color, that clean-ups of environmental disasters in these communities were slower than in wealthier, white communities and that standards for clean-up in communities of color were not as high. Marianne Lavelle, Marcia Coyle, and Claudia MacLachlan, "Unequal Protection: The Racial Divide in Environmental Law," *The National Law Journal* 21 (1994): S1. A 2007 report found that communities hosting hazardous waste facilities continue to be predominantly made up of the poor and people of color. Robert Bullard and others, *Toxic Wastes and Race at Twenty, 1987–2007* (Cleveland, OH: United Church of Christ, 2007), 49–83.

Pump Jacks, Waste Pits, and Birds

MIDGE ERSKINE lives in Midland, where she operated a well-known and respected wildlife rehabilitation facility for over twenty-five years. Through that work, she became aware in the mid-1970s of the damage to migratory birds from open oil and gas waste pits in the Trans-Pecos and elsewhere. From a decade's investigation with the U.S. Fish and Wildlife Service, it has been estimated that two million birds were killed annually by oilfield wastewater at drill sites in sixteen states owned or operated by over thirty companies. While these losses are easily and cheaply avoided, with nets and frames across waste pits, or by storing the waste in sealed tanks, she found that there was great resistance from the oil companies, as well as from the Texas Railroad Commission, which has regulatory jurisdiction over the oil industry. Frustrated by the lack of openness and cooperation, Mrs. Erskine has gone on to track and publicize municipal government's work in her hometown of Midland, to make sure that permits and payments in environmental and other programs are issued in a responsible, accountable way.

Interviewed on March 27, 2001, in Midland, Texas

Reel 2133; Time Code 00:28:32

"Almost all bones, millions and millions of birds in there. Exactly like the La Brea tar pits."

One year we decided we were going to get away and go hiking. We drove out to an area near Andrews, Texas where we hadn't been because we wanted to look at a certain formation that was out there. We happened to hear the sandhill cranes, looked up, and there was a whooping crane with them. We followed the whooping crane and it went to another lake, Lake Wayland, where the oil companies were dumping oil into this lake—what they call the BS or bottom sediment—out of the tanks, which contained oil and salt water. And that's how I first got started in the oil situation and the birds.

There were dead birds and there was oil all over much of the lake. What happens is that the birds can't tell the difference between oil and water and they would come down and land. One night there was a whole flock, seven or eight hundred ducks that had landed on this lake. and the oil slick moved over them and that was end of the ducks. If it's in the wintertime, and there's a lot of oil, the birds get hypothermia and they die. If it's just a small amount of oil and they're a nesting bird, that oil gets on the egg and the egg doesn't hatch. Just one drop of oil on an egg is enough to kill the egg. There's a lot of ramifications of this: just among the ducks' population, we were losing over a million ducks here in West Texas a year because of the oil field. At one time, every oil pump jack had a pit next to it. The birds would see this, and because we're desert, or semi-desert area, the birds would think this was water and they would come down to that. The federal game warden, Rob Lee, and I went down to a big pit by Rankin (I had been down there two or three days before with a reporter) and there were something like fifteen great blue herons just dead on top of this big pit. So I called Rob Lee, and when he got into town, we went down there and it was hot as hell. The oil was so hot that it would just burn your hands. The oil company had come in and cleaned

out one of the pits, and there was a high pile and it was almost all bones, millions and millions of birds in there. Exactly like the La Brea tar pits.

Birds have an air space between their feathers, which they can "fluff" or not, and that acts as the insulation that keeps a bird cool or warm. And it won't work if their feathers are oiled: they can't fluff or preen. Sometimes the bird would just be a black glob of oil. I was going to a Railroad Commission hearing when all this was happening and I was taking some of these oiled ducks with me.[1] They had been frozen in the freezer and I had them in a carry-on, one of these little carry-on canvas bags with ice stuffed in there, frozen bottles of ice. I was going through the airport and when it went through their x-ray machine, the lady looked at me, looked back in the machine, looked at me and looked back in there, and never said a word. I never said a

Permian Basin oil field (Courtesy Center for Land Use Interpretation)

word and we went on through. But it was a horror story out here and nobody wanted to do anything about it.

It took twelve years before we got anything really done. The Texas Parks and Wildlife really couldn't do anything because of the politics here in Texas. We had to get U.S. Fish and Wildlife involved, and they sent an agent. But then studies had to be done and one of the people that worked for the Bureau of Land Management in New Mexico started a study there. We were doing studies here in West Texas, and once it showed that this was a great killing area for birds, U.S. Fish and Wildlife could then say, "you're illegally taking birds under the Migratory Treaty Act."[2] So they gave the oil companies like a year and a half to go ahead and get netting put over the tanks and the pits, or get rid of the pits.

That was already in the 'eighties. I think it was '76 when I first started on that. I got nowhere at first, and then I was able finally to get Defenders of Wildlife to send a reporter out here, and they did a big article showing the oiled birds and the lakes. That got some attention in Washington. A year later, they followed up with another story and when that happened, then U.S. Fish and Wildlife and EPA—everybody—had to step in to do something because they were knowingly allowing contamination in the lakes and in the waters like the Colorado River and the Pecos River. These rivers were being heavily contaminated because oil companies were literally dumping into the rivers. And the [Texas] Railroad Commission wouldn't do anything. The Upper Colorado River Authority ignored the whole problem.

It just took time. But we lost all our friends here in Midland because I was bucking the big oil companies, and everybody here worked for the oil companies. So we just lost all our friends, had to make new friends. A lot of the oil field people would bring me the birds that they'd find out there. And I could never say anything about it, because it was their job at stake, so we'd have to protect them or they would lose their jobs.

We lost all our friends because they knew I was so actively working on this. And once Defenders did their articles, then we got other articles—the Dallas paper did one, *New York Times* did one, *LA Times* did one, and that put enough pressure on to get something done.[3] It focused that bad attention on the oil industry, and especially here in Midland that was a "no-no." At that time, every pump jack had a pit by it. And that was an overwhelming expense to put netting over all those pits. But once they unitized an oil field, it's computerized and you didn't have these pump jacks working all the time and they now are all connected with pipes and so you don't have those individual pits that you had to net and it was cheaper for them to do it.

And even now they aren't maintaining all the netting on the tanks because I've turned them in. I'm still doing that. We have a company now that's drilling right along the city limits on Interstate 20 and I turned them in. They're going to pay a big fine because they had this pit that all these ducks were getting stuck in about three months ago. And the people: we have to be very careful because we have to protect some jobs. They call me and I'm the one that talks to the federal game warden and either I take the "blame" for it, or the federal game warden takes the blame for it and that way the informers remain anonymous. Somebody's got to do it.

For many, many years, oil was king and there was no way you could put pressure on the industry, and nobody wanted to buck big oil. None of the environmental groups—when I first started—they wouldn't buck big oil. Audubon finally came, Dede Armentrout—she was the one that came in to help us and she was excellent. None of the other organizations here would do anything because they were not going to buck big oil. I had been a member of even the Sierra Club and I asked them for help, but they would not give help. I contacted twenty-one different environmental groups and they did not want to buck big oil because too many of the people donated to them. Plus, the fact is that most of your organizations will only get involved in something that they know they're going to win, and they didn't think that they were going to win this. And I was just dumb enough and pig-headed enough to know that

I was going to continue, because I was out here and I saw what was happening. I saw the great loss of wildlife out here. And the other thing is with that combination of dumping and of the open pits, you have water contamination and, you know, water out here is really precious but nobody cared about it. And as a consequence then, we got a tremendous amount of groundwater contamination, both with chemicals and with salt water.

The Railroad Commission and the Natural Resources Commission [Texas Natural Resources Conservation Commission], they would not enforce any rules or regulations. And no matter how hard you tried—with pictures or evidence—they would say, "Oh it's not there, it doesn't exist." In the oil fields, we would know that the Railroad Commission inspectors—if they had brand new boots on—you knew they didn't get those on their paycheck. The Railroad Commissioners, from the three guys on top, all the way down, it's cor-rupt and it's not going to change. There's too much money. It's like the drugs, there's just too much money involved. I had someone here who was a friend of mine, and at the company he worked for, he and his boss went into the Railroad Commission office here in Midland and they actually gave the guy money. And I wanted him to say something about it but he'd lose his job. And so no one would talk, no one would give affidavits. I'd learn all this from the people but they wouldn't talk—couldn't afford to lose their jobs.

1. The Texas Railroad Commission requires that oil storage tanks or pit be screened, netted, or otherwise covered to protect birds. *Texas Administrative Code,* title 16, sec. 3.22(b).

2. Robert Bryce, "Oil Waste Pits Trap Unwary Birds," *Christian Science Monitor,* March 19, 1990.

3. "Midland Journal; A Natural Home for Wildlife or a Weedy Eyesore?," *New York Times,* June 11, 1995, http://www.nytimes.com/1995/06/11/us/midland-journal-a-natural-home-for-wildlife-or-a-weedy-eyesore.html (accessed November 13, 2009).

Chihuahuan Desert, Water, and Radioactive Wastes

BILL ADDINGTON is a grocer and landowner in the small West Texas community of Sierra Blanca. Since the early 1980s, Mr. Addington has been involved in fighting proposals to dispose of sewage sludge and radioactive waste near his home in Hudspeth county. His spirited defense can be traced back through several generations of family and personal history within this unique desert region.

Interviewed on March 28, 2001, in Sierra Blanca, Texas

Reel 0136; Time Code 00:06:00

My grandmother came from Valentine, Texas, and my grandfather was on his way to California but he settled on Sierra Blanca. My grandmother I'm sure wanted to go to California because of where she was from. It had two rivers going through and it's real green. Sierra Blanca is high desert and there's not a lot of rainfall here, so she thought it was just a desolate, barren place. She didn't see the beauty when she first came here and just wanted to leave. After about a year, though, she grew to love the place and saw the beauty and the diversity that this area holds.

The diversity in this Chihuahuan Desert is just beyond belief, this region which mostly lies in Mexico—but it's in Arizona, New Mexico, and Texas as well—and rivals the rain forests in South America for diversity. People have no idea of that when they drive through Sierra Blanca on Interstate 10, at seventy miles an hour on the freeway. They see cactus, sand, and gravel and they think there's nothing that lives here. However, if they'll just get out of their cars, they would see the multitude of life that exists not only in the classic desert in which you see the prickly pear and cactus, but also into the hills and into the mountains where you actually have a different climate, more rain, different animals, different plants, a forest even. It's not the classic forest like in the Pacific Northwest, but we're talking piñon pine, oak, and cedar, which can create a high desert forest and a microclimate with springs, elk, all kinds of different endangered species of plants and animals.

As Boy Scouts, we once went to the Quitman Mountains, (they're about five miles from Sierra Blanca) and looked at an ancient village of the Native American Indians with petroglyphs—their ancient writings. We were shown how we could dig down a foot in the stream and it would fill up with water, an underground river. That's something else that people don't realize, there're actually underground rivers that flow through some of these dry creek beds. And that stood out in my mind of something really special: you could dig down a foot and it would fill up with drinkable water, really pure pristine water.

The presence of that shallow ground water would become a key piece of evidence when Mr. Addington, together with the Sierra Blanca Legal Defense Fund and other partners, successfully defeated the proposal to site a low-level nuclear waste[1] disposal facility[2] on the Faskin Ranch near Sierra Blanca. Raising concerns over an active geologic fault running through the site, the proximity to the Rio Grande River, and violations of the La Paz agreement[3] with Mexico, their hard-fought struggle took a great toll on Mr. Addington's personal life.

Reels 2137, 2138; Time Code 00:58:53

"It's about the protection of our genetic code, our 'book of life.'"

I don't want to dismiss it and paint a rosy picture that we can all do these things together and it's just easy. It's not going to be easy, but it's our responsibility to act on this as human beings. I thought I was doing this for my wife and son, protecting them. To me what they wanted to do here, the State of Texas and the Authority [Texas Low-Level Nuclear Waste Authority], is no different than if someone came into my house, some criminals waving guns, threatening my family. It's no different to me, it's just more insidious . . . This is a medical issue. What happens when a radionuclide that mimics a mineral like calcium, goes into your body and gives you bone cancer? What happens? It's not just about being an environmentalist and protecting the trees and the land. It's about the protection of life and it's about radioactive waste issues. It's about the protection of our genetic code, our "book of life." Radioactive materials disrupt the genetic code, our chromosomes, and we certainly don't want our children suffering birth defects—defects, lowered immune systems, cancer, bone disease.

Chihuahuan Desert (Courtesy Stuart Klipper)

I lost my family. I loved my wife more than life itself, and my son; she left me and they took him away. The very thing I thought I was fighting for was gone. I cried a river of tears for years over that loss. And believe me, we know about loss. So what did it do? It made me more committed and I dove further into the work and my obsessive-compulsive dysfunction overtook me. It's not something I'd advise for anybody. It's not balanced, and it's good to have a balance in your life— you're actually more efficient when you're balanced, but who can have, afford to have, a balance, when you have this breathing down your neck and there're all these deadlines and milestones coming up that could impact whether this facility got built or not.

I can only describe it as an obsession. But what a magnificent obsession: to be privileged to defend life. It's a privilege to me to work with all these people, to meet all these beautiful fine people, people that have welcomed me in their homes in Maine and Vermont,[4] in Mexico. People I don't even know, they welcome me in their homes and help me. There've been people that have sent us quarters, dimes, and nickels taped to a card, you know. Foundations would never support us, not very many of them, they never gave us much, they didn't believe in us. Case in point, the Ben and Jerry Foundation from Vermont, we applied to them. You'd think—being the social progressives they are— that they would donate part of their tax-deductible fortune from their ice cream business to help us in Sierra Blanca. After all, the radioactive waste was coming from Maine and Vermont. Guess what they told us? We're denying your grant proposal because "y'all don't have a solution." Well excuse me, we didn't start the problem of the nuclear reactors, and we don't claim to have a solution to isolate some of the most dangerous materials mankind's ever created. What we do know is it should not be buried in the ground. It should be isolated from the environment for its hazardous life, and dumping it is about the worst way to be doing it, whether it be in Maine or in Sierra Blanca, Texas.

"We're committed because it's in our heart and soul, it's a part of us."

Of course, we never got paid for any of our work. But, we weren't doing it for money, we were doing it because we believed in it and that gave us an edge. The other side, the proponents of the facility, the "forces of darkness" if you will, they don't have the same commitment because they're paid to do what they do. They just look at it as like a job to make more money. We're committed because it's in our heart and soul, it's a part of us. The land is a part of us and to move us from here, to move me from here would be like to pulling a tree or a bush up from its roots and trying to transplant it. It will usually die, you just can't do that, we're deeply rooted here and we don't want to leave, this is our home. And we'll continue to protect this land from other cities, from other states, and from other corporations. We won't allow—just like the sign I painted outside says—we won't allow companies to contaminate us and opportunistically take from us our home. We'll do everything we can; we had plans "A" through "Z" to stop this dump. If the hearings examiners had said "yes" for the dump and the state commissioners had said "yes," we had other plans, legal, legislative, political, and yes we would even go to direct action plans with other friends that could have impacted my health and safety or maybe my legal status. I was very committed to do that in defense of life.

I want people to know that the defeat of this dump at Sierra Blanca, Texas, this national dump, was no accident. It was not merely because then-Governor Bush wanted votes from the Mexican people in the United States—that helped—but this was an eight-year campaign. We worked it on a daily basis. Some of us slept, drank, ate, and breathed this issue for eight years. It was the last thing I thought about when I went to sleep, and was the first thing I thought about when I woke up in the morning. This issue cost me my family—they took a part of my life—but I don't regret it because I met some very beautiful people. I had some very beautiful experiences.

I've learned a lot. When I was growing up I was taught to believe in school that the democratic system is representative of the people and that we have a system where our legislators do what the people want and this is a democracy. I had never been to Austin, Washington, or Mexico City before all this happened in 1991. It was a rude awakening to see how our system actually works, but we've let that happen. We've let the corporations and special interests take our government from us because we're not involved.

I only hope that we can all start getting involved in our government locally, regionally, statewide, and nationally. If we don't, it's going to come back to bite us just like it did in Sierra Blanca, where some of us weren't involved in our local government. Because in the end—and it may sound corny, but I believe this—we are one earth, we are one water, and we are one soul; we're just one. I don't blame people for feeling disconnected but we have to get past that. I hope others don't have to experience what we went through in Sierra Blanca to have to realize that we're all in this together and we need to support others.

1. Low-level nuclear waste includes a variety of waste, since it is defined by exclusion: it is waste that is *not* legally high-level waste (irradiated fuel, liquids, and sludge from reactors), uranium mill tailings, and some transuranic waste (materials contaminated with elements heavier than uranium, such as plutonium, neptunium, americium, and curium). Low-level waste consists of reactor hardware and pipes, protective clothing and gloves, filters, waste paper, test tubes, syringes, linens, and other medical waste. It is generated by power plants, universities, research institutions, and hospitals. The waste can be toxic for a long time: reactor waste is contaminated with tritium (twelve year half-life), iodine-131 (eight day half-life), strontium-90 (twenty-eight year half-life), nickel-59 (seventy-six thousand year half-life), and iodine-129 (sixteen million year half-life), while the medical waste is technetium-99m (six hour half-life), gallium-67 (seventy-eight hour half-life), and iodine-131, where hazardous periods are generally ten to twenty half-lives. Nuclear Regulatory Commission, "Low-Level Waste," http://www.nrc.gov/waste/low-level-waste.html; Nuclear Information and Resource Service, "'Low-Level' Radioactive Waste," http://www.nirs.org/factsheets/llwfct.htm.

2. The first proposal for disposal of low-level radioactive waste in Hudspeth County can be traced back to the 1980 passage of the federal Low-Level Radioactive Waste Policy Act, which required creation of a waste disposal facility by 1993 (91 U.S. sec. 3347, 1980). To follow this federal mandate, the Texas Legislature passed the Texas Low-level Radioactive Waste Disposal Authority Act in 1981 (67 Tx. Leg. R.S. 713, 1981). Although McMullen and Dimmit counties in South Texas had originally been under review for disposal sites, Laredo's State Senator Judith Zaffirini intervened, inserting language barring disposal near a water reservoir (such as Amistad Reservoir or Falcon Lake on the Rio Grande). This relieved the state of the duty to pick the "best site," and gave preference to land owned by the state. (619 Tx. Leg. R.S. 2479, 1985). Attention shifted to two sites in far West Texas, in southern and northern Hudspeth county, one near Fort Hancock, the second near Sierra Blanca. In 1986, El Paso County Judge Luther Jones directed the County to challenge the Texas Low-Level Radioactive Waste Disposal Authority over the Fort Hancock site, winning an injunction against use of the site in January 1991, later endorsed under state legislation in November 1991. Philip Goodell and Deborah Caskey, eds., *Nuclear Waste Disposal Issues in the El Paso—Juarez Region: Part I—Fort Hancock, Texas,* (The El Paso Geological Society, University of Texas-El Paso, 1991). The Sierra Blanca site, however, remained in play for another seven years. On October 22, 1998, the Texas Natural Resources Conservation Commission rejected the permit for the remaining Hudspeth county waste site in Sierra Blanca, citing concerns over faulting, but also evidently responding to pressure from the Mexican government, local neighbors, and concerns over the Fall 1998 state and national elections. "Texas Agency Denies Permit for Waste Site," *New York Times,* October 23, 1998.

3. The La Paz Agreement was signed by the Mexico and the United States in 1983. Under Article 2, the Agreement commits the nations to "prevent, reduce and eliminate sources of pollution" along the border zone extending sixty-four miles on either side of the border." The proposed Sierra Blanca waste site was located sixteen miles from the Mexican border. *La Paz Agreement.* T.I.A.S. No. 10827. http://www.epa.gov/usmexicoborder/docs/LaPazAgreement.pdf.

4. Maine, Vermont, and Texas entered into a Compact agreement in 1993, providing that Texas would serve as the low-level radioactive waste disposal site for the three states, with Maine and Vermont allowed to contribute no more than 20 percent of the waste. The Compact was spurred on by the federal Low-Level Radioactive Waste Policy Act of 1980 and its 1985 amendments, which followed, in turn, on the heels of the 1979 Three Mile Island accident, and the closure of three U.S. low-level radioactive waste disposal sites in New York, Illinois, and Kentucky. The Compact made each state responsible for the disposal of its own waste, and imposed deadlines for site development. M. T. Ryan, M. P. Lee, and H. J. Larson, *History and Framework of Commercial Low-Level Radioactive Waste Management in the United States* (Washington, D.C.: U.S. Nuclear Regulatory Commission, 2007), 10, 16, 18, 23, 26. http://www.nrc.gov/reading-rm/doc-collections/nuregs/staff/sr1853/sr1853.pdf (accessed November 15, 2009); *Low Level Radioactive Waste Policy Act,* Public Law 96–573, *U.S. Statutes at Large* 94 (1980): 3347–49; *Low Level Radioactive Waste Policy Act, Amended,* Public Law 99–240, *U.S. Statutes at Large* 99 (1986): 1842.

Civil Rights and the East Austin Tank Farm

SUSANA ALMANZA is an Austin-based community organizer, activist, executive director and co-founder (with Sylvia Herrera) of PODER, People Organized in Defense of Earth and her Resources. She has worked for many years to protect her east Austin neighborhood from the environmental hazards posed by industrial developments, including a waste-recycling facility, power plant, and fuel tank farm. Zoning plans and laws dating back to 1928 allowed many of these polluting facilities to be sited in her residential neighborhood.[1] Ms. Almanza's growing awareness of environmental injustices were rooted in the nascent "brown power" and civil rights movements of the mid-twentieth century, as well as childhood experiences that she here recalls.

Interviewed on October 16, 2003, in Austin, Texas

Reel 2260; Time Code 00:02:31

". . . They said, 'Whatever you do, don't open your mouth.'"

What made me very conscious of injustice is that I grew up on the edge of East Tenth Street in east Austin.

Everyone living behind me was Mexican American. Everyone in front across the street and going further east was African American. My parents only spoke Spanish, and I felt injustice first-hand because my parents were treated as second-class citizens because they didn't speak English. We were also treated badly because we lived in poverty.

I was influenced by those experiences and looking at how African Americans were also treated because I grew up in the Civil Rights era too, and about how we were only allowed to go into certain places. I remember having African American friends—I was just a little girl—and one particular time they said, "Let's go to the movies." So we all went to the Ritz Theater, which used to be down on East Sixth Street. When we got up there to pay, the guy says, "She can't go up there. It's only for Negroes." And they said, "What?" And the guy said "No, she has to go downstairs," so we said, "Oh, okay, well then we're not going in." So we went around the corner and we waited for a while and they said, "Well what are we going to do then? They won't let you go in." So one of them says, "I know, we'll tie your hair in a scarf. We'll hide every bit of your hair. We know just how to do it so none of your hair will be showing." And I was pretty brown. At that time I was even browner because we'd been out in the sun. And they said, "Whatever you do, don't open your mouth." So we all got in together as a group and we got up to the Ritz Theaters upstairs where the African Americans had to sit and I just couldn't believe it. I just could not believe it, because I'd been downstairs before and up there the popcorn was stale. The machine was not on. The pickles were stale. It was dirty like they didn't clean it. They didn't have the theater seats and I looked at that and I said, "You know what, it's not like this downstairs." They said, "What?" I said, "No. There's fresh popcorn. The pickles are crispy. The chairs are seats: they're very nice. It's very clean."

All of these things that I've experienced, the whole issue of being looked at as a second-class citizen because you spoke Spanish or because you didn't come

from money or because of the color of your skin, it's all those life experiences that have made me feel that I had to speak out against injustice and get involved in changing a lot of these systems and policies and views that people have.

In the 1990s, Mobil Oil filed a notice of intent to expand its petroleum products tank farm[2] in east Austin. When this came to the attention of Ms. Almanza and the PODER health director Sylvia Herrera, it was a call to action that would bring the women into both conflict and collaboration with government entities, regulatory agencies, corporations, citizens, and the media. Ms. Almanza recounts the highlights of the struggle, which ultimately ended with a successful resolution for PODER and the residents of east Austin.

Reel 2260; Time Code 00:18:32

"Everybody could smell the gasoline."

It all started with Sylvia looking through the notices and giving me a call and saying, "Susana, there's a notice that Mobil wants to expand its facility and in this it says that its going to emit more xylene and toluene into the community and these are very hazardous chemicals, and so we really need to do something about it." And right after that we went down to the state headquarters of the Texas Air Control Board. It's now called the Texas Commission on Environmental Quality. We went down there and began to research the documents associated with that air permit application. We found a letter from the county health department to Mobil that says they were very concerned that Mobil was going to put out more benzene, which is a known carcinogen, because there were communities surrounding the area.

So immediately we said, "Okay, we're going to have to fight! Call for a public hearing regarding that air permit." We also decided that we needed to find out what was the health of this community, because they'd been

East Austin tank farm (Courtesy Sharon Stewart)

exposed for decades. Sylvia had looked up a lot of the health impact symptoms if you were exposed to these chemicals, such as cancer and miscarriages, nose bleeds, respiratory conditions.

And we had a public meeting and to our surprise that meeting was pretty full. We didn't expect that many people to come out, but that's when we found out there were a lot of sick people in the community. And from there we began to organize the phone trees. We asked ourselves, were there neighborhood associations in the area? If there were not any, we needed to help them form a neighborhood association. We began to meet almost weekly. We went out and did the health survey. We petitioned the agency for toxic disease and sub-

stance registry about it. We petitioned the state health department. We petitioned the county. We petitioned the city.

One thing that got us the most exposure was in February of 1992. We did a "toxic tour." We got councilman Gus Garcia, who later became the mayor, to get us two buses from Capital Metro, and we invited the state representatives, the county commissioners, the city council members, the school principals, school board members, community leaders, to come on that tour. We took them on the tour right on Alf Street next to the tank farm. We had already worked out where a couple of the residents would come out and talk out their experiences. Lupe Padilla—she was the first home we stopped at, and they listened to her. She was saying that that she was always sick. She was always taking aspirins, but that when she went to go visit her sister out in Taylor, Texas, she would be just fine. But then when she'd come back she would start experiencing those symptoms. She said, "I don't know if it's the tank farms or not. I just know that when I leave the area for a few days I'm fine and when I come back, I'm sick." Then we took them back where they could see the sheen in the runoff that would come off the tank farm and Maryann Flores talked about how her kids had played in there and they had all broken out with sores.

And so immediately State Representative Glen Maxey says, "I want air testing done out here," and State Senator Gonzalo Barrientos says "I want water testing done out here." Everybody could smell the gasoline once they got there. It was like when you go to fill up your car with gasoline and you smell those odors. Well, the people in that area were smelling those odors on a regular basis, you know, twenty-four hours a day, three hundred sixty-five days out of the year. And a lot of the children never even left that area, never went anywhere but were constantly in that area. So after everyone on the tour had that experience of smelling and seeing it for themselves, then they knew something had to be done. They knew there had to be changes done in that particular community.

We began to pressure the state to do some deep well water monitoring testing out there and they had refused. Thank goodness for Mr. Philip Gutierrez, who is now deceased. He had a little money, so he had a water well installed because there are natural springs there. He wouldn't use that water for drinking, but he'd use it to water his garden, and he noticed that his gardening and his grass were dying. So he hired a firm to come out and test his well water. And that test showed that there were petroleum byproducts in that water. That is what opened the door for us, even though the oil companies came out and said, "Well he probably is dumping motor oil down his water well." We found that very insulting. Why would anyone want to harm the water well that

they used to nourish their garden and their yard? But it was with that testing that we then told the state, "Okay, the contamination is not just on the site, it has gone off the site." And that is what opened the door to us forcing the state to come and put monitoring wells throughout the community. Of course, those monitoring wells started coming up dirty. These are the kind of insults that we were given every time we said there was contamination or Mr. Gutierrez found that his water well was contaminated. The usual thing the oil companies would say when people were saying they were sick was, "Well, it's probably because you all eat too many chilies and tortillas and smoke and you all drink—you all consume a lot of alcohol and that's probably why you all are ill."

"We speak for ourselves."

So these are just some of the things even today that we encountered as we were taking on this struggle to close down the tank farm. But one real big significant difference then and now was that the tank farm battle was at the height of the environmental justice movement, and the slogan was, "We speak for ourselves." What we were trying to tell the community is that *you've* got to speak up against what is happening here. We had a lot of the mainstream environmental groups say "We want to help, we're here to do this . . ." and we said, "We want your help, but we don't want you to be the leaders," because what happens is, when our community sees you all come in, they're going to say "Well, they have all the knowledge and they can speak for us," and then activism takes a back seat. I said, "That's not what we want. We want everybody to speak up about what's happening here. There's a role for everybody but what we want you to do is to help us to make the calls, to send out the campaign letters, to help us in this particular struggle, but not to be the leaders, not to be the spokespersons. It has to come from the community."

That began another relationship with a lot of the mainstream organizations coming to work together, but also respecting the whole movement, that what we were doing was: "We speak for ourselves." People like Mrs. Fedadina Rivera from El Salvador. She didn't speak a word of English. To this day she doesn't, but she became the Spanish spokesperson for the community. We'd take her to the Texas Air Control Board and she spoke about what was happening all in Spanish. It was up to them to find the translators to find out exactly what she was saying. We went to the Austin City Council—Gus Garcia had to translate what she was saying. We say, "No, you've got to speak up regardless if you speak English or not. You've got to say what is happening." She was very good about doing that.

And that was what we were doing: teaching the people you have to speak up and you have that right to speak up and you should take on that role. It's *your* community, it's *your* family that's being exposed here, *your* people that are dying. And that's exactly what hap-

pened. Once people got the information that it was a tank farm causing that illness or could be causing that illness, the first thing they did was they got extremely mad. The second thing they did is that they got organized and began to work to close the tank farm. So a lot of things happened in that whole struggle with the tank farm.

1. The City of Austin's 1928 Master Plan pressed for minority populations to congregate on the east side of Austin, recommending that east Austin be a "Negro district," that "all the facilities and conveniences be provided the Negroes in this district, as an incentive to draw the Negro population to this area." Elizabeth Walsh, *East Austin Environmental Justice History* (Austin: University of Texas Press, 2007), 3. http://soa.utexas.edu/work/eaejp/Papers/East%20Austin%20Environmental%20Justice%20History.pdf (accessed November 15, 2009).

2. *See* Susan G. Hadden, "The East Austin Tank Farm Controversy," in *Public Policy and Community: Activism and Governance in Texas,* ed. Robert H. Wilson (Austin: University of Texas Press, 1997), 69–94.

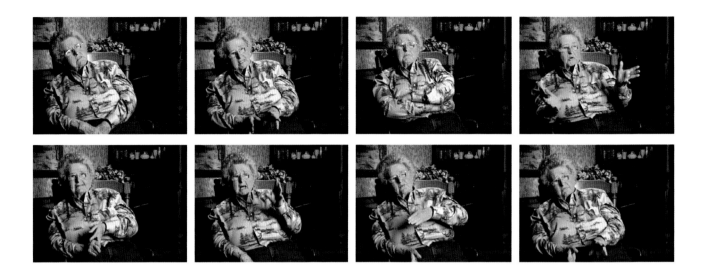

Maquiladoras, NORM Waste, and the Rio Grande

TOOTSIE HERNDON was the mayor pro-tem of Spofford, a community south of Brackettville in the Trans-Pecos of West Texas. She had been involved in a number of efforts to protect this part of the state, particularly the precious groundwater that underlies these arid lands. In the early 1990s, she and the non-profit, Citizens Against a Radioactive Environment, successfully built an alliance with the government of Mexico to stop a proposal by Texcor to construct a radioactive waste site. The site near Spofford would have been within the sixty-two mile border strip protected under the La Paz Agreement.

Interviewed February 21, 2006, in Spofford, Texas

Reel 2357; Time Code 00:04:53

In 1988 Texcor came and met with the Chambers of Commerce. I think this was in the making for several years, before the people of Spofford ever knew about it.

And they kind of got the blessing of the county judge, because they come in with their swift tongue about money. You know, you're a poor community and they offer you jobs and they offer you a hundred thousand dollars a year and that's pretty impressive to some of the people. And they come in and say "Oh, it's just a little NORM, it doesn't hurt anybody or anything." NORM stands for Naturally Occurring Radioactive Materials,[1] but see, these licenses are real funny. They use that term, but that term means that they can put several different types of waste in these facilities. The radioactive wastes were coming from mines and oil fields such. It is naturally occurring, and that's where it was all coming from. There wasn't very much known about NORM at the time. I think Utah was the only one that had one of these facilities, to my knowledge.

Charles Salsman of Texcor was the one that was promoting the idea to put the dump here. He came in pretty smooth talking, and we had a meeting here after we learned that some of the people like the Chamber of Commerce and the bank president had endorsed it. We really didn't know much about it, but my thought was I didn't really like the idea of it one half mile from my home here, with all the traffic from the trucks, and our roads aren't too good anyway. They picked this place because we are a border region. They targeted the whole border with their radioactive waste because it's got no education, no political clout in Austin. They figured they can come in and we're country people and we're going to believe what they say. They pick on mostly Hispanic and just low education people that don't have a whole lot of education and no money, and of course that's the number one problem. When you fight these big companies, you have no money to start against them.

"United we stand, divided we fall."

This rancher lady, Madge Elizabeth Belcher, she's the one who got started organizing against it. About thirty people met in the Episcopal church and then we picked a name for our group, CARE, Citizens Against a Radioactive Environment. The more we dug into it the more we realized what they were trying to do, put all this junk in there. It was hard at first because we had no money, and see, that's the big deal with these big companies. They've got so much money and there's so many lobbyists in Austin, like at the Department of Health, and they listened to the big rich investors. You know, you can't trust none of the politicians in Austin. I'm just going to be real honest, you cannot trust them, you got to get out and fight your own battle. First, you've got to get community support. Without community support, you cannot do anything. Then we had to get a resolution passed out of the nine county region, that's Middle Rio Grande Development Council, and you have to get that before they'll make a stand. They don't really like to get involved in none of this but I got on that board and we kind of put pressure on them. Then we got to Senator Judith Zaffirini. We got some of our congressmen involved in the fight. You first have to get community and then you have to get resolutions from surrounding counties, you know, like Eagle Pass, Del Rio, in the nine county region. That's what we did. The first thing we did, we tried to educate them that this

was a very big project and there was a lot of land down here that was going to be utilized for these huge massive dumps with waste coming all over this United States. We just convinced them that we thought it was bad, and then there's a fault zone laying here in Spofford. We were afraid it would contaminate all the way into the Rio Grande River and then that's when we started going over meeting with the mayors and President Salinas of Mexico, and got them involved in our fight. And they helped us a lot in this Texcor fight. You see, there was a La Paz agreement between the two countries, which says they could not put any massive dump within forty miles of the border. Spofford's within forty miles and that's why I think Mexico was just real concerned; that they were going to contaminate more of the Rio Grande River. You know, it's already contaminated with all the maquiladora factory waste. That's why there's so many babies being born down at Laredo and Brownsville without any brains.[2] It's due to the maquiladora waste being put in the Rio Grande River.

We made picket signs. We went to Austin. The signs said, "Don't dump on us," and "Del Rio opposes it." And there was lots of signs made, during that time. Even when we went over here to the civic center we had a lot of signs and a lot of people speaking out against it. You've just got to show your anger. You know, you just got to be angry about what they're doing to us! I even presented Charles Salsman of Texcor my brother's flag, the one that commemorates that he was killed in Korea, because I felt like they were taking our freedom away. It's like the Texas Department of Health said, "Well, you don't have any rights." They don't care if you oppose the dumping. You have to have science to back you up for them to deny a permit. They're not going to do it because you said, "I don't want it in my backyard." Really, as a citizen, you really don't have a lot of rights until you all band together and it's, "United we stand, divided we fall."

You know, it's amazing that this town, in Kinney County, defeated two massive toxic waste dumps in spite of all the money they had. It took a lot of praying and a lot of God's help: that opened doors for us, you know. We made tamales, we sold tamales, we did bake sales, we did anything imaginable, garage sales, recycled cans from the dump. We did everything it took to make money.

My husband J. B. spent a lot of money personally and so did Madge Belcher to fight the dump. But you just got to band together and sometimes the good people does win, they do, you know. We're living proof that you can defeat a lot of money and a lot of lobbyists up there. I think Texcor had sixty-two lobbyists up there in Austin.

Reel 2358; Time Code 00:26:34

"You got to be persistent and you got to care. You got to love your country."

When you're born and raised in a place, you have roots. My family, all my family, was here, my grandfather, my grandmother. And I think it's the love of the country. I would not even want to see any place devastated with all these massive dumps, you know, right close to your home. I think they could find a better place to put some of it, and they could cut down a lot of it that they make. And if our future generations don't do something to really think about conserving our water and everything, in fifty years, what is it going to be like? You have to instill this in your younger generation because us old people, we're going to be dead and gone. Somebody's going to have pick up the sword and fight for what they believe in. And you got to be persistent and you got to care. You got to love your country. Like these people that just throw out trash everyplace, give me a break! It's so sad now that they have no respect for the beaches or nothing. They throw all their trash right there! It seems like the lobbyists have took over our country and that's the sad part about it. You not only have to fight some of your fellow citizens here in Brackettville, but you've got to fight your state also. That's the sad part,

that we have fought so hard against our own state government because they have no mercy for us. It's whoever's got the big bucks up in Austin, that's who they look at.

1. Naturally Occurring Radioactive Materials (NORM) include discrete wastes (radium-painted watchdials, aircraft instrument panels, and some sludges and scales from petrochemical refining and manufacturing) and diffuse waste (fly ash, phosphogypsum, and bulk wastes from mining uranium ores). A. S. Paschoa, "Potential Environmental and Regulatory Implications of Naturally Occurring Radioactive Materials," *Applied Radiation and Isotopes* 49: no. 3, (1998): 189–96. In Texas, NORM is covered by the Texas Radioactive Control Act, which divides responsibility among the Texas Railroad Commission (jurisdiction over waste from exploration and production of oil and gas), Texas Department of Health Services (use, treatment, and storage of NORM), and the Texas Commission on Environmental Quality (for remaining NORM issues). *Texas Administrative Code* Title 16, sec. 3.30(d)(3).

2. From 1986 through 1991, in the lower Rio Grande Valley, there was an outbreak of spina bifida, a crippling spinal-nerve defect, and a related and fatal neural defect known as anencephaly, occurring at eight times the U.S. average. Mark Feldstein and Steve Singer, "The Border Babies," *TIME Magazine,* May 26, 1997; "Study in South Texas Finds High Birth-Defect Role," *New York Times,* sec. 1, July 12, 1992, 16. Some have claimed that the deformities and deaths of these newborn babies were due to folic acid deficiencies in the mothers' diets, or because of bunyavirus infections. Others have charged that maquiladora pollution from the Matamoros area was at fault. A lawsuit against GM, Kemet Electronics, and Trico alleging that the pollution from the factories was responsible was settled out-of-court for 17 million dollars in 1995. J. Brender and others, "Anencephaly in Texas," *Disease Prevention News,* 55, no. 13 (June 26, 1995); J. F. Edwards and K. Hendricks, "Lack of Serologic Evidence for an Association between Cache Valley Virus Infection and Anencephaly and other Neural Tube Defects in Texas," *Emerging Infectious Diseases,* 3, no. 2, (April–June 1997): 195–97.

Air Pollution, Accidents, and Health

LANELL ANDERSON is a real estate agent and citizen advocate who moved to Channelview, Texas in 1957, when she was thirteen. At that time, Channelview was a rural area, where residents could water ski and fish along the San Jacinto River. By the late 1970s, however, the local petrochemical industry began to boom, and in the decades since, the neighborhood has become surrounded by three hundred industrial facilities and fourteen thousand chemical warehouses located along the Houston Ship Channel in Harris County. Ms. Anderson's work to publicize and reduce the dangers posed by chemical emissions, toxic leaks, and other by-products of the petrochemical industry was motivated by concerns for her family's health.

Interviewed on October 5, 1999, in Channelview, Texas

Reel 2035; Time Code 00:37:53 and 00:15:59

In 1987, my mother died from bone cancer. She was barely sixty-seven years old, and she lived very close to one of these facilities. And then my father died of emphysema. And then my older sister, who is two years older than me, was diagnosed with an autoimmune disease. And I started wondering, "Why?" I started asking questions and digging for information. And then I came down with an autoimmune disease at exactly the same age as my sister had. Then, my younger sister was also diagnosed with an autoimmune disease. That means all of us in our family have been affected by environmental health issues. And that's what, what triggered my involvement. That began the journey for me.

"It's a crime. It is a crime."

What's happening is wrong. When a petrochemical corporation—or any corporation—has more civil rights than American citizens, it's just wrong. What has happened to our country? Even a foreign corporate interest can locate in our country, and its products have more "civil rights" than American citizens do. Human health is the reason I pursue this. There are numbers of people in Channelview that die daily from the effects of pollution.[1] There is an NRDC report,[2] Natural Resources Defense Council, using information from 1996, which proves that hundreds of people a year die, in Harris County, from the effects of air pollution. That's a horrible cost. If you look at conservation issues, ask yourself, "What would happen if I went and poured poison on hundreds of birds out in the Katy Prairie?" There would be an outrage in our country. But why isn't there an outrage over hundreds of people a year dying in our *county?* That's hundreds of families who pay for hundreds of funerals who look down at hundreds of caskets being covered with dirt every year in our county. It's a crime. It *is* a crime.

In this community alone, in this zip code, I have tracked the cancer rates through the Texas Department of Health, for many years. And the male lung cancer rates are one hundred percent higher than the expected incidence, based on standardized mortality ratios. That cost is too high. There are many costs when you try to understand the risks of major corporations, chemical and petrochemical, being located in your neighborhoods. But it's not only the risk from the "kill zones," or big explosions killing you, but the long-term debilitating diseases as well. There are so many people that are suffering.

There is such a public relations clamp on information that gets out to the public in Houston, that often times we are not made aware of many of the leaks that come from pipelines, for example, or from the barges that transport these chemicals up and down the Ship Channel. For example, about four years ago, I was

asleep in my brick home, air conditioned and heated, with nice windows, well sealed and insulated. And I was awakened about three o'clock in the morning by a horrific chemical odor. I could not catch my breath. I was awakened from a dead sleep with this chemical odor that was in my house. That's just something that is really frightening and should not be. That assault should not come to our community.

"We live in what I call a "kill-zone."

I've also been awakened in the middle of the night with seismic rumblings, when one of these facilities would start up one of their major production units, rattling the windows in my nice brick home. I thought maybe it's the

Lyondell facility, Channelview, Texas (Courtesy Center for Land Use Interpretation)

Swimmers, Texas City, Texas—1990 (© Sam Kittner/kittner.com)

train; maybe that's what I hear. Often times you think these rumblings are the weight of the train coming along. But this was ten times worse. I thought we were going to be blown up. And I'm not alone. Many people in this community experience the same things and have the same concerns. We don't know. Is tonight the night that our community is going to be blown off the map? And then, I learned more about the chemicals that are stored on site, which should be covered under the latest legislation of RMP, risk management programs. I understand that two hundred forty thousand gallons of ethylene oxide is stored at one of these facilities. And knowing that a twenty-five thousand-gallon tank car can explode with ethylene oxide and create a hole six-stories deep in the earth, it tells you what risk we're at in this community.

It's just insidious. We live in what I call a "kill-zone." In many communities up and down the Ship Channel, citizens are living in kill zones. There's no way to escape. If lightning hits one of those units that are holding all these on-site chemicals, we're gone. In our view, it is an unreasonable risk.

Roadside stand, Texas City, Texas—1994 (© Sam Kittner/kittner.com)

One avenue open for Ms. Anderson and other citizens who become advocates is to bring their issues before the state's environmental regulatory agency, the Texas Natural Resource and Conservation Commission or TNRCC [now known as the Texas Commission on Environmental Quality]. During the course of her work, she faced harsh realities, and learned valuable lessons, in dealing with the politics of special interest groups and corporate lobbyists, which some citizens believe have made captives of the TNRCC and other regulatory bodies charged with protecting public health, such as the federal Environmental Protection Agency (EPA) and the Occupational Safety and Health Administration (OSHA). In one instance, Ms. Anderson ended up taking her requests to the highest office in the land, with surprising results.

Reel 2036; Time Code 00:01:13 and Reel 0235; Time Code 00:34:20

There's no school that we can go to, to train ourselves to be an effective advocate. I have been advocating for Houston Ship Channel communities for some eight years now. I have aligned myself with people whom I've met at public meetings, in order to gain effective information. You have to have a taste for solving problems to even get involved in this. I've decided that what industry responds to—which I've proven—is that if you can create bad press for them, they're going to respond. For example, at public meetings, they send their representatives to see who they can "put their finger on;" to find out where the greatest opposition is coming from, if you will. And at one of the most recent meetings, concerning our State Implementation Plan,[3] I got up and spoke and among the things I said were, "I know a lot of you from industry just hate it when I get up to speak because you make allegations that I'm uninformed, that I'm angry and that you never know what I'm going to say. But you are wrong: I am informed. And you are right: I am angry. And you are dead right, you never know what I'm gonna say. I will always call a spade a spade, and until the truth is out, we will never solve the problem."

During that same meeting I turned and looked at the TNRCC commissioners, and I asked them all, counted them off one-by-one, and asked, "If I gave each one of you a hundred dollars, which I could well afford to do, would you be willing to get up and go out into the audience and beat the hell out of the corporate executives that were there?" I never got a response, and I waited a long time. And then I explained to them that that's exactly what industry is doing to us: They are using the TNRCC as their weapon. That's how fallible our system is in Texas. It is the state of "good ol' boy politicians." What do we have running our state Legislature? We have hypocrites running our state Legislature. It all gets down to the one thing that I think will change this condition in our country more than anything, and that is campaign finance reform. We have to get the money out of politics in order to regain our country from the corporations.

In 1994, I attended an EPA hearing in Pasadena, Texas, concerning the value of establishing a chemical accident safety board. I went with another environmentalist, and an environmental attorney from Austin as well. We were in a room filled with four hundred men wearing gray suits, who had perfectly combed hair, perfectly pressed pants, and who were very well prepared with the remarks that they were ready to deliver to EPA. When the second man stood up, the vice president of Monsanto, he stated from the podium that he thought that OSHA was wonderful, and that EPA was wonderful, and he wanted to remind everyone in attendance that "more regulation only costs the taxpayers more money," and that "there was no reason

for change." And when the EPA asked if anyone from the audience had anything to say, of course, I raised my hand. I went to the center microphone and I asked this vice president, in his perfectly pressed pants and his recently cut hair, how he could make that remark in light of the fact that we were sitting within five miles of two facilities where forty men had been killed.[4] And he said, of course, he couldn't justify his remarks and that "nothing could replace those lives." And I asked him why he didn't see that change was necessary, and he couldn't answer that.

Lo and behold, some years later, I see in the news that this chemical accident safety board was authorized, but they did not authorize the funding. And so once again, this authorization for funding request was coming to the forefront in Congress. And I heard in the news that President Clinton was going to veto this bill. There was something he didn't like about the bill. So I sat down and wrote him a letter. Its title was "Life in a Ship Channel Community," because I know so many of the politicians have no idea what it is like to live in these kill zones, around these corporations, where we could be killed at any moment. And within two weeks I got two letters of response, one from the Policy Director of OSHA, and one from the chemical division of EPA. And in the first paragraph of each letter it states, we're writing to you at the request of the President to let you know he has changed his mind about the funding of this board. Now I'm sure I was not the only one that wrote to the President, or who wrote about this issue, but we now have a Chemical Accident Board in Washington D.C. that functions much like the National Transportation Safety Board.[5]

1. The Scorecard database (www.scorecard.org) ranks Channelview's zip code, 77530, as first in the state, and eighth in the nation, for emission of recognized carcinogens to the air, with 637,980 annual pounds of release estimated, "Scorecard: The Pollution Information Site;" http://scorecard.org (accessed November 11, 2009). Health risks have been shown to be higher in proximity to the Houston Ship Channel. Stephen Linder, Marko Dritana, and Ken Sexton. "Cumulative Cancer Risk from Air Pollution in Houston: Disparities in Risk Burden and Social Disadvantage." *Environmental Science & Technology* 42, (2008): 4312–22.

2. An independent study commissioned by the City of Houston estimated that four hundred people die every year in the Houston area because of ozone and fine airborne particles. Bob Burtman, "The Silent Treatment," *OnEarth,* Natural Resources Defense Council, Spring 2002, http://www.nrdc.org/OnEarth/02spr/texas1.asp (accessed November 15, 2009); F.W. Lurmann and others, *Assessment of the Health Benefits of Improving Air Quality in Houston, Texas, Final Report,* STI-998460–1875-FR (Petaluma, CA: Sonoma Technology, 1999), ES-16.

3. A State Implementation Plan, or "SIP," is the set of documents and agreements laying out the measures, developed by the state and reviewed and approved by EPA, proposed to achieve state compliance with the National Ambient Air Quality Standards set under the federal Clean Air Act. C.A.A. sec. 171–193; U.S.C. sec. 7501–7515.

4. Ms. Anderson is likely referring to two lethal industrial accidents: a blast at the ARCO Chemical plant on July 5, 1990 in Channelview, that killed seventeen, and an explosion in October 1989 at the Phillips 66 chemical plant in Pasadena, that killed twenty-three. Cindy Horswell and Earnest Perry, "ARCO Refinery Explosion, Fire Kill 14," *Houston Chronicle,* July 5, 1990; Mary Ann Kreps, "Death Toll Reaches 17, Workers Recover 3 More Victims of Phillips Blast, *Houston Chronicle,* October 31, 1989.

5. Jeff Johnson 1997. "Independent chemical accident board funded." *Chemical and Engineering News* 75 (1997): 44.

Sloughs and Rivers, Lakes and Dams

RICHARD LETOURNEAU is a machinist and metal fabricator in Longview, Texas. He has long been active in hunting, fishing, camping, and protecting the forest lands and the free-flowing streams in the Sabine River basin of East Texas. He has worked particularly hard on opposition to the Little Cypress Reservoir and other major water use projects. Mr. LeTourneau has served on the board of the Texas Conservation Alliance and leads the Friends of the Sabine. Part of his interest in natural preservation can be traced to an early encounter with an uncle, whose behavior towards the environment left a distinct impression on young LeTourneau.

Interviewed on October 20, 2000, in Longview, Texas

Reel 2117; Time Code 00:58:04

". . . and I cried so hard, that I left without much more said . . ."

I was about sixteen years old and had spent a lot of time in the Sabine River bottom. My uncle ended up owning about thirteen thousand acres in the Sabine River bottom and he was a developer of unique machinery. He developed a huge machine called the "tree crusher" and it absolutely crushed trees. It didn't matter what size—it crushed them. It hit them, it knocked them over, and it plowed them in. In fact they used these tree crushers when they built Lake Texoma and they used them when they built Toledo Bend Reservoir.

But he was always improving his tree crushers and I guess he was a great entrepreneur and a great inventor. And on this river bottomland that he owned, was where he tested them. He was converting this land into a cattle ranch, but he also got away with testing the machines on it. And he had already crushed much, much, much. But there was one very specific, unique, beautiful swamp area with all this old growth forest in it that comprised about a hundred acres. I found out that they were about

Tree crusher, Four Notch Wilderness Area, Texas (Courtesy Ronald Billings, Texas Forest Service, Bugwood.org)

to crush it out to test this machine. And so I went to him and approached him and asked him, could he "test it somewhere else and not take out this hundred acres?" And he laughed so hard at me, and I cried so hard, that I left without much more said.

And he crushed out the hundred acres. A hundred out of thirteen thousand, on the banks of the Sabine River, old growth swamps and hardwoods and sloughs and even little lakes, old oxbow lakes and what not. This machine goes across the lakes, across the sloughs, knocks down everything in its path. There wasn't a lot of uses for this land after you do that, but he did that anyway. And he told me in no uncertain words that he wasn't worried about what the machine did. And I think he changed my mind for a lifetime in terms of what I was going to work toward in my life and what I was going to stand up for. I agree he had the right to do it. He owned the land, or he stole it, I don't know which, a lot of that went on back then. But theoretically at least, he had enough people to say it was his, or he had more people to say it was his than the black guy who really owned it had to say it was his. So he took it and

they crushed it. And I think I saw then that I had some standing up to do in the future.

Concerned about future development and the potential loss of ecologically sensitive bottomland habitat in northeast Texas, Mr. LeTourneau become alarmed by the plans of various regional river authorities, which operate as independent agencies, to develop dams and create reservoirs for storing surface water. As a citizen advocate to the Northeast Texas Regional Water Planning Group (Region D) he spoke out about the environmental damage and financial costs of these proposed reservoirs. It will remain for the statewide Texas Water Development Board to decide the outcome of these plans.

Reel 2117; Time Code 00:46:27

Engineering firms went out and made these studies, analyzed their problems, looked at what they had—looked at what they *didn't* have—and came up with solutions. Obviously, they were supposed to come up with economically viable solutions. Well, I've read every one of them. And, in every case, with the exception of one very small reservoir in the Sabine River basin, surface water is *not* the solution.[1] None of the engineering firms proposed that there be a large reservoir be built in Sabine basin, none of them. They did propose one on the Sulphur River, a very large reservoir, Marvin Nichols One.

But while proposing it, they've made it very clear that the people of Region D, where this reservoir lake would be created, don't need this water. Dallas doesn't need the water either, but obviously the Sulphur River Authority wants to build a reservoir and they would say, "Well, we're taking care of the future needs of our people" which, in reality, is a very, very rural area. But they want to sell the water to Dallas. Well, Dallas already has more water than they can use. They already have more water available and allocated than they can use through 2050. If you build that lake now, it will be a bog by the time anybody ever needs it.[2] All the while, you've taken good land out of the tax base, you've taken the forest out, you've taken the wildlife out and you've created a very, very expensive place to do what? Jet ski and water ski? We have plenty places to jet ski and water ski. East Texas is full of existing lakes, but Region D, which was heavily dominated by members of river authorities, is going to push this agenda down your throat whether you like it or not.

Mr. LeTourneau was often in a minority position throughout his tenure on the Northeast Texas Regional Water Planning Group,[3] but remained persistent in his beliefs and rights to assert his point of view—unwelcome though it often was.

Reel 2117; Time Code 00:52:49

On a personal level, a lot of these people know where I stand, I know where they stand, and we get along. We shake hands, we chit-chat about the weather, but they know where they're going with their program. They've got it stacked the way they need to have it stacked. So, they give me courtesy, but I'm a nuisance. Anybody that's in their way, that they can't rubber stamp with their agenda, is a nuisance.

I was on the Region D Water Planning Committee representing the environment, and on September twenty-seventh we had a public hearing and I chose to get up at the hearing and read something I had prepared. And they really tried to make me miserable, tried to cut me off in the middle of the speech because they "didn't have time." Well, I had taken off my own time for two years, one Wednesday a month, and driven to Mt. Pleasant to attend a three-hour meeting, and now because I had something to say, that wouldn't be supportive of their agenda, they wanted to limit everyone's speaking time to three minutes. I got my three minutes in and the moderator told me to "really wrap it up." I said, "I can't wrap it up." I said, "It's going to take as

long as it takes to read what I have to say. Do you want me to quit now?" And someone out in the audience said, "No, I want to hear what he has to say." And other people piped up, "Yeah, let's hear what he has to say." And, of course, now this is the public, this is certainly not the planning committee. The committee is sitting on the stage all gloom and doom. They've heard it a hundred times. They don't want to hear it again. But when I finished, I got a good reception from the people that were present and representing the public. It would just seem like maybe you would extend a little more courtesy to a member of the committee than you may to an irate citizen. I don't think I'm more deserving, but I think after having sat on this committee for a couple of years, I should be entitled to eight minutes. I think so. Then afterwards, a lot of the committee come up and pat you on the shoulder, "Oh, no hard feelings." I knew where this was going before I got involved in it two years ago. In the end, they have listened to me with a closed ear, but they've listened.

Ultimately, I don't think that the Texas Water Development Board is going to agree with the Region D plans. I'm hoping that they'll see through this for what it was. I'm hoping the Water Development Board will say, "This is not responsible, this is unreasonable." I'm hoping they'll stand up—stand up for what's right.

1. Reducing water demand can cost significantly less than increasing supplies. Advanced water conservation projects in the State Water Plan are estimated to average 234 dollars per acre-foot of water saved, while development of new supplies can reach as high as 1,186 dollars per acre-foot provided. Texas Water Development Board, *Water for Texas—2007*, Document GP-7-1 (Austin: Texas Water Development Board, 2007), 261, 265. http://www.twdb.state.tx.us/publications/reports/State_Water_Plan/CHAPTER 10 final_112706.pdf (accessed November 16, 2009); Norman Johns, *Saving Water, Rivers, and Money: An Analysis of the Potential for Municipal Water Conservation in Texas,* (Austin, TX: National Wildlife Federation, 2002), 15; Norman Johns, phone conversation with author, March 6, 2009. And the amount of water that can be saved is large; recently estimated at an additional 1,145,559 acre-feet per year statewide. Norman Johns, *The Potential and Promise of Municipal Water Efficiency Savings in Texas,* (Austin, TX: National Wildlife Federation, 2006), 5.

2. Global sedimentation rates for water reservoirs are estimated at 1 percent or more annual loss of storage capacity per year. Alessandro

Palmieri, "Sustainability of Dams: Reservoir Sedimentation Management and Safety Implications," (paper, World Bank, 1998), 2. These sedimentation problems are seen in Texas as well. On account of reservoir siltation, the total water supply of Region C alone, which includes the Dallas-Fort Worth area, is projected to fall by 9 percent, or by 135 thousand acre-feet, by 2060. Texas Water Development Board, "2007 Texas Water Plan: Summary of Region C," www.twdb.state.tx.us/publications/reports/State_Water_Plan/2007/2007StateWaterPlan/CHAPTER 2_Regional C FINAL_112706 .pdf (accessed March 9, 2009). .

3. The Northeast Texas Regional Planning Group is one of 16 such groups set up under the 1997 state law, Senate Bill 1. *Texas Water Code,* secs. 16.051, 16.053, 16.054. Coming on the heels of a severe state-wide drought during the mid-1990s, the bill initiated a process for developing a fifty-year plan for meeting the state's water needs. The 1997 process used a bottom-up, regional approach, in hopes of averting the failures of the previous four top-down, centralized plans. The earlier plans included the 1969 Texas Water Plan, which visualized importing water from the Mississippi River through a network of canals, aqueducts, and sixty-seven dams; the 1974 Plan, which proposed importing water and building twenty-seven new reservoirs; the 1981 Plan, which would have set aside half the state's budget surplus for future water projects; and the 1984 Plan, which called for forty-four new reservoirs. Texas Environmental Profiles, "Paying for the Cost of Future Water Demands," www.texasep.org/html/wqn/wqn_7pay.html (accessed January 28, 2009).

Lavaca Bay, Plastics, and Protest

DIANE WILSON is a fourth-generation shrimper from Seadrift, Texas. She first became involved in environmental issues in 1989 when she heard of neighbors' health problems, dolphin die-offs, and reduced fishery catches. At the same time, she learned from the federal Toxic Release Inventory that Calhoun County, the rural area where she lived, led the national list for toxic emissions. Ms. Wilson became more engaged when Formosa Plastics requested a wastewater permit for a major expansion in Calhoun county. Together with an affiliated non-profit, Calhoun County Resource Watch, she succeeded in pressuring the company through calls, letters, law suits, and non-violent protest to accept a zero-discharge goal, with full recycling of their wastewater stream. Other companies are now following suit. Her energy seems to be drawn from the "northers," violent cold fronts which frequently sweep across the Gulf of Mexico with little warning.

Interviewed on October 23, 2003, in Seadrift, Texas

Reel 2287; Time Code 00:02:22

". . . Wilson, you got a sense of place!"

I guess all of my work in the environmental field comes from my identity with the water. I'm a fourth-generation fisherwoman and I have spent my entire life on the bay. And when I was very young, I would go shrimping with my dad. I was probably five years old and I can remember coming to the bay, and the bay was a woman. I could see her and I could feel her personality. She was like a grandmother and she had this long gray hair, she had this long dress that kind of flowed out into the water. And when I was a kid, she was real to me. She had this personality of an old wise woman. And she really loved me. When you're one of seven kids, and women aren't considered too valuable in this part of the country, coming to the bay was like coming home; she was always, always welcoming. She would say, "Well, hello Diane, it's so good to see you down here at the bay." The bay was a person to me, and you could get a psychiatrist and he would say it was a "little bit of a mystical thing." and it was. Being on the water was like

Explosion at Formosa Plastics, Point Comfort, Texas—2005 (Courtesy Houston Chronicle)

you were a part of it. As a matter of fact, I used to feel like my skin molecules would separate and the water would move into them, there was no division. I know my environmental lawyer used to call it a "sense of place." And I never knew what that phrase was until he said it. He said "Wilson, you got a sense of place!" And I guess I do. I'm sure, when the Native Americans they talk about a mountain, or when they talk about a stream or the trees, when they say they have spirits—they're not fooling! I mean, it's real, and when I was little, I saw it and I never forgot it. And so, with my environmental battles, I fought for that woman. She wasn't a *thing* to me. She was a *person*. And so probably my passion started there when I was five years old.

When I was young, we would always spend the night out on the boat right before a "norther" storm would come blowing in. You'd be out there on the bay, on that old creaking boat (and I always slept on top of the cabin of the boat), and the whole boat would rock. Sometimes I would have a quilt and the wind would be blowing so hard it would take my quilt and it'd just pitch it out into the middle of the bay. I think my favorite time was when the water was rough. I remember one time I was shrimping and my net got caught in the block of one of the ropes. So I had to scale the mast pole with a knife in my teeth and get right to the top and that mast and the whole boat was rocking and you could just see all of that water. And it was this gray water. And it was just wild in the rain and I have never felt that free in my life. It just conveys its power and this feeling of freedom. I've seen it where it was slick calm and it was like a mirror, but I guess my favorite has always been just seeing its power, because it talks very loud.

Reel 2288; Time Code 00:37:46

". . . *You have to do something to grab people and say, 'This is not right!'*"

After a long battle against Formosa Plastics[1] and their permit for a new facility that was going to pollute our bay, I had filed this appeal in Washington with the EPA, and legally, I had stopped their permit. They could not move until a Washington federal judge decided whether they could have a discharge. So, one day I was on the phone, talking with the EPA lawyer (and my name is Diane and Formosa's lawyer's name is Diane). And so, the EPA lawyer thought I was Formosa's lawyer. And here she was, on the phone with me, just discussing about their wastewater discharge and how it was doing and how many gallons were being discharged . . . and I was like, "What?" "You're not supposed to be discharging anything. I got it *blocked.*" And yet they were still discharging. The state knew it. EPA knew it. Formosa knew it. It was just the public that didn't know it.

The reality is: whatever they're going to do, they are *going to do.* It does not matter how many laws they break. That's just the reality. That's what it boils down to. I could not stand to just let it go like this. And you have to do something to grab people and say, "This is not right!" Otherwise, people get so used to compromise, that they're finally so compromised, they might have their whole arm cut off and they look down at it like they've got a whole complete arm. And yet their whole arm is gone.

And so just off the top of my head, I knew I was going to sink something and I knew it had to be my own boat. I knew this because, while I do civil disobedience, I never do damage to anybody else. It's a personal thing. And so, I felt I had to sacrifice my boat. And in reality, the truth is, that boat is nowhere near as valuable as that bay. After all, how has it gotten to where we think a boat is more valuable than a bay? It's not. In reality, I wasn't doing that much. But, in the way life is twisted, people

think, "Oh, it's your boat. It's important, how can you do something like that?"

Of course, I took the motor out of my boat, because if I had spilled the diesel oil in the bay, everybody would've looked at the oil and said "Oh, look at that polluter." And they wouldn't have said anything about Formosa putting seven million gallons a day of wastewater out there illegally. That wouldn't have been the issue. It would've been me. So I took the engine out, because I intended to sink the boat. And I got a shrimper to pull me out in the dead of night. And I was going all the way to Lavaca Bay and I was going to get out to Formosa's discharge pipe and I was going to sink it right on top of that discharge. It was going to go down and the only thing was supposed to remain sticking up was the mast pole. It was going to be a monument to Formosa's wrong and evil deed of destruction, what they were doing to that bay. And it was just going to be a monument . . .

The only problem was that the Coast Guard got wind of the plan, so I had three boatloads of Coast Guard surrounding me and they said that I was a terrorist on the high seas and was going to get fifteen years in the federal penitentiary and five hundred thousand dollars in penalties. They said if any shrimper dared tow me out there any further (and I was almost there, I was probably about half a mile away from the discharge point), that they would confiscate their boat, too. So the Coast Guard confiscated my boat. And, matter of fact, I spent the night on the boat, tied up by the Coast Guard boats. The Coast Guard spent the night, too, and there were three truckloads of them. I guess they were afraid, somehow or another, I was going to get that boat out to the discharge and sink it. I don't know, maybe they thought I was going to fly it out there!

But the other shrimpers in the bay, they surprised me. They normally haven't been supporting me because they just quit believing. They just quit believing you can make a difference. But they were so taken by what I was doing, they all got in their shrimp boats and headed out to form a blockade. The Vietnamese and the Anglos and the Hispanics. As it was, a huge norther had come in, so it was a really rough time out in the bay. And on Lavaca Bay, when it's really rough, you can sink a tanker—that's how rough it can get. So it was very dangerous. But they all took their boats and they did this blockade and this protest. And that attracted a lot of media attention. And it was after that, Formosa Plastics said, "What is it going to take to shut her up?" And so that's how I got zero discharge.

1. Formosa Plastics is an international firm that operates a polyvinyl chloride plant in Point Comfort, Texas, on Lavaca Bay. In 1992, concern arose about a two billion dollar proposed plant expansion for several reasons. First, the company had a poor record of pollution at this plant and elsewhere, was known for contentious labor relations, and was balking at conducting an environmental impact statement for their discharge from the proposed addition to the plant complex. Secondly, the area was known to be heavily compromised already. The National Wildlife Federation had recently announced Toxic Release Inventory results indicating that Calhoun County, the site of the Formosa plant, was ranked first in the nation for the amount of hazardous waste disposed on land. James Hamilton, *Regulation through Revelation: The Origin, Politics, and Impacts of the Toxics Release Inventory Program* (New York: Cambridge University Press, 2005), 224. Moreover, Lavaca Bay sediments were contaminated with mercury discharged from the Alcoa chlor-alkali plant on its shores, leading to large parts of the bay's designation as a Superfund site, and its closure to crabbing. James Blackburn, *The Book of Texas Bays* (College Station: Texas A&M Press, 2004), 156–65.

Caddo Lake, Frog Hunting, and Dams

COL. JOHN ECHOLS grew up in Marshall and returned after retirement from the Air Force to live in Uncertain, Texas, on the shores of Caddo Lake. There he worked for Texas Parks and Wildlife at Caddo Lake State Park as a ranger, ran Long's Fishing Camp, and grew active in efforts to protect Caddo Lake through a group that he and friends formed, called the Greater Caddo Lake Association. Mr. Echols and the Association were involved in controlling harmful flood releases from the Lake O' the Pines dam, in blocking permits for effluent from a paper mill and sewage treatment plant, opposing construction of the Little Cypress Reservoir, stopping efforts by the Army Corps of Engineers to dredge a channel through the Lake, and in spearheading other efforts to protect Caddo.

Interviewed on October 23, 2000, in Uncertain, Texas

Reel 2124; Time Code 00:02:18

I guess you could say that I was kind of raised outdoors. My dad was a hunter and fisherman and ever since I can remember he took me huntin' and fishin' right along with him. I've just always loved the outdoors and it became a habit I guess. Flying in the Air Force went along with that. I was outdoors all the time, or I could look down on it anyhow.

In my childhood and up until I went into the Air Force, I hunted and I fished and I camped out and stayed in the woods as much as I could. I went to any creek, any river, anything that was available and sometimes just in the woods. I can remember taking my BB gun along, me and a friend of mine, and we'd go out and kill a bird and roast a blue jay, anything, it didn't make any difference, and it tasted good right there over a little fire. But that's been years and years ago. I wouldn't do it now, but I did it back then. Thank goodness they've got them all protected now. Going back, I fished on Caddo Lake[1] even before I was a teenager. I was born in Ranger, Texas, and then we moved to Lubbock and then to south Georgia, where my dad farmed for awhile and we almost died of malaria. So, we moved back to Texas. And he came across the border from Shreveport on what then was the Route 80 and found a job in Marshall and we've been here ever since. My dad and I fished Caddo before motors were even very big (a six-horsepower motor was a tremendous amount of motor) and most of the time we were paddling. We had an old aluminum boat and I used to have a wooden boat that was made out of cypress that we carried around for frog hunting and staying out at night.

I remember once we went up river on Big Cypress Bayou to Long's Camp, and across from Long's Camp there's a slough back in there and it opens up into a couple of lakes. Well a friend of mine and myself went out frog hunting at night. We went back in there and knew we was in the wrong place when an alligator hollered at us, so we started walking out and we got lost. And when I found myself, I was standing about this deep [neck-deep] in water and I was at Big Cypress Bayou. But it was a wonderful experience. We got frogs and we had a good time and it was just nature back then I guess, just natural to go out and not be worried about anything, before the war, when everything was just kind of loose.

Caddo Lake (Chase Fountain, courtesy Texas Parks and Wildlife Department)

Reel 2124; Time Code 00:14:32

*"When people get together, you can
move mountains."*

In 1966 the Corps of Engineers built the dam at Lake O' the Pines, that's on Big Cypress Bayou. The first thing that they built it for was flood control; second thing was the water supply; third thing, recreation. It had gotten so that when we got a lot of rain and Little Cypress was uncontrolled, we were just getting flooded three or four times a year. They were what I call "nuisance floods" for some people, but for a lot of people it was more than nuisance because it cost an awful lot of money. I had written a letter to the Corps of Engineers and said, "We've been thinking about forming an organization." And I thought, well, we can try and we can see what happens. So there was six of us that got together, and our goal was to get the Corps to shut the floodgates at the Lake O' the Pines Dam, after all, that's what it was built for.

You see, here on Little Cypress, we are quite a ways below the dam on Lake O' the Pines. And when we get a lot of rain on the watershed, we were already flooded. Well, the Army Corps was opening up *their* dam on Lake O' the Pines, which was filled from the rain, and it would come flooding down here all of a sudden overnight with six or seven feet of water. And we wanted them to keep their dam shut.

So we got together and each of us put up twenty bucks and advertised a little bit and went to school and figured that if we got a hundred and fifty people we'd have an organization. Well, we signed up a hundred and five on our first night. Our dues were five dollars a year. Greater Caddo Lake Association is what we called it, and we are a non-profit organization and registered with the State of Texas. We're over eight hundred strong now. But the first time the Corps of Engineers came up here they sent some people who said, "What's been going on twenty years, a long time, you don't change." I says to them, "When people get together,

you can move mountains." I said, "I'm going to stick a knife in your side and I'm going to twist it so much 'til you wish you'd never heard of Caddo Lake!"

Having been on the Inspector General's team in the Air Force, I kind of knew who were the proper people to write. I wrote three letters to then-president Gerald Ford. Then I got a call from Major General Lewis, who is retired down here now. And he says, "No use in writing any more letters to Ford, he doesn't see 'em." I said, "Somebody's seen 'em or I wouldn't be getting a call from you." The next thing I know, him and the district engineer was down here. They had written me letters and they had actually given me false information and I proved it. I proved 'em wrong. And Lewis claims, "Well, the district engineer said he wasn't familiar with this." And I said to him, "Well you *should* have got familiar with it." And he said, "You almost got me fired." I said, "I've been working on it." But anyhow, we finally got that straightened out!

And gradually it has worked to where, more than what we ever envisioned, the Greater Caddo Lake Association is protecting Caddo and getting things done. They tried to build a dam up there on Little Cypress for Little Cypress Utility District. And we went to Austin, fought that out.[2]

Reel 2124; Time Code 00:35:00

Caddo Lake is a very, very unique place that you don't find anyplace else in the world. It comes closer to the Okefenokee Swamp than anything I've ever seen when you get all around it and get back in the back parts of it. Even the RAMSAR Treaty, an international agreement from 1971 on the protection of wetlands, said that Caddo Lake is an ecosystem worthy of international preservation. It's one of the few left and we're losing so much of our habitat now. I know a lot of people don't believe it, but if we didn't have all of our game and other stuff, it wouldn't be the same world we're livin' in. And I tell people the one reason that I work for Caddo Lake is: I would be awful, awful disappointed if my grand-child or my great-grandchild came up to me and says, "Granddaddy, why did you let this happen to Caddo Lake?" And I get pretty sentimental. It's just a place that I dearly love and it's unique. It's different every time you go out on it. You see something new every time you go out on it, and you never know what you're going to see.

1. Caddo Lake is a 27,000–35,000 acre lake on the border of Texas and Louisiana, fed by Little Cypress Bayou, Big Cypress Bayou, Black Cypress Bayou, and Jeems Bayou. The Lake was originally formed by waters backed up from a large natural log raft in the Red River, but the raft was removed in 1873 to improve navigation, causing lake levels to fall, and to later be stabilized by earthen dams built in 1914 and in the 1970s. Fred Dahmer, *Caddo Was . . . : A Short History of Caddo Lake,* (Austin: University of Texas Press, 1995) 3–5, 20; Caddo Lake Homepage, "Caddo Lake History," http://caddolake.com/history.htm (accessed January 27, 2009).

2. In 1986, the Little Cypress Utility District proposed building the 129,000 acre-foot Little Cypress Reservoir on a fourteen thousand acre site in the Little Cypress Creek bottomlands, upstream of Lake Caddo, near Marshall, Texas. Joe N. Harle. *Report on Impact of Little Cypress Reservoir on Caddo Lake Inflow Quantity and Resultant Lake Level* (Longview, TX: Kindle, Stone and Associates, July 1987), 3. http://caddolakedata.us/media/1864/kindle stone assoc 1987.pdf (accessed November 16, 2009); Joe. N. Harle, *Report on Minimum Flow Considerations, Terrestrial Mitigation and Ecological Effects on Caddo Lake Associated with Little Cypress Reservoir Development* (Longview, TX: Kindle, Stone and Associates, April 1987), 3–2. http://caddolakedata.us/media/1764/espey huston and associates 1987.pdf (accessed November 16, 2009). The Texas Water Commission issued a permit for the dam, but local residents voted the related bond proposal down twice. Larry McKinney, "The State of Lakes," *Texas Parks and Wildlife Magazine* July 2007, http://www.tpwmagazine.com/archive/2007/jul/ed_1/ (accessed April 20, 2010). Opposition organized by the Caddo Lake Association and the Texas Committee on Natural Resources centered on the reservoir's cost, its lack of supporting infrastructure, its inundation of hardwoods and wetlands, its impact on Caddo Lake flows and levels, and its redundancy vis a vis the large nearby Lake O' the Pines. Janice Bezanson, Texas Legacy Project interview, January 20, 2007, http://www.texaslegacy.org/bb/transcripts/bezansonjanicetxt.html (accessed April 20, 2010).

Vietnam, Pantex, and Patriotism

BEVERLY GATTIS has been a key member of STAND (Serious Texans Against Nuclear Dumping) in Amarillo, a citizens' organization that was originally created to oppose plans to build a high-level nuclear waste[1] repository[2] in the Panhandle of Texas, and later evolved to provide oversight of the nuclear weapons work at the Pantex facility, sixteen miles northeast of Amarillo. As is the case with many of her generation, Mr. Gattis' views were informed by the turbulent events of the 1960s, on both the political and environmental fronts.

Interviewed on October 4, 2002, in Amarillo, Texas

Reel 2215; Time Code 00:04:46

When I went to college, I wanted to get a degree in marine biology. And I had the good fortune at the University of Texas in Austin to get to go down to the Galveston area and go out on one of the ships and found out that I have terminal seasickness, so that *wasn't* how I wanted to spend my life! But, I took a lot of science courses. I had an ecology course, a course in biology (and this would've been in 1969 or 1970), and that really made a huge difference for me. It was the first time I had formal information and training about looking at an ecological issue. And my professor was not a fan of nuclear power and I'm sure that's partly where I got that disinclination to have anything to do with this. He always considered nuclear power to be an absurd concept. It's like using a cannon to swat a fly because it's such a massive power source that it's not an appropriate match to the job you're asking it to do. And that always stuck with me.

In college, too, I took your basic government course where you have a government professor that's smart enough to tell you that, as exotic or as interesting or riveting as federal politics might seem—the presidential race, that sort of thing—the government that will affect you the most is your local city and county government, and you should never forget that. So education can teach you some things that you don't understand otherwise, or at least plant those ideas.

The book by Rachel Carson, *Silent Spring*, was one of the things that we read in my ecology course, and that was a powerful book to me. I tend to go into a state of grief over that, I'm getting choked up now just thinking about it. You worry about these things, and all the destruction. So I think you can probably see why I couldn't *not* do the work, because you just care so deeply. It's a magical world and it's being used with such carelessness and thoughtlessness. And I find it almost unbearable.

It was a tumultuous time. Being raised in this conservative area, when I graduated from high school, I was not a liberal person. I cared about ecological things, but I wasn't a liberal person. The big debate for me at that time was whether to go to college or go into the army. And I was very patriotic in the standard ways but I did decide on college and went down to the University of Texas at Austin. What I heard there—which you didn't hear here, or I didn't seek it out particularly as a high school student—completely changed how I felt about the Vietnam War.

An example was at UTA [University of Texas at Austin], where I went to the scuba diving club to get lessons, and all the folks that were teaching us were Vietnam vets. And one was missing a foot, and one had bullet holes across his chest, and one was a man that had been in the underwater demolition work and so forth. And they felt differently about the war. This was how you learned about these things and the prices that people were paying. So, it was a tumultuous time, and I'm glad that I was in some of those marches and learned some of the things I learned. It simply struck me as true when I read some of the things that I had no idea of before. For instance, Ho Chi Minh feeling that the United States, of all countries, would understand their struggle for independence. When you think of all the things you want your country to be and what you feel, ideally, in your heart, then it breaks your heart when you begin to learn what your country is and how it moves in the world. I have had a lot of dreams for the United States, but one of my dreams was never that we would be arms merchant to the world. And that's one of the things we are. So as you learn those things, you either decide to hide, or if an opportunity comes your way, you say, I have to fight for what this country is supposed to be. I think that's part of what always moved me to work on when the nuclear issue came up.

In the 1990s, proposals surfaced to increase nuclear weapons-related production and activities at the U.S. government's nuclear weapons complex outside of Amarillo, known as Pantex.[3] Ms. Gattis found herself mobilized to oppose this development.

Reel 2216; Time Code 00:23:53

The boosters for the plant pulled out the card of, "If we don't become the new Rocky Flats, if we don't accept this dangerous new work," (not that they would ever say it was dangerous), but, "if we don't accept this new work, then they'll close the plant. And Amarillo will lose one of its largest employers and it will be a devastating blow." So that was the main dynamic here. You should support your country patriotically and we should be doing this because our country needs nuclear weapons. And if we don't buy into this thing that people in Colorado and Denver drummed out of *their* neighborhood, if we don't accept that, they'll close our plant. So they were using that fear tactic of having this huge economic hit on our city as one of the ways they drove that discussion, and it polarized people. They used the slogan, "Pantex, Yes." Not a lot of detail, just say "yes." "My country right or wrong," that's what it was like. They really questioned your patriotism if you questioned them. And it's an uncomfortable position to be in.

One of the things that we would find (I generally wound up being the person who represented STAND)

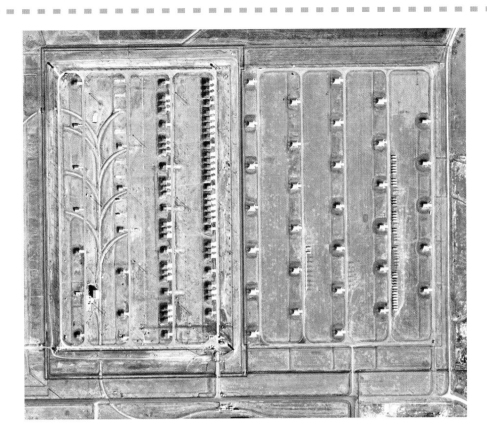

*Pantex nuclear weapons plant,
Panhandle, Texas (Courtesy U.S.
Geological Survey)*

is that an activist is always so at risk of being so cynical and so bitter that it's almost unbearable to stay inside your own skin. You begin to be unable to talk to people because you're too overwhelming to talk to. It seems too hopeless and too black and so you just don't want your spirit to go that dark route. And I always tried to take the tack of talking about what our country *should* be. We will do for our country what the country truly needs, but our government must ask for what it needs, no more, no less. And it was asking for more than it needed. It must be willing to invest in it and do the work in a top-drawer way, a safe way, so that we're not destroyed doing the work if we take it on. And it has got to give us the details, it cannot expect, should not expect, any citizen to sign on to an undefined program, to a blank check and just say, "We trust you, go ahead and do it." It's our responsibility to learn and judge and

support it if we believe in it, or question it if we think it is insufficient. And that's how I would talk to people.

*"The patriotism your country needs the most
is to be willing to think for your country."*

It was like playing a role your country needs you to play. It eventually caused me to redefine my definition of patriotism. I finally decided that in this area we were a little too inclined to the heroic version of patriotism, the willingness to die for your country. And I began to tell people that I think the patriotism your country needs the most is to be willing to *think* for your country, and to do the work, day in and day out. Anything else, anything less, and you betray your country. And people responded to that. Too often, I think, people hear too little of that kind of more sophisticated patriotism, and

I'm not uncomfortable saying it that way. It's more fleshed out: How do you maintain this thing you love? How do you bring out its best, and not let it succumb to its worst? And how do you play the role you're supposed to play?

In the early days of the nuclear waste thing, there's a tri-state fair that happens in Amarillo and we would have a booth at the fair where we would offer information. And it was during those days that I learned how powerful fear is—and I know a lot about fear myself. I am not a person who's at ease in public, and I'm not a person who ever wanted to be in the public eye or wanted to make a speech. I was not even comfortable just trying to talk one-on-one very well. But you would be at this booth, and I remember so clearly one time one woman coming up to me and just saying, "Well, it's in God's hands." And I thought that was such a debilitating thing for her to feel, and it was so dangerous for the world and the country, that I rarely did this, but I just reached across the table and I took her hands and I lifted them up. And I said, "Are these not God's hands?" And she just sort of looked at them and she said, "You might be right." It's just hard for people to believe that they are so important, each individual is so important. And it's just so true; it's the one thing that makes a difference. But getting them to believe that is a hard thing.

1. High-level radioactive waste includes four basic types of material: 1) spent nuclear fuel; 2) fission by-products from commercial nuclear power plants, nuclear submarines and ships, and from university and government research facilities; 3) weapons waste, left over from chemical reprocessing of spent nuclear fuel to recover plutonium; and 4) surplus plutonium from disassembled nuclear warheads and from defense research and development programs.

2. The Nuclear Waste Policy Act of 1982 mandated that the Department of Energy find a high-level radioactive waste disposal site to the west of the Mississippi River, and next identify a site in the eastern United States. In the West, nine sites in six states (Louisiana, Mississippi, Nevada, Texas, Utah, and Washington) were identified in 1983 as potential repositories. The Texas sites included salt beds in Deaf Smith and Swisher counties. By 1986, the list of possible western United States sites had been reduced to three: Yucca Mountain in Nevada, Hanford in Washington, and Deaf Smith County in the Texas Panhandle, and the search for an eastern site had been discontinued. In 1987, the Nuclear Waste Policy Act was amended to focus on Yucca Mountain as the only disposal site for further study. Kenneth Rogers and Marvin Kingsley, *Calculated Risks: Highly Radioactive Waste and Homeland Security* (Surrey, UK: Ashgate Publishing, 2007), 82–85.

3. Pantex is located northeast of Amarillo on a sixteen thousand acre parcel originally set aside in 1942 as the site of a conventional bomb plant for the U.S. Army. In 1951, the Atomic Energy Commission reclaimed the plant and converted it to use for assembly and disassembly of nuclear weapons. In 1989, the closure of the Department of Energy's plutonium processing program at the Rocky Flats Plant due to pollution and urban encroachment brought interim storage of the plutonium to Pantex. In 1994, Pantex was listed as a Superfund site, although operations continue there. Robert S. Norris and Hans M. Kristensen, "Dismantling U.S. Nuclear Warheads," *Bulletin of the Atomic Scientists* 60, no. 1 (2004): 72–74

Satellites
& Blueprints

OVER THE DECADE that encompassed this project, global climate change has emerged as the most profound environmental issue, affecting as it does the web of life from the largest to the smallest scales. It might be said that Texas is justifiably at the heart of the problem, having among its credentials: the greatest cluster of petroleum production and refining facilities in the Western Hemisphere; a history of large scale industrial beef production; and miles of un-zoned, low density, automobile-dependent development.

And yet, for all its contributions to the creation of greenhouse gasses, Texas does have a group of concerned, passionate innovators who are finding ways to provide for human needs while protecting the climate. Their tools include renewable energy, green building, compact city design, and their sheer imagination.

"The power of imagination makes us infinite."[1]

JOHN MUIR

1. Linnie Margh Wolfe, ed., *John of the Mountains: The Unpublished Journals of John Muir* (Madison: University of Wisconsin Press, 1938), 226.

Science, Politics, and Climate Change

GERALD NORTH is a physicist and professor in the Department of Meteorology and Oceanography at Texas A&M University in College Station, where he also served as head of the Department of Atmospheric Science from 1995 through 2003. He previously worked at the National Center for Atmospheric Research and NASA's Goddard Space Flight Center. For over three decades, Dr. North has been a student of the climate, and as concerns have grown about global warming, he has sought to educate the public and engage decision makers about the challenges we face.

Interviewed on March 4, 2002, in Bryan, Texas

Reel 2436; Time Code 00:04:48

I became very interested in a new satellite project at the Goddard Space Flight Center, and sort of helped put together the first plans for it, called the Tropical Rainfall Measuring Mission in 1984. We had the competition at NASA headquarters. I believe there were seventeen competitors for different missions, and I went down and made the presentation. We won the competition. We then began this long, arduous trail from first proposal to cutting metal to all the other steps. At any time, of course, the whole thing could be canceled. And so it had its ups and downs along the way. But I actually left Goddard a couple of years later, 1986, to come to Texas A&M. But to make a long story short, the satellite was launched in 1997. So it took thirteen years from the proposal to the launch, and it was a joint mission with Japan . . . and the satellite's still flying, actually, in 2008. It's been flying now for almost eleven years. It's been a great success helping with hurricanes, but the purpose of the satellite was to help us by getting data that can help us calibrate and test these big climate models that we hear about so much today. They were just in their infancy in the middle eighties. So there was a great need for data to help test the models, make sure they were getting things right in the present climate. And so at that time, it was a very popular venture in climate modeling to predict what would happen during an El Niño. And in order to do that, you needed to know the rainfall out over the Pacific Ocean. That's where the El Niños really start and it's the energetics related to the rainfall there that really help in predicting El Niño. And up to that time there were no measurements of rain out over the Pacific.

Reel 2437; Time Code 00:00:31:12

"It's just as bad as one of our scenarios anticipated."

What we had was less confidence in the predictions. I think now the confidence has increased. We understand the system better thirteen years later than we did then. In fact, at the time we wrote this book, *Global Warming and the Impact on Texas,*[1] we did not use the climate models to project the future temperature. We simply said, suppose the temperature goes up two degrees all across Texas. That's sort of what the climate model predicts over the next century, a couple of degrees Celsius, or three or four degrees Fahrenheit. If the temperature goes up this much, what happens in Texas? If the precipitation goes up a little bit, how does that work with it? If precipitation goes down a little bit, how does that work? And one of the things we found, which was really rather bothersome—striking, was that if the precipitation goes down, say ten percent, and if the temperature even stays the same or gets warmer, for many of the Texas rivers, there will be years when they do not reach the Gulf. They won't make it to the Gulf, because of evaporation due to the increased temperature that will dominate the inflow into the rivers. So this will have profound impact on the estuaries, all kinds of things—even nuclear power. There are nuclear power plants in Texas near the mouths of those rivers. They need that water for cooling. So if those rivers don't make it to the Gulf, they got to shut down until they do.

There will be periodic droughts. We expect that. We've had them in the past. And now, the model simulations in recent years suggest that Texas—particularly the western part of Texas—will be much drier. In fact, it will be dry compared to the 1957 drought in Texas, the

Dust storm, Stratford, Texas—1935 (Courtesy National Oceanic and Atmospheric Administration, George E. Marsh Album)

"drought of record" they would call it. That may be the normal in West Texas, west of I-35. That may become the normal climate—like the drought of the fifties—which is much more severe than the Dust Bowl drought of the thirties. This has a huge impact if it happens that way. And now the model simulation suggests that in West Texas, the precipitation will go down, temperature will go up. It's just as bad as one of our scenarios anticipated.

Now, will this happen? I mean are we going to do anything to prevent it? Well, I'm rather pessimistic. I think we'd better take the position that nothing is going to happen to change this; that it's likely to happen. So we've got to worry about what to do to provide water and other resources in this state during that period. During the next fifty years, we expect the population of Texas to double. And the [Texas] Water Development Board suggests that we'll probably need about fifty percent more water. Most of the population increase will be in the cities, not out in the agricultural areas, so they use less water. And you can recycle the water. So we're aware of that, and they know that. But maybe it will be worse—maybe it will be harder to get that fifty percent if you just use today's climate rather than if you let the temperature warm a few degrees, and cut the rainfall down a little bit. So we better worry about this. I'm not so sure I believe everything the models are saying—the models do a really great job at the global level, hemisphere level. By the time you get down to areas like Texas, they're a lot more unreliable. We just cannot pin down sharply the answers to our questions, and we would like to get good answers. We want to know the truth. And so right now, down at the scale of the area of Texas, the uncertainty is quite large. As you know, the rainfall change from year-to-year is quite large, too. So, those things go together. It's hard to predict the fluctuations from year-to-year—the noise is very high, so to speak.

We have big problems for Texas if these things really do happen. And in these thirteen years, our confidence in the models, because of more data, more means of testing, and so on, our confidence has grown. Now, this scenario about West Texas I just talked about, that was evident in 1990. That was evident in the model simulations. But nobody took it seriously because it was just too crude back then. It was there five years ago—2001. Now it's in the model simulations. Now they have much finer resolution. The little boxes on the model that makes the predictions are now finer and finer, maybe twenty or thirty of them in Texas. So now we're down to a much finer scale because of the increased computing speed and capacity, so that we can make these predic-

tions right at pretty small scale. But, you know, there's still a lot of uncertainty. But when you get the same answer you were getting with the cruder and cruder models, it starts to increase your confidence that something was right about that.

In summertime, right in here in Texas, we don't get any more "fronts." We'll see the last front coming to Austin and College Station in the middle of June. We won't see another one until September. That's when we're in the tropical mode. No more fronts, just little afternoon showers occasionally. What could happen, what's likely to happen, is that period will extend, and we'll become a more tropical climate. But it's the type of tropical climate you don't want, namely a desert. Now, the Gulf of Mexico, fortunately, is going to stay where it is in terms of climate change. So we still have all that moist air coming up from the Gulf. But all the air coming up from the south in West Texas comes from Mexico, and it's dry air. But from College Station to the east in the United States, there will probably be more rain. So the Gulf will continue feeding rain in the eastern part of the country, and in the western part of the country all the way to the coast, less rain. That seems to be how the thinking is crystallizing about what's going to happen.

1. Gerald North, Jurgen Schmandt, and Judith Clarkson, ed., "The Impact of Global Warming on Texas: A Report of the Task Force on Climate Change in Texas" (Austin: University of Texas Press, 1995).

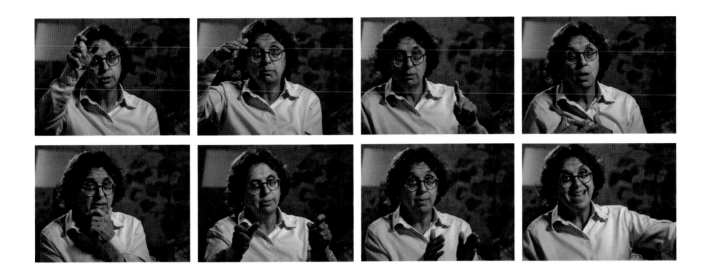

The City Beautiful, Roads, and Prairies

MARY ANNE PIACENTINI is a planner who has worked on protecting and developing open space for recreation, habitat and sustainable land use. From 1993 through 1998, she led the Friends of Hermann Park, which succeeded in restoring an historic, near-town park in Houston that includes 545 acres of land and major urban attractions. From 1998 through the present day, Ms. Piacentini has served as executive director of the Katy Prairie Conservancy, which has managed to protect twelve thousand acres of grassland to the west of Houston, for rice production, cattle raising, wildlife habitat, and flood abatement. Ms. Piacentini explores the benefits of integrating wetlands and prairies into the urban fabric, and expresses concerns over unbridled development and its long-term impacts on the quality of life, particularly in her Houston region.

Interviewed on February 26, 2008, in Houston

Reel 2414; Time Code 00:05:55

"We have to get smarter about the way we grow."

I went to school in Massachusetts and I have a master's in urban and regional planning. I had gone there because I was interested in the qualitative aspects of planning, looking at how people respond to the aesthetics of their cities. I thought a lot about the City Beautiful movement[1] in Chicago, Daniel Burnham, and about Paris and how much aesthetics impacts people and how it makes neighborhoods come together and be more cohesive. Ultimately, I felt like the program I was in sort of sold me a bag of goods, because I thought it was going to be about looking at the way you plan cities: how they work, how they look, how they function. And instead, a lot of it was about quantitative things. How do the transportation systems run? How can you move more people through? How can you pack them more densely? I felt like that wasn't really what I wanted and so it ended up that actually I took half my classes at MIT. You'd *think* MIT would be all about the numbers, but MIT was actually more about the way things

Interstate highway interchange model—1966 (Courtesy Hermann Kelly, Texas Department of Transportation)

looked, the way people interacted with it, and so it gave me another sense about why cities and areas around them should be designed in certain ways.

I happened to marry someone who teaches architecture and was very involved with architecture, and he began to bring in a lot of people like Michael Graves and Robert Venturi; people who think about how cities are built all the time. And it really kind of tested my own values and my own philosophies because I began to hear people like J. B. Jackson say, roads are the greatest impetus for development, more than anything in the world, and where people put a road, that is where people then begin to develop.[2] Road planners and engineers will tell you, "Oh, no, we put the roads there because that's where people are." But often the roads are put well before people are there. They're put there *because* other people—developers, landowners, maybe even sometimes planners—feel like that's the way they want growth to move. And so you look at all of the freeway loops that we have and you realize that a lot of those were built well before they were needed. And yes, you should do some things for anticipated growth, but I think they also direct it. So it made me start to really think about how cities grow.

Reel 2415; Time Code 00:22:43

There are two things that I think have really brought the most change to the prairie. One is the anticipation of roadways, whatever they are, whether they're the Grand Parkway or the expansion of I-10 because, as J. B. Jackson said, the thing that most fuels growth is the location of a roadway. It's not the growth itself, it's not the anticipated need, it's where you place the roadway and the roadway is often placed far in anticipation of the need for it. And there might not even be need; it actually develops the need for it. And so, you had this sense that there was going to be a Grand Parkway even though there was a lot of opposition to it. Also, with the expansion of I-10, people thought, "I can move farther west and I can still work downtown because now it's going to be an easier commute." Well, that's not true and it'll probably never be true because the use of the roadways expands as quickly as the roadways are developed, and then they're clogged again and they need more room. . .

Well, the Grand Parkway would be the *fourth* loop around the City of Houston, more loops than any other metropolitan area in the United States today. And the Grand Parkway was originally proposed as an evacuation route. It wouldn't have feeder roads and it would be really used to get people out of town. And so they decided to do it in segments and there are different segments that go across different parts of the region. And ours is "Segment E," which goes through the Katy Prairie. There have to be environmental reviews for them because there are a lot of federal funds involved, and so they're looking at the impacts just of those individual segments. They're not looking at the broader picture and asking, "What does this do to the whole area? Does it increase the chances of flooding? Does it disrupt wildlife corridors because there are no passages through? Does it destroy sensitive vegetation? Does it destroy wetlands?" And so, the proponents of it must decide the answers to these individual impacts. But they never put all the segments together to consider

what the cumulative impact of it is as a whole. I think many people in the environmental community really are conflicted on the issues. They're looking at the "need," because, truthfully, none of us in the environmental community wants to stop growth. What we want to do is manage growth and we believe that there ought to be ways to find a balance between the things that people think are wonderful about a region and the things that get you where you need to go—help you do your work, get to play, do all the things that you need to do.

Sometimes people will say to me, "Oh, if you run the Katy Prairie Conservancy, you must be against growth." And I say we're not against growth, but the truth is that I love living in the neighborhood I live in *because* there was a sense that they wanted to have green space near it. There was a sense that the features that were important, whether it was the trees or the water, were critical to the nature of that area, to the sensibilities of its community, to the people that wanted to live there. I think we have to recognize that as more and more people move to the region, we have to get smarter about the way we grow. And that may mean that not everybody gets to have a typical suburban house. Some people will, but some people, if given an option, would choose something else. I was in a meeting today about transportation and one of the things that they were saying is that the

U.S. Highway 59 under construction, Houston, Texas—1964
(Courtesy Texas Department of Transportation)

Suburban home, Houston (Courtesy Telwink-Flickr)

Department of Transportation, our TxDOT, is really not just about highways. It ought to be about "transportation" and it ought to look at what are the other opportunities for transportation. Now, you might decide you really want to drive a car, or I might say I never want to drive a car again. I love to be able to sit on a train, read my book, listen to my iPod, sleep, drink a cup of coffee, do whatever I want—and just relax to get to where I want to go. And I might be willing to take a little bit of an extra pain in that it might take longer to get there, or it might take a little more trouble. But it's an option that I have.

There are so many reasons why you wish that people who are in positions of power and influence would recognize that what they do tomorrow and what they do today really affects so many future generations. I look at certain neighborhoods and I think, wow, whoever developed those were really smart. How come they were so smart and how come we're not as smart? And one of the things that we have to think about is smarter ways to grow. I work with a lot of different groups, and a lot of the groups are looking at the Smart Growth[3]

movement, they're looking at Garden Cities.[4] And that may not be for everybody, but it may be for enough people that the people who want strictly suburban development can have it. And the people that want to be in a high-rise (who would've thought that there'd be a number of high rises in Houston where there's so much land?) can be in a high-rise. Do you want to live in a loft? Do you want to live in a highly walkable area? You know, let's give everybody options. Let's not just do kind of "cookie cutter" development.

1. The City Beautiful movement grew out of a Progressive Era concern for the impact that poverty, disease, and crime were having on the quality of life in the increasingly urban United States of the late 1800s, in the hope that beautifying U.S. cities would help inspire civic virtues among the poor. As a proponent of the City Beautiful movement, Daniel Burnham is perhaps best known for his role as director of work for the orderly "White City" of the World's Columbian Exposition of 1893. See Erik Larson, *The Devil in the White City: Murder, Magic and Madness at the Fair that Changed America* (New York: Random House, 2003).

2. J. B. Jackson, "Other-Directed Houses" in *Landscapes: Selected Writings of J. B. Jackson*, ed. Ervin H. Zube (Amherst: University of Massachusetts Press, 1970), 65.

3. Smart Growth envisions compact building designs in walkable communities with a mix of land uses and a range of housing opportunities, which preserve open space, farmland, and critical environmental areas. S. B. Beaumont, *Getting to Smart Growth: 100 Policies for Implementation.* EPA Document No. 231-R-05-001 (Washington, D.C.: Smart Growth Network and the International City/County Management Association, 2002), i–ii, 88–93. http://www.smartgrowth.org/pdf/gettosg.pdf (accessed November 16, 2009).

4. Garden Cities generally describe planned, self-contained communities with high densities and open space set-asides, typically in encircling green belts. The ideas of Garden Cities can be traced to Ebenezer Howard's 1902 book, *Garden Cities of To-Morrow* (London: S. Sonnenschein & Co., Ltd.).

Green Building, Siting, Glazing, and Massing

LAVERNE WILLIAMS is a Houston-based, registered architect whose practice has focused on green building for residential structures. He has worked since the 1970s to find better siting, design and materials for reduced energy use, more renewable resources, less toxic exposure, and reduced up-front cost and long-term maintenance. Mr. Williams has also pioneered efficient designs suited for Houston's heat and humidity. He sees this as a personal conviction and a professional obligation, strengthened by growing concerns over climate change (it is estimated that the building industry is responsible for over 50 percent of the nation's greenhouse gases).

Interviewed on February 28, 2008, in Houston, Texas

Reel 2423; Time Code 00:12:22

"We even made a corn stalk log home . . . !"

While I was growing up—I did have three older brothers—we used to do all sorts of things. We would build tree houses along side the railroad tracks, about three blocks from where we lived. There were these saplings that grew in the right-of-way of the railroad track. And we knew those saplings were going to eventually get cut down because they were just little spindly things that were growing about twenty feet tall. We actually made us a living Quonset hut out of them. We wove them into a hut that was about twenty foot long and about ten foot wide. We even made a corn stalk log home at one time! After the corn was harvested, the stalks were still up there about six foot in the air, and I just cut them off and made me a log home out of them. It was a one- or two-person room. So those were some of the things I was doing at a young age. I became a journeyman carpenter and I worked in construction—not only residential, but commercial, institutional, industrial, and manufactured housing. I went to the University of Houston architecture school and we had some great professors

Cliff dwelling, Bandelier National Monument, New Mexico (Courtesy Jan Miller)

Reel 2423; Time Code 00:39:04

I did some remodeling projects in Houston where we actually worked with *Houston Home and Garden* magazine. They were featuring some of the projects that took existing homes and remodeled them to make them perform better by adding things like passive solar greenhouses to them and so forth. And they tracked a couple of them in the magazine and so that helped give some exposure to the public.

One of the things we did was shading. Anything that you can do to shade the house to keep the sun from coming inside the house is going to be a benefit especially during the overheated months. It's called a "passive solar cooling strategy." Any time you can keep the sun from coming into a house *before* it actually hits the window can be up to seven times more effective than putting things on the inside to keep the heat out, like blinds or curtains and so forth. So you try to stop it before you get there. After I took my Permaculture[1] course, I tried to incorporate many natural ways to keep the sun out by using vegetation and trellises where you're actually growing plants that produce fruit. I try not to build much out of wood anymore. I try to use more durable products than wood down in this climate, because in the humidity nothing lasts. You may get five to ten years out of it, and if you're using treated wood, you're introducing toxins into your local environment that you really don't want to have, so we try to avoid that.

Passive design for both cooling and heating goes back for centuries, from the beginning of mankind, I would imagine. Look at the Anasazi Indians in New Mexico, how they sited their homes in the cliff sides so that in the summertime they were shaded by the overhanging cliff, but in the wintertime the sun would enter. They didn't have cliff dwellings facing north. Their cliff dwellings were all facing south. It's those kinds of siting issues you have to study. In this climate, you have to pay particular attention to ventilation. There are several months when you actually do not need any heating or cooling down here if you've got adequate ventilation.

out there. Our structures teacher used to teach us how to just build with ordinary materials. And I remember him showing us how to take gunnysacks, fill them full of cement, and build buildings out of gunnysack and cement. This was back in the late sixties. We did things like that which you are now seeing done worldwide in terms of low-cost structures, that low-skilled people can put together as far as housing. Now they have these long tubes of material and you just fill them full of sand and cement and you form your walls and then you sprinkle it with water and you've got a building. We were learning things like that way back in school.

When we design our new homes, we literally can extend the amount of time you can live without cooling or heating by two or three months over the course of a year. And that is a tremendous amount of energy savings. This has to do with shading and it has to do with orientation. It has to do with putting the windows in the right place, and making them the right size so that you get the breeze. Let's say you have a rectangular home: you want the long direction facing on the east to west axis, which is the optimum axis to have for this climate. So you have most your windows facing south and north and very few on the east and west. If you have the south windows you can open them up, but if you can open larger windows on the north sides then you actually can increase the ventilation through the house. It increases velocity of the house and it's called the Venturi effect. If you can put a roof monitor that's facing north, high on the roof where the breeze can go over the top of it, literally I have been able to create breezes in houses just from the temperature differential of air that as it heats up, creates a flow, and then exits out the top bringing in cool air from down below. I've literally helped write the book a lot on these passive solar ventilation cooling ideas. They really work!

A lot of people think that in this climate, you should build out of lightweight materials. I mean that's what all the books used to teach us. Well, I think I'm sort of rewriting that book to some degree because I found that you can incorporate mass on the inside of your home and put insulation on the outside of the mass. In other words, instead of having the brick on the outside of your house, putting it on the inside of your house. When you have the mass on the *inside* and you're designing for the microclimate of your site, you're designing to reject the heat during the summertime, and accept the heat during the wintertime. What can happen is that in the wintertime, windows can be your solar collectors. And any time you can make an element on your house like a window be a multipurpose apparatus, then you're saving dollars. Take the window, for example. The window should do several things: it not only should be a place

to look out but also should let light in, should be your passive day-lighting apparatus, it should be a place for you to get out of in case of emergency, whatever the emergency is. And it should be able to open up to let ventilation in. But the fourth thing it should be is your passive solar heating system when it's located on the south side of your house. You can let the sun come in, and if you don't have this "mass" to store this excess heat, the house will overheat and you'll be opening your windows even on the coldest day because it will get too hot in the house in this climate. But if you have a mass in there you'll be storing that heat in there, and then that heat only goes in one direction: from hot to cold. So during the daytime that heat is being stored in the cooler brick or stone that's on the inside of the house, through the windows. At nighttime, that brick or stone is giving the heat back to the space. And it doesn't have to be brick or stone. Some people have used canisters of water. And there're all sorts of other things. You can use several layers of sheet rock or you can do whatever you want to do as long as it's massive. Then, during the spring and fall, you can open up your windows at nighttime to cool down the house, when it overheats during the daytime. It's called the "mean radiant temperature effect." Even though the temperatures may get into the eighties inside your house, if the walls are cooler you're going to feel cooler. That's the principles of using mass. It just is something that most people aren't aware of. The utilities should actually be rebating people to put mass inside their homes to lower their peak demand.

1. Permaculture is a design principle joining the ideas of permanence and culture, developed first by Bill Mollison and David Holmgren, with the goal of settlement and agricultural design mimicking the structure and durability of natural ecosystems. Bill Mollison, *Permaculture A Designer's Manual* (Tyalgum, NSW, Australia: Tagari Publications, 1992), ix, 8.

Windmills, Energy, and Economics

TOM "SMITTY" SMITH has served as state director of the Texas office of Public Citizen in Austin since 1985. Prior to joining Public Citizen, he was a VISTA volunteer, a legal assistant, legislative aide, director of the Houston Foodbank, and operator of an anti-hunger advocacy program. Public Citizen is a consumer and environmental group active in issues concerning energy, environment, ethics and campaign finance reform, trade agreements with Mexico, and urban sprawl. Mr. Smith is noted as an effective public interest lobbyist, and has been most involved with pesticide use reduction and energy reform, including successfully advocating for renewable energy utilities, diesel emission reduction, clean vehicle incentives, and energy conservation standards.

Interviewed on October 14, 2003, in Austin, Texas

Reel 2253; Time Code 00:02:07

My parents were very much involved in public interest work all of their lives. My father was a social worker and when he retired after years of working with the state, he began to lobby for the Illinois Childcare Association as a volunteer for those people who were raising foster children or who were operating small day care centers, so I kind of got the bug early on from my father.

"Why don't you call your congressman? . . ."

I went to college up in northern Indiana, very close to Gary, Indiana, where the steel mills were located and the skies were a wonderful copper color when the sun set because of all the pollution. There were literally black sides to trees from all the particles that blew out of the steel mills. And I was fortunate as a college student to get a job doing air and water sampling at the local university labs. I went out and took samples out of the outfalls of the various steel mills and took the air quality samples that indicated how severe the air contamination was from these steel mills. So I learned a lot about the kinds of damage that was occurring to our environment from steel. Those steel mills no longer were able to comply with the Clean Air Act that passed in 1970 and are now shut down. The area around that part of the world is beginning to restore. The air is clean and the trees no longer have a blackened side from all the soot that used to come from those plants.

When I graduated from college, I joined VISTA, the Volunteers In Service To America, which was the domestic Peace Corps. I went to Kingsville, Texas and began to work in the legal aid office down there. And shortly after I arrived, I got the lobbying bug. A woman came to my office who was a food stamp recipient and her husband was a "hod carrier": someone who carried brick in these sort of "V" shaped pallets up the side of buildings. He was also an epileptic, and he had an epileptic fit one day while carrying brick and the bricks went flying everywhere and he was immediately fired from the job. And she went to the food stamp office to try and get her food stamps adjusted because they no longer had any income. And she was told that it would be a year before she could get her food stamps adjusted, because once you had been certified, you were locked into place. And I thought this was outrageous and tried to convince them to change their mind at the food stamp office, and was unable to do so. So the lawyers I worked with filed a suit. We went to district court and to the appellate court where the case languished for a number of years while briefs and pleadings were developed by the various parties. In the meantime, somebody said, "Why don't you call your congressman and see if he can do something about it." And, at that time, Kika de la Garza was chairman of the subcommittee in the U.S. House of Representatives that had jurisdiction over food stamps. And he thought this was outrageous and the more he began to talk to people, the more he realized there was a fatal flaw in the food stamp program. There were a number of migrant workers in his district down in the Rio Grande Valley who had come back from various places around the north who had been frozen out of their jobs picking vegetables and no longer

Pump jack and wind turbines, Sweetwater, Texas
(Creative Commons)

had the income they assumed they would have. They were also being told by the food stamp offices, "Sorry we can't adjust your allotment even though you have no income . . . you are fixed for a year." In response, we turned out close to a thousand people for a public hearing of his Congressional committee in the Rio Grande Valley, and shortly thereafter we got an amendment to the appropriations bill and shortly thereafter the food stamp laws were changed. And I thought, darn this is easy—just a couple of months, and a little old guy from central Illinois can come to Texas, change the law, and I thought, "Lobbying, it's a great way to go," so I just got the bug. From that point on, I thought that someone who could organize people could change the laws relatively quickly, and so I've been about that ever since.

Reel 2253; Time Code 00:40:21

In 1999 the electric utility industry was about ready to be deregulated and we in the environmental community had long been seeking some opportunity to develop our renewable resources here in Texas. Texas leads the nation in our ability to generate energy with renewables. And what we did was begin to pull together a coalition of the big wind companies in Texas. In those days it was Enron and the Florida Power and Light people and a number of others . . . I guess all together ten big companies. And we got them to sit with us at the table and to develop a coalition to go advocate for what's called a renewable portfolio standard or a minimum purchase requirement of renewable energy in the Texas legislature.[1] And what that coalition was able to do was to reach into communities that we typically would not be able to touch. They hired a Republican lobbyist, they hired one of the fundraisers for then-Governor Bush, who had done most of his direct mail and had worked for Karl Rove, who worked the back channels into Governor Bush's office. They were able to go into the Chambers of Commerce in small West Texas towns and ask that those who were benefiting from Texas' emerging wind industry or might be in a position to do so, contact those rural Texas legislators and talk to them about what might occur to the economics of their small town if we were able to develop the wind resources that were just outside their communities. And those kinds of economic interests were able to work miracles that we were not able to do as environmentalists and they were able to talk to the school boards and the economic development agencies who each have their own organizations that helped in the lobbying effort to pass the Texas' Renewable Portfolio Standard.

That has turned out to be a tremendous economic boom in West Texas and we're going to go back and try and do the same basic program again. What you found in West Texas is that, after the passage of the Renewable Energy Portfolio Standard, there was a major boom in construction. We built about a thousand megawatts of wind, or roughly a billion dollars worth of equipment was placed in West Texas on the tops of mesas and mountaintops in about a year and a half. And it spawned about twenty-five hundred new jobs directly in the wind industry, about twenty-nine hundred additional jobs in the cafés and the truck stops and in the welding shops around West Texas. And it enabled communities that had been economically dead for a generation to start to bring their children home, to be able to offer what one mayor said, "They're paying family raising wages again." And since the oil had dried up it was the first time that somebody could afford to raise a family in these small communities, working in the wind fields, instead of in the oil fields. And it's our hope that we can use the positive experience to argue for an expansion of the Renewable Energy Portfolio in the next legislative session. But it's had an economic boom not only for the local communities in terms of jobs, but also now in many communities the wind plants are the largest single taxpayers in the community. One little community outside of Abilene, at Trent, has been able to build a new elementary school for the first time in two generations simply because of the wind plant on the mesa up above the school. In another community outside of Fort Stockton it's the largest single taxpayer in their county, and they're beginning to be able to staff up their hospital, replace some of their fire equipment, and do a number of other things that they have not been able to do in over a generation as a result of having some new revenues coming in from these wind turbines.

1. The State of Texas enacted its Renewable Portfolio Standard in 1999 through Senate Bill 7, as part of its deregulation of the state's electricity market. The Standard required construction of two thousand megawatts (MW) by 2009 in solar, wind, biomass, or other renewable sources of energy, with market-based funding through Renewable Energy Credits that could be traded and aggregated. The 2,000 MW target amounted to a substantial increase from the 888 MW in service in 1999, but was quickly met by 2005. In that same year, Senate Bill 20 set new, even more ambitious goals (a 5,000 MW target for 2015 and a 10,000 MW mark for 2025). David Hurlbut, "A Look Behind the Texas Renewable Portfolio Standard," *Conservation Update*, March-April, 2008, http://apps1.eere.energy.gov/state_energy_program/update/feature_detail.cfm/fid=80 (accessed November 19, 2009).

Methods

The "Texas Legacy" oral history project was begun by David Todd in 1997 as an amateur and solo effort, using a DAT audio tape machine, and a hi-8 format, consumer-grade video camera. In June of 1999, a professional cameraman, David Weisman, and an experienced light and sound technician, Gary Spalding, joined the project. Backup crew included Jody Horton as cameraman and Eric Acevedo for light and sound work. Together, the bigger and more practiced crew brought better technique and equipment to the project, as described below.

Media

After the crew was organized, an early decision was made to record with the newly emerging mini-DV digital video format. This has had great benefits in editing and archiving. Using non-linear editing software on more powerful personal computers that had recently been released,[1] these digital recordings could be easily cut, copied, and spliced in new, faster, and far cheaper ways than before. Also, they could be copied to new devices, whether for editing or storage, without image quality losses and noise. From an archival standpoint, this was key: now the recordings could outlive old machines and formats, if they were transferred in a timely way to current equipment and media.

Video and Lighting Equipment

The first camera rented for work was a Sony VX-1000, then the standard for professional but low-budget productions. In addition, the team rented a kit of tungsten lights with focusing lamps, diffusion accessories, C-stands, and other associated "grip" equipment to control and direct the light.

Among the first administrative choices made was this decision to rent most of the project's equipment. Recording technology tends to evolve very rapidly,[2] and even at the lower-end of the spectrum, the cameras can be expensive. Since it was expected that these productions might be infrequent, renting allowed the producers to use the latest generation of equipment without having high overhead costs at the outset. This worked out well: by 2008, the project had moved up to using a third-generation Sony PDX-170 digital video camera, with greatly improved resolution, features and controls. Renting was also a good solution for some of the supporting equipment, such as the lighting gear, which can be quite heavy and bulky. By renting on location in Texas, the crew did not need to store this equipment between shoots, nor pay extra shipping costs, nor struggle with security issues in the post-9/11 travel world.

Decisions were also made to schedule ample time for composing and lighting the settings for the interviews. Since these interviews might last two hours or more, and were designed to have a long "shelf-life," it was important to put together an interesting and pleasing frame and backdrop, and one that might give clues to the narrator's interests. Diffused light, using gels and silk scrims, was also essential to save the interviewee from squinting or tiring during the course of a taping. In the last three years of interviews, the crew cut back on using incandescent lights, and began relying more on fluorescent lights specifically designed for video production. While more expensive to rent, they had a number of advantages. They required less space to carry and erect, created no noise, threw no heat, and provided a more even and shadowless light that was easier on the narrators' eyes.

Since the natural environment figured into the content of the interviews, preparations were made to videotape outdoors where possible. Surprisingly, even outdoor scenes need to be supplemented with artificial light. The sun is of course constantly in motion, and, as it slides behind clouds and trees, does not give a stable source of light. So, as a result, the equipment package also included large sheets of silk in four square-foot frames that could be erected above the interviewees on stands (weighted against the wind) to reduce glare and shadows. Then, either tungsten or fluorescent lights were brought in to add highlights to the narrator's eyes. Reflected light was helpful too: white boards could give a slight overall wash of light from in front and below a narrator, and a "backlight" (an aluminum surface) behind the subject ensured that the head was separated and distinctly visible against the background.

Upon arrival at a narrator's home, office, or other meeting place, and after introductions, and perhaps even the offer of coffee or snacks, the interviewee would give a tour to show what might be a good interview setting. Sometimes the choices were limited, while at other times the crew had great freedom. In all cases, the goal was to find a quiet place with ample room for all the gear, and the ability to get the camera a good distance, perhaps twelve feet, from the subject, as a telephoto lens is more flattering for portraiture. When this wasn't possible, the extreme opposite could also be used: a wide angle lens placed closer to the subject gave the feeling of intimacy, as if one were visiting across a table, over a cup of coffee. Often, creating the appropriate set involved moving some heavy furniture: sofas, coffee tables, lamps, and even paintings. Occasionally, black cloth was draped across picture windows to avoid stray light that might create shadows or reflections. In essence, a crude but workable soundstage was made and dressed for the interview.

While the technical setup continued, the interviewer would help prepare the narrator, explaining the overall project, reviewing areas for discussion, and mapping out a general course for the interview. Meanwhile, the cameraman would set the "frame" and position the camera, and the lighting technician would build the lighting rig. The crew would also work with the narrators in selecting "props," the paintings, photographs, sculptures, rocks, feathers, jetsam, books, posters, and plaques, in a way that might represent the narrator's work or interests, yet not be a distraction. A video monitor was used as a reference guide. The interviewees were shown how they appeared on this monitor, which took some of the mystery out of the process, and also allowed them the chance to adjust their own hair, makeup, or dress in a way that made them comfortable.

Sound

The last steps involved placing a condenser microphone on a stand above the subject's head. This was preferred, where possible, to the more common "lavalier" microphone that many people will recognize as the "clip-on" microphone worn by news journalists and many talk show guests. Those microphones are visible, pick up noise from clothing rustle, and need to be disconnected and reconnected every time the participant might need to leave the set. Also, the overhead microphone had a wider frequency response and recorded the voice in a more natural tone. A lavalier microphone was sufficient for the interviewer, and ensured that his interview questions could be isolated on a separate track, and well recorded for transcription.

At this point, after seating the narrator and doing a final adjustment of the lights, the interview was ready to begin. However, beyond all the technical machinations described here, and before the camera rolls, it might also be wise to include an overview of how the oral history tours were planned, and the narrators prepared.

Narrators

Starting with a raw list of fifty to seventy-five possible interviewees for a regional tour, the candidates were each contacted by phone three months before the trip was slated to begin. A shorter list was created after a preliminary discussion to gauge their interest in the project, and to get an idea of their experience, passion, memory, and eloquence. After this step, the candidates

Outdoor interview setting (Andy Sansom) (Courtesy Conservation History Association of Texas)

Indoor interview setting (Armando Quintanilla) (Courtesy Conservation History Association of Texas)

on a culled list of thirty to forty were asked about their willingness and availability to be interviewed within a tight itinerary, ultimately resulting in a group of roughly twenty actual interviewees.

Tours

At the time of preparing this book, we have completed six small interview outings and ten full tours. The longer tours were each about one thousand miles long, starting in either Austin or Houston (towns with rental houses where we could pick up video, sound, and lighting equipment), and then looping through a given region's biggest city and its nearby satellite towns. Our major trips have included Austin and the Hill Country (June 1999), Houston and the Big Thicket (October 1999), Corpus Christi and the Brush Country (February 2000), Dallas and the Crosstimbers (October 2000), Midland and the Trans-Pecos (March 2001), San Antonio and the Edwards Plateau (April 2002), Amarillo and the High Plains (October 2002), Houston and the Coastal Bend (October 2003), San Antonio and the Winter Garden (February 2006), and Houston and the Piney Woods (February 2008). Each production tour was scheduled for a ten-day to two-week period, with two interviews per working day. Four to five hours

were budgeted for each interview, including an hour for setup, two to three hours for the interview itself, and an hour for "wrapping" out of the location.

Questions

In preparing for the interviews, the producer would draft a set of interview questions based on the interviewee's history and interests. The questions were framed in a way to be open-ended, and not overly leading. At the same time, the questions were intended to be limited and specific enough that a meaningful answer would actually be possible within the short time available for the interview. The draft questions were then shared with the candidates for their review, to make sure that they were relevant and accurate. Their review helped cull the questions that might be distracting, immaterial, or uncomfortable. Also, looking over these questions gave the narrators some familiarity and confidence in preparing for the interview.

The questions were of two kinds: one that was generic and asked of all the interviewees, and another set that was specific to each narrator. The generic questions explored how the narrator might have first gotten introduced to the outdoors or conservation. This might hinge on encouragement from a parent, a friend, or a colleague, or it might turn on a connection with a nearby vacant lot or a distant hunting lodge or a long-ago camping trip. The basic purpose of this question was to give a starting point for the discussion, as well as earn a little trust that the interview was meant to create a personal history, not an inventory of public facts. The second question asked of all the narrators was to have them describe a favorite place that gave them solace and joy. This was intended to get closer to the idea that so much of conservation ties back to a love of nature or community, and to the special qualities that individual places hold for so many of us. The question also invited narrators to speak more poetically and subjectively about what animated their interest in conservation, and less clinically about the lists of names, places, events, and other facts of conservation. Finally, a third general question was asked: "if you had a message to pass on to the next generation about conservation, what would it be?" Of course, this question aimed at three goals: what was it about environmental protection that was personally important to the narrator, what should be important to the heirs of this work, and what might recruit a future generation to the work.

The specific questions of all interviews typically started with the interviewee's background, giving some leads about how he or she might be knowledgeable about their region and various local environmental topics. The specific questions might then follow several different tacks. The questions might involve queries of "what?" i.e., what are the leading air pollution, water quality, or wildlife issues in your area? Or, the questions might begin with "where?" i.e., where within this bioregion or town are the major environmental concerns of the public centered? Typically, the "where" question might hinge on the local natural resources (forests, for example), or on the major local industry (petrochemicals, for instance). Or, it might be a question of "who?" In other words, who have been the founders or leaders of the local environmental community (be they individuals or an organized group)? Conversely, sometimes this question could be framed by asking who might be the

major opponents, critics, and challengers of those perceived to be "despoilers" of the environment. The oral history could also be structured around the question of "when?" basically an effort to find the starting point of a conservation effort, and to track a sequence, and, sometimes, a conclusion. One could also begin with a question of "how?" asking for the causes and mechanics of how it is that Texas, or a particular part of the state, might have come to face a particular problem. For instance, how did it come about that the Rio Grande, a major nineteen hundred mile river draining 182 thousand square miles, would have water shortages? Or, how was it that Houston came to suffer the worst ozone levels in the country, when its strong prevailing winds would be expected to clear the air on its open, coastal prairie site?

The most critical questions, with perhaps the most elusive answers, have always revolved around the idea of "why?" Sometimes these have been very personal questions of why a given narrator cares enough about the environment to invest so much time and effort, often without the hope of gain or success, or even the realistic prospect of major change. Sometimes these have boiled down to more universal questions of why *anyone* should try to intervene in problems that are truly owned by a group, or that only affect the future most severely. It was in response to the "why" questions that the oral history process sometimes became a cathartic experience for the interviewees. Many of them had survived long, difficult struggles and had never had their stories widely heard nor recorded for posterity. Some recalled early childhood experiences of loss, poverty, or racial injustice. At other times, two hours of concentrated discussion on the ills of the planet left the narrators emotionally drained, or, conversely, angered and outraged at the bureaucracy and apathy that they felt were responsible for so many environmental problems.

After concluding the interview, the interviewer would then explain and secure a release from the narrator to ensure that the recording could be used in an open, flexible, and lasting way. The release language used by the Conservation History Association of Texas allowed future use of the recording by both the narrator and the interviewer. The Association then archived the interviews at the Briscoe Center for American History at the University of Texas, and posted copies at the website, www.texaslegacy.org. The archive has been put under a Creative Commons license that allows users to share and remix the interview materials, provided that attribution is given to the source, that the use is noncommercial, and that any resulting works are shared under the same conditions.

Landscape and Wildlife Footage

Landscape and archival footage, referred to in the video industry as "B" roll, was collected to illustrate the oral history interviews. The scenes varied, ranging from state parks, wildlife refuges, and bird sanctuaries to farms, forests, and industrial plants. Action scenes covered cotton ginning, citrus packing, harvest reaping, bird watching, recreational fishing, commercial shrimping, lignite mining, and highway and home building.

While much of the footage was captured in the mini-DV video format, 16mm black-and-white film was also used. The use of black-and-white film for some of the B-roll was both an aesthetic and pragmatic choice. The black and white film provided a distinctive contrast from the conventional "talking heads" portrayed in the color video format. The pragmatic aspect was that the images in black and white negative film, unlike color film, would not suffer color shift and fading problems. Also, the longer archival experience with the film medium itself gave greater confidence that the film acetate, emulsion, and projectors would last longer than newer video tapes and decks and computer drives and disks.

The tight schedule of taping two interviews per day did not allow for very much B-roll during the production. So, on several trips, the cameraman stayed behind on location for a long weekend. Then, armed with the video camera and cans of 16mm film, and often led by

a local narrator, he visited refineries, refuges, and inner city neighborhoods. Because much of the power in motion pictures is derived, naturally, from "motion," the B-roll tends to avoid static shots. For instance, the B-roll has included views of floating along the tranquil bayous of Caddo Lake, rafting over the rapids of the Rio Grande, or cruising past the swirling smoke from the refinery flares illuminating the Houston Ship Channel. Given the large scale of many of the environmental problems discussed by the narrators, aerial shots have been very helpful to get a full perspective. We hired helicopters and fixed-wing aircraft to get views of the expansive pivot-drip irrigation farms and cattle feedlots of the Panhandle, the petrochemical complexes girdling the Gulf, the tangle of freeways and suburbs ringing the cities, and the craggy canyons of Palo Duro State Park.

Wildlife photography would be a valuable accompaniment to our interviews, but requires a great deal of time and patience. Fortunately, we were able to link with Texas Parks and Wildlife, which has a very active media and outreach program, including a weekly television program produced by their own skilled staff. The agency kindly allowed us to search and copy material from its archives of literally thousands of tapes, many dating back even before the program began being broadcast on PBS stations in 1985. We discovered a great variety of images in the reels: Mexican free-tailed bats fluttering from a Hill Country cave and Boeing jets landing in Houston; deer hunters in the brush country and bird watchers on the coast. In short, we were fortunate to find views of all the economic and recreational uses of the flora and fauna of Texas in the Parks and Wildlife archive.

Archival Footage

Another crucial find, located high on a dusty Texas Parks and Wildlife shelf was a videotape entitled *Cavalcade of Texas*, a color 16mm film made by the state Chamber of Commerce, and produced for the

Texas Centennial of 1936. The videotape transfer itself was nearly two decades old and showing signs of decay—clogging the playback head of the video machine during the attempt to preserve it in the new digital format. Once duplicated, though, this promotional film proved to be a crucial visual bridge between Texas' past and present. Here was a film that showed a world and a mindset that might have been found in the early years of our narrators' lives. The film sought to show the state's progressive outlook, and to highlight the resources available to industry and development. The producers spared no effort in extolling the industries of Texas: logging and mining, ranching and agriculture, petrochemical extraction and refining, tourism and real estate. At first glance, such a film has value for its "camp" humor, in its trumpeting of the "untold promise of progress" that today appears naïve or ironic. Beyond that, though, it helped legitimize the stories of our narrators by documenting the origin of public works, industrialization, and population growth that would lead to environmental consequences unfolding throughout their adult lifetimes.

The archive held yet more vintage films, showing cowboys and oil wells in the Amarillo of 1929; capturing the Civilian Conservation Corps workers building the roads and cabins of Texas state parks; depicting Hill Country dams and Houston floods during the 1930s; and parading the steam trains and trolley cars of early days. Films from the 1950s and 1960s included ones made for Texas Parks and Wildlife's predecessor agencies. These included films on wildlife management, hunting, and game warden training, the scenes from which corresponded vividly with the stories told by the four veteran game wardens interviewed for this project.

Backup

Once the interviews, B-roll, and archival videotapes were collected, the work of building the library began. First, the mini-DV tapes were copied (with no quality loss) to duplicate sets of mini-DV tapes, with each stored in separate locations. They were also backed up in raw and compressed forms on pairs of computer hard drives. In addition, the originals were copied to VHS tapes, which were sent to the transcriber, the narrators, and to an off-site archive at the Briscoe Center for American History, on the University of Texas campus. In the latter years of the project, VHS was replaced by the DVD format.

Indexing

In addition to the word-for-word transcript mentioned above, the interviews and B-roll footage were also tracked in an indexed catalog, or video "log." Adapted from a standard Microsoft Excel spreadsheet, the log provided more of a thought-by-thought, phrase-by-phrase, or shot-by-shot inventory. The log categorized the interviews in one- and two-minute increments, noting the narrator's name, date, place, reel number, time code, topic, subtopic, and a 60 character description. In the case of B-roll material, there might be twenty or more specific entries per minute. By the time 225 interviews and hours of B-roll were completed, the log had nearly seventeen thousand entries, with fifteen fields of data, all of which could be sorted or searched using the keywords singly or in combination. The log has been converted to an SQL database and posted online at www.texaslegacy.org so that visitors to the site can mine the interviews in a better, quicker way.

A timeline of environmental history has also been assembled, including legislation, literature, court rulings, scientific findings, technological developments, population changes, and more, to give context and benchmarks for the interviews. While the interviews are clearly personal histories, it has seemed important to give an idea of the public events that were occurring in the backgrounds of the narrators' lives, and perhaps affecting how they acted and thought. And vice versa, the timeline could show how the efforts of these individuals often resulted in changes in public affairs. The full timeline has been posted on the website,

Scenes from the film, "Cavalcade of Texas" (Courtesy Texas World Fair Commission)

www.texaslegacy.org, but a selection of the timeline has also been included in the book as appendix 1.

Raw and Edited Video

Much of the impetus for the interview project was to give conservationists enough time to tell the long and complex environmental stories in their full detail. Too often, these issues are simplified and cut to short sound bites.[3] For that reason, there has been an effort here to circulate full transcripts and unabridged videos of the interviews. Both have been stored for viewing and downloading at www.texaslegacy.org.

However, there are limits on everyone's time and attention, so we have produced three-minute contiguous video excerpts from each narrator's interview. In addition, some longer pieces (averaging thirty minutes) have been edited and compiled from a group of narrators' interviews to join together and address shared topics such as surface and ground water, nature tourism, farming, ranching, faith, and civic advocacy.

Webpages, Maps, and Lesson Plans

As mentioned above, a good deal of effort has been put into posting archive materials on our website, www.texaslegacy.org. The ability to share digital resources on the Internet became a widespread reality with the 1994 release of the Netscape Navigator browser that allowed users to easily view the text of web pages, with graphic images, at no cost. The first recordings for the Texas Legacy Project were posted in 1998 as text profiles and transcripts, with limited images, primarily just the narrator photographs. In 2002, the Project joined with the School of Information at the University of Texas, which has kindly provided hardware and software to support streaming Real™ format video and audio to users over the Web. The increasing adoption of high-speed Internet connections, on T-1 lines, cable-modems, or DSL, has helped improve the delivery of large, high-resolution video files.[4]

The website is currently being converted to a wiki environment, to allow multiple editors to modify the site with only a browser, rather than a single webmaster using dedicated web-authoring software. As well, the video files are being reformatted in Flash, which is currently the most widely installed on computers globally. Finally, the text, database and video aspects of our texaslegacy.org site are being joined in a more unified and cross-referenced "rich-media" presentation based on the Glifos™ program.[5] Glifos™ allows video to be "tagged," in other words, linked with a table of contents and transcript, so that users can then search videos by phrase or keyword, and jump straight to that relevant part of the video.

Since the project revolves so much about the idea of "place" and each location's distinct habitat, wildlife, industries and communities, we are also introducing more use of maps. Some of the maps appear in the Glifos™ rich media section, where users can select a given location for a narrator, and be shown the interview video segment that discusses that very spot. Another use of maps to show environmental history involves "mashing up" timeline information with map coordinates, using the Timemap javascript library,[6] so that the evolution of Texas parks, or confined feeding operations, or human populations, or dams and reservoirs, can be traced through time and space.

Within our general outreach, Texas Legacy Project materials have also been prepared specifically for use in the classroom. We have built online lesson outlines and case studies based upon the archive and keyed to the Texas Essential Knowledge and Skills criteria. In this way, the environmental history of the state can be taught in tandem with language arts, social studies, humanities, economics, geography, civics, and science, with real-life, local examples.

Book

Of course, the book that you are holding is our most recent effort at sharing the stories of Texas environmen-

Table 1. Interview and log sample.

Reel	Time Code	Type	Narrator or Source	Date	City	Topic	Subtopic	Description
2257	00 43 00	Interview	Sargent, Ben	10/15/03	Austin	mass transit	cartoons	cartoon about Austin need for light rail mass transit — makes joke about birth of sprawl from autos
2257	00 45 20	Interview	Sargent, Ben	10/15/03	Austin	oil pollution	cartoons	cartoon on issue of pipeline safety for proposed gasoline pipeline through Austin; oil gushing in kitchen !
2257	00 48 15	Interview	Sargent, Ben	10/15/03	Austin	career	cartoons	his style has sharpened over the years; distinctive cross-hatching style, takes 4 1/2 hours per drawing
2257	00 51 53	Interview	Sargent, Ben	10/15/03	Austin	future	politics	TX environment facing struggle in this conservative state; profit over protection; demographic shifts
2257	00 57 30	Interview	Sargent, Ben	10/15/03	Austin	journalism	media	his brother says the internet is like a big, disorganized library; too much information, how to disseminate it?
2258	00 01 10	Landscape	CHAT	10/15/03	Austin	B Journalism	media	worker checks printing of insert coming off printing press at Austin Statesman
2258	00 02 00	Landscape	CHAT	10/15/03	Austin	B Journalism	media	details of gauges on printing press; tilt down to papers on conveyor
2258	00 02 45	Landscape	CHAT	10/15/03	Austin	B Journalism	media	follow papers on conveyor belt, tilt up to workers in control room checking results

tal history more broadly.[7] There are painful compromises in fitting the project within the covers of a book, in choosing a few representative narrators, in selecting brief individual excerpts, and in boiling down the voices and gestures of video to the mute and still lines on paper. However, books are durable, portable, accessible, and blessedly simple and direct in ways that media that depend on electricity, hard drives, cables, processors, switches, and monitors are not. In the end, we think it has been a very fair trade-off, and we are pleased and honored to be able to present these stories on these pages.

1. Widely available non-linear computer video-editing can probably be traced back to the release of the Avid 1/Macintosh system in 1989. The Avid system, and video use in general, grew exponentially in 1993 when the limit on the amount of video that the Macintosh could handle was raised from fifty gigabytes to seven terabytes, and the Avid Media 100 editor was released. The 1995 release of the Firewire IEEE 1394 bus and cable allowed much easier and faster transfer of digital video signals for editing or storage. The release of Final Cut Pro (now the market leader) by Apple in 1999 expanded use and editing of digital video still further. We currently use Final Cut Pro on an iMac laptop with two gigabytes of RAM and a 1.4 gHz processor.

2. The improvement in recording technology is dramatic when seen over the long term. In the late 1930s, the great folklore pioneer, John A. Lomax, used a 315-pound acetate phonograph disk recorder to preserve just the sounds of the ballads, love songs, and cattle calls of Panhandle cowboys and vaqueros of the Rio Grande border. By the late 1990s, when this project began, video equipment had evolved in sophistication to the point where a digital recording of video and audio could be achieved with a compact five pound unit.

3. 2008 has set new marks in brevity. Grant Barrett, head of the New Words Committee of the American Dialect Society has noted the coining of the new terms, "long photo," a video of ninety seconds or less, and "tweet," a text message of 140 characters or less. Liebovich, Mark, "Choice Syllables for 2008, You Betcha," *New York Times,* December 21, 2008, 3.

4. Broadband access is quite widely available now, although a digital gap remains for rural and poorer communities. In May 2008, 89 percent of regular Internet users in the U.S. were estimated to have broadband access. WebsiteOptimization.com, "U.S. Broadband Penetration Growth Drops to 17th Worldwide—U.S. Broadband Uptake Grows to 89.3% among Active Internet Users," http://www.websiteoptimization.com/bw/0805/ (accessed January 28, 2009). Ninety-eight percent of the users on the texaslegacy.org site in November 2008 used broadband.

5. Glifos social media software is a toolset that uses XML-based code to integrate video, text and images in a way that is independent of operating systems (Windows, Mac OS, or Linux), browsers (Explorer, Safari, Camino, etc.), and devices (PCs, PDAs, and smart phones), ensuring that the archive remains as open, portable, and durable as possible. http://www.glifos.com/wiki/index.php/Social_Media (accessed November 18, 2009).

6. The Timemap javascript library allows dynamic maps to be made from merging of Google Maps displays with Simile timeline information, loaded through JSON, KML or GeoRSS datasets. Nick Rabinowitz, "Homepage," *Timemap,* http://code.google.com/p/timemap/ (accessed November 18, 2009); David Francois Huynh, "Timeline," *SIMILE Widgets,* http://www.simile-widgets.org/timeline/ (accessed November 18, 2009).

7. We hope that this book will not only spread these stories more widely, but also preserve them for longer. The lifespan of paper is estimated to be five hundred years, while that of microfilm is 125 years, optical discs, fifty years, and magnetic tape, fifteen years. In addition to the fragility of the recording medium itself, the housing can also be short-lived: consider the fate of the once-common 5¼-inch floppy disk, the 3½-inch disk, the Zip drive, or the older wax cylinders and 16-inch lacquer-coated glass and aluminum disks. On top of the vulnerability of the medium and housing, we must recall the "ephemerae" nature of the software that interprets the recording. Remembering the long list of obsolete software in just one well-known area, word-processing can make the point. Wordstar, PFS:Write, Leading Edge, Samna, Multimate, Nota Bene and XYWrite were all popular word-processing programs in their time, but are no longer available or supported. A book, as simple and old-fashioned as it may seem, is a very durable way to preserve stories.

Afterword

"The sun has riz,
The sun has set,
And here I am,
In Texas yet."
Texas cowboy proverb

These stories are drawn from a series of ten tours over ten years, covering over ten thousand miles and 150 days on Texas roads, carrying cameras, tripods, video tapes, batteries, cables, maps, and many rolls of gaffer's tape, fueled by countless glasses of iced tea, plates of chicken fried steaks, and tanks of diesel and gasoline. We have been pleased with ourselves in returning from our big adventure intact, with recordings in hand, and with only two flat tires and one missing lens cap.

On the other hand, by studiously keeping to our schedule and dutifully following our maps, we are a little embarrassed by our robotic obedience to the clock and itinerary. We have been guilty of the same frenetic, small-minded distraction that leaves so much of our society with too little deep understanding of a given place, and too little comprehension of the consequences for that place over the long term. Watching the clock and paying attention to the traffic, we have too little knowledge of local soils, seasons, plants, neighbors and communities, and too little appreciation for how nature and community evolve in time,[1] at their own pace.[2] We should all slow down, smell the roses—or the local pollution—and pay attention.

Despite our distraction, we still do recognize what a wonderful privilege it has been to hear these narrators, and to learn from their experiences and insights. We have tried to just be an honest scribe for these people, but there is no doubt that the words and deeds of these narrators have had a strong effect on all of our crew. It is hard to be objective and unmoved by their many stories of sacrifice for the public interest and future generations. We hope that we have been changed for the better, and that we live our lives with more awareness of where we are, and with more thought and care about our shared future.

1. We see great value in the work of the Long Now Foundation, which is trying to foster long-term thinking and responsibility in the framework of the next ten thousand years, rather than our typically darting attention to thirty second commercials, twenty-two minute TV shows, eight hour workdays, quarterly fiscal periods, etc. The Long Now Foundation, "Front Page," http://www.longnow.org/ (accessed January 28, 2009).

2. We are slowly beginning to appreciate that nature's pace may not be for our own comfort and convenience. Climate change is perhaps only the most famous example of how natural change can be abrupt and dramatic.

Appendix 1

Texas Environmental History Timeline

Year	Topic	Selected Environmental Events Significant for Texas
1729	Water	San Antonio River is first diverted in the state, to be used for irrigation at Spanish missions
1836	Population	At independence from Mexico, Texas population is gauged at roughly 50,000
1840	Water	The Republic of Texas turns from the Spanish and Mexican system of water appropriation, based on the concept of first-in-time, first-in-right for beneficial water uses, and adopts the English rule of riparian right where all owners of land adjacent to a stream have water rights
1846	Wildlife	Ferdinand von Roemer notes that it is punishable by fine to kill vultures in Texas, the first mention of wildlife protection in the state, possibly under a county or common law provision
1850	Population	Texas state population is estimated to be 212,592
1852	Water	The State of Texas passes the Irrigation Act of 1852 which grants counties the authority to regulate dams and ditches, starting a Texas tradition of delegating water decisions to local governments
1856	Water	The Supreme Court of Texas recognizes a riparian system of water rights, allowing landowners adjacent to rivers to divert water
1861	Wildlife	The first game law is passed in Texas, imposing a two-year closed season on bobwhite quail on Galveston Island
1861	Parks	Texas acquires ten acres of public property at San Jacinto to commemorate the decisive battle of the Texas Revolution, designated in 1897 as a park
1873	Water	Red River log raft is removed, lowering water levels in Caddo Lake
1874	Wildlife	Texas enacts its first trespass statute, protecting enclosed lands from trespass by "shooting, hunting, fishing or fowling"
1874	Fisheries	Texas passes regulations restricting coastal seining and netting
1876	Food and Agriculture	The first local stock laws requiring fencing of cattle, sheep, goats, and other livestock are passed in Texas
1876	Water	Irrigation for farming in the Lower Rio Grande Valley begins on a small scale
1879	Wildlife	The first state-wide Texas game law is passed, protecting songbirds and establishing a season for dove and quail hunting
1879	Fisheries	Texas creates the Office of Fish Commissioner, charging it with the duties of preserving fish and building fish ladders
1881	Wildlife	Texas creates a 5-month closed season for prairie chickens and a 3½-month closed season for turkey
1883	Wildlife	The Texas Legislature exempts over half the state (130 counties) from all fish and game laws
1885	Fisheries	The Texas Legislature abolishes the Office of Fisheries Commissioner in a climate of falling farm commodity prices and conservation apathy
1887	Wildlife	Remnants of the southern buffalo herd are consolidated and protected by Charles and Molly Goodnight
1889	Wildlife	Frio County citizens petition Texas Legislature to place it under protection of state game laws, due in part to insect and rodent crop damage
1889	Water	Texas passes the Irrigation Act, replacing riparian rights with the prior appropriation system ("first in time, first in right") when diverting water from rivers
1890	Forests and Silviculture	The Texas Arbor Day and Forestry Association has its initial meeting, seeking renewal of forests and diffusion of knowledge regarding woodlands
1891	Wildlife	Against plume hunters for the hat trade, Texas enacts protection for seagulls, egrets, herons, and pelicans
1891	Water	Rice production begins on a commercial scale in Jefferson County with delivery of irrigation water from pumps on Taylor's Bayou
1893	Water	Austin Dam, the first major dam on the Colorado River, is completed (destroyed in 1900 by floodwaters)

Year	Topic	Selected Environmental Events Significant for Texas
1893	Parks	Texas authorizes funds for purchase of land at the Alamo site, Goliad, Refugio, and San Jacinto to commemorate critical battles in the Texas Revolution
1895	Fisheries	Texas Fish and Oyster Commission created to regulate fishing in the state
1897	Wildlife	77 Texas counties claim exemption from state game laws, declining from 130 in 1883
1897	Public Organization	The Texas Game Protective Association, an early wildlife conservation group, is organized
1897	Wildlife	The Texas Legislature declares that some avian species are public property
1898	Coast and Estuaries	The railroad magnate Arthur Stilwell organizes dredging of a ship canal from Sabine Lake to Gulf Pass, providing ocean access for Port Arthur
1899	Public Organization	The first Audubon group is created in Texas, in Galveston
1900	Coast and Estuaries	A hurricane strikes Galveston, inundating the island and killing 6,000 to 12,000
1900	Wildlife	The last verified Texas sighting of a wild jaguar is made
1900	Population	The Texas state census shows a population of 3,055,000
1901	Energy	The Spindletop oil well taps into a salt dome near Beaumont, and helps found Gulf Oil, Texaco, and the commercial petroleum industry
1901	Wildlife	The State of Texas prohibits nighttime waterfowl hunting
1903	Wildlife	The Texas Legislature creates a 5-year closed season on antelope, mountain sheep, and deer, and sets bag limits on turkey, quail, and dove
1903	Wildlife	The Texas Legislature passes the American Ornithological Union Model Law declaring all wildlife to be public property
1904	Water	Large-scale irrigation begins in the Lower Rio Grande Valley as the arrival of the railroad allows cost-effective delivery of produce to markets
1904	Water	A Texas Constitutional amendment is adopted authorizing the first public development of water resources in the state
1904	Water	The Texas Supreme Court adopts the "rule of capture" in *Houston Texas & Central Railway Co. v. East*, giving the surface owner generally unlimited rights to withdraw groundwater under one's land, denying that such use can be restricted by a reasonableness standard
1905	Wildlife	The Texas House establishes a Game and Fisheries Committee with jurisdiction over preservation and propagation of state game, and power to regulate fish and oyster industries
1905	Forests and Silviculture	Upon passage of a competitive bidding process in this year, only 31,978 acres of timber on public land remain out of an original 300,000 acres, much having already been distributed in an undervalued and/or fraudulent manner
1905	Fisheries	The first steam-operated shell dredge in Galveston Bay expands use of mudshell as a construction material
1907	Wildlife	A Game Department is added to the regulatory apparatus of the Texas Fish and Oyster Commission
1907	Wildlife	The first Texas game wardens are hired
1907	Forests and Silviculture	The Texas timber yield peaks at 2.25 billion boardfeet of lumber
1908	Public Organization	The Texas Conservation Association is founded
1909	Wildlife	The first requirement is imposed for Texas resident hunters to have a license
1909	Forests and Silviculture	The Yellow Pine Manufacturers Association pledges to practice sound forestry techniques and to lobby for federal and state fire protection
1910	Forests and Silviculture	The Texas Conservation Association convenes its first meeting, with 200 state officials, lumbermen, and conservationists in attendance, and adopts proposals deploring waste of all natural resources, particularly forests, and recommending creation of a state forestry agency
1911	Water	Irrigation from wells near Plainview begins, likely the first such operation in the High Plains
1911	Forests and Silviculture	The Texas House creates a standing committee to investigate forestry legislation

Year	Topic	Selected Environmental Events Significant for Texas
1913	Water	The Texas Legislature creates the Board of Water Engineers to monitor and regulate water development
1913	Water	Texas passes the General Irrigation Act of 1913, making it illegal to take water from a public stream without first having a permit from the Board of Water Engineers
1914	Water	Caddo Lake water levels are stabilized by earthen dams
1914	Coast and Estuaries	Dredging of the 50-mile long Houston Ship Channel is completed and the canal is opened for navigation
1914	Forests and Silviculture	The Texas Forestry Association is created with a charge to lobby for a state forestry agency
1915	Coast and Estuaries	The Texas City dike is constructed, trapping nutrients and sediments and raising the salinity of Galveston's West Bay
1915	Forests and Silviculture	The Legislature establishes the Texas Department of Forestry (renamed the Texas Forest Service in 1926)
1916	Water	The Texas Constitution is amended to authorize creation of river authorities and water conservation districts to help rationalize administration of water use, and to augment bonding power for irrigation and flood control projects
1917	Water	The Conservation Amendment to the Texas Constitution is adopted, declaring that conservation of all natural resources of the state is a public right
1917	Water	Texas adopts the Texas Water Code, providing for termination of riparian water rights in cases where water is not put to a beneficial use within 3 years, and giving the Board of Water Engineers the power to adjudicate water rights and to appoint a water master
1917	Energy	The Texas Railroad Commission is given the power to regulate oil pipelines as common carriers, like railroads, and empowered to prevent the waste of oil and gas
1918	Wildlife	An agreement between the U.S. government and southern coastal states, including Texas, temporarily suspends game, fish and oyster laws as a wartime measure, but is reimposed in 1919 after a Texas protest
1921	Energy	The Gulf-Burnet No. 2 well produces the first Panhandle oil and encourages further exploration
1923	Parks	Audubon begins a network of coastal island sanctuaries in Texas, to protect wading birds decimated by the millinery trade
1923	Energy	Construction of a carbon black plant in Stephens County signals the creation of the Texas petrochemical industry
1923	Public Organization	The Outdoor Nature Club in Houston, a non-profit group for study and protection of nature, is formed
1923	Wildlife	The Texas Legislature approves the Game, Fish and Oyster Commission to make full use of license and fee revenue, formerly diverted to the General Fund, doubling the Commission's disbursements, and allowing it to hire 50 additional game wardens
1923	Public Organization	The Texas State Parks Association organizes for "encouraging and assisting in the establishment of a systems of State parks," and proposes parks in the Davis Mountains, Palo Duro Canyon, Frio Canyon, Junction, Bosque County, and Rabb's Palm Grove in Brownsville
1923	Parks	Texas State Parks Board is created by the Legislature and empowered to solicit donations of tracts of land for the "purpose of public parks" and to investigate and locate tracts suitable for use as state parks
1924	Wildlife	The Texas Game, Fish and Oyster Commission uses movies of native wildlife to promote conservation
1925	Wildlife	The Texas Legislature approves a game preserve act empowering the Game, Fish and Oyster Commission to lease land from private landowners to create sanctuaries where hunting would be restricted and populations could recover
1926	Water	*Boyd v. Motyl Heirs* ruling asserts that state of Texas has control over storm and flood waters, and that the Board of Water Engineers has authority to make appropriations for water projects
1926	Coast and Estuaries	Dredging of the Corpus Christi ship canal is completed, providing a port for ocean-going vessels
1927	Industrial Accident	The *Gulf of Venezuela*, an 85,000-barrel gasoline tanker, explodes in Port Arthur, killing 29
1927	Pollution	The Texas Game, Fish and Oyster Commissioner receives legal authority to prosecute violators of pollution statutes
1929	Water	The Texas Legislature authorizes creation of the Brazos River Conservation and Reclamation District, the first of the major river authorities that were organized for irrigation, flood control, and hydroelectricity development
1930	Forests and Silviculture	Angelina County Lumber Company plants 200,000 seedlings, one of the first examples of reforestation in the state

Year	Topic	Selected Environmental Events Significant for Texas
1930	Wildlife	The first importation of exotic game from foreign lands to Texas begins with the release of nilgai antelope on the King Ranch
1930	Energy	H. L. Hunt's Daisy Bradford #3 well in Kilgore taps into the huge East Texas oil field
1930	Parks	Muleshoe National Wildlife Refuge, the first federal refuge in Texas, is set up as a wintering area for migratory waterfowl and sandhill cranes
1930	Wildlife	The Texas Game, Fish and Oyster Commission launches predator control effort aimed at "any animal that is known to do more harm than good" and including wolves, coyotes, jaguars, mountain lions, foxes, and eagles
1931	Energy	The Texas Railroad Commission begins making monthly production allowance announcements, dictating what percentage of maximum production Texas wells could pump, helping control supply and price worldwide until the 1960s, when Middle Eastern production and OPEC grew more important
1932	Parks	Texas makes its first purchases of land for state parks in the acquisition of Longhorn Cavern and Palo Duro Canyon
1932	Forests and Silviculture	Texas timber yield falls to 350 million board feet, the lowest since 1880, and 15% of the 1907 peak
1933	Parks	Civilian Conservation Corps organizes 12 camps in East Texas to work on tree planting, fire protection, trail building, and other projects
1933	Water	The Guadalupe-Blanco River Authority and the Lower Neches River Authority are created
1933	Parks	The Texas Legislature creates Texas Canyons State Park on fifteen sections of land in the vicinity of Santa Elena, Mariscal, and Boquillas canyons on the Rio Grande in southern Brewster County, later to be expanded by the federal government and renamed Big Bend National Park
1934	Forests and Silviculture	The Texas Legislature passes SCR-73, authorizing the U.S. to buy cut-over private timberlands to create national forests in the state
1935	Energy	Conoco, Texaco, Shell, and others bring in oil and gas wells that develop the Permian Basin oil field near Midland and Odessa
1935	Water	The Lower Colorado River Authority, Nueces River Authority and Upper Colorado River Authority come into being
1935	Parks	Federal acquisition of Davy Crockett, Sam Houston, Angelina, and Sabine national forests begins
1935	Water	Texas creates the Texas Planning Board to build a coordinated state-wide plan for conservation and use of water
1936	Water	U.S. Army Corps of Engineers begins stream surveys in Texas for possible flood control projects
1936	Parks	H. B. Parks and V. L. Cory write the *Biological Survey of the East Texas Big Thicket Area*, among the first organized efforts to protect the Thicket, then estimated at 1 million acres in size
1937	Parks	Aransas National Wildlife Refuge is established to protect the wintering grounds of the endangered whooping crane
1937	Forests and Silviculture	Construction of a pulpwood plant in Houston leads to commercial use of wood for Kraft pulp in container board, wrapping, and magazines, creating a larger wood products market, and one that allows use of younger, smaller-diameter trees
1937	Water	The San Antonio River Authority and the San Jacinto River Authority are organized
1938	Water	The U.S. Army Corps of Engineers begins construction of the Denison dam, impounding the 89,000-acre Lake Texoma on the Red River, its first major project in Texas
1938	Public Organization	Founding of the Texas Federation of Nature Clubs
1939	Water	The Upper Guadalupe River Authority is created
1939	Forests and Silviculture	First commercial use of southern pine for newsprint production, contributing both to the pressure for reforestation and the replacement of diverse forests by pine plantations
1939	Parks	The National Park Service surveys the Big Thicket and recommends inclusion of 400,000 acres in the National Park System, a proposal cut short by the outbreak of WWII
1939	Water	The Rio Grande Compact, which dictates how Texas, Colorado, and New Mexico shall share the river, is ratified by the Texas Legislature
1941	Water	The Mansfield Dam is completed on the Colorado River, creating Lake Travis in central Texas
1942	Data and Literature	The Texas Game, Fish and Oyster Commission publishes the first issue of the magazine, *Texas Game and Fish*

Year	Topic	Selected Environmental Events Significant for Texas
1943	Wildlife	First escaped nutria, a South American furbearing rodent indicted in wetland erosion and fragmentation, are documented in Texas
1944	Parks	Big Bend National Park is created, with 708,000 acres within its boundaries
1944	Water	The Rio Grande Treaty is signed, allocating water between the U.S. and Mexico below Fort Quitman
1944	Forests and Silviculture	The Texas Forestry Association, Texas Forest Service, East Texas Chamber of Commerce, Southern Pine Association, and American Forest Products create the Texas Tree Farm System to promote commercial reforestation and silviculture
1944	Water	The Texas Water Conservation Association is organized
1944	Water	The 89,000-acre, 1,321,000 acre-foot Lake Texoma is completed on the Red River in northeast Texas, near Denison
1944	Wildlife	The wild population of whooping cranes dips to an historic low of 21
1945	Water	The Legislature authorizes the Texas Department of Health to enforce drinking water standards for public water supply systems
1945	Water	The Texas State Board of Water Engineers reports appreciable declines in the water table in parts of the High Plains where irrigators had pumped significant volumes of groundwater, indicating that the aquifer was limited
1947	Industrial Accident	A cargo of ammonium nitrate fertilizer aboard the *Grand Camp* freighter explodes in Texas City, killing over 600
1947	Data and Literature	*Adventures with a Texas Naturalist*, by Roy Bedichek, is published
1947	Water	The Lavaca-Navidad River Authority is created
1948	Parks	The Texas Game, Fish and Oyster Commission purchases original 54,000 acres of Black Gap Wildlife Management Area
1949	Water	The Sabine River Authority is organized
1949	Coast and Estuaries	The Gulf Intracoastal Waterway's dredging is completed and the canal is opened to navigation from Brownsville, Texas to Carrabelle, Florida
1949	Water	State legislation declares that groundwater is private property
1949	Water	The Texas Legislature passes the Underground Water District Act, authorizing the creation of such districts on the approval of local voters
1950	Population	The Texas state population estimated to be 7,776,000
1951	Public Organization	The Texas Ornithological Society is formed
1951	Water	Local voters approve the High Plains Water Conservation District, No.1, the first groundwater district in the state
1951	Coast and Estuaries	The Texas Supreme Court, in *J.W. Luttes et al. vs. The State of Texas*, extends the boundary line of beachfront private property from the vegetation line to the line of mean high tide
1952	Pollution	The Texas Department of Health conducts its first study of air pollution in the state
1953	Water	Falcon Dam is completed on the Rio Grande, in south Texas near Zapata
1953	Water	Legislature creates the Texas Water Pollution Control Advisory Council, in the Department of Health, as the first state body charged with dealing with pollution related issues
1953	Fisheries	Mudshell dredging is banned within 457.2 meters of living oyster reefs in Texas
1953	Water	Steinhagen Reservoir completed on the Neches River in East Texas
1954	Wildlife	A whooping crane's summer nesting site is discovered at Wood Buffalo National Park in Canada
1955	Water	The Trinity River Authority is formed
1955	Water	In the *City of Corpus Christi v. City of Pleasanton* case, the Texas Supreme Court rules that groundwater withdrawals and uses cannot be restricted by waste, even where 70% of the delivered water is lost, and notes that its policy is not to intervene in groundwater
1955	Public Organization	The Sportsmen's Clubs of Texas, representing most of the major conservation, hunting, and fishing groups in the state, is organized

Year	Topic	Selected Environmental Events Significant for Texas
1955	Coast and Estuaries	The Texas Game and Fish Commission dredges a channel across Rollover Pass to improve fishing, releasing salt water to Galveston's East Bay, killing major seagrass stands
1955	Wildlife	The Tri-County Game Preserve Association, located in Bee, Goliad, and Karnes counties, is organized as the first wildlife management organization in Texas
1956	Energy	M. King Hubbert, a Shell petroleum geologist, predicts a 1966–72 peak, and subsequent decline, in petroleum production within the lower 48 states, which in fact does occur in 1970
1956	Pollution	The Texas Department of Health performs its first air sampling in the state
1956	Water	The seventh year of a severe state-wide drought (though ended in this year with wide-spread flooding) gives impetus for dam construction throughout Texas in the ensuing two decades
1956	Industrial Accident	A Shamrock pentane tank ignites in Solray, Texas, killing 19
1957	Water	The Texas Water Planning Act is enacted in response to the severe statewide drought of 1950–56
1957	Water	The 18,700-acre, 239,000 acre-foot Lake O' the Pines is completed in northeast Texas, near Longview, on Big Cypress Creek, a tributary of the Red River.
1957	Water	The 20,300-acre, 111,000 acre-foot Wright Patman Reservoir is completed on the Sulphur River in northeast Texas, near Texarkana
1958	Wildlife	To protect against the spread of nonnative fire ants, a quarantine of selected Texas counties is imposed
1959	Water	The Red River Authority is organized
1959	Coast and Estuaries	Texas Beaches Unlimited is formed to lobby for public access to the Texas coast
1959	Public Organization	The Texas chapter of the Nature Conservancy is organized
1959	Public Organization	The Texas Conservation Council is incorporated as a non-profit lobbying group
1959	Data and Literature	*Goodbye to a River*, by John Graves, is published
1959	Coast and Estuaries	The Texas Legislature passes the Open Beaches Act, overruling the 1951 decision, *J.W. Luttes et al v. The State of Texas*, and creating a national model for ensuring public access to the shore
1961	Pollution	Colorado River experiences a massive pesticide-related fish kill extending 140 miles from Austin to Matagorda Bay
1961	Pollution	Creation of the Texas Water Pollution Control Board
1961	Pollution	The Legislature passes the Injection Well Act, authorizing the Texas Board of Water Engineers to regulate waste disposal (other than that from the oil and gas industry) into the subsurface
1962	Data and Literature	*Silent Spring*, by Rachel Carson, is published
1963	Fisheries	The required buffer around mudshell dredging is reduced from 457.2 to 91.4 meters of living oyster reef
1963	Parks	93,243 acres of state-owned submerged lands is deeded to the Padre Island National Seashore
1963	Wildlife	The first exotic wildlife census by the state indicates that 13,000 individuals from 13 non-native species are present in Texas
1964	Parks	The Big Thicket Association is formed to press for protection of this area in southeast Texas
1965	Water	Congressman George Mahon of Lubbock requests the Bureau of Reclamation to investigate the feasibility of a coastal canal project to divert surplus water from southeastern Texas to the Rio Grande Valley
1965	Water	The 2,876,000 acre-foot Sam Rayburn Reservoir is completed on the Neches River in East Texas
1965	Pollution	Texas Clean Air Act establishes the Texas Air Control Board, in the Department of Health, to monitor and regulate air pollution in the state
1966	Parks	The 150-square mile Guadalupe Mountains National Park is established
1966	Public Organization	The Buffalo Bayou Preservation Association is organized, leading to success in stopping flood-control related dredging of Buffalo Bayou in Houston

Year	Topic	Selected Environmental Events Significant for Texas
1966	Parks	Senator Ralph Yarborough introduces the first Big Thicket National Park Bill, which succeeds in passing the Senate, but later dies
1966	Parks	Texas adopts the Statewide Comprehensive Outdoor Recreation Plan, enabling it to receive funds from the federal Land and Water Conservation Fund for park planning, acquisition and development
1966	Water	The Texas Water Development Board incorporates the Bureau of Reclamation's 1965 proposal for a coastal canal, and adds a proposal for importing water through northeast Texas, across the High Plains into eastern New Mexico, and into the Lower Rio Grande Valley
1967	Data and Literature	Justice William O. Douglas writes *Farewell to Texas: A Vanishing Wilderness*
1967	Pollution	Texas Air Control Board adopts its first air quality regulations
1967	Water	The Texas Water Pollution Control Board is replaced by the Texas Water Quality Board with increased funding and staff, but no laboratory facilities, hampering prosecutions
1967	Water	The Texas Water Rights Adjudication Act requires registration of all unrecorded surface water rights, limiting claims to actual use
1967	Water	Water Quality Standards are adopted under the Federal Water Pollution Control Act and the Texas Water Quality Act
1967	Wildlife	The whooping crane is listed in the U.S. as threatened with extinction
1968	Water	The first Texas State Water Plan is adopted, with a recommendation for moving water from the Mississippi River to Texas
1968	Water	The 1,742,000 acre-foot Lake Livingston is completed on the Trinity River in southeast Texas
1969	Water	The 3,274,000 acre-foot Amistad Reservoir is completed on the Rio Grande, near Del Rio, in South Texas
1969	Parks	The Legislature creates the Texas Conservation Foundation to act as trustee for gifts of land, cash, or historic sites
1969	Water	Texas voters narrowly reject a $3.6 billion bond package intended to fund the '68 Texas Water Plan's delivery of water across northeast Texas to the High Plains and eastern New Mexico, as well as to the Lower Rio Grande Valley
1969	Water	The 4,477,000 acre-foot Toledo Bend Reservoir is completed on the Sabine River in southeast Texas
1970	Recycling	Ecology Action opens Austin's first recycling center
1970	Public Organization	The Citizens' Environmental Coalition, an information clearinghouse and communication network for environmental issues in the Houston and Galveston area, is formed
1970	Parks	Representative Bob Eckhardt sponsors a bill to establish a 191,000-acre Big Thicket bill, which fails
1970	Energy	The Texas Railroad Commission, recognizing the decline of the state's oilfield production, approves unlimited pumping
1970	Wildlife	The U.S. Fish and Wildlife Service establishes a red wolf captive breeding program
1970	Public Organization	The first Earth Day is celebrated
1971	Public Organization	The Texas Environmental Coalition is organized
1971	Pollution	The Texas Air Control Board issues its first air pollution permits
1971	Pollution	The Texas Clean Air Act is passed, grandfathering pre-existing plants from requirements to obtain permits or reduce pollution
1972	Parks	The Texas Legislature authorizes the Dedicated Park Fund, allocating a distinct and reliable stream of funding for state and metropolitan parks
1972	Energy	Texas oil production peaks at 1.3 billion barrels per year
1973	Parks	Congressman Charlie Wilson introduces a bill to protect 75,000 acres in the Big Thicket
1974	Energy	North American oil production peaks
1974	Parks	President Ford signs legislation creating the Big Thicket National Preserve, the first tract in the National Park System acquired chiefly for biological reasons. Originally authorized for 84,550 acres, the Preserve has grown to later consist of 97,000 acres of protected public land
1974	Pollution	The ocean-going incinerator, *Vulcanus I*, does its first test burns in the Gulf of Mexico

Year	Topic	Selected Environmental Events Significant for Texas
1975	Water	The Texas Water Development Board is directed to study relationships between freshwater inflows and biological productivity of Texas bays and estuaries
1976	Wildlife	Following restocking with eastern wild turkeys, the first legal turkey hunting season in Texas is opened in more than a half-century
1976	Energy	The Texas Solar Energy Society is formed
1978	Food and Agriculture	Safer Way Natural Food, which later evolves into Whole Foods Market, is started in Austin, helping popularize natural and organic foods
1978	Parks	The Nature Conservancy of Texas purchases Enchanted Rock, selling it in turn to Texas when the state receives matching money from the federal Land and Water Conservation Fund
1978	Water	The Texas Supreme Court rules in *Friendswood Development Co. v. Smith-Southwest Industries* that a landowner is liable for the subsidence on another's land caused by the negligent withdrawal of groundwater, creating an exception to the absolute rule of capture
1979	Energy	2.6 million gallons of oil are spilled in the collision of the *Burmah Agate* and the freighter *Mimosa* southeast of Galveston Bay's entrance to the Gulf
1979	Fisheries	The use of single-strand monofilament nets is outlawed in Texas
1980	Fisheries	Gill net use in Texas bays is prohibited
1980	Water	The 27,690-acre, 604,000 acre-foot Lake Fork reservoir is completed on a tributary of the Sabine River in northeast Texas, near Quitman
1981	Parks	The Big Thicket National Preserve is designated an International Biological Preserve by UNESCO in recognition of its ecological diversity and richness
1981	Pollution	The Legislature creates the Texas Low-Level Radioactive Waste Disposal Authority, charged with siting, operating, and de-commissioning a disposal facility for commercial low-level radioactive waste (generally, all types other than military and reactor core waste)
1981	Water	Voters reject a proposed Texas constitutional amendment setting aside one-half of the state's surplus revenues for a permanent water fund
1982	Water	The 26,000-acre, 695,000 acre-foot Choke Canyon reservoir is completed on the lower Nueces River, in central Texas near Three Rivers
1982	Fisheries	Mudshell dredging ends after the last permit expires
1982	Recycling	Austin begins the state's first curbside recycling program for a major urban area
1982	Wildlife	Reintroduction of the desert bighorn sheep, once extirpated in Texas, is begun in the Sierra Diablo Wildlife Management Area
1983	Pollution	U.S. and Mexico adopt the La Paz Agreement, pledging to prevent, reduce and eliminate any contaminating sources along the border zone
1984	Pollution	EPA denies a permit for ocean incineration in the Gulf of Mexico
1984	Parks	Five wilderness areas in East Texas (Big Slough, Indian Mounds, Little Lake Creek, Turkey Hill, and Upland Island), totaling 37,000 acres, are designated
1984	Wildlife	A Texas Parks and Wildlife Department survey reports that 75 non-native species of foreign big game, including 120,000 individuals, are found in Texas
1985	Water	Texas imposes environmental conditions on water rights to be granted in the future
1987	Wildlife	The first captive-bred red wolf is reintroduced into the wild, at Alligator River National Wildlife Refuge, starting the first successful breeding/reintroduction of a mammal
1987	Water	The Texas Water Development Board and Texas Parks and Wildlife Department are directed to jointly study effects of freshwater inflows on coastal bays and estuaries
1988	Forests and Silviculture	The Texas Committee on Natural Resources, Sierra Club, and Wilderness Society obtain an injunction against the Forest Service, banning clear-cutting on 200,000 acres of national forests in Texas to protect the endangered red-cockaded woodpecker

Year	Topic	Selected Environmental Events Significant for Texas
1988	Energy	The South Texas Nuclear Project's Unit 1 and 2, twin 1251 MWe pressurized water reactors, come on line near Bay City
1988	Food and Agriculture	The Texas Department of Agriculture begins voluntary organic certification program of food and fiber
1989	Recycling	Ecology Action begins Texas' first plastics recycling program
1989	Fisheries	The State of Texas bans possession of illegal fishing devices on or near Texas waters
1989	Industrial Accident	An explosion at a Phillips 66 polyethylene facility kills 23 in Pasadena
1990	Energy	Comanche Peak's Unit 1, an 1150 MWe pressurized water nuclear reactor, comes on line near Glen Rose
1990	Industrial Accident	A pump room explosion and fire aboard the *Mega Borg* releases 5.1 million gallons of oil some 60 nautical miles south-south-east of Galveston
1990	Industrial Accident	A chemical reaction at an ARCO Chemical plant causes an explosion, and kills 17 in Channelview
1990	Fisheries	Trammel nets are banned in Texas
1992	Public Organization	The Environmental Fund for Texas (later renamed Earth Share of Texas) is created, providing a workplace fundraising campaign for Texas environmental non-profits
1992	Recycling	Houston becomes the first major U.S. city to initiate a curbside motor oil recycling program
1993	Energy	Comanche Peak's Unit 2, an 1150 MWe pressurized water nuclear reactor, comes on line near Glen Rose
1993	Pollution	The Texas Natural Resources Conservation Commission is created, for the first time merging Texas air, water, and solid waste regulatory programs
1993	Parks	Texas Parks and Wildlife initiates the Texas Coastal Birding Trail
1993	Pollution	Texas, Maine, and Vermont enter into the Compact agreement, providing that Texas will serve as the low-level radioactive waste disposal site for the three
1994	Water	Lavaca Bay is designated a Superfund site, due to mercury discharges from the Alcoa Point Comfort plant
1994	Pollution	Pantex is listed as a Superfund site
1994	Public Organization	The private property rights group, Take Back Texas, is formed, partly in response to endangered species regulation
1995	Data and Literature	The Texas Center for Policy Studies publishes the Texas Environmental Almanac
1995	Food and Agriculture	The Texas Natural Resources Conservation Commission issues Subchapter K rules streamlining permitting for CAFOs
1995	Pollution	*The Impact of Global Warming on Texas*, edited by Gerald North, Jurgen Schmandt, and Judith Clarkson, is printed
1996	Wildlife	The Texas Organization of Wildlife Management Associations, a statewide federation of more than 100 wildlife co-ops, is formed
1996	Water	Texas Supreme Court reaffirms the rule of capture, while upholding expanded powers of underground water districts, in *Barshop v. Medina County Underground Water Conservation District*
1997	Water	The Texas Legislature adopts Senate Bill 1, mandating development of 50-year regional water plans that protect agricultural and natural resources
1999	Food and Agriculture	On invalidation of 1995 Subchapter K regulations, the Texas Natural Resources Conservation Commission issues Subchapter B rules for CAFOs, still contested as weak
1999	Energy	Texas adopts one of the nation's first renewable energy portfolio standards, requiring utilities to purchase 2.7% of their energy from renewable sources by 2009
1999	Water	The Texas Supreme Court again affirms the rule of capture for groundwater in *Sipriano et al v. Ozarka Natural Spring Water, et al.*
2000	Water	The San Marcos River Foundation applies for surface water rights of 1.15 million acre-feet per year from the Guadalupe River to protect freshwater inflows to San Antonio Bay
2000	Population	The Texas population is calculated to be 20,949,316, ranking it as the second most populous state in the nation, with 80% of its population to be found in urban areas
2001	Water	The Guadalupe-Blanco River Authority applies for all the remaining unappropriated flow of the Guadalupe River

Year	Topic	Selected Environmental Events Significant for Texas
2001	Forests and Silviculture	International Paper announces plans to sell 800,000 acres of forestland in East Texas, as part of an industry move to lower debt and property taxes, and take advantage of higher land values
2001	Water	Rio Grande ceases flowing to the Gulf of Mexico, for the first time in recorded history
2002	Water	The Lower Colorado River Authority and San Antonio Water System agree to study the feasibility of providing water to San Antonio from the Colorado River
2002	Water	A State Water Plan is released under Senate Bill 1, compiling 16 regional plans, envisioning 8 major new reservoirs, and costing $18 billion
2003	Parks	The Conservation Fund acquires 33,000 acres of bottomland forest in the Neches River valley of East Texas, to be managed for sustainable forestry and habitat protection
2003	Water	The first donation of a water right is made to the Texas Water Trust, protecting 1,236 acre-feet of stream flow from the Rio Grande, upstream of Big Bend National Park
2003	Forests and Silviculture	Louisiana-Pacific sells 475,000 acres of East Texas forestland to Molpus Woodlands Group, part of a trend of divestment among traditional east Texas timber owners and operators
2003	Pollution	Texas passes HB 1567 and SB 824 allowing for two privately-operated radioactive waste sites in Andrews County
2003	Food and Agriculture	The Texas Department of Agriculture initiates certification of organic beef, pork, poultry, and dairy
2005	Industrial Accident	A major explosion at BP's Texas City Texas City oil refinery kills 15 and injures 70
2005	Coast and Estuaries	Rita makes landfall as a category 3 hurricane near Sabine Pass in southeast Texas, causing $11 billion in damage
2005	Fisheries	The Texas Legislature imposes a moratorium on the issuance of commercial oyster and Gulf shrimp licenses
2005	Food and Agriculture	Whole Foods and HEB's Central Market groceries agree to list any genetically engineered ingredients in their private-label products
2005	Energy	Texas legislation increases the mandate for renewable energy to 5880 megawatts by 2015, and 10,000 MW by 2025
2007	Forests and Silviculture	Temple-Inland sells 1.5 million acres of forestland in Texas and elsewhere to the Campbell Group
2008	Coast and Estuaries	Ike, a category 2 hurricane, strikes the upper Texas coast, causing roughly $22 billion in economic damage, with extreme harm to Galveston Island and Bolivar Peninsula
2008	Recycling	The Texas Legislature mandates free e-waste recycling
2009	Water	The Lower Colorado River Authority refuses to continue water export consideration, due to projected in-basin shortages, triggering a law suit by the San Antonio Water System
2009	Coast and Estuaries	Public vote amends the state Constitution to guarantee open access to the Texas coast
2010	Industrial Accident	BP Deepwater Horizon offshore rig explodes, kills 11, and releases large oil and gas spill in the Gulf of Mexico

Appendix 2

List of Narrators

This book is a small piece of a much larger archive, consisting of a handful of carefully but nevertheless somewhat randomly chosen excerpts, and from only a few narrators. Many more wonderful people have participated in the Texas Legacy Project and they deserve much more attention. We urge you to read their stories and learn about their lives and contributions at the website, www.texaslegacy.org.

At this time, November 2009, the full collection consists of interviews with the following individuals:

A

Marjorie Adams
Bill Addington
John Ahrns
Richard Alles
Susana Almanza
Tony Amos
Jim Bill Anderson
LaNell Anderson
George Archibald
Dede Armentrout
Bob Armstrong
Mary Arnold
Georgia Auckerman

B

Sue Bailey
David Bamberger
Malcolm Beck
Mavis Belisle
Maria Berriozabál
Janice Bezanson
Alan Birkenfeld
Darryl Birkenfeld
Jim Blackburn
David Blankinship
Deyaun Boudreaux
Mike Bradshaw
Betty Brink
George Bristol
Al Brothers
John Bryant
Winnie Burkett
Bob Burleson
Mickey Burleson
Alma Burnam
Earl Burnam

C

T. C. Calvert
Mary Lou Campbell
Neil Carman
John Carpenter
Scooter Cheatham
Russel Clapper
H. C. Clark
Bessie Cornelius
Ernie Cortes
Felix Cox
David Creech
David Crossley
Carol Cullar
Susan Curry
Tom Curry

D

Fred Dahmer
Walt Davis
Bill Dawson
Larry DeMartino
Donnie Dendy
Delbert Devin
Alfred Dominic
Richard Donovan
Robin Doughty
Louis Dubose
Helen Dutmer

E

Jim Earhart
John Echols
Bob Eckhardt
Jim Eidson
Jane Elioseff
Victor Emanuel
Midge Erskine
Ted Eubanks

F

John Fairey
Sissy Farenthold
Shudde Fath
Bebe Fenstermaker
Martha Fenstermaker
Mary Fenstermaker
Merriwood Ferguson
Ben Figueroa
Pliny Fisk
Hal Flanders
David Freeman
Johnny French
Carl Frentress
Ned Fritz

G

Nacho Garza
Beverly Gattis
Hana Ginzbarg
Phyllis Glazer
Katherine Goodbar
Jeanne Gramstorff
Jesse Grantham
John Graves
J. D. Graves
Meg Guerra
Pete Gunter

H

Ann Hamilton
Grover Hankins
Richard Harrel
Adlene Harrison
Ed Harte
Stuart Henry
Tootsie Herndon
Sylvia Herrera

Terry Hershey
Jim Hightower
Henry Hildebrand
Tim Hixon
Dennis Holbrook
Buddy Hollis
Clark Hubbs
Susan Hughes

J

Reggie James
Pat Johnson
Maxine Johnston

K

Don Kennard
Marie Killebrew
Michael King
Walt Kittelberger
Tonya Kleuskens
Stephen Klineberg
Ken Kramer
Frank Kurzaj

L

David Langford
Dan Lay
Rob Lee
Marvin Legator
Richard LeTourneau
Ruth Lofgren
Rick Lowerre
Kamlesh Lulla
Jim Lynch
Mary Lynch
Susan Lynch

M

Roy Malveaux
Brandt Mannchen
David Marrack
Carla Marshall
Leroy Matthiesen
James Matz
Craig McDonald
Bob McFarlane
Terry McIntire
Billy Pat McKinney
Bonnie McKinney
Pleas McNeel
Ike McWhorter
Martin Melosi
Susan Mika
Char Miller
Genevieve Miller
Joe Moore, Jr.

N

Jim Neal
Bill Neiman
Gerald North

O

Clarence Ogle
Gary Oldham
Bill Oliver
Gary Oliver
Terry O'Rourke
Keith Ozmore

P

Marcos Paredes
Howard Peacock
Larhea Pepper

Mary Anne Piacentini
Mary Anne Pickens
Ellis Pickett
Tom Pincelli
Billy Platt
Sue Pope
John Praeger

Q

Daniel Quinn
Armando Quintanilla

R

Bob Randall
Campbell Read
George Rice
Susan Rieff
Chester Rowell
George Russell

S

Fran Sage
Andy Sansom
Ben Sargent
Carol Ann Sayle
John Scanlan
Ed Scharf
Irene Scharf
Jim Schermbeck
David Schmidly
Carl Schoenfeld
A. R. "Babe" Schwartz
Peggy Sechrist
Richard Sechrist
Kenneth Seyffert
Carroll Shaddock
Bill Sheffield
Dwight Shellman

Larry Shelton
Mike Shoup
Ted Siff
Fay Sinkin
Lanny Sinkin
George Smith
Russel Smith
Smitty Smith
Steve Smith
Carmine Stahl
David Stall
Linda Stall
Jim Steiert
Kerrie Steiert
Sharron Stewart
Jim Stinebaugh
Pat Suter

T

Jim Teer
Ellen Temple
Lucie Todd
Benito Trevino
Carlos Truan
Merlin Tuttle

U

Nancy Umphres

V

Genevieve Vaughan
Tom Vaughan
George Veni
Gail Vittori
Gary Vliet

W

Geraldine Watson
Evangeline Whorton
Andy Wilkinson
Fred Wills
Diane Wilson
Billie Woods

Z

Ken Zarker
Barrie Zimmelman

Index

(Names in **bold** indicate Texas Legacy Project narrators; page numbers in **bold** denote their narration excerpts included in this book. Page numbers followed by *n* indicate notes.)

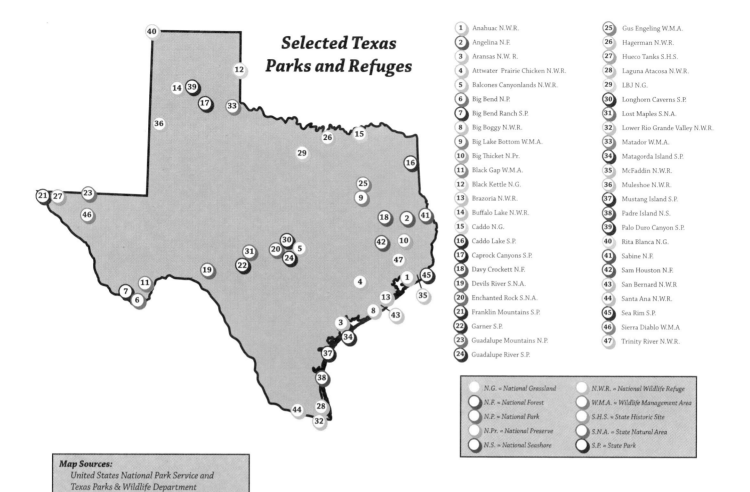

Selected Texas Parks and Refuges

1	Anahuac N.W.R.	25	Gus Engeling W.M.A.
2	Angelina N.F.	26	Hagerman N.W.R.
3	Aransas N.W.R.	27	Hueco Tanks S.H.S.
4	Attwater Prairie Chicken N.W.R.	28	Laguna Atacosa N.W.R.
5	Balcones Canyonlands N.W.R.	29	LBJ N.G.
6	Big Bend N.P.	30	Longhorn Caverns S.P.
7	Big Bend Ranch S.P.	31	Lost Maples S.N.A.
8	Big Boggy N.W.R.	32	Lower Rio Grande Valley N.W.R.
9	Big Lake Bottom W.M.A.	33	Matador W.M.A.
10	Big Thicket N.Pr.	34	Matagorda Island S.P.
11	Black Gap W.M.A.	35	McFaddin N.W.R.
12	Black Kettle N.G.	36	Muleshoe N.W.R.
13	Brazoria N.W.R.	37	Mustang Island S.P.
14	Buffalo Lake N.W.R.	38	Padre Island N.S.
15	Caddo N.G.	39	Palo Duro Canyon S.P.
16	Caddo Lake S.P.	40	Rita Blanca N.G.
17	Caprock Canyons S.P.	41	Sabine N.F.
18	Davy Crockett N.F.	42	Sam Houston N.F.
19	Devils River S.N.A.	43	San Bernard N.W.R
20	Enchanted Rock S.N.A.	44	Santa Ana N.W.R.
21	Franklin Mountains S.P.	45	Sea Rim S.P.
22	Garner S.P.	46	Sierra Diablo W.M.A
23	Guadalupe Mountains N.P.	47	Trinity River N.W.R.
24	Guadalupe River S.P.		

N.G. = National Grassland
N.F. = National Forest
N.P. = National Park
N.Pr. = National Preserve
N.S. = National Seashore

N.W.R. = National Wildlife Refuge
W.M.A. = Wildlife Management Area
S.H.S. = State Historic Site
S.N.A. = State Natural Area
S.P. = State Park

Map Sources:
United States National Park Service and
Texas Parks & Wildlife Department

Created by: Kevin Schwartz 2009

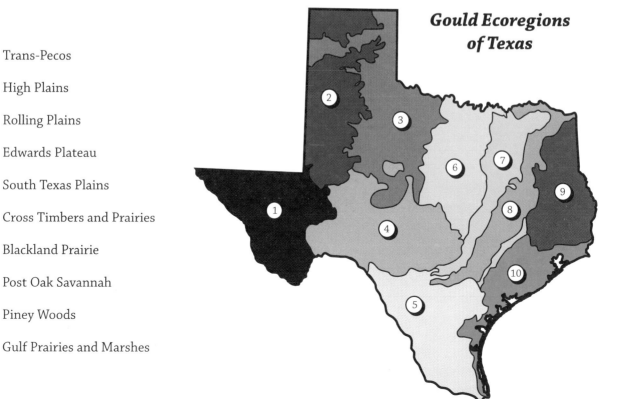

Gould Ecoregions of Texas

1. Trans-Pecos
2. High Plains
3. Rolling Plains
4. Edwards Plateau
5. South Texas Plains
6. Cross Timbers and Prairies
7. Blackland Prairie
8. Post Oak Savannah
9. Piney Woods
10. Gulf Prairies and Marshes